The Idea of Development in Africa

The Idea of Development in Africa challenges prevailing international development discourses about the continent by tracing the history of ideas, practices, and "problems" of development used in Africa. In doing so, it offers an innovative approach to examining the history and culture of development through the lens of the development episteme, which has been foundational to the "idea of Africa" in western discourses since the early 1800s. This study weaves together an historical narrative of how the idea of development emerged with an account of the policies and practices of development in colonial and postcolonial Africa. This book highlights four enduring themes in African development, including their present-day ramifications: domesticity, education, health, and industrialization. Offering a balance between historical overview and analysis of past and present case studies, Corrie Decker and Elisabeth McMahon demonstrate that Africans have always co-opted, challenged, and reformed the idea of development, even as the western-centric development episteme presumes a one-way flow of ideas and funding from the west to Africa.

Corrie Decker is Associate Professor of History at the University of California, Davis. She is the author of *Mobilizing Zanzibari Women: The Struggle for Respectability and Self-Reliance* (2014) and numerous articles in the *Journal of Women's History*, the *International Journal of African Historical Studies, Past and Present, Africa Today,* and the *American Historical Review.* She is currently writing a book on the history of puberty in twentieth-century East Africa.

Elisabeth McMahon is Associate Professor of History at Tulane University. She is the author of *Slavery and Emancipation in Islamic East Africa: From Honor to Respectability* (2013) and numerous articles in *International Labor and Working-Class History, Slavery and Abolition,* the *International Journal of African Historical Studies, Women's History Review,* the *Journal of Women's History, Africa Today,* the *Journal of Social History,* and *Quaker History.* She led the digital humanities African Letters Project in conjunction with the Amistad Research Center, making letters written by Africans during decolonization accessible globally.

New Approaches to African History

Series Editor
Martin Klein, *University of Toronto*

Editorial Advisors
William Beinart, *University of Oxford*
Mamadou Diouf, *Columbia University*
William Freund, *University of KwaZulu-Natal*
Sandra E. Greene, *Cornell University*
Ray Kea, *University of California, Riverside*
David Newbury, *Smith College*

New Approaches to African History is designed to introduce students to current findings and new ideas in African history. Although each book treats a particular case and is able to stand alone, the format allows the studies to be used as modules in general courses on African history and world history. The cases represent a wide range of topics. Each volume summarizes the state of knowledge on a particular subject for a student who is new to the field. However, the aim is not simply to present views of the literature but also to introduce debates on historiographical or substantive issues, and individual studies may argue for a particular point of view. The aim of the series is to stimulate debate and to challenge students and general readers. The series is not committed to any particular school of thought.

Other Books in the Series

The Idea of Development in Africa
A History

Corrie Decker
University of California, Davis

Elisabeth McMahon
Tulane University

CAMBRIDGE
UNIVERSITY PRESS

CAMBRIDGE
UNIVERSITY PRESS

University Printing House, Cambridge CB2 8BS, United Kingdom

One Liberty Plaza, 20th Floor, New York, NY 10006, USA

477 Williamstown Road, Port Melbourne, VIC 3207, Australia

314–321, 3rd Floor, Plot 3, Splendor Forum, Jasola District Centre, New Delhi – 110025, India

79 Anson Road, #06–04/06, Singapore 079906

Cambridge University Press is part of the University of Cambridge.

It furthers the University's mission by disseminating knowledge in the pursuit of education, learning, and research at the highest international levels of excellence.

www.cambridge.org
Information on this title: www.cambridge.org/9781107103696
DOI: 10.1017/9781316217344

© Corrie Decker and Elisabeth McMahon 2021

First published 2021

A catalogue record for this publication is available from the British Library.

ISBN 978-1-107-10369-6 Hardback
ISBN 978-1-107-50322-9 Paperback

Cambridge University Press has no responsibility for the persistence or accuracy of URLs for external or third-party internet websites referred to in this publication and does not guarantee that any content on such websites is, or will remain, accurate or appropriate.

Contents

PART III "PROBLEMS" IN THE DEVELOPMENT EPISTEME

Figures

Tables

Maps

Boxes

Acknowledgments

We faced many challenges writing this book, in part because of the strongly held belief among some scholars that a history of development in Africa should convey a teleological history of economic progress. We were never going to write that book. Nonetheless, we appreciate all the feedback we received from anonymous reviewers – both positive and negative – as it helped us articulate our intentions more clearly and ground our arguments more firmly in the historical evidence. We are especially grateful to our series editor, Martin Klein, and to Cambridge University Press editors Maria Marsh and Dan Brown for their encouragement and guidance throughout the process. In particular, Martin Klein's painstaking reading of multiple drafts offered invaluable insights. Also, we are very thankful to Stephanie Taylor, Atifa Jiwa, Allan Alphonse, and Ami Naramor for making the final production of this book possible.

We are grateful to Melissa Graboyes for reading and offering feedback on Chapter 11, to Garrett Ingoglia for speaking openly about his work with AmeriCares during the 2014–2015 Ebola crisis in Liberia, and to Laurence Maka for sharing our work with his students at Stawa University in Kampala, Uganda. For her helpful work in framing the early chapters of this book, we would like to thank Margaret Puskar-Pasewicz of MargaretEdits. Thanks to Donald Treiman for allowing us the use of one of his photographs.

We wrote this book for students and anyone else interested in development in Africa. For this reason, we are truly indebted to the students at Tulane University, UC Davis, and Stawa University who took our courses, debated the topics addressed in this book, and/or read and critiqued draft chapters.

Corrie offers special thanks to Sheikha Abdulla, Mouna Albakry, Garrett Ingoglia, Laurence Maka, Stephan Miescher, Marissa Mika, Martha Saavedra, Sarah Zimmerman, and numerous other colleagues and friends for the many thought-provoking discussions about development that informed this book in some way. Thanks also go to my UC Davis community for their moral and intellectual camaraderie. This book would not have happened without the unending support of my family and, in particular, the patience and understanding of my partner, Chris.

Liz offers special thanks to her community of African historians on Facebook for their encouragement and excitement about the project. Numerous shared discussions, ideas, and articles have helped in writing this book. Thanks also go to my colleagues at Tulane who have been enormously helpful and to the provost's office for holding regular writing retreats. Special thanks to my entire family, who endured me writing when I came to visit rather than actually spending time with them. Thanks to Vera Lester for keeping me sane and flexible. And of course, Chris and Wheeler, who make everything possible.

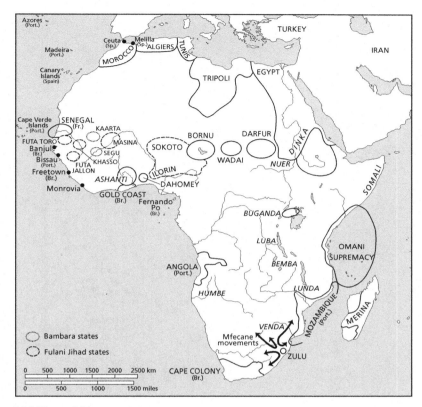

MAP 0.1 Africa ca. 1830

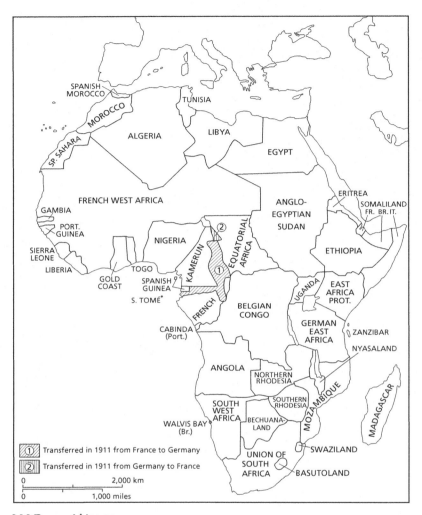

MAP 0.2 Africa ca. 1914

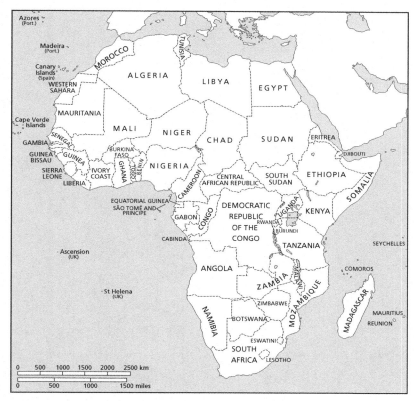

MAP 0.3 Africa ca. 2020

Introduction

The pictures show smiling children in western-style clothing, writing in school notebooks with their decorated pencils; one little girl wears a cross dangling from a silver chain and the headlines bleat "Invest in Uganda's Youth" and "Investing in Ethiopia's People." Welcome to the Africa page of the World Bank website. The World Bank is the largest international financial institution dedicated to supporting global economic development through capitalist projects. A quick glance at the World Bank website offers some insight into how institutions with the economic means to determine international aid policies define development. At the time we write this, the World Bank in Africa website offers an overview of current growth rates for sub-Saharan African economies in a section titled "Africa at-a-Glance."[1] An "Overview" distinguishes "resource-intensive" countries from those that are "non-resource-intensive" and notes that "many challenges remain" in African nations' efforts to grow their economies. Among these challenges are unemployment, poverty, and "fragility." The "Data" section of the World Bank in Africa page includes graphs showing per capita gross national income (GNI), along with population and other statistics. The "Project" section features a summary of a plan to extend access to electricity in West Africa. Other links on the website navigate to discussions of public health, violence, and challenges and opportunities for entrepreneurs. The bottom of the page highlights two "Experts" at the World Bank who are economists from

---

[1] www.worldbank.org/en/region/afr, accessed June 12, 2019. The plan referenced is the "West African Power Pool" project.

Egypt and Cameroon. The reports and data referenced on the front page of the World Bank in Africa website define development in narrow economic terms around resources and wealth, while the images of and stories about African children reify a particular vision of what underdevelopment looks like in Africa: poverty, poor nutrition, and limited access to schooling. This vision is based in what we call the development episteme, the knowledge system that has shaped ideas of development for Africa over the past two centuries.

While providing a broad overview of sub-Saharan Africa's social, economic, and political conditions, the World Bank narrowly defines underdeveloped economies as a problem for the global economy. The World Bank suggests this problem can be fixed through the collection of "Data" that feed into western-style scientific solutions. "Experts" then translate the scientific results into "Projects" meant to expand the national economies of African countries and thus bring Africa's youth into a future defined in terms of neoliberal capitalism and western modernity. Each piece of the World Bank in Africa website represents a piece of the development episteme that advocates this western-style modernity, a modernity that is constantly changing and thus always out of reach.

To the majority of Africans today, "development" does not necessarily mean GNI, growth rates, or statistical assessments of infrastructure in their countries. Development is both more tangible on an individual level – a measure of a mother's ability to pay school fees for her children, for example – and less concrete – such as a general sense of "moving forward" (Swahili, *maendeleo*) or embracing change. Nonetheless, the World Bank's definition of development and, in particular, the idea that some nations lag behind others, has informed and continues to inform international development policies for Africa. *The Idea of Development in Africa* offers an overview that explores where this idea of development came from and how it has shaped Africa's past, present, and visions for the future.

The title of this book is a nod to Congolese philosopher V. Y. Mudimbe's *The Idea of Africa* (1994).[2] Mudimbe argues that the "idea of Africa" now pervasive globally materialized during the era of European colonialism starting in the nineteenth century. This idea

---

[2]   V. Y. Mudimbe, *The Idea of Africa* (Indiana University Press, 1994). See also V. Y. Mudimbe, *The Invention of Africa: Gnosis, Philosophy, and the Order of Knowledge* (Indiana University Press, 1988).

became ingrained, co-opted, and reformed – though not completely transformed – by Africans themselves who inherited the language of othering from colonialism and turned it into a language of solidarity in the twentieth century. This "idea of Africa" portrays the continent and its people as stuck in the past and embroiled in poverty and, therefore, the target of necessary and justified intervention. This idea of Africa was thus inherent to the development episteme, and vice versa. The terminology has changed over time, and the speakers now include Africans as well as westerners, but the basic assumptions about the difference between those who are developed and those who need development have not changed. This book provides an overview of the historical foundations of those assumptions (the development episteme) and how it gave shape to the idea of development. Our intention is to engage readers in a conversation about how and why international development efforts in Africa have historically had ambiguous results, and why we need to challenge the basic assumptions underlying our contemporary idea of development.

THE DEVELOPMENT EPISTEME

The development episteme has been an essential component of the "idea of Africa" in western discourses since the early 1800s. The word "episteme" means knowledge system or the creation of knowledge. Episteme is not merely the creation of knowledge but the hegemony of that knowledge and the idea that a particular epistemology, or way of knowing, is the *only* way of getting at the truth. The "development episteme" thus refers to the knowledge system that claims there are real, measurable differences in "development" between nations, societies, or social groups. It is the "scientific" concept that some societies are "developed" and others are "undeveloped," "less developed," or in the process of "developing." The development episteme promotes the impression that development is the *only* lens through which one can understand African cultures and societies.[3]

Africa's modern history has been a history of development. By this, we do not mean the capitalist economic growth, the expansion of

---

[3] For more on the hegemony of the development discourse see Arturo Escobar, *Encountering Development: The Making and Unmaking of the Third World* (Princeton University Press, 2012 [1995]).

infrastructure, or the emergence of democratic nation-states that many African countries have experienced. We investigate the history of the ideas, practices, and "problems" of development as the episteme that has shaped the way westerners perceive African people, societies, and environments. Many diplomats, professionals, practitioners, and scholars assert that international development began with the Bretton Woods Conference of 1944 and the creation of the World Bank and the International Monetary Fund (IMF) the following year.[4] According to the standard narrative, these institutions initially raised funds for Europe's recovery in the wake of World War II and then gradually shifted their attention toward development of the "Third World," or what today is often called "the global south." This book offers a different take on the history of development by examining the origins of the development episteme itself.[5]

The development episteme emerged out of Enlightenment philosophies that justified a sense of racial and cultural superiority among Europeans and instilled in them the impulse to "civilize" the rest of the world. This civilizing mission, which some people in the late nineteenth century described as the "white man's burden," laid the groundwork for many of the development discourses and practices directed toward Africa and Africans today. Assumptions about racial difference remained foundational to the development episteme between the 1880s and the 1950s, when more than 90 percent of the African continent was under European colonial control. Gradually after the Second World War, the development discourse shifted its focus from race to culture, but the othering of Africans racially, culturally, and geographically has not disappeared. This othering is not necessarily a reflection of racial biases or nefarious intentions among individuals engaged in development work – quite the opposite. Most people working toward developing Africa aim for justice and equality globally. However, the structures of the development industry nonetheless perpetuate ideological and material inequalities. The central argument of this book is that this logic of difference and differentiation is built into the foundations of the development episteme itself. We offer an overview of how the idea of development, or the development

[4]   See, for example, Barrie Ireton, *Britain's International Development Policies: A History of DFID and Overseas Aid* (Palgrave Macmillan, 2013); Corinna Unger's *International Development: A Postwar History* (Bloomsbury Academic Press, 2018).
[5]   Aram Ziai, *Development Discourse and Global History: From Colonialism to Sustainable Development Goals* (Routledge, 2016).

episteme, came into being, and how this idea has shaped particular policies and practices in Africa over the past two centuries. Each chapter also provides examples of how the development episteme endures into the present day.

VERNACULAR DEVELOPMENT

While the development episteme has dominated western ideas about Africa, Africans themselves have generated their own diverse meanings of development. Vernacular development, or the words and phrases Africans have used to describe development, highlights the ways in which development became translated and redefined in African languages and cultures and how the targets of development interventions have designed their own paradigms for understanding economic, political, and social change.[6]

In the Shona language of Zimbabwe, the word *budiriro* is used as a translation for "development." *Budiriro* literally means "physical and material success." Anthropologist Erica Bornstein argues that this concept has moral implications in addition to practical ones. Success in material or physical form is not enough. One who is successful must also be humble and generous, for there is a negative connotation to *budiriro*, an underside to development that refers to the potential to corrupt by desire, greed, or envy. Thus, built into the Shona concept of development is both the idea of striving for material gain and the warning about the negative consequences this success might bring.[7]

Elsewhere, development is understood as a process of transforming from one thing into another. For example, the word for "development" in Xhosa, a language spoken in South Africa, is *uphuhliso*, which refers to renewal or improvement of a current condition. This word is also used to indicate empowerment or the ability to overcome challenges. Closer to the English word "development" in its literal sense is the Wolof word *yokute*, which comes from the root *yokk*, meaning to "add" or "increase." In the *yokute* form, however, the word takes on a new connotation. For example, Senegalese president Macky Sall has

---

[6] The authors thank Dr. Carolyn E. Vieira-Martinez and the Asili Collaborative Research Group for providing a list of African-language terms related to development, which was compiled from their databases.

[7] Erica Bornstein, *The Spirit of Development: Protestant NGOs, Morality, and Economics in Zimbabwe* (Routledge, 2003), 155.

employed the slogan "*Yoonu Yokute*" to describe his national development plan. *Yoonu Yokute* translates as "The Way Forward" or "The
Pathway to Development." Though the Wolof root word for "development" evokes accumulation or growth – a concept that might imply
personal, material success – the word *yokute* has a broader connotation
referring to progress for all.[8]

"Moving forward" is a common sentiment conveyed by African-
language terms for "development." As mentioned earlier, the Swahili
word *maendeleo*, used widely across eastern Africa, comes from the root
word *kuenda* ("to go"), as well as the word *kuendelea* ("to go on" or "to
continue"). Anthropologist James Smith notes that in Kenya *maendeleo*
can refer to movement in space *or* to movement in time. As such,
maendeleo can indicate anything from an individual traveling to
a foreign land to a community planning for its future.[9] Similar words
and phrases referencing mobility include the Hausa term *ci gaba* used
in Northern Nigeria and the Malagasy word *fampandrosoana* common
in Madagascar. These phrases have different meanings in different
contexts, but they all connote a general sense of heading in a certain
direction toward the future. Some scholars have interpreted this as
"modernity" rather than "development." Along these lines, anthropologist James Ferguson has argued that, as development appears to
have failed Africa, modernity has replaced development as the goal for
those who want to improve their lives and communities.[10]

African concepts of development must also be understood in terms
of philosophies about humanity and social change. One common ideal
in African philosophies is the notion of *ubuntu*, generally translated as
"I am because we are." This idea originated from southern Africa in
the nineteenth century and became widely popular across the continent in the 1950s. It celebrates communal well-being over individual
prosperity. African nationalist leaders in particular embraced *ubuntu* as
a symbol of pan-African solidarity, and today the word *ubuntu* appears
in the names of nongovernmental organizations (NGOs), religious
movements, political parties, and even computer software. Africans
across the continent evoke this ideal in order to explain their shared

---

[8]   Jean Léopold Diouf, *Dictionnaire wolof-français et français-wolof* (Karthala, 2003).
[9]   James Smith, *Bewitching Development: Witchcraft and the Reinvention of Development
      in Neoliberal Kenya* (University of Chicago Press, 2008), 4–7.
[10] James Ferguson, *Global Shadows: Africa in a Neoliberal World Order* (Duke University
      Press, 2006).

values and goals for development and to capitalize on its global currency.[11]

Whether African-language words for development imply the amassing of wealth, globalization, individual transformation, community values, or simply heading into the future, they provide insight into the nuances of meaning Africans have brought to development ideas and practices. Alternative visions of development can also reveal some of the assumptions and misconceptions built into western ideals and top-down development policies. Comedic interpretations of international development initiatives on television or the Internet, especially by Africans, poignantly highlight common fallacies about Africa. Before he became the host of Comedy Central's *The Daily Show*, South African comedian Trevor Noah did a bit as a guest on a show called *Spot the Africa*, which poked fun at western stereotypes about African poverty and underdevelopment.[12] Other artists and activists ridicule the development industry itself. The web series entitled *The Samaritans* features a fictional NGO called "Aid for Aid" based in Nairobi, Kenya. In order to access episodes of the show, which is "about an NGO that does nothing," visitors make a small donation to fund the production of future episodes.[13] Government development organizations have even funded efforts to flip the script on the development discourse. The Norwegian Agency for Development Cooperation funded a student group to run an annual competition, the "Radi-Aid Award," for commercials that highlight stereotypes in NGO advertising, most famously producing a video asking Africans to send radiators to the poor freezing Norwegians because "frostbite kills too."[14] Another winning Radi-Aid video mocks people and organizations seeking to "save Africa."

The amount of money generated from development and the number of people profiting from it, however, is no joke. Development is its own multibillion-dollar industry, and has spawned what Nigerian-American writer Teju Cole has labeled the "White Savior Industrial Complex" that drives much of the western urge "to do something" in Africa.[15] For

---

[11] Michael Onyebuchi Eze, *Intellectual History in Contemporary South Africa* (Palgrave Macmillan, 2010), 89–192.

[12] *Spot the Africa*, www.youtube.com/watch?v=AHO1a1kvZGo, accessed June 12, 2019.

[13] *The Samaritans*, www.aidforaid.org/, accessed June 12, 2019.

[14] "The Rusty Radiator," http://radiaid.com/, accessed June 12, 2019.

[15] Teju Cole, "The White-Savior Industrial Complex," *The Atlantic*, March 21, 2012, www.theatlantic.com/international/archive/2012/03/the-white-savior-industrial-complex/254843/, accessed June 12, 2019.

well-off people in the global north who struggle with how to tackle societal problems within their own countries, offering "aid" to African countries puts distance between their own lives and those "in need" while assuaging their guilt. It is no wonder that development continues to be the primary lens through which the world sees Africa and Africans.

A BRIEF HISTORY OF DEVELOPMENT IN AFRICA

Development has and still is frequently packaged as a gift from the haves to the have-nots. During the nineteenth century, the humanitarian efforts of missionaries and Europeans who embraced the "white man's burden" portrayed "civilization" as a gift to Africans. This civilizing mission set the tone for colonial and postcolonial international interventions in Africa. Colonial-era development was never simply about helping Africans, but was also an ideological, economic, and political project that sought to exploit African land, labor, and resources. This is not our judgment on development, but was built into the very conceptualization of colonial development policy. The French term for colonial development in Africa was *mise en valeur*, a phrase world systems scholar Immanuel Wallerstein has pointed out literally translates as "making into value."[16] Similarly, Britain's Colonial Development Act of 1929 stated explicitly that colonial development funding must promote "commerce with and industry in the United Kingdom."[17] The colonial policies of self-sufficiency dictated that the costs of administration, infrastructure, health care, education, and other social services had to come out of local revenues rather than metropolitan resources.[18] Many colonial administrations relied on philanthropic organizations like the Rockefeller Foundation and the Carnegie Commission to offset the cost of development programs.[19]

---

[16] Immanuel Wallerstein, "After Development and Globalization, What?" *Social Forces* 83:3 (2005) 1263–1278 at 1263.

[17] Great Britain Colonial Office, *First Interim Report of the Colonial Development Advisory Committee Covering the Period 1st August 1929–28th February 1930* (His Majesty's Stationary Office, 1930), 7.

[18] Crawford Young, *The African Colonial State in Comparative Perspective* (Yale University Press, 1994), 97.

[19] Edward H. Berman, *The Influence of Carnegie, Ford, and Rockefeller Foundations on American Foreign Policy: The Ideology of Philanthropy* (State University of New York Press, 1983), 133–136.

After World War II, new development policies addressed the demands Africans, colonial officials, missionaries, and humanitarians made for more attention and funding toward "social welfare." Metropolitan funding schemes like Britain's Colonial Development and Welfare Fund, established in 1940, and France's Fonds d'investissements pour le développement économique et social (FIDES), inaugurated in 1946, funneled new life into development and welfare programs that appeared to focus more on Africa than on Europe. European imperial powers offered this "gift" of development in order to quell anticolonial sentiment and convince Africans that their European overseers had their best interests at heart. This was Europe's desperate attempt to prevent what was perhaps already a forgone conclusion, the closing chapter on colonialism. Development was repackaged once more in the postcolonial era, this time as a "gift" from wealthy nations to newly independent African countries and, in trickle-down economics fashion, from nationalist elites to their constituencies. Just like its colonial precedents, the gift of nationalist development was exposed as a broken promise in the 1970s and 1980s when the World Bank and IMF's Structural Adjustment Programs devastated African economies. Even as the policies and practices changed, the fundamental definition of development remained static.

Despite the extractive nature of development policies, Africans were adept at making development work for them. Colonial and postcolonial administrators pushed back against restrictive policies that limited spending on welfare programs. Many advocates for development in Africa believed wholeheartedly that they were altruistic endeavors to combat poverty, disease, or other calamities. However, even where development agents and policies prioritized African interests, they had to contend with the fact that, ultimately, development was required to be profitable. The "gift" of development always had strings attached.

During the nationalist era, some African political leaders debated whether international development interventions in Africa constituted a form of neocolonialism. In his 1965 book titled *Neo-colonialism: The Last Stage of Imperialism*, Kwame Nkrumah defined neocolonialism as a situation in which a state is "in theory, independent and has all the outward trappings of international sovereignty," but "[i]n reality its economic system and thus its political policy is directed from outside."[20] Some argue that neocolonialism is evident in the fact

[20]   Kwame Nkrumah, *Neo-colonialism: The Last Stage of Imperialism* (Thomas Nelson, 1965), ix.

that, at the time we write this, some former French colonies' currencies and public financing are still determined by the French treasury.[21] African political leaders have also expressed concern that postcolonial international organizations such as the British Commonwealth of Nations or the Comunidade dos Países de Língua Portuguesa (Community of Portuguese-Speaking Countries) (CPLP), founded in 1997, constitute cultural or political forms of neocolonialism.[22] Even where former colonial powers no longer have control over African national economies, they often attempt to influence African politics by leveraging development aid. When an anti-homosexuality bill appeared before the Ugandan parliament in 2011, Britain threatened to withdraw development funding to its former colony.[23] Other donor nations followed suit after a version of the bill passed in 2014, though they backed off when the Ugandan constitutional court revoked the law. In these ways, wealthy countries (often former colonizers) lord their financial power over poorer countries (often their former colonies). Accusations of neocolonialism in Africa were not reserved for former imperial powers. Many Africans have argued that World Bank and IMF policies have increased Africa's dependency on the global north and replicated colonial-era political relationships.

Whether referring to the colonial or postcolonial era, one of the primary aims of the development enterprise has been to make African countries look more like western ones economically, politically, and culturally. Development interventions strive to encourage neoliberal capitalist trade and investment and to pressure African leaders to

---

[21] The currency used in francophone West and Central Africa (the Colonies Francises d'Afrique [CFA] franc) was pegged to the French franc and later to the euro. Since 1959, the central banks of West and Central Africa have collected foreign exchange reserve funds from these territories (now independent nations) in order to pay a tax to the French treasury. In 2020, eight West African countries will stop using the CFA franc and change their currency to the eco. The nations using the eco will no longer be required to keep a portion of their foreign reserves in France. The Comoros Islands, a former French territory, also pays into this tax fund, even though it is not a member of either bank. The French government can seize these funds at any time for economic or political reasons. Anne-Marie Gulde and Charalambos Tsangarides, eds., *The CFA Franc Zone: Common Currency, Uncommon Challenges* (International Monetary Fund, 2008).

[22] Norrie Macqueen, "A Community of Illusions? Portugal, the CPLP and Peacemaking in Guiné-Bissau," *International Peacekeeping* 10:2 (2003) 2–26.

[23] "Uganda Fury at David Cameron Aid Threat over Gay Rights," BBC News, October 31, 2011, www.bbc.com/news/world-africa-15524013, accessed January 12, 2018.

institute democratic reforms. On the surface, these are laudable aspirations designed to improve the lives of Africans and make African nations more equal partners in the global market. However, the underlying impetus behind these efforts has always been to facilitate foreign investment and trade and to ensure the continued prosperity of wealthy countries as much as to help African nations become wealthier. One of the fundamental beliefs behind international development is the notion that everyone has the potential to prosper in a capitalist system. This idea has been fiercely challenged by world systems theorist Immanuel Wallerstein and historian-activist Walter Rodney, as well as university graduates whose degrees are not recognized in the global north, entrepreneurs shut out of business deals in their own countries, public employees who only occasionally receive paychecks from bankrupt African governments, and others who have yet to see the promised benefits of neoliberal capitalism.[24]

Development funding comes in many different forms, ranging from capitalist investments designed for profit to aid that may or may not require a return on investment (ROI). Humanitarian aid, conditional loans from international institutions, foreign direct investment (FDI), collaborative profit-yielding ventures, and country-to-country assistance are just some examples of development funding. Development projects may be short or long term, one-time transactions or ongoing relationships. The benefits and pitfalls of development projects are not always clear. For example, infrastructural development may be welcomed by some but considered a burden by others if the project requires ongoing maintenance that the state or society is unwilling or unable to perform. Much development assistance consists of humanitarian efforts focused on poor relief, responses to health crises, and other emergency aid that effectively deal with catastrophes, but fail to address the sources of the problems themselves.

Development often seems like a game of Whack-a-Mole: tackling one problem as another one pops up, then going after that problem while a new one emerges, and so forth. Piecemeal action and the emphasis on development "projects" force development agents to focus on one village, one issue, or one initiative at a time. Thus, even

---

[24] See, for example, Immanuel Wallerstein, *World-Systems Analysis: An Introduction* (Duke University Press, 2004), and Walter Rodney, *How Europe Underdeveloped Africa* (Howard University Press, Revised ed. 1982 [orig. Bogle-L'Ouverture Publications, 1972]).

as the development discourse promises equality (by transforming the have-nots into the haves), the ad hoc nature of development intervention perpetuates inequalities through differential access to health care, education, clean water, and other services. Development interventions have been often reactive rather than proactive and solutions are often touted as one size fits all. When development projects fail, the "experts" often offer new development solutions rather than questioning their assumptions about the development "problems." Development is self-perpetuating. *The Idea of Development in Africa* is not a comprehensive listing of which development projects have or have not worked, but an overview of development in Africa supplemented with case studies that demonstrate the fundamental characteristics of the development episteme and its influence on the present.

Africans have long created their own ingenious methods for sustaining their environments, promoting their economic interests, and protecting themselves from various forms of oppression or exploitation. In the age of international development, many people circumvent governments, multinational corporations, and international financial institutions in order to promote local interests and grassroots initiatives. The turn toward neoliberalism in development since the late 1990s has led to an increase in pan-African, national, and local nongovernmental organizations (LNGOs), such as the Forum for African Women Educationalists/Forum des éducatrices africaines (FAWE),[25] the conservationist NATURAMA group[26] in Burkina Faso, and the Mwambao Coastal Community Network[27] in Tanzania, to name a few. While international development institutions and agents maintain considerable power over financial decisions and planning, African NGOs have helped communities maintain control over local funds and have given African recipients of development aid a stronger voice in defining what development means for them.

The early years of the twenty-first century ushered in much optimism about Africa's development prospects. This "Africa Rising" narrative proclaimed new opportunities on the horizon associated with increasing gross domestic product (GDP), the emergence of financial environments conducive to FDI, and the rapid industrialization of African

---

[25] See http://fawe.org/home/, accessed June 12, 2019.
[26] See www.naturama.bf/web/index.php/naturama/2016-04-15-18-25-59/organisa tion, accessed June 12, 2019.
[27] See www.mwambao.or.tz/, accessed June 12, 2019.

economies.[28] The African Development Bank, established by the Organization of African Unity (the African Union) in 1964, and the New Partnership for African Development (NEPAD), formed in 2001, have trumpeted this message of positivity. In 2016, the African Development Bank laid out the following "High 5" development priorities: Light Up and Power Africa, Feed Africa, Industrialize Africa, Integrate Africa, and Improve the Quality of Life for the People of Africa.[29] That same year, NEPAD declared four similar investment schemes in Human Capital Development; Industrialization, Science, Technology and Innovation; Regional Integration, Infrastructure and Trade; and Natural Resources Governance and Food Security.[30] Whereas the African Development Bank is more focused on development financing, NEPAD seeks to coordinate African countries' national development agendas in order to identify common goals across the continent. The development plans for both entities align closely with the United Nations Development Programme's (UNDP) Sustainable Development Goals.[31] With the exception of greater emphasis on renewable energy and environmental protection, these development objectives are not new. Reducing poverty, building infrastructure, providing clean water and electricity, expanding modern education and training programs, drawing more Africans into wage employment, integrating African economies into the world market, encouraging foreign investment and trade, and improving the health of women and children have been the goals of development interventions since at least the 1930s, and many of them much earlier. The financial arrangements – colonial government investment, bilateral aid between nations, grants and loans from the World Bank and the IMF, and FDI through private companies and individuals – have varied; however, the essential definition of development in all of these approaches has not changed. We argue for a deeper historical understanding of the idea of development in

---

[28] *The Economist* dedicated its December 3, 2011, issue to the theme "Africa Rising: The Hopeful Continent," www.economist.com/leaders/2011/12/03/africa-rising, accessed February 4, 2020.

[29] African Development Bank, *African Economic Outlook, 2017: Entrepreneurship and Industrialisation* (African Development Bank, Organisation for Economic Co-Operation and Development, United Nations Development Programme, 2017).

[30] "About NEPAD," http://nepad.org/content/about-nepad, accessed June 12, 2019.

[31] United Nations Development Programme (UNDP) Sustainable Development Goals, www.undp.org/content/undp/en/home/sustainable-development-goals.html, accessed June 12, 2019.

Africa in order to break the cycle generated by the development episteme.

BEYOND AN ECONOMIC HISTORY
OF DEVELOPMENT

Until recently, the history of development in Africa has been a teleological story of national economic growth, industrialization, infrastructure building, capitalist enterprises, per capita income, and changing standards of living since World War II. Foundational studies of Africa's economic history recognize that colonial extraction and exploitation of African labor negatively impacted African economies.[32] However, these works often embrace the notion that now-independent African nations can and should aspire toward the western industrialized model of development. They assume a primarily economic and capitalist definition of development. More recent scholarship has critically examined the specific ideas, policies, and practices carried out in the name of development and evaluated their impact on Africa and Africans. These works include studies on socialist development in Tanzania, witchcraft and ideas about development in Kenya, unsuccessful agricultural development schemes in Mali, gender and social development in Nigeria, women's professionalization and colonial development in Zanzibar, the centrality of NGOs to development polices in the Sahel, development of the oil industry, creation of scientific knowledge for development, colonial development, and gender and development.[33] *The Idea of Development in Africa* builds on these efforts

[32] Anthony Hopkins, *An Economic History of West Africa* (Routledge, 2014 [orig. Addison Wesley Longman, 1973]); Ralph Austen, *African Economic History: Internal Development and External Dependency* (James Currey, 1987).

[33] Priya Lal, *African Socialism in Postcolonial Tanzania: Between the Village and the World* (Cambridge University Press, 2015); Smith, *Bewitching Development*; Monica van Beusekom, *Negotiating Development: African Farmers and Colonial Experts at the Office Du Niger, 1920–1960* (Heinemann, 2002); Abosede A. George, *Making Modern Girls: A History of Girlhood, Labor, and Social Development in Colonial Lagos* (Ohio University Press, 2014); Corrie Decker, *Mobilizing Zanzibari Women: The Struggle for Respectability and Self-Reliance in Colonial East Africa* (Palgrave Macmillan, 2014); Gregory Mann, *From Empires to NGOS in the West African Sahel: The Road to Nongovernmentality* (Cambridge University Press, 2015); Jesse Salah Ovadia, *The Petro-developmental State in Africa: Making Oil Work in Angola, Nigeria and the Gulf of Guinea* (Hurst, 2016); Helen Tilley, *Africa As a Living Laboratory: Empire, Development, and the Problem of Scientific Knowledge, 1870–1950* (University of

to move beyond a narrow economic history of development in order to identify the key development ideas, practices, and "problems" that have shaped Africa's past and present. We address the following questions: What has driven the development impulse in Africa over time? How has development been defined and who has defined it? How did the development episteme become the dominant framework for understanding African political, economic, and social dynamics?

Development has come in many different forms and was not always called "development," but we define it in three ways. First, development entails the development episteme, or the creation of knowledge about Africa's social, economic, political, environmental, intellectual, and physical conditions and how to improve them. These ideas have been generated primarily by non-African governments and individuals located in the global north. Second, development refers to the specific policies and practices arising from this "knowledge" imposed onto African communities. Third, because it is based in an unequal relationship between the "haves" and the "have-nots" (that is, those who claim to have development and those they proclaim do not have and therefore need development), development is a discourse of power that "experts" have inflicted on Africans, though Africans have also challenged, redefined, subverted, or engineered development theories and practices.[34] In short, development entails knowledge production, the power to implement this knowledge, and the impact this knowledge and power have on the experience of individuals caught in the system. Parts I, II, and III of this book correlate with these three definitions of development, respectively, and historicize the relationship between them. *The Idea of Development in Africa* thus maps out the origins of the development episteme in nineteenth-century imperialism and colonialism (Part I), how the development episteme determined the trajectory of colonial and postcolonial international development policies and practices for Africa (Part II), and how it shaped approaches to specific development "problems" in Africa during the twentieth and twenty-first centuries (Part III). Each chapter presents the reader with an introductory overview of the topic and specific examples from the past and present that represent the issue discussed in the chapter. By

Chicago Press, 2011); Joseph M. Hodge, Gerald Hödl, and Martina Kopf, eds., *Developing Africa: Concepts and Practices in Twentieth-Century Colonialism* (Manchester University Press, 2014); April Gordon, *Transforming Capitalism and Patriarchy: Gender and Development in Africa* (Lynne Rienner, 1996).

[34] Escobar, *Encountering Development*, 10.

putting the past and present into dialogue, this book offers readers a new way to think about the relationship between development, power, and the creation of knowledge about Africa and Africans.

★★★

Development has become its own industry invested as much in its continued existence as it is in eradicating poverty, generating growth, and facilitating global trade. This does not discount the fact that many African individuals and societies have benefited directly from development and many have embraced fully the ideology that Africa and Africans need development. Despite the rhetoric on saving, helping, and equalizing, the development industry has done more to maintain global and local inequalities than it has to dismantle them. This is part of the legacy of European colonialism in Africa, a legacy international development has yet to shed, regardless of the intentions of development experts and advocates. We analyze the ways in which development has been conceptualized and implemented in order to expose the inequalities embedded in the development episteme, and thus spark a conversation among development experts, investors, volunteers, and local, national, and international leaders about the inadequacy of viewing Africa through the development lens. It may be impossible to decolonize development fully or disentangle Africa from the development discourse; nevertheless, we believe it is worthwhile to imagine other ways of understanding Africa's place in the world.

Part I

Origins of the Development Episteme

CHAPTER 1

From Progress to Development

The smoked monkeys brought the point home. During my first day on a boat on the Congo River, I'd embraced the unfamiliar: how to bend under the rail to fill my wash bucket from the river, where to step around the tethered goat in the dark and the best way to prepare a pot of grubs. But when I saw the monkeys impaled on stakes, skulls picked clean of brains and teeth thrusting out, I looked otherness in the face – and saw myself mirrored back.

–Maya Jasanoff, "With Conrad on the Congo River," 2017

On August 18, 2017, historian of British imperialism Maya Jasanoff wrote in the *New York Times* about her journey along the Congo River that followed the route Joseph Conrad took in the 1880s.[1] Jasanoff's expectations, reactions, and language demonstrate the rhetorical loop of ideas about development in Africa that has existed for more than 250 years. Echoing Conrad, whose book was "a meditation on progress," Jasanoff herself asked, "what counts as progress?" Her goal was to "take the measure of what has and hasn't changed since his time." By using the language of "progress" Jasanoff offered to modern readers an analysis that directly linked the nineteenth-century concept of progress with twenty-first-century notions of development.

Joseph Conrad published his novella *Heart of Darkness* in 1899, which told the story of a steamboat captain sent up the Congo River to bring back an ill ivory trader, known as Kurtz. The story's narrator questions

---

[1] Maya Jasanoff, "With Conrad on the Congo River," *New York Times*, August 18, 2017, www.nytimes.com/2017/08/18/opinion/joseph-conrad-congo-river.html, accessed February 4, 2020.

whether the experience of colonization in the Congo drove Kurtz, a highly respected European, to madness before he died. As Jasanoff noted in her article, Conrad was as critical of European colonial exploitation in the Congo as he was of the "backwardness" of the Congolese people he encountered. Conrad's representation of Africans as backward or savage was typical of European opinions at the time.

This view evolved out of the eighteenth-century Enlightenment idea that all societies progressed in a linear fashion toward modernity, the pinnacle of which was European civilization. In this construction "modern" or "progressive" societies were those that mimicked European cultural, social, economic, and political structures. While Conrad questioned the costs of European progressivism in 1899, Jasanoff accepted this concept at face value. The idea of progress defined in terms of western modernity had become so pervasive by the twenty-first century that even as Jasanoff recognized Conrad's criticism of colonialism, she did not call into question the concept of progress itself. Either the Democratic Republic of Congo (DRC) had progressed (implying that it more closely resembled western civilization) or it had moved backward; Jasanoff offered no other option.

Conrad's novella gave witness to the rush of late nineteenth-century European colonialism in Africa. The move to colonize Africa was based on the founding idea that European civilization was superior to all other forms of civilization and would bring enlightenment as it spread across the globe. European explorers, missionaries, and colonists saw Africa as a "dark continent" because it did not have the "light" of western civilization shining within it; they saw themselves as the humanitarians who could bring modernity to Africa. As to the question of whether the civilization Europeans envisioned in the nineteenth century had finally come to the modern country of the DRC, Jasanoff's response was a resounding "no." Instead, she decried that "measured in relative terms, most people in Congo were probably better off 100 years ago" than in the present day.[2] This statement was remarkable for its overlooking of the rapacious nature of Belgian colonialism in the region, in particular the period between 1887 and 1907 during which an estimated ten million Congolese were killed and forced to work in a brutal quest to extract rubber and line the pockets of King Leopold II.[3]

---

[2]   Ibid.
[3]   Adam Hochschild, *King Leopold's Ghost: A Story of Greed, Terror, and Heroism in Colonial Africa* (Houghton Mifflin, 1998).

Throughout her narrative of the boat trip, Jasanoff defines for her readers what she means by progress or, in the case of the DRC, the absence of progress. First and foremost, she references the lack of speed with which anything is achieved in the country. Instead of embracing the rapid modern convenience of air travel, Congolese continue to travel primarily by boat. Given the riverine environment of the DRC, boat travel is the most economical and environmentally friendly means of movement within the country. Jasanoff also laments that Congolese river towns lack visible progress by comparing them to the fake towns from "the set of a western" film. Twenty-first-century Congolese towns, in her opinion, cannot even measure up to the Hollywood fantasies of a nineteenth-century US frontier. Furthermore, Jasanoff tells the reader that while the Congolese people are very friendly, they are still culturally backward. She points to foods such as monkey brains and grubs to demonstrate the deficiency of Congolese cuisine, culture, and civilization. It is no wonder that Jasanoff concludes that the DRC was "better off" under Belgian colonialism; according to her, the Congolese have failed to develop because they are not westernized.

Jasanoff's article illustrates the persistence of ideas about linear progress in western discourses on development in Africa, but one thing has changed since the nineteenth century. During the nineteenth century European ideas of progress centered around Christianity. The European "civilizing mission" of the 1800s entailed efforts to modernize, westernize, and Christianize non-western societies, especially in Africa. By the 1920s the civilizing mission, as it had been known, morphed into the concept of "development," which continued to define progress in terms of the remaking of African societies in the mold of the west. Even though Jasanoff does not use the language of the civilizing mission or of Christianity, she still frames her idea of development within a language of linear progress that is directly linked to the adoption of western cultural values. This chapter explores the nineteenth-century origins of the language that Jasanoff uses to describe the DRC and how it became foundational to development studies in present-day Africa.

MAKING THE PROGRESSIVE WEST

During the medieval period many Europeans explained events as God's will. The flow of life – birth, youth, maturity, old age, and death – became a metaphor for civilizations, which were believed to go through a similar cycle as humans. With the Scientific Revolution, Europeans slowly moved out of the "dark ages" into the "light" of knowledge based on empirical studies rather than tradition or super-stition. Enlightenment philosophy introduced the notion that social evolution and progress resulted from scientific inquiry and techno-logical advancements. "Modern" European civilization, especially that of Western European countries, became the model of progress for all societies around the world.

The definition of the word "civilized" evolved over time, but Europeans of the early modern era adopted the word to describe "the west" as distinct from other societies they considered "primitive," or less developed. Martin Lewis and Kären Wigen argue the concept of "the west" began with divisions between the eastern Orthodox and western Latin Christian churches. By the eighteenth century the occi-dent (the west) was mostly defined as Western or Central Europe.[4] However, "the east" was much less clearly defined and usually incorp-orated Islamic societies near Europe. It was in the nineteenth century that the terminology of the west came to mean societies descended from Western Europeans, including colonial settler states such as Canada and the United States. In European discourses the meaning of the orient (the east) expanded from "non-western civilization," such as Islamic societies, to societies "lacking civilization." "The east" then incorporated larger Asia and came to be defined phenotypically, or in racial terms.[5] This racialized geographic distinction between "the west" and "the east" became part of a stratified racial hierarchy that positioned "the west" above all other regions of the world and that placed Africa on the bottom rung. Simultaneously, western societies defined their form of civilization as "modern" based on their adherence to progressivist ideas.

Those progressivist ideas came from Enlightenment thinkers who detached philosophical and scientific ideas from theology. No longer beholden to theology for explaining the world around them, they emphasized the creation of knowledge based on empirical evidence. The rise of scientific knowledge and technological developments brought the notion of progress to the center of Enlightenment theory. Philosophers such as Anne Robert Jacques Turgot, Antoine-Nicolas

---

[4]   Martin W. Lewis and Kären E. Wigen, *The Myth of Continents* (University of California Press, 1997), 49.

[5]   Ibid., 50–55.

de Condorcet, and Immanuel Kant argued that societies moved in a linear fashion toward modernity. Immanuel Kant described the Enlightenment as a "maturity of thinking" that used science and empiricism to fundamentally reframe the episteme of European societies.[6] The foundation of progressive intellectual growth allowed European theorists to see themselves at the forefront of knowledge creation globally. Europeans perceived their civilizations as the yardstick against which all other societies should be measured.[7]

European explorers of the eighteenth and nineteenth centuries began to distinguish themselves as more "civilized" and developed in comparison with the diverse human communities they encountered around the world. Edward Said labeled this process as Orientalism, the racial "othering" of "eastern" people and the eroticization of Arab culture in particular. Othering was a tool of modern European imperialism because it mapped non-European cultures and people onto a global racial hierarchy that reified white men as the pinnacle of progress.[8] European efforts to collect ethnographic data about "other" cultures were not merely a sign of their ethnocentrism or curiosity. Enlightenment progressivism made it imperative for Europeans both to empirically document their knowledge about other societies and to transform these societies into "civilized" ones modeled after the west.

The scientific turn in the development discourse was not entirely disconnected from religion. American sociologist Robert Nisbet argues that the "idea of progress" was actually Christian doctrine secularized.[9] The Protestant religious revivals of the nineteenth century both fueled the rise in missionary societies across Europe and the United States and linked Protestant beliefs with progressivist ideas of labor and economic reward. The new missionaries of the nineteenth century were interested in spreading the gospel and bringing a "civilizing mission" to Africa and Asia. Civilizing primarily required conversion to Christianity, but also the adoption of western cultures and technologies. Progressive ideas allowed westerners in Africa to see

[6]   Immanuel Kant, "An Answer to the Question: What Is Enlightenment?" (1784), in Allen W. Wood, ed., *Basic Writings of Kant* (Modern Library, 2001), 133–142.

[7]   Robert Nisbet, *History of the Idea of Progress*. Fourth edition (Routledge, 2017 [orig. 1980]), 171–316.

[8]   Edward Said, *Orientalism* (Pantheon Books, 1978); Mary Louise Pratt, *Imperial Eyes: Travel Writing and Transculturation* (Routledge, 1992).

[9]   Nisbet, *History of the Idea of Progress*, 172.

themselves not as colonizers exploiting other societies but as humanitarians sharing the gift of their civilization and bringing economic
development to their new converts.

Western Christian missionaries worried about "backsliding" among
their African converts and the threat of "regression" among westerners
who embraced African traditions or beliefs. To return to Conrad's
Heart of Darkness, Kurtz, the brilliant ivory trader, was driven "mad"
by the savagery around him. This brutality represented the dangers of
"going native" by adopting the social and cultural practices of "less
civilized" societies. Enlightenment philosophers argued that regression meant simply becoming less civilized; however, by the end of the
nineteenth century, European distinctions between *who* was civilized
and *who* was not had an implicit racial connotation.[10] Lewis and Wigen
note that in the nineteenth century, "non-western cultures came to be
dismissed as entirely stagnant, if not barbaric, while racism came to be
cloaked with a new intellectual respectability."[11] Thus, western progressivist ideas of "civilizing" slowly adopted racist implications without ever explicitly marking progressivism as a racial ideology.

PROGRESS, MISSIONARIES, AND THE CIVILIZING MISSION

The nineteenth century saw major changes in how European missionaries and governments engaged the civilizing mission and sought to
develop African societies to look like western ones. Western portrayals
of Africans transformed over the century from those featuring a simple,
innocent people bound by the shackles of slavery to those depicting
savages and cannibals who *needed* to be introduced, by force if necessary, to the European model of progressive civilization.[12] An early
effort made by British abolitionists to develop a westernized African
community failed dramatically when the African participants refused
to embrace the capitalist exploitation of their labor. In response, the
colonial government imposed a framework where missionaries did the
work of social and cultural development while the government focused

---

[10]   Patrick Brantlinger, "Victorians and Africans: Genealogy of the Myth of the Dark
        Continent," *Critical Inquiry* 12:1 (1985) 166–203.
[11]   Lewis and Wigen, *The Myth of Continents*, 76.
[12]   Brantlinger, "Victorians and Africans."

on economic development; this framework would come to dominate colonial social and political structures into the twentieth century.

Religious revivalism in Europe and America during the late eighteenth and mid-nineteenth centuries sparked the abolitionist and missionary causes in Africa. One of the earliest examples of the European civilizing mission in West Africa was the founding of the colony of Sierra Leone. In 1787 Granville Sharp, a leading British abolitionist, helped to establish the colony with 340 Black ex-slaves from North America. Sharp envisioned a colony where the Black settlers, all of whom were already Christians, would own their land, create their government, and slowly bring Christianity and western values to Africans. He hoped for a self-sufficient, model society that would demonstrate to Europeans the humanity and dignity of ex-slaves, thereby reinforcing efforts to abolish the slave trade. After four years and the death of 292 settlers, other British abolitionists declared the experiment a disaster.

Henry Thornton, an associate of Granville Sharp, took over control of the Sierra Leone colony but incorporated it into a charter company called the Sierra Leone Company (SLC). The new company's stated goal was to "promote civilization in Africa," but as a company that had to generate profit for its investors, its central aim was economic development.[13] The company took ownership of all the land and assets of the original colony, imposed a white British governor on the surviving Black settlers, and set economic goals for anyone living in the settlement. Thornton instituted a model wherein the civilizing of Africa would be achieved through western-style "disciplined work" done by Black people and supervised by white Europeans. Civilizing Africans may have been the stated intention of the SLC, but the primary outcome was the introduction of western-style economic development.

Twelve hundred new settlers, originally ex-slave maroons from Jamaica who had settled in Nova Scotia, agreed to move to Sierra Leone in 1792 with hopes of leaving behind the racial bias they encountered in Canada. These settlers, all of whom were Protestant Christians, viewed themselves as free British subjects, not Africans. However, the white founders of the SLC insisted on

---

[13] Cassandra Pybus, "'A Less Favourable Specimen': The Abolitionist Response to Self-Emancipated Slaves in Sierra Leone, 1793–1808," *Parliamentary History* 26:4 (2007) 97–112 at 99.

calling them Africans.[14] As Thornton decreed, the settlers were treated as economic laborers without rights of representation in the government. Over the course of the next decade the settlers resisted the actions of the SLC governor, Macaulay. Macaulay blamed resistance not on his economic policies but rather on the influence of Black ministers among the Methodist settlers. Macaulay brought European teachers and religious leaders to the colony in an effort to undermine the Black ministers and control the Black settlers. Eventually, when he left the colony in 1799, he took twenty-five African children to be educated in England. He viewed African children as the future of civilizing in the continent because they were more malleable than the ex-slaves. Macaulay, much like many other abolitionists of the time, had come to believe that enslavement fundamentally corrupted Africans' ability to become civilized or develop economically.

The British government took over Sierra Leone from the SLC in 1808 and officially designated it a colony of Britain. After the British abolition of the transatlantic slave trade in 1807, British naval vessels began "liberating" Africans by intercepting slave ships. Many of these "liberated" Africans were deposited in Sierra Leone and handed over to the Church Missionary Society (CMS) missionaries to be educated in the "civilized" ways of Europeans.[15] From the perspective of British officials, freeing Africans from slavery also meant freeing them from the "savagery" of a society that accepted slavery. Numerous liberated Africans brought to Freetown, Sierra Leone, tried to leave the missions, and government officials and missionaries eventually imposed apprenticeships and indenture contracts to discourage flight and "teach" them how to "work."[16] They needed to keep the liberated Africans in the colony as workers in order to make the colony cost-effective. This policy demonstrates the direct link between the civilizing mission and economic aspects of colonization.

---

[14] Ibid., 100.
[15] Bronwen Everill, *Abolition and Empire in Sierra Leone and Liberia* (Palgrave Macmillan, 2013).
[16] Everill, *Abolition and Empire*, 20, 36. See also Philip D. Curtin, *African Remembered: Narratives by West Africans from the Era of the Slave Trade* (Waveland Press, 1967), 289–316.

1.1 Samuel Ajayi Crowther

Before quinine became widely used as a prophylaxis against malaria in the late nineteenth century, European leaders worked to find alternative means of spreading Christianity in Africa because of the high rate of mortality among European missionaries. At Freetown and other mission stations missionaries began training African converts to proselytize. One of the most well-known indigenous West African missionaries was Samuel Ajayi Crowther. The British Navy took Crowther off a slave ship in 1822 and transported him to Freetown to live with the CMS. Crowther quickly proved himself adept at learning English, and within four years he was sent to England on one of several trips to study. He was the first student to register at Fourah Bay College in Sierra Leone in 1827, and he soon became a teacher. However, Crowther is better known for his work with the British Niger Expeditions of 1841, 1854, and 1857. The initial expedition of 1841 ended disastrously with most of the white participants dying from disease. Thus, the leaders of the later expeditions insisted that the majority of the participants were of African descent. The 1857 mission was unique among other CMS missions of the time because of its all-African staff, most of whom were from the settler and liberated African community in Sierra Leone. In 1864 Crowther was consecrated as the first African Anglican bishop for the territory of western Africa outside of the "Queen's control."

Sadly, toward the end of Crowther's life, white missionaries began to feel threatened by an all-African Christian church. By the late 1880s most white missionaries had embraced the view that Africans represented an inferior race. Accused of malfeasance by white missionaries, Crowther was forced to resign his position in the Anglican church and died two years later in 1891. His life came to represent the different stages of the civilizing mission in Africa – from the partnership between Africans and Europeans at the beginning of the nineteenth century to Africans as "the White Man's Burden" by the end of the century. Africans could be taught western civilization, but they could no longer be partners in the process of becoming "progressive."[1]

[1] Curtin, *Africa Remembered*, 289–316.

Setting a precedent for future colonies in Africa, European missionaries in Sierra Leone took responsibility for civilizing Africans through education, medicine, and social welfare work while the British colonial administration promoted economic development through "legitimate" trade in the agricultural and mineral commodities wanted in western countries. Government officials and white missionaries did not always see eye to eye during the colonization of Africa, but this division of responsibilities in Sierra Leone became the norm in European colonies across the continent. The civilizing mission of missionaries went hand in hand with government-led economic development. Western missionaries often had good intentions in bringing the civilizing mission to Africa. Some missionaries, however, became uncomfortable with Africans who wholly embraced European cultures because this blurred the line between the "civilized" and those in need of civilizing.

LEGITIMATE TRADE, COMMODITY PRODUCTION, AND THE CIVILIZING MISSION

The calls for ending the slave trade and shifting to "legitimate trade" existed decades before British abolitionist Thomas Buxton published his book on the topic in 1840.[17] However, it was Buxton's influence on a young missionary, David Livingstone, that brought England the pithy call for "Christianity, Commerce & Civilization" in order to bring progress and modernity to Africa. In 1857 Livingstone published his first book about his travels in Africa to great acclaim. In it he laid out his vision to "civilize" Africa and Africans.

Sending the Gospel to the heathen must ... include much more than is implied in the usual picture of a missionary, namely, a man going about with a Bible under his arm. The promotion of commerce ought to be specially attended to, as this, more speedily than any thing else, demolishes that sense of isolation which heathenism engenders. ... My observations on this subject make me extremely desirous to promote the preparation of the raw materials of European manufactures in Africa, for by that means we may not only put a stop to the slave-trade, but introduce the negro family into the body corporate of nations, no one member of which can suffer without the others suffering with it ... for neither

---

[17]   Robin Law, Suzanne Schwarz, and Silke Strickrodt, "Introduction," *Commercial Agriculture, the Slave Trade and Slavery in Atlantic Africa* (James Currey, 2013), 1–27 at 1–3; Thomas Fowell Buxton, *The African Slave Trade and Its Remedy* (John Murray, 1840), 306.

civilization nor Christianity can be promoted alone. In fact, they are inseparable.[18]

Livingstone envisioned social and economic development emerging from the combined influences of civilization, Christianity, and (legitimate) commerce. Livingstone journeyed across the United Kingdom between his trips to Africa, calling on British men and women to close the "open sore of Africa" by ending the continent's slave trades and facilitating trade with Europe. Although he railed against the slave trade in his numerous letters, travelogues, and public speeches, he often had to rely on slave traders for protection, guidance, and information during his travels. Nonetheless, he hoped Africans would barter raw materials instead of people in exchange for the products of European industrial capitalism, and consequently develop a desire to become civilized.

Livingstone and other Europeans either did not understand or ignored the reality that much of the "legitimate commerce" produced in Africa during the nineteenth and early twentieth centuries relied on locally enslaved labor.[19] This was true of the trades in spices from the Zanzibar Islands, palm oil from West Africa, and rubber from the Congo. While Europeans eventually ended slavery in the continent in name, they endorsed forced labor in deed. As Eric Allina argues in the case of Portuguese company rule in central Mozambique, forced labor was "slavery by any other name."[20] In 1899, Portuguese officials argued that "the state, not only as a sovereign of semi-barbaric populations, but also as a trustee of social authority, should have no scruples in obliging and, if necessary, forcing them [Africans] to work, that is, to better themselves through work, to acquire through work means for a more prosperous existence, to civilize themselves through work."[21] Even the International Labour Organization's 1930 statute banning forced labor included a caveat for certain types of coercion necessary for "educational purposes"

[18] David Livingstone, *Missionary Travels and Researches in South Africa, Including a Sketch of Sixteen Years' Residence in the Interior of Africa, and a Journey from the Cape of Good Hope to Loanda on the West Coast; Thence across the Continent, Down the River Zambesi, to the Eastern Ocean* (John Murray, 1857), 28.

[19] Landeg White, *Magomero: Portrait of an African Village* (Cambridge University Press, 1987), 23. European officials clearly understood that legitimate trade was produced by locally held slaves. In an 1874 report, Frederic Holmwood reported "legitimate" items being produced by slaves. See United Kingdom National Archives (hereafter UKNA), Foreign Office (FO) 881/2572.

[20] Eric Allina, *Slavery by Any Other Name: African Life under Company Rule in Colonial Mozambique* (University of Virginia Press, 2012).

[21] Ibid., 33.

and "the public benefit."[22] The socialization of Africans into western modes of capitalist trade and labor coincided with the intersecting causes promoting Christianity and development in Africa.

In contrast to the religious foundations of the British civilizing mission in Africa, the French civilizing mission, or *mission civilisatrice*, was an overseas expression of broader French republican ideals. French imperialists interpreted the civilizing mission as an extension of the political concepts of equality and freedom that emerged from the 1789 French Revolution. The French believed that if Africans embraced French culture, they would be free from their own forms of oppression, such as slavery. Historian Alice Conklin argues that French liberalism was not merely rhetoric designed to obscure capitalist greed and colonial exploitation. Much as Granville Sharp had envisioned for Sierra Leone, early French colonizers intended for Africans under their stewardship to gain basic human rights denied them by their "uncivilized" societies. After the federation of French West Africa in 1895 the government "aimed at ending slavery and eroding the power of chiefs – in true republican spirit – in the name of the rights of the individual."[23]

Conklin's work on French colonialism is a good reminder to examine the motivations of European colonizers (or all historical actors, for that matter) from their own perspectives as well as their historical impact. Whether inspired by French political liberalism or Christian universal humanism, many Europeans embraced the progressive ideas of the civilizing mission and the development discourse as a means to *welcome* Africans to a new modern humanity. However, contradictions between these universalist ideologies and late nineteenth-century racial othering persisted in all European efforts to colonize Africa. It is also important to remember that the economic side of the civilizing mission, especially the effort to develop commodity production, buttressed the capitalist foundations of European colonialism in Africa.

[22] Daniel Roger Maul, "The International Labour Organization and the Struggle against Forced Labour from 1919 to the Present," *Labor History* 48:4 (2007) 477–500.

[23] Alice Conklin, "Colonialism and Human Rights, a Contradiction in Terms? The Case of France and West Africa, 1895–1914," *American Historical Review* 103:2 (1998) 419–442 at 424. See also Alice L. Conklin, *A Mission to Civilize: The Republican Idea of Empire in France and West Africa, 1895–1930* (Stanford University Press, 1997). French West Africa expanded to include the region covering the contemporary nations of Benin, Burkina Faso, Guinea, Ivory Coast, Mali, Mauritania, Niger, and Senegal.

EVOLUTION OF SOCIETIES TOWARD DEVELOPMENT

Charles Darwin's theory of evolution explains changes in biological species over the course of millennia, but during the nineteenth century many scholars interpreted evolution in social terms. Social evolution is the belief that societies, like species, evolve from simple to more complex forms over time. Nineteenth-century social evolutionists argued that different contemporary societies represented separate stages of a single evolutionary ladder depending on their level of progress. This flattening of evolutionary time onto social or geographical difference in the present resulted in the highly racialized distinction between "primitive" and "civilized" societies. Western concepts of social evolution associated capitalism, technology, and whiteness with "civilization," development, and modernity, an association still prevalent in contemporary ideas of development.

While many historians have referred to social evolution as "social Darwinism," it was not Darwin but other scientists and writers who promoted the theory. In 1857, two years before the release of Charles Darwin's *On the Origin of Species*, Herbert Spencer published an article titled "Progress: Its Law and Cause."[24] He offered a pseudoscientific "Natural Law," which argued for a linear progression of evolution in all aspects of the universe. When *On the Origins of Species* made its debut Spencer incorporated Darwin's theory of natural selection into his own theory of social evolution and coined the phrase "survival of the fittest." Social Darwinists argued that the strongest societies survived, gained power, and developed while the weak were destined to disappear. Some social Darwinists believed that class stratification was also a product of natural selection and that the poor and weak were undeserving of help. Social evolutionists employed Darwin's ideas about natural selection to justify colonizing "weaker" societies. Some argued that colonization would help other societies develop, thereby preventing their extinction. Whether or not they bought Spencer's "survival of the fittest" concept, many nineteenth-century Europeans used the theory of social evolution to explain racial difference, which

---

[24]   Herbert Spencer, *Essays: Scientific, Political, and Speculative, Volume I* (D. Appleton, 1910), 8–62. The chapter, titled "Progress: Its Law and Cause," was first published in *The Westminster Review* in April 1857.

generated a brand of racism that culminated in the eugenics movement of the early twentieth century.

Nineteenth-century artistic and scientific images conveying the theory of social evolution reinforced the association of development with whiteness and industrialization. One notable example is John Gast's 1872 painting *American Progress* (see Figure 1.1). It portrays "primitive" hunting-based societies (in this case, Native Americans) fleeing in the path of "advanced" white agriculturalists (who are also shown as progressing over time as they embrace industrialization and capitalism). As American society expanded westward, white Americans believed they were taming the landscape with new technologies. In Gast's painting white men overcome the foreboding darkness of untamed nature with the bright light of civilization, represented by trains and telegraph wires. The popularity of Gast's painting, which was reproduced and distributed widely, demonstrates the salience of the social evolution theory and scientific progressivism among European and European-descended people around the globe in the late nineteenth century.

FIGURE 1.1 George A. Crofutt. *American Progress*. Chromolithograph, ca. 1873, after an 1872 painting by John Gast. Source: Prints and Photographs Division, Library of Congress

AFRICAN DEVELOPMENT AS THE "WHITE MAN'S BURDEN"

By the end of the nineteenth century European powers claimed that colonialism was the best means for spreading "civilization" in Africa. The major shift toward colonization came after the Berlin Conference held between November 1884 and February 1885. The conference was organized by German chancellor Otto von Bismarck to quell imperial rivalries. In attendance were representatives of all major European imperial powers, the Ottoman Empire, and the United States. The participants agreed that imperial powers' "spheres of influence" in Africa would be recognized once these powers demonstrated occupation of their claimed territories. The meeting sparked an era of "New Imperialism" that, when combined with the Christian abolitionist movement and social evolutionist thinking, sped up European colonization of the African interior in the name of progress and the civilizing mission.

Late nineteenth-century poetry, paintings, and political cartoons provide insight into how westerners envisioned this New Imperialism. One of the most iconic representations of the civilizing mission was a poem entitled "The White Man's Burden: The United States and the Philippine Islands," written by British author Rudyard Kipling and published in an American newspaper in February 1899.[25] Kipling sought to encourage the United States to fulfill what he saw as its imperialist *duty* in the Philippines. In the poem he urged the "White Man" to carry those people untouched by western civilization "toward the light" even though it may appear to him a futile and thankless endeavor. This poem was read widely in Europe and the United States and sparked a wave of poetry, paintings, and political cartoons with similar themes. These works suggested that non-western people were ignorant, superstitious, brutal, and cruel perpetuators of vices such as sexual promiscuity and drinking. In contrast they portrayed colonialism as a philanthropic movement, arguing that "uncivilized" people would only learn how to develop and become modern with the help of whites. The religious undertone of spreading the "light" of civilization was intentional, though here the "light" referred as much to the

---

[25] Rudyard Kipling, "The White Man's Burden," *New York Sun*, February 10, 1899. The poem was originally written about British imperialism but for publication in the United States Kipling switched its focus to the Philippines.

Enlightenment, industrialization, and the white race as it did to Christian salvation.

Not everyone agreed with Kipling's representation of the "White Man" in contrast to the "Others" he wanted to save. A compelling critique of Kipling's poem was H. T. Johnson's "The Black Man's Burden," published in an American missionary magazine in April 1899.[26] Johnson was a middle-class, African American minister who argued that the "Black Man's Burden" was that people of color around the world had to endure the atrocities and oppression of white imperialism. While artists and writers such as Johnson brought criticism of imperialism to the fore, many still believed in the superiority of western societies and viewed Africans on the continent as distinctly underdeveloped. Some African Americans resented the racial distinction made between the "White Man" and the "uncivilized man" in Kipling's poem and argued for the inclusion of African Americans as part of the "civilized" world by virtue of their geography, social status, economic class, and other markers of modernity.[27]

Americans actively participated in the construction of racial stereotypes of Africans as people who need westerners to bring them civilization and development, a trend that continued into the twentieth century. For example, the first Tarzan movie, a 1918 US silent film, sparked a "jungle film" trend that exploded in the 1930s and 1940s. Many of these films were ostensibly set in "Africa" though exact locations were not specified and filming usually took place somewhere in the Americas. They often featured a white savior rescuing either people or the environment from evil, "tribal," or "cannibalistic" Africans. Africans thus appeared in the films as either naïve innocents or treacherous cannibals, but always unmodern and in need of western intervention.[28] As such, they contributed to the racist discourses that legitimated the missions to "civilize" Africans through imperialism, trade, and Christianity. European and American literature, art, film, and other media captured the ethos of the day and presented a lasting

---

[26] H. T. Johnson, "The Black Man's Burden," *Voice of Missions* 7 (Atlanta: April 1899), 1. Reprinted in Willard B. Gatewood Jr., *Black Americans and the White Man's Burden, 1898–1903* (University of Illinois Press, 1975), 183–184.

[27] Michele Mitchell, "'The Black Man's Burden': African Americans, Imperialism, and Notions of Racial Manhood 1890–1910," *International Review of Social History* 44:7 (1999) 77–100.

[28] N. Frank Ukadike, "Western Film Images of Africa: Genealogy of an Ideological Formulation," *Black Scholar* 21:2 (1990) 30–48.

image of Africans as underdeveloped in the western imagination. This image continues into the twenty-first century with Hollywood productions such as *The Last King of Scotland* and *Blood Diamond* that portray saving Africans from the savagery of evil dictators and greedy capitalists as the modern "white man's burden."

POVERTY AS A DEVELOPMENT PROBLEM

During the late eighteenth and nineteenth centuries Europeans became more concerned about the problem of urban poverty that emerged in tandem with the Industrial Revolution.[29] Previously, the middle and elite classes of Europeans had viewed poverty as a part of the natural social order and thus it required no intervention on their part. Individual poverty was viewed as a moral failing rather than a symptom of the systemic exploitation of poor people. According to Gareth Stedman Jones, this idea faded when thinkers such as Thomas Paine and Antoine-Nicolas Condorcet argued that the elimination of poverty was central to creating a progressive society.[30] In the progressive ideologies of the late nineteenth-century poverty became a development problem. Reformers rendered distinctions between the "deserving" and "undeserving" poor based on hierarchies of race or ethnicity and the willingness of the poor to conform to modern bourgeois standards of respectability.[31] European discourses associated poverty with savagery and the discourses on class and race echoed one another. By the twentieth century poverty was much more than the absence of food and shelter; it became a problem that development needed to solve.

[29] William Olejniczak, "Royal Paternalism with a Repressive Face: The Ideology of Poverty in Late Eighteenth-Century France," *Journal of Policy History* 2:2 (1990) 157–185; James Symonds, "The Poverty Trap: Or, Why Poverty Is Not about the Individual," *International Journal of Historical Archaeology* 15 (2011) 563–571.

[30] Jones, however, argues that the structure for ending poverty offered by Paine and Condorcet looked very different from the charitable and state-sponsored policies of the present day that generally end up reinforcing poverty. Gareth Stedman Jones, *An End to Poverty: A Historical Debate* (Columbia University Press, 2005).

[31] Mary Poovey, *Making a Social Body: British Cultural Formation, 1830–1864* (University of Chicago Press, 1995), 87; Michael B. Katz, "The Urban 'Underclass' As a Metaphor of Social Transformation," in Michael B. Katz, ed., *The "Underclass" Debate: Views from History* (Princeton University Press, 1993), 10–11.

While poverty reform was necessary for modernizing the "social body" as a whole, after 1800 governments and many affluent people defined "the poor" as those who were unwilling or incapable of progress or becoming modern.[32] By this definition poverty was not an economic state but rather a "state of mind." In the twentieth century scholars used the term "relative poverty" to denote how economically poor a person is in comparison to the rest of the population in their country. A person could be "poor" in their country but considered economically affluent in another country; thus poverty is often understood in social rather than economic terms.[33] These concepts have endured in contemporary studies of poverty.

As European colonization gained momentum in Africa, people in Europe expressed fears about degeneration of the white race. This fear showed up in debates on the so-called poor white problem beginning in the late nineteenth century. Churches that actively participated in urban reform movements in the west brought this same approach to their overseas missions. Reformers who sought to "civilize" poor whites later advocated the civilizing mission for Africans. However, these reforms were distinctly racialized. Poverty relief was the primary tactic for "civilizing" poor whites, but Christianity and colonization were the tools for "civilizing" Africans. Furthermore, it was not until the end of World War II that missionaries, reformers, and colonial officials fully came to recognize the Black poor in Africa as deserving of economic aid.

In the early twentieth century, white political leaders in South Africa discovered their own "poor white problem." South Africa's poor whites lived in close proximity to Black Africans geographically and culturally. Thus, political leaders feared poverty would increase incidents of miscegenation, the sexual union of people from different racial groups. Miscegenation challenged the notion that western civilization was and would remain superior, undermining the primary justification for European rule in Africa. Political leaders believed that if whites began "regressing" by intermarrying with "less civilized" groups such as Black Africans, then they could no longer claim superiority. The history of western responses to poverty around the globe reveals the

---

[32]   See Poovey, *Making a Social Body*; Steven Beaudoin, *Poverty in World History* (Routledge, 2007).

[33]   Grace Davie, *Poverty Knowledge in South Africa: A Social History of Human Science, 1855–2005* (Cambridge University Press, 2014), 4.

inherent racialized aspect of colonization. The foundations of present-day definitions of poverty lie with nineteenth-century racialized conceptions of respectability, progress, and what it meant to be "civilized."

In the early 2000s David Everatt conducted a survey in South Africa to measure the percentage of households living in poverty. He asked how many households were headed by females, what were the rates of illiteracy and unemployment, which households suffered from a very low annual income, how crowded were households, what kinds of building materials were used in housing, and whether they had sanitation, water, and electricity.[34] These survey questions make clear that poverty has come to be defined by the absence of certain markers of modernity rather than merely the absence of food and wealth alone. Such studies imagine a modern household headed by a man with a formal-sector job and a modern home large enough to afford privacy for individuals. The western ideal of a heteronormative nuclear family structure has come to signify both wealth *and* progress. As long as poverty is defined in terms of western ideas of modernity and standards of living, certain societies and cultures in the world will always be categorized as "poor."

This paradigm of poverty is beginning to change as new research challenges the racial and cultural connotations of impoverishment. Over the past decade Martin Burt has sought to dissociate assessments of poverty from western norms of modernity. His organization, Poverty Stoplight, surveys communities to find out whether and how people see their households and communities as impoverished. This approach prioritizes local knowledge and values regarding standards of living. The organization also maps community responses so that other organizations can adjust their interventions according to what local communities want.[35]

★★★

Missionaries' efforts in the nineteenth century to bring "Christianity, commerce & civilization" set in motion a progressive ideology that led to modern development practice in Africa. These three words captured the Enlightenment ideology of social progress, the capitalism of the Industrial Revolution, and the mating of Christian doctrine with secular social Darwinism. These concepts are the bedrock on which all future ideas of modern development theory would be built. At their heart they

---

[34] David Everatt, "The Undeserving Poor: Poverty and the Politics of Service Delivery in the Poorest Nodes of South Africa," *Politikon* 35:3 (2008) 293–319.
[35] See www.povertystoplight.org/en/, accessed August 2, 2018.

presume that western civilization is the highest form of social development, that all societies must progress in a linear fashion to attain this
status, and that development will come through an economic transformation that will reshape social and cultural aspects of societies. Moreover,
as Maya Jasanoff's *New York Times* article reminds us, westerners continue to dictate the development discourse that assesses the progress of
Africans today. The foundations of international development did not
emerge from post–World War II global economic relationships, as
common knowledge often presents; rather, this book demonstrates
that international development ideas and interventions emerged in the
wake of the European Enlightenment and in the context of European
imperialism. Nineteenth-century liberalism, which promulgated both
a singular, linear notion of progress measured in terms of western
modernity and a hierarchy of social evolution that ranked contemporary
societies around the world, still forms the guiding premises of modern-
day development discourses about Africa.

Further Reading

On concepts of progress see Hamza Alavi and Teodor Shanin, *Introduction to
   the Sociology of "Developing Societies"* (Palgrave, 1982); Robert Nisbet,
   History of the Idea of Progress (Transaction, 1994); Leslie Sklair, *The
   Sociology of Progress* (Routledge & Kegan Paul, 1970); Isser Woloch and
   Gregory S. Brown, *Eighteenth Century Europe: Tradition and Progress,
   1715–1789.* Second edition (W. W. Norton, 2012).
On ideas of the civilizing mission see Osama Abi-Mershed, *Apostles of Modernity:
   Saint-Simonians and the Civilizing Mission in Algeria* (Stanford University
   Press, 2010); Tunde Adeleke, *UnAfrican Americans: Nineteenth-Century
   Black Nationalists and the Civilizing Mission* (University of Kentucky Press,
   1998); Patrick Brantlinger, *Rule of Darkness: British Literature and Imperialism,
   1830–1914* (Cornell University Press, 1990); Patrick Brantlinger, *Dark
   Vanishings: Discourse on the Extinction of Primitive Races, 1800–1930* (Cornell
   University Press, 2003); Waibinte E. Wariboko, *Race and the Civilizing
   Mission: Their Implications for the Framing of Blackness and African Personhood*
   (Africa World Press, 2010).
On ideas of poverty see Felicitas Becker, *The Politics of Poverty: Policy-Making
   and Development in Rural Tanzania* (Cambridge University Press, 2019);
   Grace Davie, *Poverty Knowledge in South Africa: A Social History of Human
   Science, 1855–2005* (Cambridge University Press, 2014); John Iliffe, *The
   African Poor: A History* (Cambridge University Press, 2009 [orig. 1987]).

CHAPTER 2

Knowledge and the Development Episteme

In 1799 Scottish explorer Mungo Park published an account of his travels in the West African interior. Park's narrative featured maps created by one of Britain's preeminent cartographers of the day, James Rennell. In his journal entry for August 23, 1796, Park referenced a distant mountain range, which locals said belonged to the kingdom of Kong. Rennell rendered Park's brief and nondescript notation about the "Kong Mountains" as a long mountain range stretching across much of western Africa in a west-east direction. Earlier maps of the region showed only vast areas of blank space in this territory. By drawing a mountain range into this blank space, Rennell lent epistemological legitimacy to this geographic feature and set the stage for European expertise as the basis for knowledge about Africa for the next two centuries.

By the end of the nineteenth century European scholars realized that Rennell's map was not an accurate representation of West African topography, but the story of how he came to draw the Kong mountain range demonstrates the significance of how Europeans constructed knowledge about Africa. Rennell extrapolated from Mungo Park's declaration that the Niger River flowed from west to east. According to nineteenth-century European understanding of geography, a river the size of the Niger needed to have a significantly large geographic source such as a lake or mountain range. James Rennell literally drew Park's speculation about the mountain and assertion about the directional flow of the river onto the map of West Africa (see Map 2.1). This was how the European scientific imagination gave birth to the

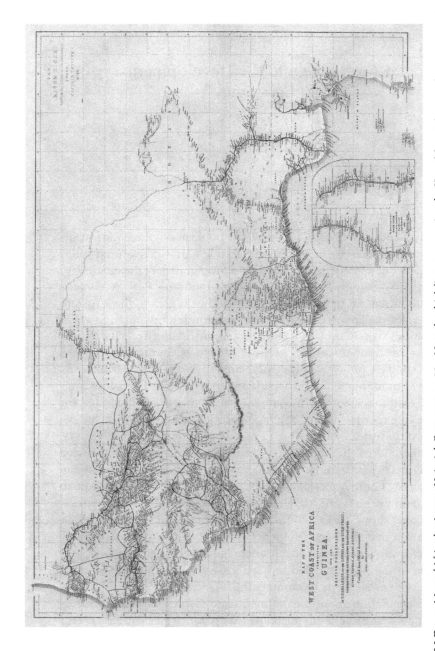

MAP 2.1 Map of Africa by August Heinrich Petermann, 1880. Note the thick line representing the Kong Mountains running across western Africa. Source: Stanford University Libraries, https://exhibits.stanford.edu/maps-of-africa/catalog/fx703zs6529, accessed August 2, 2018

nonexistent Kong Mountains in western Africa. Although Rennell had no firsthand knowledge of the mountains and no evidence they existed, his position as a leading cartographer, combined with Park's apparent expertise in geography, lent "scientific" legitimacy to the Kong Mountains, which the Europeans believed were real for almost 100 years.

As Thomas Bassett and Philip Porter have argued, maps offer "authoritative power [because] the inherent quality of maps as images gives them a unique role in shaping knowledge. The authority of maps is based on the public's belief that these images are accurate representations of reality, or 'true' maps."[1] European epistemologies, or ways of knowing, have constructed ideas about Africa through maps, travelogues, ethnographies, and other documents. European imaginations, such as Rennell's fabrication of the Kong Mountains, produced an idealized version of Africa ripe for western economic and cultural development. Into the twenty-first century a western development episteme, or knowledge system, continues to shape the way Africa was and is understood in international discourses.

This chapter explores the ways Europeans created knowledge of African societies while discounting and ignoring African knowledge systems throughout the nineteenth and twentieth centuries. African societies had their own epistemologies, and Europeans were certainly aware of African written and oral traditions, art, architecture, and other forms of intellectual production. The Egyptian and Sudanese pyramids, the rock-hewn churches of Ethiopia, the monumental walls of Great Zimbabwe, and many other features that dotted the continent's landscape testified to the existence of advanced ancient and medieval African civilizations. Yet by the late nineteenth-century Europeans questioned whether these civilizations were truly African. They perpetuated the mythology that ancient Semitic societies visited the continent, founded these civilizations, and then disappeared. As Europeans discovered more evidence of these precolonial civilizations, they became less convinced that Africans could have produced them.[2] Despite being sympathetic to African communities or curious about

---

[1] Thomas J. Bassett and Philip W. Porter, "'From the Best Authorities': The Mountains of Kong in the Cartography of West Africa," *Journal of African History* 32:3 (1991) 367–413 at 370.

[2] Richard J. Reid, *A History of Modern Africa: 1800 to the Present* (Wiley-Blackwell, 2009), 167; Curtis Keim, *Mistaking Africa: Curiosities and Inventions of the American Mind*. Third edition (Westview Press, 2013).

African cultures, nineteenth- and early twentieth-century explorers and colonizers were men and women of their time. As Europeans imbued with the notion that their cultures and technologies represented the pinnacle of civilization, they viewed themselves as culturally superior to Africans.

During the nineteenth century Europeans developed scientific methodologies that generated new knowledge about Africa. This knowledge reflected Eurocentric ideas about progress and became the foundation for the development episteme. More recently, scholars of the global north have introduced forms of knowledge about Africa that do not perpetuate the notion of western superiority, but that still rely on some of the same assumptions built into nineteenth-century European epistemologies. To appreciate the way western ideas of development evolved in Africa, it is crucial to look at the trajectory of how nineteenth-century Europeans formulated their knowledge about the continent. A better understanding of how this "knowledge" came to dominate global paradigms about "science" and "development" in the twentieth and twenty-first centuries illuminates the remnants of nineteenth-century thinking in more recent development discourses.

THE PRODUCTION OF EUROPEAN SYSTEMS OF KNOWLEDGE

The American and French Revolutions embodied Enlightenment ideologies that declared "all men are created equal." Enlightenment ideals offered an egalitarian way of approaching the world, yet they also helped to solidify racialized discrimination within western societies. At the same time that the American revolutionaries could claim "all men are created equal," they instituted the three-fifths clause in the American Constitution. This rule acknowledged the (partial) personhood of enslaved men and women, but it also enshrined and legitimized their subjecthood as noncitizens. In the revolutionary American imagination people of African descent were not equal to whites. This contradiction undergirded attitudes toward Africa and Africans in the global north, even those of white abolitionists who worked to end the slave trade and slavery.

While "knowledge" itself may be based on objective facts and information, its collection and construction by individuals was deeply subjective. Many stereotypes and biases against African epistemologies

crept into the way this scientific evidence was constructed. This knowledge shaped the subsequent project to develop African societies along
"scientific" lines. While different forms of knowledge coexist in any
society, it is how those forms of knowledge are valued and categorized
that prioritizes their use. Carl Linnaeus, a Swedish botanist, came up
with the classification system for defining the natural world that is still
used today across the world. The Linnaean system was critical to both
European exploration and empire building, as Mary Louise Pratt
argues, because it allowed westerners to create order out of the perceived chaos of non-western societies.[3] Colonial and postcolonial
development specialists, in particular, employed Linnaeus's method
for categorizing the natural world in producing knowledge about
Africa.

Carl Linnaeus's 1735 book, *The System of Nature*, used
a binominal nomenclature or taxonomy for describing objects of
the natural world according to first their "genus" and then their
"species." All animals, plants, and rocks could be classified within
this system based on a set of characteristics. By the 1750s Linnaeus
had perfected his method for categorizing plants, animals, insects,
and minerals, and he began sending his students to collect data
from all over the world to add to this database of knowledge. As
Europeans moved out into the rest of the world, the "knowledge"
they compiled using the Linnaean system gave them the sense that
they "knew" these regions of the world.[4] In theory anyone familiar
with the Linnaean system of categorization could become an amateur scientist and participate in the creation of knowledge by
searching for and cataloging new specimens. In practice this job
was available almost exclusively to middle- and upper-class white
men. From this point forward scientific inquiry became central to
all European-led expeditions to other parts of the world. However,
as Johannes Fabian has demonstrated, these amateur scientists
practiced the Linnaean system very haphazardly.[5]

Before Linnaeus's classification system different systems and forms
of knowledge coexisted. When Europeans traveled beyond their continent they learned about new cultures, societies, and environments

---

[3] Mary Louise Pratt, *Imperial Eyes: Travel Writing and Transculturation* (Routledge,
     1992).
[4] Ibid.
[5] Johannes Fabian, *Out of Our Minds: Reason and Madness in the Exploration of Central
     Africa* (University of California Press, 2000).

from their own observations and also from engaging with people from those regions. People communicated knowledge about their societies and value systems to newcomers. Once the Linnaean system became the primary method for cataloging information about the natural world, Europeans tended to base their knowledge of Africa on their own observations and classifications rather than on indigenous epistemologies. While some still asked Africans for local names of plants and animals, they also assigned names to these objects in Latin in order to fit within the Linnaean system. Europeans' belief in the superiority of their own epistemologies meant that they engaged less and less with local systems and forms of knowledge.[6] Western explorers and scientists concluded that Africa was epistemologically deficient and that valuable knowledge about Africa could be produced only by Europeans.

European imperial expansion during the nineteenth century facilitated the creation of more "knowledge" about Asia and Africa, and in turn this knowledge facilitated imperial conquest.[7] European epistemologies created the academic fields of study about non-western places and people that still shape scholarship on these societies today. For example, nineteenth-century European writings constructed the idea that "the Maasai" of Kenya and Tanzania were a "warrior tribe," though they actually consisted of disparate groups of people with complex relationships to cattle herding, agriculture, and trade.[8] The power to "know" and therefore define another as a one-dimensional "Other" was instrumental to claiming superiority over that "Other." European travelers, missionaries, traders, and colonial officials simplified and stereotyped African societies, codifying which kinds of knowledge were "useful" for colonial rule and discarding the rest. Oversimplified descriptions of African people and societies continue in some development discourses of the present day, as Dorothy Hodgson explains in the case of "the Maasai."[9] A simple internet search returns countless websites describing the "Maasai warrior," not to mention the numerous published works (including

6   Pratt, *Imperial Eyes*.
7   V. Y. Mudimbe, *The Invention of Africa: Gnosis, Philosophy, and the Order of Knowledge* (Indiana University Press, 1988).
8   Thomas Spear and Richard Waller, eds., *Being Maasai: Ethnicity and Identity in East Africa* (Ohio University Press, 1993).
9   Dorothy L. Hodgson, *Once Intrepid Warriors: Gender, Ethnicity, and the Cultural Politics of Maasai Development* (Indiana University Press, 2001).

autobiographies) on the topic.[10] Understanding the imperialist origins of discourses on African cultures and communities reveals the problematic assumptions and misunderstandings that continue to shape development "knowledge" about Africa and Africans today.

VISUALIZING EUROPEAN SCIENTIFIC PROGRESS ACROSS AFRICA

Cartography, or mapping, was one of the first scientific endeavors to shape how modern Europeans would engage with Africa scientifically, economically, and culturally. In 1788 a group of wealthy British men formed the Association for Promoting the Discovery of the Interior parts of Africa (better known as the African Association) in order to investigate the "unknown" regions of the continent. This group of explorers, scientists, abolitionists, and bankers intended both to further European knowledge of Africa and to reshape the lives of Africans. They argued, "by means as peaceable as the purposes are just, the conveniences of civil life, the benefits of the mechanical and manufacturing arts, the attainments of science, the energies of the cultivated, and the elevation of the human character, may be in some degree imparted to nations hitherto consigned to hopeless barbarism and uniform contempt."[11] Their goals for transforming Africa anticipated the colonial development plans of the twentieth century. The African Association funded projects like Mungo Park's expedition to find the source of the Niger River that sought to produce scientific knowledge designed to facilitate future economic exploitation.

Besides inventing the Kong Mountains, Park also dramatically recounted in his book how he nearly starved to death, was reduced to rags, and was even enslaved at one point. While Park's book was not the first European travel narrative about Africa, it became immensely popular

---

[10]   See, for example, "Life of a Maasai Warrior," www.bush-adventures.com/maasai-warriors/, accessed December 26, 2017; Olivia Yasukawa and Thomas Page, "Lion-Killer Maasai Turn Wildlife Warriors to Save Old Enemy," CNN World, February 8, 2017, www.cnn.com/2017/02/07/africa/maasai-tanzania-wildlife-warriors/index.html, accessed December 26, 2017; Tepilit Ole Saitoti, *The Worlds of a Maasai Warrior: An Autobiography* (University of California Press, 1986); Corinne Hofmann, *The White Masai* (Bliss, 2005).

[11]   Kate Ferguson Marsters, "Introduction to Mungo Park," in Kate Ferguson Marsters, ed., *Travels in the Interior Districts of Africa* (Duke University Press, 2000), 1–28 at 9.

and helped to spur generations of western men (and a few women) who wished to expand European knowledge of Africa and gain fame for exploring what they considered a "barbaric" land. In the following years increasing numbers of western men embraced the adventure of traveling into the interior of the continent to "discover" new things, people, and places. These men named landmarks – real and imagined – that brought the Africa they "discovered" into existence for the European imagination.

Europeans visualized Africa as a space devoid of people. It was a tabula rasa (blank slate) ready for Europeans to conquer and develop. Cartography was key to European conquest of Africa. Maps defined and named spaces, allowing for Europe's intellectual appropriation of the continent.[12] Europeans labeled African lakes, mountains, and other natural landmarks with European names in order to solidify their claims to those territories. For instance, David Livingstone reported that he "discovered" the massive waterfall along the border of present-day Zambia and Zimbabwe, which he named "Victoria Falls" after Queen Victoria of England. Ignoring the Kololo name Mosi-oa-Tunya ("The Smoke That Thunders"), Livingstone believed he had the right to name this natural wonder because he was the first European to set eyes on it. By applying an English name to the falls, he claimed the "scientific" expertise to catalog and characterize Africa's geographic wonders without recognition of the African epistemologies that had already done so.[13] This was the first step toward conquest.

Maps filled with European names for Africa's physical features were a crucial by-product of scientific exploration. They represented the ways in which Europeans planned and developed spaces. They were central to the work of military officials, missionaries, colonial officials, and merchants, all of whom contributed to the early project of building colonial knowledge about Africa. Nineteenth-century European expeditions in Africa often lacked trained surveyors, and not until after 1870 was any kind of systematic surveying done of the African continent. As the discussion of the Kong Mountains demonstrates, nineteenth-century European maps of Africa were drawn from the published accounts of missionaries and explorers. Mapmakers relied on geographers and their theories about cartographic features to locate specific landmarks. As such, they reflected European imaginations more than actual African landscapes.

---

[12]   Fabian, *Out of Our Minds*, 180–208.
[13]   JoAnn McGregor, "The Victoria Falls 1900–1940: Landscape, Tourism and the Geographical Imagination," *Journal of Southern African Studies* 29:3 (2003) 717–737.

The Kong Mountains are not the only example of European mis-mapping of Africa. Until 1850 most maps of the eastern cape of South Africa, for instance, were wildly inaccurate. Again, cartographers repro-duced the mistakes of their predecessors, as well as those of travel narratives. William Cornwallis Harris created a new map in 1834 based partly on his own travels and partly on the accounts of other travelers. Harris was not a trained surveyor, neither did he have survey-ing equipment with him on his journey. He ended up excising an area of approximately 60,000 square kilometers from his map of South Africa. The absence of this region, which was in the shape of a pie piece, foreshortened the territory between the coast near Maputo, Mozambique and Pretoria, South Africa. Over the next twenty years other cartographers repeated this mistake, which led to the excision of the Pedi ethnic group from numerous nineteenth-century maps of southern Africa. This seemingly small mistake had a big impact during the 1830s when Boer (Dutch-descended) settlers flooded the region. By foreshortening this area Boers came into conflict with people they did not even know existed. Boers traveling into the area anticipated entering the Portuguese colony of Mozambique, out of the control of the British Cape colony. Instead they found themselves roughly 250 kilometers away from their desired destination. A few years later, in 1839, the Natal Association of the Eastern Cape replicated the error in a map of South Africa it included with an investors' prospectus. This report created the perception that land in the area was fertile and uninhabited. These advertising maps designed to lure investors and settlers in turn informed other scientific maps produced by the Arrowsmith and James Wyld cartography firms of London. These repeated mistakes in map-making reproduced European capitalist visions of African spaces rather than the actual contours of African geographies and societies.[14]

APPROPRIATING AFRICAN KNOWLEDGE AND LABOR

Searching for the source of the Nile River was one of the main obses-sions of nineteenth-century European explorers and geographers. This

---

[14] Norman Etherington, "A False Emptiness: How Historians May Have Been Misled by Early Nineteenth Century Maps of South-Eastern Africa," *Imago Mundi* 56:1 (2004) 67–86.

quest set off a series of rival European expeditions in which African guides and interpreters played a central role. The labor of Africans in the process of European exploration is often overshadowed by the celebrity of European explorers who claimed to have "discovered" African landmarks. Richard Burton was a quintessential example of a European explorer who appropriated the knowledge of Africans without giving them credit. When Burton decided to search for the source of the Nile River he was already famous for his pilgrimage to Mecca and Medina as the first European nonbeliever in more than 300 years to sneak into the Hajj. In 1854 Burton and a small entourage that included John Hanning Speke started off on their first expedition to East Africa to search for the source of the Nile. Their expedition was a disaster, and both men were wounded. Two years later they set off again in search of the great "sea of Ujiji" they had heard about from Africans living on the East African coast. This "sea," which Burton believed to be the source of the Nile, turned out to be Lake Tanganyika bordering the present-day countries of the Democratic Republic of Congo, Tanzania, Burundi, and Zambia. Both men fell ill, but Speke recovered enough to continue traveling when they heard about another "great sea" in the interior. Eventually, in 1858, Speke's African guides led him to a large freshwater lake bordering the present-day countries of Uganda, Kenya, and Tanzania. Speke "named" Lake Victoria (also after Queen Victoria) and claimed it was the true source of the Nile. As it turned out, Lake Victoria is the source of the White Nile, while the Blue Nile originates in the Ethiopian Highlands. Speke's development set off a rivalry between him and Burton, who also sought fame and recognition for their geographic discoveries. Neither man mentioned in his books and lectures the many Africans who made their "discoveries" possible. They excised from history the African geographic experts who told them where and how to find the lakes and the numerous African employees who carried their equipment, translated for them across the region, negotiated for food and supplies from local communities, and nursed them when they were too sick or injured to travel.[15]

From the time of the first major European explorations of sub-Saharan Africa in the fifteenth century to the period of conquest in the nineteenth century, Europeans relied on Africans to mediate the transfer of knowledge. During the first centuries of contact, many of the African "informants" were the African wives or romantic partners

[15] For similar examples from Central Africa see Johannes Fabian, *Out of Our Minds*.

of European men. These women educated European men who traded and in some cases settled in African territories such as modern-day South Africa, Senegal, Guinea, Angola, and Mozambique.[16] Later, during the scientific and political scramble for Africa, most European explorers (women and men) turned to African men as their main informants. As African individuals moved across the continent with Europeans, mediating cultures and information, they brought both insider and outsider perspectives of various communities. Gender, class, religion, and ethnicity affected the ways in which Africans understood information and shared it with Europeans. For example, Europeans labeled one southern African ethnic group the "Matabele" based on what their Sotho and Tswana interpreters called the people. However, the "Matabele" actually referred to themselves as "Ndebele." Thus, while European explorers learned about the Ndebele from an African perspective, it was a non-Ndebele viewpoint that shaped European production of knowledge about them for almost a century.

Many Africans working for Europeans as interpreters and other assistants during the early twentieth century were educated in western, most often missionary schools. As such, African assistants were adept at filtering information through a western lens in order to translate it to Europeans. This filter transformed African knowledge into European "facts." James Christie, a medical doctor located in East Africa, noted with appreciation the help he received from indigenous informants in researching his 1876 book.[17] French West African colonial officials depended on a network of African ethnographers, many of whom were teachers in the colonial service and graduates of the Ecole Normale William Ponty (an important high school) in Senegal.[18] The case of these ethnographers again demonstrates how much knowledge Africans were producing, not only about their own communities but also about other African societies and cultures.

Europeans often viewed knowledge produced by Africans as less valuable, even when their research depended on it. As James Christie admitted, "Europeans are very apt to discredit or undervalue

[16] George Brooks, *Eurafricans in Western Africa: Commerce, Social Status, Gender, and Religious Observance from the Sixteenth to the Eighteenth Century* (Ohio University Press, 2003).

[17] James Christie, *Cholera Epidemics in East Africa* (Macmillan, 1876), ix.

[18] Amadou Hampâté Bâ, *The Fortunes of Wangrin*, transl. by Aina Pavolini Taylor (Indiana University Press, 1987).

information from natives."[19] At times European scholars acknowledged African assistants for collecting "facts" but not always for
their interpretations of these "facts." In most cases European scholars
did not share credit with African contributors to knowledge production or, worse, assumed Africans were less knowledgeable about their
own societies than European scholars. Examples abound of Europeans
critiquing the work of African scholars, such as Paul Marty, who
"regretted the author's [Moctar Diallo's] lack of knowledge ... and
utter misunderstanding" of Islam in West African societies.[20] Often
Europeans made the choices about the type of information collected
and the methods used. This created a particular vision of what constituted viable knowledge about Africa. Johannes Fabian argues that
many Europeans believed that African knowledge lacked precision.[21]
Europeans "corrected" the findings of African scholars or outright
appropriated the knowledge Africans produced, and thus claimed the
mantle of legitimate knowledge and expertise about Africa and
Africans.[22]

2.1 Mary Kingsley

Mary Kingsley was one of the earliest European female explorers to
visit Africa. She took her first trip to west central Africa in 1893 after
receiving an inheritance at the death of her parents. Kingsley had
spent her twenties caring for her ailing parents. She was inspired by
reading her father's library and hearing of his own global travels.
Scientific exploration of Africa during the nineteenth century was
generally a masculine venture. Kingsley, a single woman in her
thirties, was quite unusual for her time. She traveled with only a few
African porters and an interpreter, shocking both Europeans and

---

[19] Christie, *Cholera Epidemics in East Africa*, ix.
[20] Jean-Hervé Jezequel, "Voices of Their Own? African Participation in the Production
      of Colonial Knowledge in French West Africa, 1910–1950," in Helen Tilley, ed.,
      with Robert J. Gordon, *Ordering Africa: Anthropology, European Imperialism, and the
      Politics of Knowledge* (Manchester University Press, 2007), 119–144; Ruth Ginio,
      "Negotiating Legal Authority in French West Africa: The Colonial Administration
      and African Assessors, 1903–1918," in Benjamin N. Lawrance, Emily Lynn Osborn,
      and Richard Roberts, eds., *Intermediaries, Interpreters, and Clerks: African Employees
      in the Making of Colonial Africa* (University of Wisconsin Press, 2006).
[21] Fabian, *Out of Our Minds*, 186–190.
[22] Jezequel, "Voices of Their Own," 148.

Africans with her disinclination to be "protected" by western men. When one French consul refused to give her permission to pass through a region because she lacked a husband, she noted, "neither the Royal Geographical Society's list in their 'Hints to Travellers' nor Messrs. Silver, in their elaborate lists of articles necessary for a traveler in tropical climates, make mention of husbands."[1] While Kingsley challenged imperialist notions of masculinity, she rejected the label of being a New Woman or having an interest in women's suffrage, as she was represented in the press. She insisted she was interested in exploring Africa for purely scientific reasons.

Kingsley represented a generation of colonial scholars who were sympathetic to their African subjects yet remained avidly imperialist and implicitly racist. She was opposed to the imposition of European cultural ideas on Africans, such as the missionary requirement that their converts practice monogamy. Kingsley argued that African wives had too much work to do all by themselves and that they needed co-wives. Moreover, as missionaries forced African male converts to repudiate all but one wife, other wives and children were left without the support of a husband. This created social breakdown in some societies. Kingsley also lamented that the type of education missionaries offered Africans had little resonance in their cultures. For example, teaching girls of the Fang ethnic group to sew, wash, and iron western clothing made little sense when most girls would never wear this kind of clothing. She did not question the right of Europeans to "educate" Africans, only that they needed to readjust their approach.

Kingsley's books and speaking tours popularized the new science of anthropology. She encouraged anthropologists to expand beyond a focus solely on physical anthropology and embrace cultural ethnology by studying African religions, legal codes, and medical systems. Her own account is filled with analyses of the biological, geographical, spiritual, social, political, and economic phenomena she encountered. Kingsley has come to represent empathetic Europeans who recognized the contradictions inherent to European imperialism, but who also viewed European cultures as superior to those of Africans.

[1] Mary Kingsley, *Travels in West Africa* (Macmillan, 1897), reprinted in Patricia W. Romero, ed., *Women's Voices on Africa: A Century of Travel Writings* (Markus Wiener, 1992), 43.

DEVELOPING KNOWLEDGE FOR CONQUEST

During the period between 1870 and 1900, the era of the European scramble for Africa, scientific exploration was central to the mission of colonization. By the early 1880s European nations were rushing to send expeditions to claim African territories before they fell into the hands of rival imperial powers. Knowledge created by European scientists and scientific societies helped to define the terms of colonization. These scientific societies also determined the future terms of development by emphasizing particular areas of study for economic and political interest. As historian Helen Tilley explains, "Geographical societies made an essential contribution to the conditions that precipitated the scramble for Africa, acting not in isolation but precisely through their intricate connections with economic, diplomatic and military forces."[23] While scientists generally were not concerned about government agendas, by the 1870s they became more embroiled in the imperialist efforts of the European governments that financially supported their expeditions into Africa. For example, Louis-Gustave Binger's excursion to West Africa in the late 1880s had both the scientific purpose of surveying western Africa and the diplomatic authority to sign treaties with African leaders in order to "claim" territory on behalf of the French government.[24]

Scientific societies supporting European exploration of Africa in the nineteenth century set the stage for scientific research into the twentieth. One of the many prominent intellectual societies that emerged in the 1800s was the Royal Geographical Society of London. This organization was formed in 1830 and eventually absorbed the African Association, the same group that sponsored Mungo Park's travels. In 1870 another scientific organization called the Epidemiological Society of London approached Dr. James Christie about inquiring into the spread of cholera in East Africa. Christie explained that tracking a cholera epidemic necessitated the study of "the geography of the localities, the ethnology, commercial connections, and the manners and customs of the tribes through which the epidemics passed before the subject was comprehended in a satisfactory manner."[25] Scientific organizations, their

---

[23] Helen Tilley, *Africa As a Living Laboratory: Empire, Development, and the Problem of Scientific Knowledge, 1870–1950* (University of Chicago Press, 2011), 37.
[24] Bassett and Porter, "'From the Best Authorities.'"
[25] Christie, *Cholera Epidemics in East Africa*, xiii–xiv.

research journals, and their international meetings created a cohesive genre of development scholarship. As the nineteenth century came to a close, scholars and scientists realized that national and commercial needs would always come first in the race to document African lands and societies.

In 1876, in a step to consolidate his claim to the Congo, King Leopold II of Belgium held an exclusive meeting in Brussels to discuss the creation of an International African Association (IAA) for geographical studies. He invited thirty-seven delegates from seven European countries, the power brokers of various scientific fields who were charged with mapping out a program for creating new knowledge about the continent of Africa. These geographical leaders established specific guidelines for all expeditions in Africa. They hoped to set up five "scientific stations" across the continent that, according to Helen Tilley, would focus on

astronomical and meteorological observations, collecting specimens of geology, botany and zoology, mapping the surrounding country, preparing a vocabulary and grammar of the languages of the natives, making ethnological observations, collecting and report the accounts of indigenous travelers in unknown regions, and in keeping a journal of all events and observations worthy of note.[26]

The depth and breadth of studies envisioned for the scientific stations indicates the enormous scope of Europeans' fascination with Africa. Scientists at King Leopold's conference envisioned the IAA as a pan-European commission with quasi-oversight of scientific expeditions into the continent. However, nationalist interests drove many of these expeditions and kept the IAA from ever fully functioning.

Within a few years of King Leopold's 1876 geographical conference, the race between European nations to explore and claim territory in Africa intensified almost to the brink of war. In order to avert conflict, Otto von Bismarck of Germany invited delegates from European countries, the United States, and the Ottoman Empire to meet in Berlin in 1884. In what came to be known as the Berlin Conference, King Leopold II of Belgium and other European countries including Britain, France, Germany, Portugal, Spain, and Italy laid out their claims to different parts of the continent and the rules by which they would recognize the claims of other imperial powers. The United

---

[26]   Tilley, *Africa As a Living Laboratory*, 43.

States remained as an ally but not a colonizer of Liberia, an independent colony in West Africa founded in part by freed American slaves. King Leopold II claimed the Congo Free State (today, the Democratic Republic of Congo) for scientific, religious, and commercial purposes. It was to be free for exploration, evangelization, and trade by individuals from any nation as well as a slave trade-free zone. The Congo Free State came to represent the worst of colonial exploitation, with an estimated ten million people dead from forced labor, mutilation, torture, disease, and environmental degradation during the twenty years of Leopold's rule over the region.[27] When western powers challenged Leopold's rule in the first decade of the twentieth century, they learned the powerful lesson that colonial powers must act with civility toward their subjects in order to engage them in the modernizing project.

THE DEVELOPMENT EPISTEME

European colonialism relied not only on the production of knowledge deemed necessary for developing Africa economically and politically but also on the dissemination of European "knowledge" to Africans as part of the civilizing mission. While the former required help from scientists, the latter depended extensively on missionaries. Scientific societies published the work of amateur and professional scholars who amassed a body of knowledge useful for colonial rule, while missionaries offered their assistance in constructing principles and procedures for creating "civilized" or "modern" African communities. The combination of the two established an episteme, or knowledge system, that would undergird modern development into the twenty-first century. This is what we call the development episteme.

The cadre of experts King Leopold II invited to participate in his 1876 Brussels conference attempted to address the first question by producing a plan for a scientific approach to colonization.[28] Fourteen years later Arthur Silva White, the secretary of the Scottish Geographical Society, published his book, *The Development of Africa*, which laid out a framework for what the west needed to know in order to economically exploit the continent. His table of contents included

[27] Adam Hochschild, *King Leopold's Ghost: A Story of Greed, Terror, and Heroism in Colonial Africa* (Houghton Mifflin, 1998).
[28] Tilley, *Africa As a Living Laboratory*, 41–42.

sections on geography and geology, climate, ethnology, linguistics, political structures, religion, and commercial resources.[29] Throughout the late nineteenth century experts from the many scientific societies across Europe vied to expand their knowledge about Africa and to assemble a framework for the operation of colonial power.

The transfer of knowledge from Europeans to Africans produced the other side of the development episteme. Since the late nineteenth century the development episteme has shaped most development work done in Africa. Nineteenth-century Europeans assumed their knowledge was valuable to Africans. Even missionaries, whose primary focus was religious conversion, believed in "civilizing" Africans by introducing them to western epistemologies. Their efforts to reshape African societies also shaped the development episteme westerners continued to reproduce over time. Medical and education work came first as a means to entice Africans to the mission stations and communicate religious ideas. As mission communities grew, missionaries focused on teaching new methods of agriculture and industrial education. These four areas (medical, educational, agricultural, and industrial) came to structure the forms of knowledge westerners felt were necessary for Africans to progress into civilized people and developed societies. Africans would be judged on how well they adapted to and adopted the development episteme that came with European colonization.

At the same time Africans were partners in creating the development episteme.[30] Europeans offered different skills to the communities they entered and many noted what evoked the most interest from Africans. For example, European travelers in southern Africa quickly learned that Zulu leaders appreciated the practices in western medicine that appeared to have a direct or immediate impact on healing. As Karen Flint argues, "healing the body became a means by which Europeans sought to demonstrate the superiority of western medicine and, by extension, western culture, civilization, and religion."[31] Missionaries without extensive medical skills relied on books they brought with them to Africa to introduce basic western medical

[29] Arthur Silva White, *The Development of Africa* (George Philip & Son, 1890), ix–xi.
[30] Jean Comaroff and John Comaroff, *Of Revelation and Revolution: Christianity, Colonialism, and Consciousness in South Africa* (University of Chicago Press, 1991).
[31] Karen Flint, *Healing Traditions: African Medicine, Cultural Exchange, and Competition in South Africa, 1820–1948* (Ohio University Press, 2008), 95.

principles to their congregations.[32] Africans may or may not have seen western medicine as superior, but they definitely found it useful in certain situations. At each stage in the establishment of the development episteme, Africans embraced knowledges and technologies when they offered specific values. Like medicine, acquiring a western education and industrial skills led directly to employment opportunities. Accepting western agricultural education or jobs offered landless Africans access to land, seeds, and tools. The development episteme was not an invention solely of westerners; rather it evolved in conversation with Africans who differentiated between the elements of western knowledge or technologies they found valuable and those they did not.

★★★

The development episteme emerged in the nineteenth century out of both the scientific endeavor to produce new knowledge about Africa *and* the missionary-imperialist project to disseminate European Christianity, commerce, and "civilization" to Africans. The knowledge explorers, cartographers, medical doctors, biologists, economists, ethnologists, and other scientists produced about Africa facilitated colonization by claiming mastery over the continent's environment and people. Missionaries and colonial officials drew on this scientific information to assert their technological expertise and moral right – even obligation – to "civilize" Africans. Scientific research also facilitated the imperialist development and exploitation of Africa's raw materials and industries. European scholars suggested their expertise was needed because they *knew* Africans best, better than Africans knew themselves. Yet the development episteme was formulated in dialogue with Africans whose own knowledge and interests often determined which development efforts would succeed and which would fail.

Further Reading

On the creation of knowledge about Africa, see Joseph Morgan Hodge, *Triumph of the Expert: Agrarian Doctrines of Development and the Legacies of British Colonialism* (Ohio University Press, 2007); V. Y. Mudimbe, *The Invention of Africa: Gnosis, Philosophy, and the Order of Knowledge* (Indiana University Press, 1988); Mary Louise Pratt, *Imperial Eyes: Travel Writing and*

---

[32] Landeg White, *Magomero: Portrait of an African Village* (Cambridge University Press, 1987), 40.

Transculturation. Second edition (Routledge, 2007); Helen Tilley, *Africa As a Living Laboratory: Empire, Development, and the Problem of Scientific Knowledge, 1870–1950* (University of Chicago Press, 2011); Helen Tilley, ed., with Robert J. Gordon, *Ordering Africa: Anthropology, European Imperialism, and the Politics of Knowledge* (Manchester University Press, 2010).

On European mapping of the African continent, see Thomas J. Bassett and Philip W. Porter, "'From the Best Authorities': The Mountains of Kong in the Cartography of West Africa," *Journal of African History* 32:3 (1991) 367–413; Denis Cosgrove and Stephen Daniels, eds., *The Iconography of Landscape: Essays on the Symbolic Representation, Design and Use of Past Environments* (Cambridge University Press, 1988); Philip D. Curtin, *The Image of Africa: British Ideas and Action, 1780–1850* (University of Wisconsin Press, 1964); Isabelle Surun, "French Military Officers and the Mapping of West Africa: The Case of Captain Brosselard-Faidherbe," *Journal of Historical Geography* 37 (2011) 167–177.

The most prolific British author in the genre of exploration literature was Richard F. Burton. For examples of his work, see Richard F. Burton, *First Footsteps in East Africa, or, An exploration of Hārar* (Longman, Brown, Green, and Longmans, 1856); *The Lake Regions of Central Africa: A Picture of Exploration* (Longman, Green, Longman and Roberts, 1860); *Wanderings in West Africa from Liverpool to Fernando Po* (Tinsley Brothers, 1863); and *Zanzibar: City, Island, and Coast* (Tinsley Brothers, 1872). Other explorers' works include Mary H. Kingsley, *Travels in West Africa: Congo Francais, Corisco and Cameroons* (Macmillan, 1897); Mary H. Kingsley, *The Story of West Africa* (H. Marshall & Son, 1899); David Livingstone, *Missionary Travels and Researches in South Africa [electronic resource]: Including a Sketch of Sixteen Years' Residence in the Interior of Africa, and a Journey from the Cape of Good Hope to Loanda on the West Coast, Thence across the Continent, Down the River Zambesi, to the Eastern Ocean* (John Murray, 1857); John Hanning Speke, *Journal of the Discovery of the Source of the Nile* (Harper, 1864); and Henry Morton Stanley, *The Congo and the Founding of Its Free State: A Story of Work and Exploration* (Harper, 1885).

CHAPTER 3

Eugenics and Racism in the Development Episteme

In 1949 the United Nations Educational, Scientific and Cultural Organization (UNESCO) held a meeting of cultural anthropologists, sociologists, and other scientists from around the world to attack the problem of racial prejudice. The atrocities of the Holocaust made it politically expedient to discredit racist theories about the inherent inferiority or superiority of racial groups. UNESCO asked the meeting participants to study "scientific materials concerning questions of race" and to devise "an education campaign based on this information."[1] The scholars firmly believed that non-westerners were less developed than westerners, but they debated whether it was because of racial or cultural differences. Sebastián Gil-Riaño argues, "the participants in the 1949 meeting were located within traditions of human science that attached conceptions of race to discussions about the improvability of so-called backward peoples."[2] The outcome of the meeting was the 1950 UNESCO Statement on Race that debunked earlier "scientific" theories about the essential connections between race, intelligence, and development. For instance, they contended that intelligence tests "do not in themselves enable us to differentiate safely between what is due to innate capacity and what is the result

---

[1] United Nations, United Nations Educational Scientific and Cultural Organization, "The Race Question, 1950," 1, https://unesdoc.unesco.org/ark:/48223/pf0000128291, accessed February 5, 2020.

[2] Sebastián Gil-Riaño, "Relocating Anti-racist Science: The 1950 UNESCO Statement on Race and Economic Development in the Global South," *British Journal for the History of Science* 51:2 (2018) 281–303 at 287.

of environmental influences, training and education."[3] The scientists concluded, "'race' is not so much a biological phenomenon as a social myth."[4] The debate over difference was no longer one of race but now one of social and cultural influences.

The 1950 statement immediately garnered significant global debate, especially among European and American physical anthropologists and geneticists who strongly disagreed with its scientific implications.[5] The dissenting scholars worked on their own Statement on the Nature of Race and Race Differences, which UNESCO published in 1951. They argued, "Man, we recognized, is distinguished as much by his culture as by his biology."[6] Despite their disagreements over the biological nature of race, all of the scientists involved in the debate emphasized that intelligence and corresponding stages of social development were influenced by cultural factors. As such, they defined the "difference" between Africans and westerners as one between "primitive" or "tribal" cultures and "modern civilization." "Culture" replaced "race" as the marker of developmental difference, but "culture" never completely abandoned its racial connotations. The UNESCO debates reinforced the "scientific" argument that (white) western modernity was the benchmark for measuring the developmental status of all other cultures.

This shift in discourse from "race" to "culture" in the UNESCO scientific debates points to World War II as a watershed moment in the history of international development. Indeed, many historians date the emergence of development to the end of the war, when the World Bank, the International Monetary Fund (IMF), and the United Nations (UN) came into existence. The policies and practices of these institutions have both reshaped and been shaped by the development episteme. They have contributed to the foundation of knowledge that has determined and continues to determine international development policies in the present. By pulling back the veil on how social Darwinist and eugenic ideas undergirded international development policies before and after World War II, this chapter demonstrates how

[3] United Nations, United Nations Educational Scientific and Cultural Organization, "Text of the Statement Issued 18 July 1950," 7, https://unesdoc.unesco.org/ark:/482 23/pf0000128291, accessed February 5, 2020.

[4] Ibid., 8.

[5] Jenny Bangham, "What Is Race? UNESCO, Mass Communication and Human Genetics in the Early 1950s," *History of the Human Sciences* 28:5 (2015) 80–107.

[6] United Nations, United Nations Educations Scientific and Cultural Organization, "Statement on the Nature of Race and Race Differences," Paris, June 1951, 37, https://unesdoc.unesco.org/ark:/48223/pf0000122962, accessed February 5, 2020.

racist assumptions of African inferiority were embedded in the development episteme itself.

SCIENCE, RACE, AND THEORIES OF EVOLUTION

Carl Linnaeus's *The System of Nature* (1735) classified all humans and primates under the category of *anthropomorpha*. This move was controversial because it placed humans on equal footing with animals in the natural world. Christian theologians believed that humans were made in the "image of God"; therefore to equate humans with animals was, by extension, to debase God. Linnaeus eventually refined his system of classification and organized humans into four "races" based on their skin tone and continental origins. These four "races" were European, American, Asian, and African. Linnaeus's secularization of knowledge classification built the foundation for "scientific" constructs of race.

Johann Friedrich Blumenbach, a German scholar often credited with being the "father" of physical anthropology, expanded on Linnaeus's categorization in the multiple editions of his book *On the Natural Variety of Mankind* (1775, 1782, and 1806). He identified five distinct "races" based on his study of sixty skulls: Caucasian, Mongolian, Malayan, Ethiopian, and American. While his argument was ostensibly grounded in his investigation of the skulls, the evidentiary support for his classification presumed categories based on skin tone. Blumenbach argued that all humans derived from a single origin and that environmental factors degenerated the human stock, resulting in the different skin tones and other attributes of the five races.

During the nineteenth and twentieth centuries many western scholars drew on the work of Linnaeus and Blumenbach to "prove" the superiority of the "white race."[7] Over time numerous scientists attempted to claim that race is genetically linked to behavior. This is called biological determinism or racial essentialism. Often these ideas blended into social Darwinist thinking of the late nineteenth century

---

[7] Blumenbach used the term "Caucasian" to describe a "white race" – yet his terminology was deeply flawed. Using the term "Caucasian" replicates the theories of pseudoscientific racism. See Carol Mukhopadhyay, "Getting Rid of the Word 'Caucasian,'" in Mica Pollock, ed., *Everyday Anti-racism: Getting Real about Race in School* (New Press, 2008).

that applied biological concepts of natural selection to social phenomena in order to justify white and western domination and imperialism.[8]

Many of these theories originated in the study of anthropology.
Anthropology, which some scholars in the 1970s accused of being the
"handmaiden of colonialism" because of its historic role in exploration
and conquest, was a product of nineteenth-century European and
American interest in the study of other humans and their cultures.[9]
Long before the separation of the discipline into subfields, which we
discuss further in Chapter 5, anthropologists did not distinguish
between studies of human origins and studies of "other" cultures; in
fact, they were two sides of the same coin. The establishment of the
French Société ethnologique de Paris in 1839 and the Ethnological
Society of London four years later formalized the academic field of
anthropology. Over the next few decades scholars from these and other
anthropological organizations generated a robust debate about human
genesis and evolution. The major anthropological debates of the day
concentrated on two questions: whether all humans had one common
ancestor (genesis) and whether they evolved from earlier proto-
humanoids (evolution). The answers anthropologists of the late nineteenth century gave to these questions helped to shape early colonial
perceptions of Africans as racially inferior.

In the 1840s intellectuals debated whether all humans share
a common descent (monogenesis) or whether the "races" of humanity
represent separate species unique to their environments (polygenesis).
This question engendered disagreement for more than a century, and
not until after World War II, when work on early humans by paleon-
tologists provided incontrovertible proof for monogenesis, did this
theory become the standard hypothesis for human evolution. The
reasons for individual belief in monogenesis or polygenesis ranged
widely. For example, Christian leaders were monogenists based on
a biblical understanding of Adam and Eve as the common progenitors
for all of humanity. On the other hand, Charles Darwin was convinced
by the theory of monogenesis because he knew that interbreeding
between different species causes infertility, which did not happen
among different groups of humans.[10] Many monogenists like

---

[8]   Curtis Keim, *Mistaking Africa: Curiosities and Inventions of the American Mind*. Third
      edition (Westview Press, 2013), 42–43.
[9]   Talal Asad, ed., *Anthropology and the Colonial Encounter* (Ithaca Press, 1973).
[10] Henrika Kuklick, "The British Tradition," in Henrika Kuklick, ed., *A New History of
      Anthropology* (Blackwell, 2008), 55.

Blumenbach believed in a single human species even though they identified biological varieties of human "races" based on physical appearance.[11]

In contrast to monogenists, polygenists believed that different human "races" represented distinct "species." Polygenist arguments were found on both sides of the Atlantic, but the strongest proponents were located in the United States. Swiss biologist Louis Agassiz, who gave a series of lectures across the United States in 1847, argued "that the unity of species does not involve a unity of origin, and that a diversity of origin does not involve a plurality of species."[12] Agassiz and other polygenists used the example of dog breeds to make their case. Did all dogs come from the same ancestor, or did they evolve out of similar species in different locations over time? Dogs can interbreed and at the same time appear to have very different physical traits. Polygenists argued similarly that humans evolved separately in different places, adapting to their environments to create different species and races (see Figure 3.1). Many Southerners in the United States used the theory of polygenesis to justify slavery by arguing that Africans are not the same species as Europeans. To them, owning slaves was not unlike owning dogs, cows, horses, or other species. Both groups, monogenists and polygenists, generally viewed Africans as fundamentally inferior to Europeans, but they had different justifications for the inferiority.

While some disagreements continued to exist in the late nineteenth century over the origins of humans, Darwin's theory of evolution eventually united monogenists and polygenists by making the case for a unified human evolution with later environmental influences that created regional differences. When Charles Darwin published his book *On the Origin of Species* in 1859, he was not the first scholar to offer an evolutionary theory to explain the natural world. As mentioned in

---

[11]   Various intellectuals of the eighteenth and nineteenth centuries set up different categorizations of races. Most systems (including that of Linnaeus) had either four or five divisions that were generally grouped geographically: European, African, Asian, and American. Some systems included a fifth category that subdivided Asians into East Asians and South/Central Asians. For a discussion of racial classification systems see Saul Dubow, *Scientific Racism in Modern South Africa* (Cambridge University Press, 1995), 20–65.

[12]   Original citation Louis Agassiz, "The Diversity of Origin of the Human Races," *Christian Examiner*, 4th Ser., 14, 110–145, cited in Thomas Glick, "Anthropology, Race, and the Darwinian Revolution," in Henrika Kuklick, ed., *A New History of Anthropology* (Blackwell, 2008), 225–241 at 225–227.

From Nott and Gliddon *Types of Mankind* (1856)

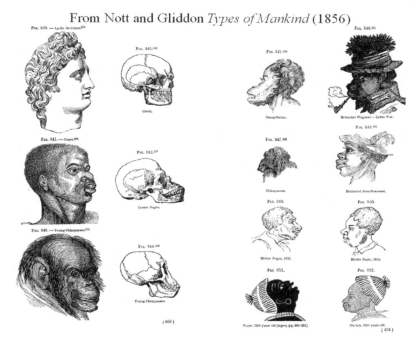

FIGURE 3.1 Chart of the "Types of Mankind". Source: Josiah Clark Nott, George R. Gliddon, Samuel George Morton, Louis Agassiz, William Usher, and Henry S. Patterson, *Types of Mankind* (J. B. Lippincott, Grambo, 1854), 458–459

Chapter 1, Herbert Spencer also coined an evolutionary system for understanding human development that was based on his interpretation of the differential levels of human and societal progress. Darwin's book used the idea of natural selection to explain how different species evolved over time in response to their environment. Not until his 1871 book, *The Descent of Man*, did Darwin address the issue of human evolution. He argued that "those groups who displayed the greatest social cohesion would be advantaged in the struggle for life over those who had less."[13] Evolution, according to Darwin, was not necessarily a progressive ideology. As Darwin noted, societies do not always act rationally for the survival of the species, evident by the fact that many societies send their fittest young men into warfare. Nonetheless, Darwin employed Occam's razor (see Box 3.1) to argue that all humans evolved from one progenitor and that "races," or visible biological and cultural

---

[13] Glick, "Anthropology, Race, and the Darwinian Revolution," 227.

differences, were formed by surrounding environments. He argued, "The great variability of all the external differences between the races of man, likewise indicates that they cannot be of much importance; for if important, they would long ago have been either fixed and preserved, or eliminated."[14] Darwin was not devoid of racialist thinking; he believed in a racialized, hierarchical distinction between "civilized" and "savage" societies and that, over time, the former would either absorb the latter or otherwise cause them to become extinct.[15] Whether categorized as different species or as different groups within the human species, both monogenists and polygenists subscribed to this hierarchical mapping of race during the nineteenth century.

While scientific debates around evolutionary ideas eventually brought Africans into the family of humans, they were consistently defined by nineteenth-century scientists as less than equal to other "races." In *On the Origin of Species* Darwin wrote of "evolutionary dead ends." These dead ends represented traits that either evolved poorly for the environment or did not evolve at all in response to environmental change. Many influential Europeans such as novelist Charles Dickens came to see Africans as poorly evolved versions of the human species and as such an evolutionary dead end. Thus, even as Africans were finally incorporated into the family of humanity, they lost their future as Europeans presumed they would "die out." The only means to save Africans was by creating a civilized environment around them that would allow them to "evolve" to the level of Europeans.

ANTHROPOLOGY, PSEUDOSCIENTIFIC RACISM, AND EUGENICS

During the nineteenth century many Europeans believed in a hierarchy of races ranging from the most "civilized" to the most "primitive" with Europeans located at the top and Africans at the bottom. Pseudoscientific racism, the teleological practice of using scientific techniques to justify a belief in the racial inferiority of non-European

---

[14] Charles Darwin, *Descent of Man, and Selection in Relation to Sex*. Second edition revised and augmented (John Murray, 1874), 198.
[15] Charles Darwin, *Descent of Man, and Selection in Relation to Sex*, Vol. I (John Murray, 1871), 236–240. Darwin believed extinction would result from the poor health of "savage" races and their inability to adapt to changing environmental and political conditions.

people, provided "scientific" evidence to justify this hierarchy. Well-regarded scientists such as Robert Knox and Paul Broca employed anthropological methodologies including craniometry (measurement of the size and shape of the cranium) and phrenology (correlating skull measurements to personality) in order to confirm their beliefs about racial difference. Modern scientists have long debunked the notion that racial difference can be explained in terms of phenotype or cranio-metrics. Nonetheless, early physical anthropologists were determined to "scientifically" prove that Africans, as a race, were less intelligent than Europeans. By the end of the century pseudoscientific racism had helped to shape Francis Galton's theory of "eugenics," the science of determining how to "improve" human groups. European colonial officials in Africa drew on these and other pseudoscientific theories about race to transform Africans from evolutionary "dead ends" into "uncivilized" people.[16] The work of all of these "apostles of objectivity" was founded on the premise that the veracity of their theories would be confirmed by collecting mountains of data.[17] Nineteenth-century scientists failed to understand that no amount of data could correct for misinterpretation and confirmation bias.

3.1 Scientific method and confirmation bias

What we call the scientific method has evolved over many centuries and cultures into a system based on observation, measurement, and experimentation. Darwin's theory of evolution is a classic example of the scientific method. During his time in the Galapagos archipelago he observed that similar species of birds and other animals differed across each island. Darwin pondered his observations for four years before he came to the idea of natural selection. He then spent the next twenty years

---

[16] Many hierarchies existed within this larger framework, such that some Europeans were defined as lower than others, most famously the Irish; likewise, some Africans were defined as "more civilized" than others – often based on physical appearance or social status within their regions. For further discussion of how different white "races" were defined, see David Roediger, *The Wages of Whiteness: Race and the Making of the American Working Class* (Verso, 1991).

[17] Paleontologist Stephen Jay Gould described Francis Galton and other pseudoscientists as "apostles of objectivity" because of their belief that scientific research would prove them correct about their theories of race. Stephen Jay Gould, *The Mismeasure of Man* (Norton, 1981), chapter 3.

gathering the evidence to support this theory. Darwin was very careful to look at different theories and ideas about evolution that were in vogue during his time (the 1830s and 1840s) so that he could avoid confirmation bias in his work. Confirmation bias occurs when scientists approach their data with outcomes already determined and look only for evidence that supports those outcomes. For example, many nineteenth-century physical anthropologists examined the size and shape of human skulls in order to confirm their belief that Europeans were superior to all other "races." Their work was eventually discredited.

Two methods in particular have helped scientists avoid or at least become more aware of confirmation bias. One is Occam's razor, the principle that if more than one hypothesis can explain a particular phenomenon, then the simplest hypothesis is probably correct. Another useful concept is reproducibility. If another scientist can successfully reproduce the experiment and come to the same conclusions, the results may be confirmed. Reproducing another scientist's research may also reveal that person's biases. For example, during the 1970s paleontologist Stephen Jay Gould attempted to replicate the work of nineteenth-century craniometrist Paul Broca. Gould demonstrated that, despite Broca's rigorous data collection, his biases about racial inequality led him to incorrectly interpret the evidence and argue that race determines intelligence.[1] Biases are still present in some scientific work today, of course, and may be inadvertently introduced at various points in an experiment: research design, data analysis, and/or publication. Awareness of the potential for confirmation bias helps scientists to mitigate this problem in their research.

[1]   Gould, *The Mismeasure of Man.*

The career of Robert Knox, a Scottish doctor and scientist, demonstrates the deep connections between the history of imperialism and racism in South Africa and pseudoscientific research in nineteenth-century physical anthropology. Knox was a military doctor based in the Zuurland region of South Africa between 1817 and 1820, at a time when the British and the Xhosa were fighting in the Cape-Xhosa Frontier Wars.[18] Knox and other scientists working in South Africa during this period

[18]   Kevin Shillington, *History of Southern Africa* (Macmillan, 1987), 21–42.

collected the skulls of the Xhosa people killed in the war and used them to test out their theories about race, intelligence, and evolution. The victims of colonial violence became the specimens of study for scientists like Knox who sought to prove that Africans and Europeans were separate species with distinct biological and cognitive attributes. Building on his experiences in South Africa and the earlier work of Linnaeus and Blumenbach, Robert Knox published his book *The Races of Men* in 1850, which argued that race determines behavior and character. He classified races based on attributes such as skin color, hair texture, head shape, and other physical features. The origins of the science of physical anthropology was entangled with the history of conquest and bolstered a white supremacist ideology that dominated South African politics until the end of apartheid in 1994.[19]

Knox's work measuring cranial capacity deeply influenced French anthropologist Paul Broca, who founded the Society of Anthropology of Paris in 1859. Broca firmly believed in the superiority of Europeans and the inferiority of Africans based on the notion that human intelligence correlates to a linear, hierarchal scale of racial difference. To prove this theory, Broca measured the ratio of the radius to the humerus bones (the lower to upper arm bones) among the skeletons of different "races." Initially, he was pleased to find a significant difference between the European and African skeletons held at the Musée de l'Homme in Paris. However, when confronted with the skeleton of Sara Baartman, a Khoikhoi woman brought from South Africa to France in the 1810s, Broca found that Baartman's ratio placed her significantly higher on his scale than Europeans.[20] Having failed to prove his theory, Broca started over, this time following Knox's work to argue that cranial capacity was both racially determined and corresponded directly with intelligence.

In 1861 another anatomist, Louis Pierra Gratiolet, challenged Broca by arguing that brain size is not indicative of intelligence. Rather than using scientific evidence to respond to Gratiolet, Broca used "logic." He contended, "In general, the brain is larger in mature adults than in the elderly, in men than in women, in eminent men than in men of mediocre talent, in superior races than in inferior races. ... Other things equal, there is a remarkable relationship between the development of intelligence and the volume of the brain."[21] Most of Broca's peers in the

---

[19]   Dubow, *Scientific Racism*, 27–29.
[20]   Gould, *The Mismeasure of Man*, 86–87.
[21]   Quoted in Gould, *The Mismeasure of Man*, 83.

scientific community, predominantly white men themselves, were easily convinced that women, people of color, the elderly, and the poor were "naturally" less intelligent than wealthy and healthy white men. As long as he provided "scientific" arguments about racial and gender differences, Broca and his colleagues believed their work was without bias and based in sound evidence; they were convinced their work was "objective." Scientists of the nineteenth century were unaware of their confirmation bias. They did not see that they relied on assumptions to interpret evidence instead of allowing the evidence to drive their conclusions.

3.2 Sara (Saartjie) Baartman

An 1810 advertisement in London's *Morning Herald* announced, "The Hottentot Venus. – Just arrived, and may be seen between the hours of one and five o'clock in the afternoon, at No 225, Piccadilly, from the banks of the river Gamtoos, on the borders of Kaffraria, in the interior of South Africa, a most correct and perfect specimen of that race of people . . . the Public will have an opportunity of judging how far she exceeds any description given by historians of that tribe of the human race . . . Admittance 25 each."[1] "The Hottentot Venus" was the exhibition name of Sara Baartman, a Khoikhoi woman from South Africa. Baartman had agreed to travel with Hendrick Cezar to Europe, but whether she fully understood the ways in which she would be displayed is unclear. Starting as early as the seventeenth century, European travelers brought human "exotics" home to display to the public. By the mid-nineteenth century racialized and sexualized "Others" had become regular curiosities at world's fairs, circuses, and other exhibitions.[2] With the scientific revolution under way, many amateur and professional scientists were fascinated by people from other parts of the world. Traveler's tales of steatopygia (a particular shape of buttocks) and an "apron" of skin in front of the genitalia of some Khoikhoi women had preceded Baartman's appearance in London. Scientists of the day were obsessed with studying Baartman's body and particularly her genitalia, while to European men and women she symbolized stereotypes (and fantasies) of the hypersexual African woman.

When Sara Baartman died in France in 1815 she was dissected by French anatomist George Cuvier. Her skeleton was kept for future scientific experiments, her genitalia put in jars of formaldehyde, and parts of her body left on display in the Musée de l'Homme until 1974. Cuvier studied Baartman's genitalia in order to prove that Baartman was actually a "lower primate" and not fully human.[3] He discovered that the "apron" on Baartman's genitalia was an extended labia minora, prompting him to conclude that all women in Africa naturally had extended labia minora. The closer one moved toward the Mediterranean Sea, he argued, the smaller the labia minora on women's bodies. He surmised that the reason female circumcision was practiced in Ethiopia was to remove this "disgusting" elongation. Cuvier assumed that Khoikhoi (and African) women were less than human based on his assertion that Baartman's genitalia were an aberration from those of the typical (white) woman. Cuvier's reputation as the greatest scientist in France of his time gave him the power to co-opt Baartman's body for scientific study and lent legitimacy to his theories about racial difference.

[1] Rachel Holmes, *African Queen: The Real Life of the Hottentot Venus* (Random House, 2007), 6–7.

[2] The 1851 Great Exhibition in London had Inuit, Native Americans, and Africans. In 1853 displays of "Zulu Kaffirs" and "Aztec Lilliputians" were posted in the *Illustrated London News*. See other references in Barbara Harlow and Mia Carter, eds., *Archives of Empire*, Vol. 2 (Duke University Press, 2003), 134. See also Dana S. Hale, *Races on Display: French Representations of Colonized Peoples, 1886–1940* (Indiana University Press, 2008).

[3] Stephen Jay Gould, "The Hottentot Venus," *Natural History* 91:10 (1982) 20–27 at 26.

The work of Knox and Broca became the basis for Francis Galton's theory of eugenics. In his 1883 book, *Inquiries into Human Faculty and Its Development*, Galton coined the term "eugenics" from the Greek word meaning "well born." Eugenics is the science of improving population groups through the manipulation of breeding. Combining Knox's views on race and Darwin's concept of natural selection, Galton proposed that human races could be improved through the careful selection of "positive" traits and the weeding out of "undesirable" or "inferior" traits. Many of the "traits" that Galton viewed as genetic were actually social or economic. Galton's theory of eugenics was designed to deal with the "problem" of the degeneration of the white race, which was defined at the time in terms of the problem of "poor whites." The late nineteenth century in Europe was a time of rapid industrialization and an ever-expanding population of urban poor. Several decades before colonial officials used the ideas of eugenics to transform the lives of Africans, eugenicists targeted "poor whites." As discussed in Chapter 1, the "poor white problem" seemed to arise wherever people of non-European and European descent lived in close proximity, such as in the settler colonies of South Africa, Kenya, and Algeria.[22] "Poor whites" were seen as more vulnerable to degeneration because of concerns about the impact of the environment and miscegenation ("race mixing"). Eugenic ideas quickly gained in popularity among middle-class Europeans who linked degeneration to interracial contact, poverty, and prostitution.

Eugenics would come to play an important role in colonial development policies in Africa. In the first decade of the twentieth century eugenicists focused their efforts on the impoverished white communities of settler colonies. By the 1920s eugenic ideas began to filter into colonial development policies for Black Africans. During this period two broadly construed camps of eugenics emerged, and these positions – positive and negative eugenics – originated from the nurture versus nature debate. Positive eugenicists aimed to improve the white race through the increased reproduction of people with ideal traits and improvement of the race in general through social welfare. The efforts of positive eugenicists were based on the Lamarckian theory of inheritance. Jean-Baptiste Lamarck was an early nineteenth-century biologist who developed the idea of soft inheritance, or the inheritance of acquired characteristics. One way that positive eugenicists sought to improve the race was by bettering the lives of the working class through more sanitary housing, nutrition, and education. Maternal welfare was also important to positive eugenicists because they believed it ensured the healthy development of

---

[22] For further discussion of the "poor white problem" see Dubow, *Scientific Racism*, 120–165; Chloe Campbell, *Race and Empire: Eugenics in Colonial Kenya* (Manchester University Press, 2007); Susanne Klausen, *Race, Maternity, and the Politics of Birth Control in South Africa, 1910–39* (Palgrave Macmillan, 2004); Lundy Braun, *Breathing Race into the Machine: The Surprising Career of the Spirometer from Plantation to Genetics* (University of Minnesota Press, 2014), 109–138; William Schneider, "Toward the Improvement of the Human Race: The History of Eugenics in France," *Journal of Modern History* 54:2 (1982) 268–291.

the next generation of humans.[23] Positive eugenic policies fit well within the development episteme and helped to shape colonial development policies.

The key component of negative eugenics was controlling the fertility of "less desirable" populations. The scientific theories behind negative eugenics came out of the work of German biologist August Weismann. According to Weismann's germ plasm theory, acquired characteristics cannot be inherited. Only innate qualities can be passed to the following generation. In order to cull negative elements from society, negative eugenicists believed, government policies should control reproduction among less desirable groups. Traits viewed as heritable included criminality, poverty, alcoholism, mental deficiency and illness, and prostitution. Eugenicists argued that these cultural, economic, and social characteristics were driven by biology. They attempted to limit the growth of "undesirable" populations through legal and medical procedures such as birth control, forced sterilization, marriage restrictions, antimiscegenation and segregation laws, and generally discouraging reproduction among lower social classes and non-Europeans.

Eugenic ideas "coincided with the rising intensity of imperialist feeling from the 1880s, helping to stoke nationalist fervor and providing a convenient rationale for the colonial subjugation of non-Europeans."[24] This was especially true for settler colonies. In South Africa eugenics research targeted the improvement of the white community, efforts that were replicated in the budding settler colonies of Kenya and Rhodesia at the beginning of the twentieth century. Historian Chloe Campbell argues that calls for eugenic policies in the British Empire came to be far more virulent than in the metropole. The underlying argument of eugenics, that elite Europeans were racially superior to the rest of humanity, was used to justify settlers' claims over land and right to rule. Campbell explained, "as well as expressing the cultural fears of colonialism, eugenics also expressed the modernity of the colonial project in Africa: the newness of settler society and the perceived rawness of African development presented an ideal opportunity to create a society modelled on eugenic insights."[25] In colonial Africa eugenic development policies became cultural practices as much as scientific programs. As occurred with physical

---

[23]   Schneider, "Toward the Improvement of the Human Race."
[24]   Dubow, *Scientific Racism*, 121.
[25]   Campbell, *Race and Empire*, 3.

anthropological theories of race, eugenicists masked cultural assumptions as scientific evidence designed to make the case for European racial superiority.

EUGENICS, RACE, AND LABOR IN COLONIAL AFRICA

European colonial powers implemented eugenic ideas and practices among poor white settlers in Africa as early as the 1890s. Soon after the French began isolated eugenic programs for Africans around the turn of the century. However, it was after World War I that colonial governments throughout Africa expanded their efforts to create the healthiest, most effective labor force through eugenic practices. Colonial efforts in housing, public health, education, and agriculture – the four areas of intervention that we examine more closely in Part III of this book – contributed toward eugenic efforts to improve the quality of the African workforce.

Colonial officials drew on positive eugenic theories and practices in the late nineteenth and early twentieth centuries to address fears about declining population in African colonies. Medical and public health departments implemented eugenicist ideas to create healthier workers for the state and healthier living spaces for European settlers. For example, early twentieth-century mosquito eradication and inoculation schemes in the Zanzibar Islands were explicitly designed to improve the "quality" of the African labor pool.[26] During the early years of colonial development officials sought to increase African life expectancy not merely for its value to African societies but, more importantly, to improve the health and productivity of labor for the colonial economy.

The work of General Gallieni in Madagascar offered one of the first models for employing positive eugenic methods in Africa's colonial development practices. Initially, Madagascar was to serve as a crucial site for improving the white race through outmigration based on the notion that the island's climate would foster more rapid population growth than would occur in France.[27] Within a few years a different eugenics project to improve the indigenous Merina community

---

[26]   Elisabeth McMahon, "Becoming Pemba: Identity, Social Welfare and Community during the Protectorate Period" (PhD diss., Indiana University, 2005), 167–198.

[27]   By the turn of the century the French government regularly fretted over the declining fertility amongst the white population of France.

preoccupied the colonial administration. Gallieni was concerned about the Merina because he considered them the most likely labor pool for colonial industries. Gallieni sought to increase the Merina population from three million to ten million by increasing rates of reproduction and decreasing infant mortality. These pronatalist efforts became the basis for the island's colonial public health system and the cornerstone of French imperial policies for *mise en valeur* (development). In 1897 Gallieni established hospitals, leprosariums, maternity wards, venereal disease treatment centers, orphanages, and a medical school for indigenous students. By 1901 a Pasteur Institute was opened with the capacity to vaccinate 30,000 people a month. The medical school also indoctrinated locals into western ideas about health and hygiene. Indigenous midwives studied for two years and doctors for five years, all at the cost of the state. Midwives visited the homes of indigenous women and gave advice on best practices for prenatal and postnatal care and infant welfare in order to increase infant life expectancy.[28]

The Belgian administration instituted a similar pronatalist program in the Congo. In 1912 Madame van den Perre of Belgium founded the League for the Protection of Black Children in order to combat high infant mortality in the colony. The League opened the first milk station (*goutte de lait*) to provide Congolese women supplementary food for their infants, teach mothers how to "properly" raise their children, and spread other western ideas about cleanliness and hygiene.[29] These milk stations had been used in Belgium and other European nations in the previous decades to improve the health of working-class whites. By 1910 colonizers shifted their concerns toward declining birth rates among labor populations in the colonies. As with Gallieni's pronatalist project in Madagascar, these "scientifically based" Lamarckian social welfare policies were designed to ensure a larger, healthier, and more productive African workforce.

Initially, the Belgian and French governments brought eugenic policies to Africa to improve their white population, just as the British in South Africa, Rhodesia, and Kenya sought to improve their

---

[28] Margaret Cook Andersen, "Creating French Settlements Overseas: Pronatalism and Colonial Medicine in Madagascar," *French Historical Studies* 33:3 (2010) 417–444.

[29] Nancy Rose Hunt, "'Le Bebe en Brousse': European Women, African Birth Spacing and Colonial Intervention in Breast Feeding in the Belgian Congo," *International Journal of African Historical Studies* 21:3 (1988) 401–432 at 405.

"poor whites." Colonial officials quickly realized, however, that the same policies used to improve "poor whites" could be implemented to improve the quality of African laborers as well. Lamarckian or positive eugenic ideas reinforced the ethos of the development episteme through a secular "civilizing mission" described as racial improvement. Such ideas and practices of social engineering informed development policies across the continent well into the twentieth century.

POPULATION CONTROL AND THE IMPLICIT RACISM OF POSTWAR DEVELOPMENT THEORIES

Julian Huxley, the first director general of UNESCO, took the reins in 1946 determined to bring his ideas of evolutionary humanism to this new international organization. Huxley had been a well-known eugenicist before the Second World War. During the 1920s and early 1930s he urged the British Colonial Office to take a "biological approach in native education" in East Africa because biology was important for teaching "personal hygiene," "social hygiene," and what he called "the eugenic ideal."[30] An earlier version of his recommendations stated more overtly that biology was crucial for teaching "racial hygiene [in order] to inculcate a knowledge of heredity."[31] Huxley gradually abandoned references to "race" and "tribe" in favor of "culture," but he maintained a strong belief in social evolutionary theory. Before World War II Huxley was both an avowed eugenicist and anti-Nazi. Huxley renounced the overtly racialist ideas of many eugenicists of his time and argued that the improvement of humanity was an issue of culture rather than skin tone.[32] Huxley promoted evolutionary humanism, which was the theory that "more evolved" societies in the west could and should facilitate the development of "less evolved" societies through a combination of cultural, economic, and social interventions. When he took up the reins as the director of UNESCO most of sub-Saharan Africa was still under

[30] UKNA Colonial Office (CO) 879/123/11, Professor Julian Huxley, MA, "Biology and the Biological Approach to Native Education in East Africa" (Printed for the Colonial Office, April 1930), 21.
[31] UKNA CO 879/121/4, Memorandum Prepared by Professor Julian Huxley and Dr. W. K. Spencer for Advisory Committee on Education in Tropical Africa, 1928, 214.
[32] Paul Weindling, "Julian Huxley and the Continuity of Eugenics in Twentieth-Century Britain," *Journal of Modern European History* 10:4 (2012) 480–499.

European colonial rule, and Huxley accepted that colonialism was the vehicle for developing African societies.

After World War II scholars such as Julian Huxley helped to remove the racialized discourse from the idea of western cultural supremacy and reframe the discourse on development to one about societies and cultures. However, as evident in the 1950 and 1951 UNESCO statements discussed in the beginning of this chapter, race did not entirely disappear from debates about comparative differences. By the 1950s evolutionary humanism itself became redefined as international development and modernization, and the discourse on eugenics had morphed into one about population control.

Other eugenicists imitated Julian Huxley's post–World War II pivot away from the explicit language of race. These eugenicists, particularly those in the United States such as Frederick Osborn, transformed their prewar focus on sterilization and limiting the fertility of "unfit" (usually nonwhite) populations into a cornerstone of modern development policy. Beginning in the late 1940s governments in colonial Africa and elsewhere were no longer concerned about population decline, but about what eventually came to be known as the "population bomb."[33] Neo-Malthusian arguments that global food supplies could not keep up with the exponential pace of population growth fed the panic. Western eugenicists urged the need to control population expansion, especially in the global south, through widespread distribution of birth control.

Much to the gratification of colonial officials, their ongoing colonial vaccination campaigns and other health interventions across Africa in the preceding decades created a population boom on the continent.[34] While officials on the ground valued the birth of more laborers, some scholars and activists located in the European imperial metropoles and in the United States raised the alarm over the booming population in Africa. In 1948 two neo-Malthusian books published in the United

---

[33] Paul R. Ehrlich, *The Population Bomb* (A Sierra Club Ballantine Book, 1968).

[34] For more information on population expansion and vaccination campaigns in colonial Africa see Hannah-Louise Clark, "Administering Vaccination in Interwar Algeria: Medical Auxiliaries, Smallpox, and the Colonial State in the Communes Mixtes," *French Politics, Culture & Society* 34:2 (2016) 32–56; Tiloka de Silva and Silvana Tenreyro, "Population Control Policies and Fertility Convergence," *Journal of Economic Perspectives* 31:4 (2017) 205–228; William Schneider, "The Long History of Smallpox Eradication: Lessons for Global Health in Africa," in Tamara Giles-Vernick and James L. A. Webb Jr., eds., *Global Health in Africa: Historical Perspectives on Disease Control* (Ohio University Press, 2013), 25–41.

States warned of a coming environmental collapse. William Vogt's *Road to Survival* and Henry Fairfield Osborn Jr.'s *Our Plundered Planet* both spoke to the concern that expanding populations would permanently damage the earth's environment. Vogt was an activist for population control and eventually a president of Planned Parenthood. Osborn was the son and nephew of two leading eugenicists, Henry and Frederick Osborn. While both books have been credited with helping to found the modern environmental movement, their influence was also felt in the new field of demographics.

Frederick Osborn, the longtime secretary of the American Eugenics Society, feared nonwhites in the global south would overrun the white populations of the global north. He used his positions on the Rockefeller and Milbank Foundation boards to finance the emerging field of demography. In the 1930s Osborn was opposed to birth control because the primary users of birth control in the United States at the time were middle- and upper-class white women, exactly the people eugenicists wanted to procreate. In the postwar era Osborn transformed his view on birth control, at least in terms of where it should be deployed. Through financing from the Rockefeller and Milbank Foundations, he helped to establish a major demographic institution known as the Population Council in 1952.[35] The Population Council oversaw the development and distribution of inexpensive birth control in Africa, Asia, and South American countries, work it continues to do into the present day. Demographers at the Population Council did not frame their work in terms of limiting the growth of nonwhite populations; instead, they employed neo-Malthusian rhetoric about the dangers of overpopulation.

The Population Council sought to make fertility reduction a cornerstone of future development policies. In 1963 the Population Council drafted the language for the UN statement on access to family planning services as a human right. As a follow-up to this statement, the UN created the Fund for Population Activities (UNFPA) in the late 1960s. The UNFPA institutionalized fertility control as part of all future development paradigms. In the present day advocacy for birth control is a central plank in development programs supporting women in African countries. Contemporary advocates of international birth control programs certainly do not view their work as an example of

---

[35]   Emily Klancher Merchant, "A Digital History of Anglophone Demography and Global Population Control," *Population and Development Review* 43:1 (2017) 83–117.

negative eugenics. When eugenicists removed overt references to "race" from their policies in the 1950s they shrouded the original intentions of birth control campaigns. For far too long, forced and coercive sterilization has been used to control population growth among "undesirable" groups in Africa and elsewhere, most recently among HIV-positive women in South Africa during the height of the HIV crisis in the 1990s.[36] Many women around the world find access to birth control liberating, but the "right" to birth control also includes the "right" to have children. Awareness of these rights and of reproductive justice debates generally is crucial for understanding the family planning policies that continue to be foundational in contemporary international development discourses.

★★★

The emerging discipline of physical anthropology in the nineteenth century challenged the notion in Darwin's evolutionary theory that all human beings are part of the same species. Combined with social Darwinist ideas of the time, this set the stage for racialist discourses that linger in the development discourse. Anthropological studies of human evolution also sparked the eugenics movements of the early twentieth century, creating new theories of race that pathologized Blackness. This racialist thinking viewed Africans and people of African descent as biologically different from whites and in need of either eradication or evolutionary intervention. The problem with eugenic theories, whether positive or negative, is that they envisioned Africans as a separate and distinctly lesser race than Europeans.

Positive eugenicists advocated social welfare to "improve" Africans because they believed environmental factors affected their ability to "evolve" – or in twentieth-first-century terms, "modernize." The vast majority of social welfare and development initiatives over the past 100 years have focused on the improvement of education, nutrition, and housing. These are laudable goals taken at face value. However, when combined with discourses on racial inequality, they have other implications. Eugenic efforts to improve poor white and Black communities have their origins in racist ideas of the late nineteenth century. The postwar evolutionary humanist notion that cultural difference determines ability drew on earlier racial hierarchies that viewed people of

---

[36] Vicci Tallis, *Feminisms, HIV and AIDS: Subverting Power, Reducing Vulnerability* (Palgrave Macmillan, 2012), 100–105.

European descent as the evolutionary standard to which all races should strive. This eugenic history of early development policies has largely been forgotten, but the rhetoric on racial difference, now masked as "culture," has stubbornly endured.

Further Reading

On the history of evolution theories and pseudoscientific racism see Lundy Braun, *Breathing Race into the Machine: The Surprising Career of the Spirometer from Plantation to Genetics* (University of Minnesota Press, 2014); Saul Dubow, *Scientific Racism in Modern South Africa* (Cambridge University Press, 1995); Sandra Herbert, *Charles Darwin and the Question of Evolution: A Brief History with Documents* (Bedford St. Martins, 2011); John P. Jackson Jr., *Science for Segregation: Race, Law, and the Case against* Brown v. Board of Education (New York University Press, 2005); Dov Ospovat, *The Development of Darwin's Theory: Natural History, Natural Theology, and Natural Selection, 1838–1859* (Cambridge University Press, 1981); Diana Wylie, *Starving on a Full Stomach: Hunger and the Triumph of Cultural Racism in Modern South Africa* (University of Virginia Press, 2001).

On the history of eugenics and physical anthropology see Andrew Bank, "Of 'Native Skulls' and 'Noble Caucasians': Phrenology in Colonial South Africa," *Journal of Southern African Studies* 22:3 (1996) 387–403; Philip L. Bonner, Amanda Esterhuysen, and Trefor Jenkins, eds., *A Search for Origins: Science, History and South Africa's "Cradle of Humankind"* (Wits University Press, 2007); Chloe Campbell, *Race and Empire: Eugenics in Colonial Kenya* (Manchester University Press, 2007).

CHAPTER 4

Decolonizing the Idea of Development

In 1981 Kenyan novelist and playwright Ngũgĩ wa Thiong'o called for Africans to "decolonize their minds" by embracing African languages, literatures, and cultures.[1] He criticized the first president of Kenya, Jomo Kenyatta, for collaborating with western governments to continue neocolonial policies that disempowered Kenyans. Ngũgĩ (to which he often referred) argued that Kenyatta's education in colonial schools made him more accepting of the western development paradigm, which, in turn, promoted the extension of western-style schooling and westernization more generally in postcolonial Kenya. Acceptance of western cultures and languages, he explained, subjugated Africans to the interests of western governments. Kenyatta, like most early African leaders, was a product of missionary and colonial education, and he used his western education to challenge colonialism. Yet in the postcolonial period he was constrained by both the limited economic power of his country in the face of neocolonial forces and his own efforts to reinforce and institutionalize his political power.

Kenyatta's earlier experiences negotiating with the British government illustrate the difficulty in assuming a binary collaborator/resister framework by distinguishing Africans who collaborated with (former) colonizers from those who resisted colonialism and neocolonialism. In

---

[1] Ngũgĩ wa Thiong'o, *Decolonising the Mind: The Politics of Language in African Literature* (East African Educational Publishers, 1981). Ngũgĩ's argument paralleled Frantz Fanon's earlier call to physically and intellectually decolonize Africa. Ngũgĩ made the case that even after colonization ended, elite Africans remained confined by their western educations and framed their power structures on western models that perpetuated the disenfranchisement of most Africans.

1929 Jomo Kenyatta (known at the time as Johnstone Kenyatta) arrived in England for the first time as a representative of the Kikuyu Central Association (KCA) of Kenya. He came to petition the secretary of state for the colonies to address the land issue in the Kikuyu territory. Kenyatta's requests to meet with the secretary of state were repeatedly denied. Officials in England were reluctant to publicly acknowledge the KCA's grievances over land, but in private conversations they considered meeting with Kenyatta. The British hoped to capitalize on his influence among the Kikuyu to deal with what they viewed as a pending crisis over female circumcision.[2] Kenyatta went back to Kenya in September 1930 but returned to England within a year. Between 1931 and 1946 Kenyatta remained in Europe (mostly England) where he worked on a farm, took courses at several universities, completed a social anthropology degree at the London School of Economics, and published his ethnographic book *Facing Mount Kenya*. During his time in England Kenyatta associated with whites whom the British government viewed as radical, such as Sylvia Pankhurst (see Figure 4.1), further arousing government officials' suspicions of him. After Kenyatta returned to Kenya he became a leader in the Kenya African Union, a nationalist political party, until his arrest and imprisonment by the colonial government in October 1952. As colonialism ended in the early 1960s across much of West and East Africa, Kenyatta was one of several political leaders on the continent who went from being a colonial prisoner to serving as the head of the country's government; he was elected Kenya's first prime minister in 1961 and the president of independent Kenya in 1963, a position he held until his death in 1978. Kenyatta's varied experiences – from education in western schools to election as an African nationalist leader – illustrate the complicated loyalties African elites held during the colonial and postcolonial eras.

Ashis Nandy noted in *The Intimate Enemy* that "[m]odern colonialism won its great victories not so much through its military and technological prowess as through its ability to create secular hierarchies incompatible with the traditional order. These hierarchies opened up new vistas for many, particularly for those exploited or cornered

---

[2]   UKNA CO 533/384 Johnstone Kenyatta. In order to maintain historical accuracy, we use the term "female circumcision" in reference to the period before 1970, and "female genital cutting (FGC)" in reference to the period since 1970. See Box 4.2 for a discussion of the term "female genital cutting."

FIGURE 4.1 Jomo Kenyatta shakes hands with Sylvia Pankhurst at the "Abyssinia and Justice" conference, September 9, 1937. Pankhurst was an anticolonial activist and a supporter of Emperor Haile Selassie and Ethiopian independence in Ethiopia's conflict with Italy.

within the traditional order. To them the new order looked like the first step towards a more just and equal world."[3] Nandy recognized the ways in which the colonial social and economic systems encouraged Africans to prioritize western cultures over indigenous cultures as the means for social mobility. Consequently, that some Africans appeared to move up the social ladder by embracing western cultures furthered the illusion that such cultures were more useful than African systems of social status. By privileging western cultures as "superior" the civilizing mission undergirded the development episteme, a racialized framework that shaped colonial policies.[4] Those who felt they had less power in local hierarchies, often women, young people, and formerly

---

[3]   Ashis Nandy, *The Intimate Enemy: Loss and Recovery of Self under Colonialism* (Oxford University Press, 1983), ix.
[4]   Richard Reid argues that racism was central to European colonialism in Africa and it is "dangerous to overlook the subject, because in many ways it goes to the very heart

enslaved people, sought out these new opportunities for social mobility. Jomo Kenyatta was a classic example of this strategy. He was orphaned young and held a subservient position in his uncle's household. He eventually decided to move to the Church of Scotland Mission in Kenya. There he converted to Christianity and received a western education, preparing him to move up the colonial social ladder. Yet he also broke many of the missionaries' rules about appropriate conduct for Christian converts. Even as he worked within British colonial structures, he began anticolonial political organizing among the Kikuyu ethnic group. Kenyatta quickly discovered, as did other African leaders, that even if they embraced Christianity and the civilizing mission Africans were never included on the higher rungs of colonial hierarchies. Their disillusionment became the platform for various nationalist movements.

Nationalists like Jomo Kenyatta who fought for independence in Africa drew on their westernized education to combat colonial arguments that Africans were not prepared for independence. Most of the leaders in the newly independent nations of postcolonial Africa were products of missionary and government schools. Some like Jomo Kenyatta, Kwame Nkrumah of Ghana, and Hastings Banda of Malawi were also products of educational institutions in the global north. Westernized education in the postcolonial era in Africa represented both modernity and development but continued to tie African educational systems to the colonial past. Ngũgĩ's call to "decolonize the mind" was as much about decolonizing power structures created during the colonial period as it was about reforming individual Africans. In the twenty-first century, the call to decolonize African education systems and power structures has expanded. The South African #RhodesMustFall protest movement (depicted in the cover image for this book) began in 2015 as an effort both to remove a statue of Cecil Rhodes from the University of Cape Town campus and to decolonize the educational system in South Africa and across the continent. The call for the decolonization of power structures in Africa has also moved into the realm of international development. In November 2017 the University of Sussex held a workshop to explore the influence of colonial power constructions in its international development studies program. The workshop considered

of the historical relationship between Africa and Europe." Richard Reid, *A History of Modern Africa: 1800 to the Present*. Second edition (Wiley-Blackwell, 2012), 143.

the epistemological and racial legacies of colonialism in how western institutions teach about development. The Rhodes Must Fall campaign and the University of Sussex workshop reconfigure Ngũgĩ's call. No longer is the call to decolonize the minds of Africans; rather these efforts demand that we decolonize the whiteness of the power structures based in white supremacy that shape relationships between the global north and south.

ASSIMILATION AND CULTURAL IMPERIALISM

The expansion of colonial rule into the interior of the continent introduced Africans to the civilizing mission through the policy of assimilation. Assimilation arose out of the colonial powers' ethnocentric assumption that Africans would want to become more like their European colonizers once introduced to European cultures. Assimilation, the stated colonial policy for French, Portuguese, and Italian colonies, pressured Africans to attend western-style schools, wear European clothing, learn western languages, and adopt the cultural norms of their European overseers. In essence, assimilation was cultural imperialism. Cultural imperialism had a dramatic impact on Africans across the continent because it encouraged Africans to devalue their own cultures in order to embrace westernization, even as most Africans did not perceive such a clear distinction or conflict between African and western cultural practices.

Assimilation came in different forms and had its advantages and disadvantages. In francophone Africa, Africans who spoke the French language, attended French schools, wore European clothes, and demonstrated fluency in French culture – those who identified themselves as Frenchmen – were promised French citizenship. An 1848 law recognized the residents of the four "communes" or settlements in Senegal (Gorée, Saint-Louis, Rufisque, and Dakar) as French citizens. However, this law did not extend into the other regions of French West Africa, neither did it give them full protection of the law if they chose to remain within African and/or Islamic legal systems. Another law passed in 1848 gave the *originaires*, as the original inhabitants of the communes were called, the right to elect a representative to the French Assembly in Paris. Elected representatives included those of mixed African and French heritage, and in 1914 Blaise Diagne became the first black African to occupy the position. Diagne fought for expanded rights for Africans, encouraged Africans to embrace French colonialism, and urged the French to recognize them as full citizens.

Blaise Diagne's vision of expanded citizenship did not come to fruition. French assimilation policies distinguished between the *évolué* (the "evolved" or "civilized") and those governed by the Code de l'indigénat, the set of rules that applied to colonial subjects but not to citizens. The vast majority of Africans under French rule were denied the rights of citizenship until 1946 when France overhauled its colonial policy and declared all of its African subjects "citizens" of the French government. While these new "citizens" could no longer be forced to labor for the government, Africans still did not share the same rights as Frenchmen. French colonial policy never fulfilled the promise of equality in the original conception of the civilizing mission.[5]

Nevertheless, attempts to assimilate Africans into French culture permeated colonial societies. Assimilation was in the French cuisine served to soldiers, workers, and students; the French language examinations required for government jobs; the French films, magazines, and music available for consumption; and even in the French-style streets, public squares, and homes people encountered in their daily lives.[6] French urban planners sought to assimilate Africans through the reinforcement of western spatial ideas. For example, in the early nineteenth century French colonizers took over the villages of Ndakaru in present-day Senegal and made them into the city of Dakar, the headquarters of French West Africa. Maps of Dakar from 1862 show only the "French" quarters of the city, which were designed by Jean Marie Émilie Pinet-Laprade, and ignored non-French sections of the city such as the Medina where the indigenous Senegalese were forced to live. The names of the streets were French, and only those spaces drawn into "the city" were given modern amenities like electricity. Defining Dakar as a French city equated Frenchness with modernity and urbanity. The many Senegalese who did not live in the French part of the city but passed through this space daily were constantly reminded of the modernity of European cultures. Likewise, the Senegalese children who grew up within the assimilated city spaces

---

[5] Patrick Manning, *Francophone Sub-Saharan Africa 1880–1995* (Cambridge University Press, 1988).
[6] Ambe J. Njoh, "The Experience and Legacy of French Colonial Urban Planning in Sub-Saharan Africa," *Planning Perspectives* 19 (2004) 435–454.

eating baguettes and speaking French learned to see Frenchness as their culture.[7]

Although very few Africans in French colonies actually achieved the legal assimilation that gave them the benefits of French citizenship, in all colonies Africans had to assimilate to colonial cultures in order to attain the highest forms of education and government employment. The French viewed assimilation as their "gift" to Africans. In his satirical novel *L'étrange destin du Wangrin* (*The Strange Destiny of Wangrin*) Amadou Hampâté Bâ recounts this idea through the words of the French colonial commandant who informed his new African clerk:

You must pay the debt you owe France by ensuring that she is loved and that her language and civilization are spread far and wide. In the whole history of mankind, these are the two most beautiful gifts ever bestowed on African Blacks. Yes, it is our mission to bring happiness to the Black peoples, if need be against their own wishes.[8]

Bâ understood well the contradictions of the French civilizing mission, being himself a product of African and western schools. An intellectual, Bâ spent twenty years working in the colonial government across the French Empire before joining the IFAN research institute (for more information, see Chapter 5). Bâ saw clearly the mechanics of French colonization of Africans and ridiculed this process in his post-colonial writing. His novels and memoirs emphasized the equipoise many Africans sought between honoring their own cultures and acquiring western languages and cultural accoutrements.

In the late colonial era, the most well-known and powerful critiques of assimilation came from Frantz Fanon, a man from the French Caribbean island of Martinique who worked as a psychologist in the French colony of Algeria during the 1950s. One of his books, entitled *Black Skin, White Masks*, recounts how colonized people were forced to don figurative white masks in order to survive in a European-made world. He argued that colonization deformed all members of a colonized society, both white and black. Fanon wrote that language shapes our understanding of culture; thus, one who is forced to learn the language of another group (that is, a colonizer) is more likely to come to

---

[7] Liora Bigon, "Urban Planning, Colonial Doctrines and Street Naming in French Dakar and British Lagos, c. 1850–1930," *Urban History* 36:3 (2009) 426–448.
[8] Amadou Hampâté Bâ, *The Fortunes of Wangrin*, transl. by Aina Pavolini Taylor (Indiana University Press, 1987), 17.

value aspects of that culture above his or her own. "Every colonized people – in other words, every people in whose soul an inferiority complex has been created by the death and burial of its local cultural originality – finds itself face to face with the language of the civilizing nation; that is, with the culture of the mother country."[9] In particular, western languages such as French and English assign values to the colors that symbolize racial difference; white/White is associated with purity and black/Black is associated with evil. For assimilated Africans, learning these languages helped them to understand European cultures, but it also threatened to alienate them from their own societies.

4.1 Frantz Fanon

Frantz Fanon was born in the French Caribbean colony of Martinique in 1925 to a middle-class black family. Several formative events occurred in his teenage years that led him to question the value of assimilation. Perhaps the most important was his good fortune to have Aimé Césaire, one of the leading proponents of the African cultural revivalist movement called Négritude and an ardent critic of colonialism, as his high school teacher. Césaire's teaching encouraged Fanon to question the racialized aspects of colonialism. In 1940, when Fanon was fifteen years old, Martinique became the Caribbean stronghold of the Vichy government, the French fascist government that collaborated with the Nazis during World War II. The colonial administration instituted an oppressive regime on the island. Three years later Fanon fled to Dominica, a nearby island, and joined the Free French army stationed there. He was sent to North Africa and eventually fought in Europe toward the end of the war. After World War II Fanon decided to study medicine in France, receiving his degree in psychiatry in 1951. His first book, *Black Skin, White Masks*, was published in 1952. Based on the work he did for his dissertation, his book looked at the psychological effects of colonialism on black people. Fanon worked in France until 1953 when he moved to Algeria to become the chief of a hospital psychiatry ward. Within a year of

---

[9]   Frantz Fanon, *Black Skin, White Masks* (Grove Press, 1967), 18.

his arrival in Algeria, the Algerian war for independence broke out and Fanon found himself increasingly on the side of the resistance group, the Front de Liberation Nationale (FLN). In his psychiatric treatment of soldiers fighting for the French and the tortured Algerian prisoners of war, he came to see colonialism as the root of the violence. Fanon secretly joined the FLN and in 1956 quit his job to spend his time working for the FLN. He published a group of essays in 1959 titled *A Dying Colonialism*, but his most famous book came out shortly before his death from leukemia in 1961. *The Wretched of the Earth* was a foundational text for resistance movements in Africa seeking their independence from European colonizers. In this book Fanon argued that the colonized had to violently resist their subjugation by European colonizers in order to free themselves psychologically from the effects of colonialism. After treatment in both the Soviet Union and the United States, Fanon died in December 1961 in Maryland.

INDIRECT RULE AND THE INVENTION OF "TRIBES"

Whereas assimilation was the stated policy in francophone and lusophone Africa, Britain imposed a policy of indirect rule in its African territories. Frederick Lugard laid out the formal policy of indirect rule in his *Dual Mandate in Tropical Africa*, published in 1922. Lugard stated that the primary mission of the British Empire was to secure "liberty and self-development" to all of those under the British flag. These ideals "can be best secured to the native population," he explained, "by leaving them free to manage their own affairs through their own rulers, proportionately to their degree of advancement, under the guidance of the British staff, and subject to the laws and policy of the administration." Lugard qualified his statement by urging that colonial administrations must be able to "preserve law and order."[10]

Although Lugard was the first to articulate indirect rule in detail, the policy had been standard practice in most of Britain's African colonies

---

[10]   Frederick D. Lugard, *The Dual Mandate in Tropical British Africa* (Frank Cass, 1922), 94.

since their establishment. Lugard designed the policy based on his experience as the governor of Northern Nigeria, where the Sokoto Empire, founded in 1804 by Usman dan Fodio, had been incorporated into the Nigerian colonial administration. Rather than assimilation through complete adoption of European political, social, and cultural practices, the primary goal of indirect rule was to "teach" Africans about self-government by preserving, wherever possible, indigenous political and social structures. Indirect rule was also a convenient way to offset the overhead costs of colonial administration.

Indirect rule policies recognized two types of African societies: centralized states and decentralized "tribes." The administration of centralized states was modeled after Frederick Lugard's experience in Northern Nigeria (the Sokoto Empire). This was also the policy for the kingdom of Swaziland (present-day Eswatini) and the Buganda kingdom in Uganda since the late nineteenth century. Where they found no centralized state, the British sought out allies among local chiefs or other African men (indeed, leaders were always male from the patriarchal perspective of British colonizers) who laid claim to political authority in a particular region. Often conflict arose over who could claim to rule over a territory or group of people, and the British usually did not know enough about local culture and politics to interpret such conflicts. They resolved these issues simply by naming the most loyal African leaders as "paramount chiefs" regardless of their status in their communities. Other "chiefs" or local leaders had to answer to the paramount chief, who, in turn, answered to the colonial administration. Everywhere in colonial Africa, African kings, sultans, and other rulers who were disloyal or who otherwise disobeyed colonial officials were replaced with loyal ones. The French government eventually adopted similar policies to British indirect rule around the turn of the century as it moved toward a system of colonial rule known as association.

One outcome of indirect rule policies was the solidification of the concept of the "tribe" as the primary social unit in Africa. Historically, in Africa as elsewhere, ethnic identities were formed out of particular social or political circumstances and their meanings and associations shifted over time. Ignorant of these historical forces, European travelers, colonial officials, and ethnographers assumed that the "tribe" represented Africans' primary means of connecting to the world around them. In European discourses the "tribe" represented a lower stage of development than the nation-state or empire. For instance English traveler

Nathaniel Isaacs described the Zulu as one of the many "uncivilised tribes" of southern Africa in his 1836 book *Travels and Adventures in Eastern Africa.*[11] In fact, at the time of Isaacs' visit, the "Zulu" had only recently come into existence out of an amalgamation of many different ethnolinguistic communities. The "Zulu tribe," as it came to be known, gradually emerged after Shaka founded the Zulu kingdom in the 1820s. To nineteenth- and early twentieth-century Europeans, all African societies, even centralized states, were made up of "tribes." Isaacs wrote that Africa was a place where "civilisation has not yet made any strides; – where rational man has not yet trodden to shed the light of truth among the ignorant, nor to inculcate a knowledge of religion."[12] Imperial discourses fixated on "tribes" as shorthand for Africans' lack of civilization.

The organization of Africans into "tribes" was also part of the divide-and-rule approach of indirect rule. Colonial officials often privileged some ethnic groups over others. In British colonial Kenya, educated Kikuyu men (and some women) had greater access to colonial education and thus occupied many of the intermediary positions, or government jobs, in greater proportion than other Kenyans, the effect of which is still perceptible in Kenya today. Similarly, Belgian colonial discourses about the distinction between Hutus and Tutsis helped to fuel the conflict that led to the 1994 genocide in Rwanda. The Belgians incorporated Tutsis into the colonial administration based on their claim that the "racial stock" of Tutsis was more evolved than that of neighboring Hutus.[13]

During the twentieth century British indirect rule solidified the notion that African ethnicities were static, unchanging, and bounded by particular geographies. Today the term "ethnic group" is often preferred to "tribe," yet the notion that African societies can and should be identified primarily by ethnicity rather than other markers of identity remains common in development work. When development organizations use ethnicity as a defining characteristic for their work they reinforce colonial constructs about Africa's lack of modernity.

---

[11] Nathaniel Isaacs, *Travels and Adventures in Eastern Africa, Descriptive of the Zoolus, Their Manners, Customs, Etc. Etc. with a Sketch of Natal* (Bradbury & Evans Printers, 1836).
[12] Ibid., vi.
[13] Catharine Newbury and David Newbury, "A Catholic Mass in Kigali: Contested Views of the Genocide and Ethnicity in Rwanda," *Canadian Journal of African Studies* 33:2/3 (1999) 292–328.

RESISTING CULTURAL IMPERIALISM IN COLONIAL KENYA

While British indirect rule policies upheld certain African customs in an effort to secure loyalty from African patriarchs, officials were expected to outlaw customs they considered "repugnant to justice, equity, and good conscience."[14] Missionaries often pressured the colonial government to do so when they strongly disagreed with specific traditions. In late 1920s Kenya dissent erupted among the Kikuyu, Kamba, and Meru communities when first Christian missionaries and then the colonial government attempted to change the practice of female circumcision. In these regions of Kenya and in other regions of Africa both girls and boys went through circumcision as part of their transition to adulthood. Circumcision made one eligible for marriage because, as many people argued, it prepared young bodies for sex and reproduction. Uncircumcised persons, regardless of their biological age, could not marry, start their own household, or participate in the decision-making of their community. Circumcision practices and the rites of passage of which they were a part formed a crucial component of the age-grade systems that determined acquisition of status over a lifetime. While missionaries and the colonial state strongly supported male circumcision, some missionaries and medical officers argued that female circumcision was dangerous and oppressive to girls and women.[15] When the missionaries and colonial officials attacked the practice of female circumcision, they challenged the foundation of the communities' social and cultural systems.[16]

Missionaries and colonial officials were not entirely coordinated in their plans to challenge what today is generally called "clitoridectomy" or "female genital cutting" (FGC). Missionaries wanted to phase out the practice because they believed it was savage. From a Victorian perspective, clitoridectomy represented the atavistic element in African societies as a holdover of "primordial" culture. Colonial officials had other concerns related to the production of

---

[14] See Kristin Mann and Richard L. Roberts, eds., *Law in Colonial Africa* (Heinemann Educational Books, 1991), 13.
[15] Paul Ocobock, *An Uncertain Age: The Politics of Manhood in Kenya* (Ohio University Press, 2017).
[16] Lynn M. Thomas, *Politics of the Womb: Women, Reproduction, and the State in Kenya* (University of California Press, 2003).

labor; they believed that health issues associated with clitoridectomy could limit procreation. Officials also feared an increase in abortions if girls waited until their late teens or twenties to be circumcised because this was a common response to pregnancies that occurred before the girl's circumcision. Officials were anxious not to limit the number of children, the future laborers for the colonial state.[17]

The response of the Kikuyu to British efforts to change their cultural norms demonstrates some of the tactics of resistance Africans used to combat colonialism. Kikuyu Christians did not challenge their religious conversion, though many did refuse to participate in schools and churches run by missionaries who banned these practices. A group of Kikuyu Christians initiated the "Kikuyu Independent Schools Association" in the 1930s. Jomo Kenyatta himself was an active advocate for the Kikuyu resistance to interventions on this issue. His 1938 book *Facing Mount Kenya* devoted a significant portion of a chapter on boys' and girls' initiation to a defense of female circumcision.[18] Yet Kenyatta was the same person who, as the first president of Kenya, Ngũgĩ wa Thiong'o accused of acquiescing to western neocolonialism. The line between embracing westernization and fighting cultural imperialism was not always clear and the meaning of particular actions changed over time. Historian Lynn Thomas argues that when the Meru Local Native Council attempted to ban female circumcision during Kenya's Mau Mau anticolonial war of the 1950s, a group of girls "circumcised themselves" as a statement of both their rejection of Meru elders' authority and their solidarity with the Mau Mau warriors.[19] In the past and today, the battle over FGC in Kenya and elsewhere has been so heated because it has represented resistance to cultural imperialism to some, and the fight for protection of girls and women to others.

---

[17] Ibid.
[18] Jomo Kenyatta, *Facing Mount Kenya: The Tribal Life of the Gikuyu* (Vintage Books, 1965 [1938]).
[19] Thomas, *Politics of the Womb*, 79–102.

4.2 Female genital cutting

The issue of female genital cutting (FGC), sometimes referred to as female circumcision or female genital mutilation (FGM), has been fiercely debated across Africa and has become a cause célèbre of western feminists. Female genital cutting entails the piercing, cutting, or removal of part or all of the external genitalia of females for cultural purposes. Male and female circumcision is found among a number of African societies that include Christians, Muslims, and other faith communities. The majority of African communities do not practice FGC.[1]

Clitoridectomy and infibulation are two of the more invasive forms of female genital cutting. Clitoridectomy refers to the partial or complete removal of the clitoris; in extreme versions the labia are also removed. Infibulation is when the labia are sewn together to make the vaginal opening smaller, and in some cases the labia are sewn completely shut until marriage. In African societies that practice FGC generally an uncut woman cannot marry or become a full social adult within the community. In most cases women manage girls' rites of passage and perform the genital cutting itself. However, many activists in Africa (as well as in the west) are working to change these practices because of the health implications for African women, and many African nations have passed laws banning the practice. Furthermore, where they continue to exist, the form and meaning of FGC practices have adapted to meet new health requirements or cultural demands.

In 2004 Senegalese filmmaker Ousmane Sembène made the fictional film *Moolaadé* about a woman in a village in Burkina Faso who refuses to allow her daughter to be circumcised. Throughout the film villagers debate arguments for and against ending the practice of female circumcision. Eventually, the women of the community collectively refuse to continue the practice and protect their daughters from it. The film was a joint production sponsored by the governments of Senegal, Burkina Faso, Cameroon, Morocco, Tunisia, and France in an effort to end the practice in their countries.

The debates around female genital cutting center around medical, cultural, and linguistic issues. Medical debates argue that most often FGC is practiced on children, without

anesthetic, and often in unsanitary situations that allow for significant blood loss, infection, and at times death. However,
medical objections rarely consider the cultural framework of
FGC and the role it fulfills socially and culturally. African
scholars, even those who oppose the practice, note that objections to the practice from westerners are often framed in terms
reminiscent of colonialism and redolent with racism. The linguistic distinction between the terms "female genital cutting"
versus "female genital mutilation" is a case in point – activists
who use the word "mutilation" evoke an image of barbarism and
demonize Africans as atavistic and in need of western intervention. Some African activists and scholars argue that western
societies impose similar medical procedures on women's bodies,
such as breast enhancement and vaginal "tightening," that
encourage women to reshape their bodies for male pleasure.

---

[1]   For an excellent book with many perspectives from African activists trying to end
     female genital cutting, see Rogaia Mustafa Abusharaf, *Female Circumcision:
     Multicultural Perspectives* (University of Pennsylvania Press, 2006).

DECOLONIZING THE MIND

Ngũgĩ wa Thiong'o described culture as the "spiritual eyeglasses through
which people come to view themselves and their place in the universe."[20]
From the moment Europeans stepped onto the continent of Africa as
"explorers" they began the process of delegitimizing and decentering
African knowledge. Efforts to indoctrinate Africans into European languages and cultures sought to destroy the essence of African identity by
replacing African religious beliefs, morality, clothing, and languages with
foreign ones. In *Decolonising the Mind* Ngũgĩ argued that because most
African literature was still written in western languages "African children
who encountered literature in colonial schools and universities were thus
experiencing the world as defined and reflected in the European experience of history. Their entire way of looking at the world, even the world of
the immediate environment, was Eurocentric."[21] For instance French

---

[20]   Ngũgĩ wa Thiong'o, *Moving the Centre: The Struggle for Cultural Freedoms* (James
      Currey, 1993), 14.
[21]   Thiong'o, *Decolonising the Mind*, 93.

colonial history lessons for African schoolchildren in francophone regions
of the continent, even those taught by Africans, began with "our ancestors
the Gauls."[22] Wangari Maathai, the first African woman to win a Nobel
Peace Prize, recalled how the Catholic school she attended in the 1950s
punished girls who spoke their native languages by making them wear
a sign that shamed them.[23] The influences of the civilizing mission in
African schools remained strong into the postcolonial era.

The first step to "decolonising the mind" was to dismantle the legacies
of colonialism in African education systems. Kwame Nkrumah, the first
president of independent Ghana, turned his attention to university education in 1963 when he created the Institute of African Studies at the
University of Ghana.[24] Nkrumah recognized that education in and
about Africa had been centered on European models. He argued for an
Africa-centered model of higher education that taught about Africa outside the colonial framework. The first director of this new Institute of
African Studies argued that knowledge about Africa needed to be
researched, written, and taught on the continent rather than in the west.
As historian Jean Allman points out, "In the history of knowledge production about Africa, this constituted an extraordinary moment . . . a moment
bursting with possibilities, in which engaged and rigorous debate, African-
centered and Africa-based, was the prerequisite, no epistemic paradigm
was hegemonic, and 'African Studies' was envisioned as the site for a full
re-imagining of higher education in an African postcolonial world."[25]
Nkrumah saw the development of a vibrant intellectual and *African* knowledge base as central to overthrowing colonial epistemological domination.

On the other side of the continent and influenced by thinkers like
Frantz Fanon, Ngũgĩ wa Thiong'o became a vocal critic of the continued
influence of European culture in African schools and universities after the
end of colonialism. As a faculty member in the English department at the
University of Nairobi in the 1960s, he, along with several African colleagues, questioned the Eurocentric approach to teaching literature. In
1969 this group of faculty circulated a proposal, *On the Abolition of the*

---

[22] Tukumbi Lumumba-Kasongo, "Rethinking Educational Paradigms in Africa:
      Imperatives for Social Progress in the New Millennium," in Philip Higgs,
      Ntombizolile Vakalisa, Thobeka Mda, and N'Dri Thérèse Assié-Lumumba, eds.,
      African Voices in Education (Juta, 2000), 143.
[23] Wangari Maathai, *Unbowed* (Anchor Books, 2007), 59–60.
[24] Jean Allman, "Kwame Nkrumah, African Studies, and the Politics of Knowledge
      Production in the Black Star of Africa," *International Journal of African Historical
      Studies* 46:2 (2013) 181–203 at 183.
[25] Ibid., 193.

English Department, to fundamentally transform the British-centered English department into one focused on African literature and its engagement with the rest of the world. According to Ngũgĩ, Africans needed an epistemological revolution in order to liberate their minds from the effects of colonialism. Fanon, Ngũgĩ, and others calling for cultural and psychological decolonization in the 1950s, 1960s, and 1970s argued that, as long as Africans learned through institutions that prioritized western cultures over African ones, Africans could gain political freedom but could never achieve true liberation from the west.

Education and cultural reform was also a major factor in the antiapartheid movement in South Africa, where activist and writer Steve Biko led the Black Consciousness Movement during the 1960s and 1970s. Biko's call for Black Consciousness was a response to the student antiapartheid activism led mostly by whites. Biko urged black students to take charge of their own causes, not only to obtain freedom from political oppression from the apartheid South African government but also to reclaim their identities and rebuild their sense of self-respect.[26] Black Consciousness had its precedents in the Harlem Renaissance in America, Négritude in francophone West Africa, and cultural nationalism across the continent. Steve Biko's tragic death at the hands of the police in 1977 made him a legend and a martyr for the antiapartheid struggle.

In the 1980s and 1990s a debate developed between those who favored Ngũgĩ's argument against writing in European languages and the position of Nigerian writer Chinua Achebe, who argued for the value of using a widely known language as a lingua franca to reach a broader audience. Achebe acknowledged the problem that "the telling of the story of black people in our time ... has been the self-appointed responsibility of white people, and they have mostly done it to suit a white purpose."[27] He agreed with Ngũgĩ that western narratives about African societies have sought to devalue African cultures and epistemologies and Africans must fight to tell their own stories, in their own words, even if those words are in a European language.

All of these movements and debates aimed to repair the cultural and psychological damage of colonialism. They coalesced around one point: as long as Africans were taught that western values were better than African values, Africans could never fully be independent socially,

---

[26] Steven Biko, *I Write What I Like* (Harper & Row, 1979).
[27] Chinua Achebe, *The Education of a British-Protected Child: Essays* (Alfred A. Knopf, 2009), 61.

economically, or culturally. This concept has resurfaced more recently in criticisms of postcolonial international development. The notion that expertise in healthcare, education, agriculture, and other areas of development originates from outside the continent devalues African knowledge systems and dismisses local, homegrown initiatives. Moreover, by handing ownership of African civil society over to international nongovernmental organizations (INGOs), a theme explored further in Chapter 8, African leaders are beholden to westerners rather than to their own constituents.

DECOLONIZING DEVELOPMENT

The problem of a colonized mindset is not only for Africans but for citizens of the global north as well. Many people who came to Africa from western countries over the past two centuries have viewed the differences between Africa and the west not as cultural differences but as problems that should be fixed. While this mindset might seem well-meaning, it perpetuates a sense of African inferiority among people from the west.[28] The notion that westerners need to bring development to Africa reinforces the ethnocentrism that drove Europeans to attempt colonization of the minds and bodies of Africans in the first place. Nigerian-American writer Teju Cole noted the powerful drive for Americans to do good.

[The American's] good heart does not always allow him to think constellationally. He does not connect the dots or see the patterns of power behind the isolated "disasters." All he sees are hungry mouths, and he . . . is putting food in those mouths as fast as he can. All he sees is need, and he sees no need to reason out the need for the need.

Cole makes the case that white Americans respond to the problems without understanding the historical, political, economic, and racialized causes.[29]

In March 2015 South African students began the Rhodes Must Fall movement, in order to challenge the hegemony of western education

---

[28]   Kathryn Mathers, *Travel, Humanitarianism, and Becoming American in Africa* (Palgrave MacMillan, 2010).

[29]   Teju Cole, "The White-Savior Industrial Complex," *The Atlantic Monthly*, March 21, 2012, www.theatlantic.com/international/archive/2012/03/the-white-savior-industrial-complex/254843/, accessed February 4, 2020.

systems and their dominance by a culture of whiteness. Removing a statue of Cecil Rhodes from the front of the University of Cape Town's campus represented the broader movement to decolonize education and dismantle the legacies of white supremacy in South Africa. In the twenty-first century university education has come to represent the key to success, modernity, and development, yet globally universities remain bastions of hegemonic power. As South African scholar Sebeka Richard Plaatjie has noted, development must first "decolonize the white man" before change can truly come to the field of international development studies. "No matter how much we try to decolonize the racialized peoples of the world," he argues, "without decolonizing the white man, the gaze of supremacy of a heterosexual patriarchal white male will forever hang above radicalized peoples ... reminding them of their inferiority and where they belong in the hierarchy of the world system."[30]

Over the past decade, scholars across the global south have argued that the call for Africans to "decolonize the mind" is problematic because it suggests that decolonization must happen on the individual level rather than on a systemic level.[31] Given the association of development and its many facets (multilateral organizations, international NGOs, etc.) with the global north and westernization, development institutions have become ground zero for decolonizing efforts. One approach to decolonizing development has included embracing China as a development partner. Chinese investment in Africa has expanded rapidly over the past two decades. Many believe this offers an alternative to the pitfalls of western morality and western ideas of modernity that have permeated International Monetary Fund (IMF) and World Bank interventions in Africa. Another approach has been to create alternatives to the IMF and the World Bank. In 2014 the BRICS countries (Brazil, Russia, India, China, South Africa) founded the New Development Bank (NDB). The core purpose of this multilateral organization was "to mobilize resources for infrastructure and sustainable development in BRICS countries." A fundamental piece of the NDB was to create an equal playing field for all members of the institution. Each member of the organization has an equal vote, and

[30]   Sebeka Richard Plaatjie, "Beyond Western-Centric and Eurocentric Development: A Case for Decolonizing Development," *Africanus* 43:2 (2013) 118–130 at 128.

[31]   Sara Estrade-Villalta and Glenn Adams, "Decolonizing Development: A Decolonial Approach to the Psychology of Economic Inequality," *Translational Issues in Psychological Science* 4:2 (2018) 198–209.

none holds a veto power over the other members. These policies contrast sharply with other multilateral organizations such as the World Bank and the African Development Bank (AfDB). In the AfDB, voting power is based on the number of shares held by individual countries. African countries own 60 percent of the voting shares in total; however, among the top ten share owners, African countries only constitute 50 percent. For example, Nigeria is the largest share owner, while the United States is second, Japan is fourth, and Germany, Canada, and France are seventh, eighth, and ninth, respectively.[32] While African countries hold the majority of the votes in the AfDB, non-African countries play a significant role in the decision-making of the institution. Likewise, the United States holds veto power in the World Bank over all other members, giving the United States extraordinary power to steer loans and to decide the direction of the organization. The intention of the BRICS in creating the NDB is to break the power of western banks and offer a new balance of power in the realm of international development. However, some theorists argue that the NDB still reinforces capitalist exploitation of underdeveloped economies.

International nongovernmental organizations (INGOs) remain some of the most important development institutions globally. While decision-making in most INGOs based in Europe and the United States remains primarily in the hands of its global north leadership, recent efforts to decentralize decision-making demonstrates a first step toward decolonizing these organizations. By decentralizing, institutions such as CARE and Save the Children are beginning the process of power-sharing. Organizations like Oxfam and ActionAid have gone further by diversifying their leadership and moving their headquarters to the global south. ActionAid hired Salil Shetty in 1998, its first CEO from the global south. He spearheaded the move of the international headquarters from London, England to Johannesburg, South Africa in 2003. Since then, ActionAid has had several CEOs from both the global south and the global north. The organization has also continued to further decentralize their structures with an emphasis on south-south partnerships.[33] Likewise,

---

[32]   African Development Bank, *Board Documents*, "Statement of Voting Powers As at 28 February 2019," www.afdb.org/en/documents/document/afdb-statement-of-voting-powers-as-at-28-february-2019–108964, accessed February 4, 2020.
[33]   Kirsten C. Williams, "INGOS Relocating to the Global South," *K4D Helpdesk Report*. UK Department for International Development, September 10, 2018, https://assets

Oxfam set about building more legitimacy in the global south through its Oxfam 2020 campaign. It hired a Ugandan engineer, Winnie Byanyima, in 2013 as its executive director. Byanyima led Oxfam's move to Nairobi, Kenya in 2019.

These efforts to decolonize the structures of international development, such as the NDB or ActionAid and Oxfam's moves to Africa, seek to transform the development episteme by placing African leaders at the helm of development policy making. Yet these efforts to decolonize development will remain piecemeal as long as assumptions about backwardness based on race or culture remain central to the development episteme. Under African leadership a new episteme may emerge, but it will have to be one that values African cultures and knowledge as modern and relevant to development.

★★★

Decolonizing the idea of development entails much more than pointing out the legacies of the civilizing mission or colonialism in contemporary development discourses on Africa. While colonial discourses often pit westernization against African cultures, people like Jomo Kenyatta did not fit so easily into one camp or the other. Colonial experiences reflect multiple, overlapping, and sometimes contradictory forces of change. Both western and African cultures have transformed over time, but what has not changed is the perception that the former is "modern" and the latter "traditional." The false dichotomy between the "developed" west (or "the global north") and the "less developed" or "developing" countries of Africa (as part of "the global south") reifies colonial-era stereotypes and continues to fuel the development industry.

This chapter has outlined the connections between resistance to cultural imperialism during the colonial era, the call to "decolonize the mind" in the 1970s and 1980s and, finally, debates about decolonizing development today. All of these movements have challenged the racial and cultural inequalities built into the development episteme. Whether seeking to transform a "backward" custom or making decisions about expenditure, hierarchies of power are foundational to the development episteme. As long as Africans remain the targets of intervention rather than the policy makers or drivers of development, and as long as

.publishing.service.gov.uk/media/5bb226d9e5274a3e10bd9394/438_INGOs_relocating_to_the_South.pdf, accessed February 4, 2020.

development remains an industry whose power base remains in the global north, efforts to decolonize development will fail to restructure the development episteme.

Further Reading

On the civilizing mission and colonial policies, see Alice Conklin, *A Mission to Civilize: The Republican Idea of Empire in France and West Africa, 1895–1930* (Stanford University Press, 1997); Martin Chanock, *Law, Custom, and Social Order: The Colonial Experience in Malawi and Zambia* (Heinemann, 1998); Benjamin N. Lawrance, Emily Lynn Osborn, and Richard L. Roberts, eds., *Intermediaries, Interpreters, and Clerks: African Employees in the Making of Colonial Africa* (University of Wisconsin Press, 2006); and Lynn Thomas, *Politics of the Womb: Women, Reproduction, and the State in Kenya* (University of California Press, 2003).

On the creation of "tribes" in the context of imperialism and colonialism, see Mary French-Sheldon, *Sultan to Sultan: Adventures among the Masai and Other Tribes of East Africa* (Arena Publishing Company, 1892); Nathaniel Isaacs, *Travels and Adventures in Eastern Africa, Descriptive of the Zoolus, Their Manners, Customs, Etc., Etc., with a Sketch of Natal* (Edward Churton, 1836); Frederick D. Lugard, *The Dual Mandate in British Tropical Africa* (Frank Cass, 1922); Leroy Vail, ed., *The Creation of Tribalism in Southern Africa* (James Currey, 1989).

On the psychology of colonialism and decolonizing the mind, see Frantz Fanon, *Black Skin, White Masks* (Grove Press, 1967); Paulo Freire, *Pedagogy of the Oppressed* (Bloomsbury Publishing, 2014 [1970]); Albert Memmi, *The Colonizer and the Colonized* (Orion Press, 1965); Ashis Nandy, *The Intimate Enemy: Loss and Recovery of Self under Colonialism* (Oxford University Press, 1983); and Ngũgĩ wa Thiong'o, *Decolonising the Mind: The Politics of Language in African Literature* (East African Educational Publishers, 1981).

Part II

Implementation of the
Development Episteme

CHAPTER 5

The Salvation of Science

On December 9, 1920, British explorer and botanist Sir Harry Johnston promoted the work of the Royal African Society (RAS) in his address as president of the organization. The RAS was a nonprofit organization dedicated to scientific exploration and study in Africa. It mobilized a new cadre of scientific specialists. Johnston bemoaned the lack of financial support for the RAS.

During the past eighteen years I have lectured and privately pleaded ... on the need for a Society like ours, which undertakes the scientific study of Africa. I have pointed out that to maintain successfully and permanently our enormous commerce with Africa and our rule over such a large proportion of that continent, we must come to understand Africa, and to understand, not only British Africa, but also self-governed South Africa, French Africa, Italian, Spanish, Belgian, and Portuguese Africa, and the native states that are either independent or at any rate self-governing. But I have preached to deaf ears. Individual men and commercial associations that are making thousands a year – a million a year, maybe – out of Africa will not contribute even a guinea a year to our maintenance, though if they read our Journal diligently they might light upon many a notion for making Africa an even better paying proposition than it already is.[1]

The cost of research, Johnston explained, fell on the shoulders of "poorly paid workers in Africa itself, who are building up the vast wealth of our African commerce." Though he was referring to European researchers and colonial officials like himself, it is difficult not to think of the many thousands of Africans whose labor directly

---

[1] Harry H. Johnston, "Sir Harry Johnston's Address on Retirement from the Presidency," *Journal of the Royal African Society* 20:78 (1921) 83–88 at 86.

fueled colonial industries. Johnston's call to businessmen spoke to the prevailing idea then and now that significant and lasting economic development was only possible with ongoing investment in scientific research. This was especially important for those interested in "unfamiliar" regions of Africa.

Understanding the continent's environments and societies was crucial to colonial development, but colonial scientists were not the first or only people to record information about African societies. For centuries before European conquest Africans in the kingdoms of Ethiopia, Ghana, Mali, the Swahili Coast, and many other places wrote about their own histories and cultures and those of their neighbors. Foreign travelers, explorers, merchants, missionaries, and early colonizers had been cataloguing their journeys to Africa for centuries as well. Early European representations of Africans, such as seventeenth-century drawings of Khoikhoi people in southern Africa, vacillated between depicting them as "grotesque" and "noble" and became emblematic of ideas about the "savage" in Africa.[2] Napoleon Bonaparte's invasion of Egypt in 1798 emphasized scientific study as a vital component of European conquest. He employed dozens of researchers to study linguistics, geography, biology, medicine, and poetry. By 1829 the project included more than 150 scholars contributing to twenty-three volumes of material discussing Egyptian culture and history. Napoleon's military and scholarly invasion of Egypt initiated the academic field of Egyptology and was, as Edward Said described it, "the very model of a truly scientific appropriation of one culture by another."[3] The desire for knowledge was instrumental to the business of imperialism.

As Europeans consolidated colonial control in Africa, scientists from across the disciplines found a whole new world to explore and experiment, new terrain on which to test out old theories, and further scientific knowledge about the natural and social world. The pseudosciences of race that emerged during the late nineteenth century (discussed in Chapter 3), along with the capitalist demands on research and technology, set the course for foregrounding scientific study in the development projects of the twentieth century. As social Darwinism and eugenics gave way to sociology and (ethno)psychology, and physical anthropology expanded to include social and cultural

---

[2] George Steinmetz, *The Devil's Handwriting: Precoloniality and the German Colonial State in Qingdao, Samoa, and Southwest Africa* (University of Chicago Press, 2007), 75–134.

[3] Edward Said, *Orientalism* (Pantheon Books, 1978), 42.

anthropology, development discourses on race morphed into those about culture. Economics, agriculture, veterinary sciences, environmental studies, and industrial technologies informed colonial government and private investment in monocrop production, dairy farms, mining ventures, and public works projects. Geographers, naturalists, biologists, medical doctors, nutritionists, sociologists, economists, and anthropologists employed scientific methods to exploit African resources and to modernize African societies. Collectively, these sciences produced their own genre of knowledge, which formed the foundation of the development episteme.

Furnished with their own mission to modernize, the scientific development experts of the twentieth century supplanted the Christian missionaries as the moral and intellectual authorities on progress for Africa. Despite its humanitarian origins, the majority of development funding during the early colonial era was designed to jump-start the decimated economies of post–World War I Europe – not Africa, especially during the Great Depression of the 1930s. Development policies of the interwar period focused on large-scale infrastructure, industrialization, and agricultural projects that would generate sizeable returns for the metropoles and employment opportunities for Europeans. Colonial development funding bolstered the budgets of colonial departments of public health, agriculture, forestry, mining, commerce, and education. Tasked with facilitating the exploitation of African resources and labor, colonial technologies offered scientific salvation for Africa.

These scientific studies were not merely imposed on Africa and Africans but were often the product of western engagement with African systems of knowledge. As historian Helen Tilley explains,

[S]cientific research began to decolonize Africa by challenging stereotypes, destabilizing Eurocentric perspectives, and considering African topics on their own terms. . . . By misapprehending, mislabeling, and facilitating new forms of control, emerging sciences had the potential to coerce. Yet, by introducing new concepts, new ways of knowing, and new methods for understanding, these disciplines had the potential to liberate. In the end, they did both.[4]

The scientific work of the development episteme was sometimes subversive, even anticolonial, but it always reinforced development as the organizing principle of the colonial project.

---

[4] Helen Tilley, *Africa As a Living Laboratory: Empire, Development, and the Problem of Scientific Knowledge, 1870–1950* (University of Chicago Press, 2011), 24–25.

Africa served as a vast and diverse laboratory for research and experimentation. For scholars and officials like Harry Johnston, the quest for knowledge drove scientific projects as much as the promise of profitable results, but financial support would only come where the potential for profit existed. To be sure, some businesses saw large returns, though many endeavors were unsuccessful and companies went bankrupt. Researchers and officials regularly misunderstood African environments and European scientific knowledge often failed to secure its desired outcomes; yet faith in the salvation of the development episteme endured.

THE RISE OF THE DEVELOPMENT SPECIALIST

As European colonialism took hold across the continent of Africa in the late nineteenth and early twentieth centuries the prevailing idea of progress shifted from one rooted in the civilizing mission to one dependent on scientific research. This ideological shift brought about a change in the focus on intervention, from the building of churches, schools, and hospitals by private organizations or religious groups to the building up of colonial infrastructure, the extraction of resources, the recruitment of labor, and the modernization of African subjects. European Christian missionaries and explorers who came to Africa during the eighteenth and nineteenth centuries defined progress in terms of the abolition of slavery, the spread of literacy, improved health, and Africans' adoption of western norms. Some like Mungo Park, Paul Du Chiallu, David Livingstone, and Johannes Ludwig Krapf fancied themselves botanists, geographers, zoologists, ethnographers, and biologists. They recorded volumes of information about newly "discovered" people, places, plants, and animals. By the late 1880s a cohort of specialists trained in Europe derided the amateurism of these earlier generations of travelers and missionaries. Scientific curiosity had been integral to European engagement with Africa for centuries, but it did not become the primary tool for engineering the continent's progress until the colonial era solidified the scientific approach to the development episteme.

Much of the early twentieth-century scientific research in Africa was geared toward identifying potential sources of profit. The French term for development in the colonies, *mise en valeur*, or "making value" out of the colonies, captured the capitalist ethos of European colonial states. Before the Second World War colonial development meant the expansion of infrastructure for economic and political functions and, more importantly, revenue from the production, harvesting, and export of cash crops and raw materials. A capitalist approach prevailed in South Africa, which was in the process of transforming from a British colony into a nascent nation-state under the terms of the 1910 Union of South Africa. There the white minority government shared with colonial officials elsewhere on the continent certain administrative goals: consolidation of territory and the segregation and control of migrant labor for the lucrative industries of mining, agriculture, and other extractive schemes. From studies calculating the precise motions of workers in factories and mines to those determining the best extraction and cultivation methods, scientists were at the forefront of capitalist endeavors across the continent in the early twentieth century.[5]

Large-scale development initiatives had been a central feature of European colonialism since at least the time of the Scramble for Africa in the 1880s. King Leopold II of Belgium planned to build research stations across Africa in order to exploit the natural resources of the continent. He failed to implement this vision because he could not convince rival European states to cooperate in the project. To this end individual European colonizers constructed their own research stations. The English opened a botanical station in Lagos, Nigeria in 1887.[6] A year later the Royal Niger Company began an experimental plantation at Asaba, which reverted to the colonial government in 1901. Germany created one of the best-funded research stations on the continent when it opened the Kwai Farm in the Usambara region of German East Africa (present-day Tanzania) in 1896. The success of this experiment inspired them to establish the Amani Research Institute in 1902.[7]

---

[5]   Brett M. Bennett and Joseph M. Hodge, eds., *Science and Empire: Knowledge and Networks of Science across the British Empire, 1800–1970* (Palgrave Macmillan, 2011); Joseph Morgan Hodge, *Triumph of the Expert: Agrarian Doctrines of Development and the Legacies of British Colonialism* (Ohio University Press, 2007).

[6]   Europeans developed botanical gardens across their colonies in Asia and Australia in the earlier part of the century. By the 1860s the Cape colony in South Africa had several botanical societies, but none of these were fully experimental stations as founded in Nigeria. See Kate B. Showers, "Prehistory of Southern African Forestry: From Vegetable Garden to Tree Plantation," *Environment and History* 16:3 (2010) 295–322.

[7]   Christopher A. Conte, *Highland Sanctuary: Environmental History in Tanzania's Usambara Mountains* (Ohio University Press, 2004), 41–67. During the German period, the Amani Research Institute was known as the Biologisch-Landwirtschaftliche Institut.

5.1 The Amani Research Institute

The Amani Research Institute (see Figure 5.1) held a unique place in colonial development in Africa. The scientific goals of the Institute were both theoretical and practical. German scientists experimented with varieties of coffee, sisal, rubber, and cucumbers in search of economic gains in German East Africa. They studied plant pathology and the chemistry of soils in the tropical environment. As Andrew Zimmerman explains, the scientists also examined labor issues by testing "the speed at which these workers could perform various tasks, such as clearing land or planting seeds, and determined the cost in wages per hectare."[1]

FIGURE 5.1 The Agricultural College, Amani Institute, German East Africa, ~1910s. Source: Haeckel collection/ullstein bild via Getty Images

At the end of the First World War Britain took over the Amani Institute when it took control of German East Africa, which then became the League of Nations Mandated Territory called Tanganyika. Alex Holm, the director of agriculture in Kenya, believed the Institute should be used primarily for technical support of colonial industries while Dr. David Prain, the director of the Royal Botanic Gardens at Kew in London, emphasized its value as a center for scientific research. Tensions between agricultural officials and researchers continued. Alleyne Leechman, who became the director of the Amani Institute in 1920, brought in employees from the Royal Botanic Gardens at Kew and the University of London's Royal School of Science in order to bolster the Institute's scientific reputation. After a few years of uncertainty Amani was rebranded as the premier center for agricultural research in East Africa, though its long-term funding remained in jeopardy.[2]

Under both German and British administrations Amani was one of the few independent, government-sponsored research institutions on the continent. The Amani Institute represented a new model in which specialists collaborated on issues common across a broad region including multiple colonial territories. Directly funded by metropolitan grants and the Empire Marketing Board instead of individual colonies' budgets, Amani was free to take on scientific studies that might otherwise have been dismissed as frivolous spending by local administrations. The Institute's academic associates stressed the applicability of scientific research to the day-to-day work of the departments of agriculture in the territories of Tanganyika, Kenya, Uganda, Zanzibar, and Nyasaland (Malawi). Amani scientists advised the local European settler communities, the colonial technical departments, and other researchers investigating continent-wide development problems. As a scientific body exempt from the constraints of specific colonies' needs, the Amani Institute could invest in building abstract knowledge for improving commodity production. It was a manifestation of nineteenth-century European scientific ideals realized with twentieth-century colonial development funding.[3]

[1]   Andrew Zimmerman, "'What Do You Really Want in German East Africa, Herr Professor?' Counterinsurgency and the Science Effect in Colonial Tanzania," *Comparative Studies in Society and History* 48:2 (2006) 419–461 at 436.
[2]   UKNA CO 533/601, East Africa, Reestablishment of the Amani Institute, May 1926.
[3]   Conte, *Highland Sanctuary*, 55–67.

Early twentieth-century colonial economic initiatives had mixed results. Colonial officials had to be experts in multiple fields. Europeans' unfamiliarity with African environments, farming practices, and cultures of labor checked their successes. The rudimentary colonial surveys of the early twentieth century necessarily ballooned into all-out scientific investigations by the interwar period in order to better inform officials and scientists. Increasingly after the First World War colonies established government departments for agriculture, forestry, public health, medicine, and education with highly technical and specialized staff.

The interwar period was the age of expansion for scientific research in Africa. In British territories the number of technical officers rose from around 600 in 1919 to nearly 2,000 in 1931. The colonial administration's interests in science culminated into the African Survey under the directorship of Lord Hailey, the results of which were published in 1938. Bucking the trend among colonial officials who regarded the work of academics with suspicion, Lord Hailey consulted with social scientists like Audrey Richards for the project.[8]

Likewise, French colonial officials took more interest in academic and scientific research. The French government brought the Academy of Colonial Sciences under the purview of the Ministry of Colonies in the mid-1920s. In 1931 a colonial exhibition in Paris became the premier venue for parading the scientific discoveries of the French Empire. Louis Hubert Lyautey, the son of an engineer who helped Joseph Gallieni secure French rule in Madagascar at the turn of the twentieth century, oversaw the exhibition. His work in Madagascar planting rice, cotton, coffee, and tobacco and building western schools convinced him that science was crucial to empire.[9]

By the end of the interwar period faith in science had come to replace faith in religion as the means to "convert" and "civilize" Africans. When it came to development planning, western scientific discourses often delegitimated African knowledge even as they relied on African "informants." Many European specialists based their assessment of African conditions on mere days or

---

[8]   Tilley, *Living Laboratory*.
[9]   Elizabeth Ezra, *The Colonial Unconscious: Race and Culture in Interwar France* (Cornell University Press, 2000), 13–16.

weeks of research in the field, and sometimes they relied on only secondhand information provided by people with limited experience of their own. In the absence of deeper understandings of African economic ideologies, decision-making practices, and knowledge of their own environments many Europeans relied on preconceived notions of Africa and Africans based in nineteenth-century social Darwinism. They formulated complex, long-term, and transformative schemes out of snapshots of the people and places. As we elaborate further in Part III of this book, European scientists and officials brought to Africa their own assumptions and visions for the construction of domesticity, the rearing and socialization of children, health and healing, and productive use of the environment, which were the essential components of the development episteme. At the same time, African responses to these interventions and their own development initiatives often forced European scientists to rethink their approaches.

The scientific turn in colonial Africa produced a cadre of technical experts who genuinely believed in the power of science to improve the lives of Africans. The rise of the scientific expert in African development helped to shift colonial attention toward the welfare of Africans during the interwar period. In particular, development schemes singled out women, children, and others considered vulnerable to poverty, disease, or abuse. The cry of development specialists in 1930s Africa was for "social welfare," the "welfare of women and girls," and "infant and child welfare," themes that coincided with the global response to the Great Depression and grabbed the attention of western feminists. Many European and American women came to Africa in the 1920s, 1930s, and 1940s to work in anthropology, nutrition, hygiene, child and maternal health, and education. In the Belgian Congo, for example, this work began when the Ligue pour la Protection de l'Enfance Noire (The League for the Protection of Black Children) took up the issues of breastfeeding and birth spacing.[10] However, metropolitan development funding was only available for such endeavors when direct economic

---

[10]   Nancy Rose Hunt, "'Le Bebe en Brousse': European Women, African Birth Spacing and Colonial Intervention in Breast Feeding in the Belgian Congo," *International Journal of African Historical Studies* 21:3 (1988) 401–432.

benefits were evident. Investment in the health of wives and mothers, for instance, flowed only after officials recognized that this would increase the productivity of laborers, generate wealth for colonial industries, and reinforce the racialized colonial economy. In one way or another, the science of development always served interests in profit.

COLONIAL DEVELOPMENT AND THE SOCIAL SCIENCES

Scientific development in colonial Africa emerged simultaneously with the specialization of the modern social sciences of anthropology, sociology, psychology, economics, and political science. Ethnography (the study of people and cultures) in particular permeated colonial development research. Evolutionary anthropology, which dominated European discourses on African culture until the interwar period, echoed the biological racist arguments of nineteenth-century physical anthropologists discussed in Chapter 1. The new branch of social anthropology that emerged in the 1920s challenged these theories of race, evolution, and social hierarchy, yet cultural racism – that is, the assumption that white societies are more "civilized" than so-called primitive, nonwhite societies – endured in anthropology until at least the 1960s. This theme of backwardness gave shape to the idea of development. The western superiority perpetuated by the development episteme still haunts the contemporary development discourse when organizations report that economies are "stunted" or "stagnant" or that certain African "tribes" reject "modernization" for cultural reasons.

Ethnography was essential to colonial development projects. During the twentieth century it was commonplace for European colonial officials to study the languages and cultures relevant to their posts. French officials such as Maurice Delafosse, based in French West Africa, integrated ethnographic and linguistic fieldwork into their administrative work and helped to found L'Institut ethnographique international de Paris (The International Ethnographic Institute of Paris) in 1910.[11] As early as 1908, Harry Johnston, the colonial official

---

[11]   Emmanuelle Sibeud, "The Elusive Bureau of Colonial Ethnography in France, 1907–1925," in Helen Tilley, ed., with Robert J. Gordon, *Ordering Africa:*

and anthropologist quoted at the beginning of this chapter, urged the British government to provide a grant for ethnographic research as part of its administration in Africa. The grant request was denied, but such interventions positioned the science of anthropology as part of the practical work of development. Similar to the French, the British government established the International Institute of African Languages and Cultures in 1926 to facilitate the fieldwork of colonial officials. The Paris and London institutions managed their own journals, *Revue d'ethnographie et de sociologie* and *Africa: Journal of the International Institute of African Languages and Cultures*, respectively. In the inaugural issue of *Africa*, British colonial official Sir Frederick Lugard outlined its agenda. The "distinctive characteristic of the Institute," Lugard explained, was to bring about

a closer association of scientific knowledge and research with practical affairs. All of the work of the Institute will be based on strictly scientific principles and carried out by scientific methods. It will undertake and assist in anthropological and linguistic investigations. But it will at the same time attempt to relate the results of research to the actual life of the African peoples, and to discover how the investigations undertaken by scientific workers may be made available for the solution of pressing questions that are the concerns of all those who, as administrators, educators, health and welfare workers, or traders, are working for the good of Africa.[12]

Colonial officials' research at times rivaled that of professional anthropologists and sociologists, though they struggled to gain scholarly recognition for their work within academic circles.

In reality, most European officials and researchers working for colonial governments in Africa did not stay long enough in one territory to become fluent in local languages or acquire a solid understanding of local customs. The few officials with personal experience or deeper knowledge of African communities acted as cultural liaisons. For example, Louis Descement, the *métis* (mixed-race) secretary to the French governor of Senegal in West Africa, published a Wolof-French dictionary in 1864 in aid of the colonial administration.[13] As Fiona

Anthropology, European Imperialism, and the Politics of Knowledge (Manchester University Press, 2007), 49–66.

[12] Frederick D. Lugard, "The International Institute of African Languages and Cultures," *Africa: Journal of the International African Institute* 1:1 (1928) 1–12 at 2.

[13] Fiona McLaughlin, "Can a Language Endanger Itself? Reshaping Repertoires in Urban Senegal," in James Essegbey, Brent Henderson, and Fiona McLaughlin,

McLaughlin points out, Descement promoted a particular elite, urban form of Wolof that included words of French origin. Colonial officials who became more integrated into local cultures prided themselves on their expertise. Charles Dundas, author of *Kilimanjaro and Its Peoples* (1924), was a district official stationed in the Mount Kilimanjaro region of the Tanganyika Territory (Tanzania) then under British rule. Dundas claimed that his knowledge of Chaga customs earned him the honorary title of "elder."[14] Colonial officials and professional anthropologists tended to consult with elder men and chiefs as the premier experts on local cultures. African men in positions of power often reified patriarchal interpretations of tradition as the means to control the behavior of women and young people. Colonial interventions, academic ethnography, and cultural nationalism thus reinforced patriarchal interpretations of custom.

Ethnographic information facilitated the codification of customary law where colonial powers implemented indirect rule, which helped district or provincial officials mediate between local communities and central colonial authorities. Officials and scholars employed social scientific theories and methods in order to generate this knowledge. Often social scientists – anthropologists in particular – saw themselves as defenders of African rights and interests in the face of colonial encroachment and westernization. Africans were not mere objects of study but active participants in this knowledge production. African interlocutors shaped western anthropologists' understanding of their cultures, and African scholars often initiated academic debates about custom.

Ethnographic information about Africans directly informed colonial development policies. In Anglo-Egyptian Sudan, for example, research conducted by Egyptian social scientists helped to formulate the government's economic and social reforms of Sudanese peasant life.[15] The establishment of the Institut français d'Afrique Noire (French Institute of Black Africa) (IFAN) in Senegal with branches across French West Africa in 1936, the Rhodes-Livingstone Institute

---

eds., *Language Documentation and Endangerment in Africa* (John Benjamins, 2015), 131–152 at 136.

[14] Charles Dundas, *Kilimanjaro and Its People: A History of the Wachagga, Their Laws, Customs and Legends, Together with Some Account of the Highest Mountain in Africa* (H. F. & G. Witherby, 1924).

[15] Omnia El Shakry, *The Great Social Laboratory: Subjects of Knowledge in Colonial and Postcolonial Egypt* (Stanford University Press, 2007).

(RLI) in Northern Rhodesia (today Zambia) in 1937, and the East African Institute of Social Research (EAISR) in Uganda in 1948 enabled collaboration between anthropologists, sociologists, African scholars, indigenous experts on custom, and colonial policy makers. Government officials consulted with researchers at these institutes as they drew up plans for community development programs during the 1940s and 1950s.[16]

As mentioned in Chapter 3 some scholars have argued that anthropology is the "handmaiden" of empire. V. Y. Mudimbe explains, "Only from the eighteenth century on is there, thanks to the Enlightenment, a 'science' of difference: anthropology. It 'invents' an idea of Africa. Colonialism will elaborate upon the idea."[17] James Ferguson has expanded on this point to argue that development is the "evil twin" of anthropology, both being derived from social Darwinist ideologies.[18] The new branch of social anthropology emerging in the 1920s and 1930s sought to distance itself from this legacy. Unlike western imperialists, missionaries, and colonial officials, interwar social anthropologists did not wholeheartedly embrace the civilizing mission. While they employed the language of the day to describe African cultures as "primitive" and western cultures as "civilized," many rejected the idea that the former needed to transform into the latter. Anthropologists often butted heads with government officials over what they saw as the negative impact of westernization and "modernization" on Africans. For instance, Godfrey Wilson, the first director of the RLI, brought to the attention of colonial officials the fact that migrant labor systems introduced by European companies were destabilizing families and devastating rural communities.[19] These modern colonial development efforts undermined progress in Africa.

The new branch of social anthropology that emerged during the 1920s and 1930s thus complicated the relationship between ethnography, colonialism, and development. Innovative scholars Franz Boas at Columbia University and Bronislaw Malinowski at the London

[16]   Today IFAN stands for Institut fondamental d'Afrique noire, the Fundamental Institute of Black Africa.
[17]   See also V. Y. Mudimbe, *The Idea of Africa* (Indiana University Press, 1994), 30.
[18]   James Ferguson, "Anthropology and Its Evil Twin: 'Development' in the Constitution of a Discipline," in Frederick Cooper and Randall Packard, eds., *International Development and the Social Sciences* (University of California Press, 1997), 150–175.
[19]   Godfrey Wilson, *An Essay on the Economics of Detribalization in Northern Rhodesia*, Rhodes-Livingstone Papers No. 5–6 (Rhodes-Livingstone Institute, 1941–1942).

School of Economics promoted the theory of cultural relativity, which solidified the shift from race to culture in the science of anthropology. The theory of cultural relativity stated that the only way to understand other cultures is to examine them not in comparison to one's own but from the perspectives of those who live within those cultures. Malinowski introduced a new research method for achieving this level of understanding called "participant observation," which became the backbone of British social anthropology. Participant observation required the researcher to live among his/her research subjects, learn their language, and participate in their normal day-to-day activities, important rituals, and other aspects of work or leisure. At the same time, the researcher had to maintain objectivity through observation in order to interpret the cultural logic of the community and translate it for a general audience. Observation ensured the anthropologist's allegiance to the scientific method while participation allowed for a deeper understanding of the observed cultures. The end result was a new type of ethnography, the systematic study of a people's history, beliefs, and customs. Anthropologists and other Africanists have since challenged some of the assumptions built into participant observation methods, such as the concept that one could or should categorize Africans into distinct cultural units or "tribes," as many scholars have done. While contemporary anthropologists are aware of these biases, the basic principle of cultural relativity and the method of participant observation continue to shape anthropological research today.

Like their British counterparts, leading francophone Africanist scholars of *ethnologie* (ethnology/anthropology), *ethnosociologie* (ethnosociology), *ethnohistoire* (ethnohistory), *ethnolinguistique* (ethnolinguisitics), and *ethnogéographie* (ethnogeography) challenged the racist assumptions of evolutionary anthropologists. Scholars such as Marcel Griaule, who served as the chair of anthropology at the Sorbonne starting in the 1940s, promoted both a cultural relativist approach for understanding African societies and a universal humanism that challenged essentialist arguments about racial difference.[20] After World War II, as British social anthropology became increasingly structural functionalist, francophone anthropologists like Griaule

---

[20]   Pierre Alexandre, "Introduction," in Pierre Alexandre, ed., *French Perspectives in African Studies: A Collection of Translated Essays* (Oxford University Press for the International African Institute, 1973), 1–10.

researched "values, beliefs, and Weltanshauung (world view), rather than kinship systems and political structures."[21]

Many anthropologists believed that, due to their deep knowledge of African cultures, they were better suited than colonial officials to devise long-term policies for Africa's social, economic, and political development. At the same time, colonial and postcolonial state officials contended that anthropologists were more adept at developing abstract theories than concrete plans, even as officials increasingly adopted ethnographic methods (participant observation, study of local languages, and the attempt to understand cultures from their own perspectives). The tensions between anthropologists and colonial administrators increased with the rise of cultural nationalism starting in the 1930s. The popularity of works such as Léopold Senghor's Négritude poetry and Jomo Kenyatta's *Facing Mount Kenya* demonstrated the growing influence of African cultural nationalists in shaping debates about the impact of colonialism on Africa and Africans during the interwar period. It was no coincidence that both Senghor and Kenyatta went on to become the leaders of their newly independent nations in the early 1960s. Across the continent, Africans who became literate in European languages and trained in anthropology, sociology, economics, and other social sciences contributed to – and at times reshaped – anthropological knowledge about Africa and Africans.[22] By the 1950s and 1960s Africans fighting for independence from colonialism employed African authored works about local customs, histories, and beliefs as tools of nationalism. African cultural nationalists sometimes also drew on western scholarly works and amateur anthropological research conducted by colonial officials to assert Afrocentric interpretations of modernity and development. The relationship between anthropology, imperialism, and development was ambiguous and always in flux.

Anthropology was not the only social science to mature alongside colonialism in Africa. The African continent also served as a site for the development of sociology, economics, political science, and psychology. During the early twentieth century the delineations between different social sciences were still somewhat artificial in that anthropologists, sociologists, economists, political scientists, and psychologists working

---

[21]   Ibid., 4.
[22]   Gaurav Desai, *Subject to Colonialism: African Self-Fashioning and the Colonial Library* (Duke University Press, 2001).

in Africa often employed the same methodologies, mainly ethnology, ethnography, and linguistics. Colonial officers, translators, and intermediaries acted as government "sociologists" until the Second World War when academics became more willing to lend their services to colonial administrations. The colonial administration in German South West Africa directly sponsored sociological studies during the time of the Herero genocide (1904–1908) when colonial concentration camps transformed quite literally into laboratories for studies of eugenics, evolution, and racial difference.[23] Starting in the late 1930s colonial government-funded studies of "race relations," ethnopsychology, poverty, and social and economic development contributed to the professionalization and specialization of social scientists.

The social sciences simultaneously fostered colonialism, justified colonial development interventions, and problematized the assumptions behind both. They became a tool for implementing colonial policies of economic exploitation and political oppression, but they also carved a path for scientifically based criticism of development policies.

5.2 The Rhodes-Livingstone Institute

The Rhodes-Livingstone Institute opened in Northern Rhodesia (Zambia) in 1937 and became the iconic center for social scientific research in British colonial Africa. The first director, Godfrey Wilson, was a social anthropologist who studied at the London School of Economics under the guidance of Bronislaw Malinowski. He and his wife, Monica Wilson – a South African anthropologist, did fieldwork in Tanganyika, Nyasaland, and Northern Rhodesia. They and other academics based at the Institute sought to document the history and customs of African communities as well as the impact of colonialism. The British colonial administrations of central Africa provided the bulk of funding for the RLI, though some researchers came to Africa on individual scholarships or grants. Private companies and individuals with varied interests in the region also contributed financially to the work of the Institute. The RLI expanded

---

[23]   Steinmetz, *The Devil's Handwriting*.

rapidly to include a museum that doubled as a cultural center. The museum displayed art and artifacts collected from fieldwork across the region, including what is today the countries of Zambia, Zimbabwe, Malawi, Tanzania, Botswana, and South Africa. The museum featured exhibits, dances, and other performances to celebrate African customs and history. Fieldwork, however, remained the central focus.

Initially the scope of work at the RLI included both social and biological sciences, but the latter pursuits did not pan out and the Institute remained a center for social anthropology and sociology. The Institute published a journal that was read widely among European and American social scientists. The primary issue facing the RLI and Northern Rhodesia more generally, according to Director Wilson, was that 44 percent of the "able-bodied male population ... are always at any one time in European employment," which usually required long stints far from home.[1] Wilson, like other anthropologists of the time, was concerned about the economic, social, and cultural disruptions associated with the colonial migrant labor system. His research ruffled the feathers of colonial development officers and mining company officials, an affront that led to his resignation in the early 1940s.

South African social anthropologist Max Gluckman, who joined the Institute while conducting fieldwork in Zululand (South Africa) during the 1930s, replaced Wilson as director. His influence continued well after he left in the late 1940s to pursue an academic career in Britain. Thereafter, the RLI became a hub for the type of social anthropology that promoted the theory of structural functionalism. First promoted by Gluckman and E. E. Evans-Pritchard, an anthropologist who conducted research in the Upper Nile region of Sudan, structural functionalism was a macro-level study of societies designed to demonstrate how all of a society's components (customs, beliefs, and institutions) coordinate in order to maintain the stability of the whole structure. Scholarly fascination with African social structures shone a light on the economic and social disruptions that colonialism brought to these systems.

Under the directorship of American anthropologist Elizabeth Colson (1947–1951), the RLI continued to foster ethnographic research that illuminated social conflict. Colson's own fieldwork traced the long-term transformations of Tonga families in Zambia and Zimbabwe sparked by displacement from the building of the Kariba Dam. The RLI scholars documented not only the cultural and social logic of African societies but also Africans' impact on, perceptions of, and reactions to the colonial economy. In doing so RLI publications served as an invaluable resource in administrative debates about colonial development policies.

Lyn Schumaker recounts the history of the RLI and, in particular, how the Institute engaged Africans who facilitated and sometimes directed the ethnographic and sociological research. Schumaker argues that Africans who participated in fieldwork, whether as research assistants, interlocutors, or cultural experts, directly shaped the anthropological theories and methods western scholars developed. In doing so they "Africanized" anthropology at the RLI.[2]

Today, the RLI lives on as the Institute of Economic and Social Research at the University of Zambia. After Zambia's independence in 1964 research sponsored by the Institute became more interdisciplinary and academic. However, its tenuous relationship with the government and its ability to directly shape development policies remained.

[1]   Godfrey Wilson, "147. Anthropology in Northern Rhodesia," *Man* 38 (1938) 130.
[2]   Lyn Schumaker, *Africanizing Anthropology: Fieldwork, Networks, and the Making of Cultural Knowledge in Central Africa* (Duke University Press, 2001).

★★★

By the interwar period the western scientist replaced the Christian missionary as the savior of Africans in development discourses. The colonial drive for profit through "modern" technological advancement sparked this move. At the same time, innovations in social research brought about colonial investments in social welfare. Science was integral to both. Academics, government officials, humanitarians, and private investors argued over whether anthropology should be practical or theoretical, whether subsistence farming or migrant labor was to blame for African poverty, and whether to prioritize technology and profit or social and political stability. The methods and goals of development were in flux, but reliance on science became a cornerstone of the development episteme in the twentieth century.

The sciences employed in colonial Africa were not necessarily cutting-edge. Governments and researchers had to contend with tiny budgets, and private companies looked for the most immediate return on investment. Yet research hubs like the Amani Research Institute, IFAN, and the RLI offered a broader perspective. They brought academics and government officials together and forced compromises between practical and theoretical pursuits. Harry Johnston recognized these tensions in his 1920 speech referenced at the beginning of this chapter. Though scientific research was intended primarily to secure profit in colonial Africa, ultimately it became an end of its own as the continent became a "laboratory" for researchers. Scientific research sometimes brought economic and political inequalities into sharp focus. As the next chapter details, African frustrations with the colonial economy ultimately led to a wave of protest in the late 1930s, 1940s, and 1950s demanding a shift in colonial development policies. Social scientists took notice of these issues and drew attention to the intersection between colonial labor systems, poverty, disease, and political upheaval. Despite the ambiguous impact of scientific progress in Africa, the emphasis on science as *the* solution to development problems remains unchallenged.

Further Reading

On the rise of the development specialist and the role of science in colonial and postcolonial Africa, see Saul Dubow, ed., *Science and Society in Southern Africa* (Manchester University Press, 2000); Toyin Falola and Emily Brownell, eds., *Landscape, Environment and Technology in Colonial and Postcolonial Africa* (Routledge, 2012); and Joseph Morgan Hodge, *Triumph of the Expert: Agrarian Doctrines of Development and the Legacies of British Colonialism* (Ohio University Press, 2007).

For a history of social sciences and colonialism in Africa see Lyn Schumaker, *Africanizing Anthropology: Fieldwork, Networks, and the Making of Cultural Knowledge in Central Africa* (Duke University Press, 2001); George Steinmetz, *The Devil's Handwriting: Precoloniality and the German State in Qingdao, Samoa, and Southwest Africa* (University of Chicago Press, 2007); and Helen Tilley, ed., with Robert J. Gordon, *Ordering Africa: Anthropology, European Imperialism, and the Politics of Knowledge* (Manchester University Press, 2007).

CHAPTER 6

Challenges to Development

The British governor of Nigeria, Bernard Bourdillon, wrote to the secretary of state for the colonies in October 1941 to request colonial development funding free from the stipulation that it should be matched by local revenues. He warned the Colonial Office in London that many military officers returning from visits to Italian-occupied Ethiopia, Vichy French-controlled Senegal, and other colonies of Britain's enemies were "impressed" with the amount of money these European powers spent on African welfare. In contrast to these regions, the poor living conditions of British West Africa, such as the "Lagos slums" of Nigeria, were "absolutely shocking." In the propaganda sphere of the Second World War (1939–1945) European powers demonized their enemies as oppressors and sought to convince Africans that their version of imperialism was benevolent. Bourdillon worried that Britain was losing this battle over the "hearts and minds" of colonial subjects because the Colonial Office had not entirely "overthrown the fetish of the Balanced Budget." Bourdillon argued that Britain might see new labor strikes like those that spread across the Caribbean and Africa during the 1930s if it did not address the situation. Destabilization in the colonies could spread through colonial armies and result in British losses on the actual battlefronts as well.[1]

The passing of the Atlantic Charter in August 1941 put colonialism on the defensive. The Atlantic Charter recognized that all people had a right

---

[1] UKNA CO 859/81/15, B. H. Bourdillon to Lord Moyne, October 24, 1941, correspondence marked "secret and personal."

to "self-determination." Though the Charter sought to address Germany's aggression against its neighbors, nationalist leaders in Asia and Africa began to adopt the language of self-determination to argue for their independence. The years during and immediately after the Second World War saw the rise of nationalism in French Indochina (Vietnam, Laos, and Cambodia), Italy's forced withdrawal from Libya and the Horn of Africa, Indonesia's declaration of independence from the Netherlands, and the ending of nearly ninety years of British colonial rule in India. The threat of nationalism was real and it was spreading. In Africa the threat was also an economic one. Social scientific surveys of the 1920s and 1930s alluded to the economic problems arising from policies of self-sufficiency in Africa, but labor protests that erupted in the late 1930s and 1940s made it impossible to ignore (see Table 6.1). The development episteme had to

Table 6.1 Comparative timeline of events, 1929–1948

Dates	Labor Strikes	Colonial Development Plans	International Political Events
1929		Colonial Development Act (Britain)	Great Depression (to 1933)
1935	Copperbelt Labor Strike		
1936	Dakar Labor Strike		
1938	Caribbean Labor Strike		
1939	Copperbelt Labor Strike; Mombasa General Strike		World War II begins in Europe
1940	Copperbelt Labor Strike ends	Colonial Development and Welfare Act (Britain)	
1941			Atlantic Charter; the United States enters World War II
1943			Widespread famines
1944		World Bank and International Monetary Fund founded	

Table 6.1 (cont.)

Dates	Labor Strikes	Colonial Development Plans	International Political Events
1945			World War II ends
1946	South African Mine Workers Strike	FIDES (France) established	
1947	Gold Coast Port Strike; Mombasa General Strike; beginning of Dakar Railroad Strike		Indian independence
1948	Dakar Railroad Strike		

adjust to the new political reality on the continent, and European colonial powers had to demonstrate a sincere interest in the welfare of their subjects in order to justify their continued rule in Africa.

Great Britain's Colonial Development and Welfare Act (CDWA), passed in 1940 and expanded in 1945, was a start. France followed suit with the establishment Fonds d'investisse-ments pour le développement économique et social (the Investment Fund for Economic and Social Development) (FIDES) in 1946. Unlike pre–World War II colonial development policies that demanded self-sufficiency, these new initiatives pro-vided significant metropolitan funding for economic and social programs in Africa without the stipulation that they result in a direct return on investment. As Chapter 7 explains, the end of World War II was also the moment when international devel-opment expanded beyond formal colonialism with the establish-ment of the International Monetary Fund (IMF) and the World Bank. European colonial development in Africa was no longer simply investment in colonial industries; now it claimed to pro-mote the welfare and general well-being of African people. Imperial powers envisioned postwar development as a solution to growing dissent in Africa and budding anticolonial movements across the globe at the end of the war. The new colonial devel-opment policies signaled a desperate attempt to keep colonialism alive at a time when it seemed perilously out of date.

ECONOMIC CRISIS BEFORE AND DURING THE SECOND WORLD WAR

The Second World War was a turning point in the history of development in Africa, but not only because of the emergence of CDWA, FIDES, the IMF, or the World Bank. The war brought to light the severe economic devastation facing African communities, and European powers could no longer deny that colonialism was at least partly to blame. From the time of Europe's conquest of Africa under the guidance of concessionary companies in the late nineteenth century, African territories were expected to be both self-sufficient and profitable. Very often they were neither. The policy of self-sufficiency dictated that African colonial administrations maintain budgets based on the revenues earned from local taxes and profits; however, the reality was more complicated. Colonial expenditures varied, but in many regions payroll for European staff was the most expensive item in the budget. Roughly half of the colonial budgets in West Africa went toward the salaries of European officials.[2] Everywhere the salaries of European employees far exceeded those paid to non-European employees because both positions and salary rates were racially determined. Table 6.2 shows the racial breakdown of wages in British colonial Zanzibar as an example.

Table 6.2 Salaries by ethnicity in the Zanzibar Protectorate, interwar era

Employee	Ethnicity	Salary in Rupees per Year
Public Health Department sweeper; court policeman; Sanitation Department pumper	African	Rs. 19–20
Clerks Grades I–III	Asian	Rs. 200–400
District Officer	European	Rs. 7,980–12,236
British Resident (top official)	European	Rs. 31,920

Source: UKNA CO618/40/2, Pensions and Gratuities of non-Europeans and CO850/16/5, Pensions of Europeans in Zanzibar[3]

---

[2] Anthony Hopkins, *An Economic History of West Africa* (Routledge, 2014), 190.
[3] Calculations are based on the 1930 Zanzibar Annual Report that pegged the rupee at 1 shilling, 6 pence. In that period the pound was the equivalent of 20 shillings, thus 13.3 rupees to 1 pound. British salaries were calculated in pounds but African and Asian salaries were paid in rupees.

Exorbitant European salaries bloated colonial budgets with high overhead that could not be met by revenues from customs duties or taxes imposed on Africans.[4] Moreover, some tax revenue from exports went directly to the metropoles, where the raw materials from Africa were manufactured into consumer products. In reality, "self-sufficiency" meant colonies had to pay for colonial extraction.

During the Second World War declining imports and exports, increasing demands for labor, decreasing or stagnant wages, and redirection of resources toward the "war effort" resulted in widespread poverty and outbreaks of famine across the continent. Decades of redirecting labor efforts away from subsistence farming and toward cash crops resulted in severe malnutrition, famines, and droughts even before the war broke out. Investments in the production of coffee, tea, cotton, sisal, tobacco, and other exports left African territories dependent on food imports. Africans suffered the devastating consequences when these products became scarce during the Second World War. The price of meat, flour, sugar, oil, and other staples shot up. Famines erupted globally, for example in Bengal in 1943 when Winston Churchill redirected rice from Bengal to Europe in order to stockpile food supplies for the military. By the mid-1940s thousands had perished from starvation in Mozambique, Tanzania, Kenya, Nigeria, Burundi, Cape Verde, and Somalia.[5]

The African food crisis during the Second World War owed a lot to the decline in availability of rice, the favored staple in many regions of the continent. When Japan occupied French Indochina in 1940 and British Burma in 1942 it cut off the main supply of rice to much of sub-Saharan Africa. The rice industry in India, which fed many East Africans, suffered its own environmental and economic crisis during the war. In French West Africa (AOF) rice imports all but disappeared, decreasing from about 63,000 metric tons in 1940 to just 1,000 metric tons two years later. In British territories as well local production of rice was minimal compared to the amount imported. In Zanzibar

---

[4] Hopkins, *An Economic History*, 190.
[5] Lizzie Collingham, *The Taste of War: World War II and the Battle for Food* (Penguin, 2011); Judith A. Byfield, Carolyn A. Brown, Timothy Parsons, and Ahmad Alawad Sikainga, eds., *Africa and World War II* (Cambridge University Press, 2015); Nicholas Westcott, "The Impact of the Second World War on Tanganyika, 1939–49," in David Killingray and Richard Rathbone, eds., *Africa and the Second World War* (Palgrave Macmillan, 1986), 143–159 at 147–148; Daniel Nyambariza, "Les Efforts de Guerre et la Famine de 1943–1944 au Burundi, d'Après les Archives Territoriales," *Cahiers CRA Histoire* 4 (1984) 1–18.

90 percent of locally consumed rice was imported before World War II. In South Africa rice imports decreased from about 70,000 tons of rice per year before the war to 31,000 tons in 1943, and then down to the lowest levels at about 20,000 tons in 1945.[6]

In order to deal with shortages of rice, colonial administrations urged local production with varying success. Some African regions like Niger had been producing rice of their own but at a much higher cost and lower output than the production in Asia. The French government also cultivated rice in the Ivory Coast, Senegal, and elsewhere in AOF, requiring farmers to meet quotas in order to replace the lost imports. In Nigeria and Tanganyika Britain's wartime Grow More Food campaigns included local rice cultivation. As part of the "war effort," African farmers were forced to grow food crops, and soldiers and laborers had to work on farms engaged in food production.[7] The Southern Rhodesian Compulsory Native Labour Act, for example, redirected African labor away from private industries toward government-run food farms. The government provided enormous subsidies to white farmers to offset their loss of labor. Generally labor recruitment laws applied only to able-bodied men, but in Northern Rhodesia women were compelled to work as well. Some of the mandatory crops grown in Africa went toward feeding the soldiers fighting in European armies. Forced food production reduced the amount of land and resources devoted to export crops and small farm production, thus contributing to overall economic decline. Despite the "war effort," high labor costs and low output prevented colonial industries from meeting Africa's demand for food during the war.[8]

Amidst the crisis European administrators urged people to consume locally produced crops like cassava and maize in place of rice. Cassava had been a safeguard against famine since the nineteenth century. However, many Africans had an aversion to consuming cassava because they did not like its taste and considered it the food of the poor. It is also much less nutritious than sorghum or millet and

---

[6] Judith A. Byfield, "Producing for the War," in Byfield et al. eds., *Africa and World War II*, 24–42; Collingham, *The Taste of War*.

[7] Elisabeth McMahon, "Developing Workers: Coerced and 'Voluntary' Labor in Zanzibar, 1909–1970," *International Labor and Working-Class History* 92 (2017) 114–133.

[8] David Killingray, "Labour Mobilisation in British Colonial Africa for the War Effort, 1939–46," in David Killingray and Richard Rathbone, eds., *Africa and the Second World War* (Macmillan, 1986), 88.

poisonous if not cooked properly. In order to help address the food crisis, Ethiopia and Egypt provided wheat, maize, and millet to other territories of Africa and the Middle East, and Dakar imported wheat from France and Morocco.[9] Maize production intensified in places like Kenya and South Africa where maize-based "mealie rice" became the primary substitute for imported rice. In South Africa supplies of wheat for human consumption were limited by the high demand for livestock feed. In 1944 the South African government inaugurated the Food Control Organization and imposed new regulations on the Livestock and Meat Industry Control Board in order to help manage the supply and price of produce and meat for local markets.[10]

6.1 Cooking cassava

In the Zanzibar Islands of East Africa during the early 1940s, female teachers from Zanzibar Town conducted food demonstrations for women in villages across the islands in order to promote the consumption of cassava and maize. One teacher, Zeyana Ali Muhammad, recalled a demonstration in Mangapwani where she and her colleagues explained to a group of eighty women why they needed to learn how to cook cassava to survive the war. Access to food staples was difficult in Zanzibar at that time, and the government required all able-bodied adults to grow cassava. The government also instituted price controls on locally produced goods. Muhammad remarked, "Had it not been for the government keeping a watchful eye on shopkeepers, prices of goods would be deadly."[1] While she painted a positive picture of the government interventions and the teachers' cooking lessons, some people resented the government's insistence that they eat cassava and maize instead of rice. Cassava and maize were generally associated with poverty, and in wartime Zanzibar food rations were determined based on ethnicity. As historian Laura Fair explains, rice was a staple for nearly everyone on the islands before the war,

---

[9] Byfield, "Producing for the War," 35–36.
[10] James Maddison Tinley, *South African Food and Agriculture in World War II* (Stanford University Press, 1954).

but only those with ration cards classifying them as "Asians" or "Arabs" were eligible to purchase rice during the war, while "Africans" were expected to eat cassava and maize.[2] Wartime ration policies exacerbated ethnic and class tensions that erupted with increasing violence after the war. The link between economic hardship, wartime rations, and ethnic politics in Zanzibar echoes the growing politicization of economic issues across the continent during and after the Second World War.

[1] Zeyana Ali Muh'd, "Wartime in Zanzibar," in Amandina Lihamba, Fulata L. Moyo, M. M. Mulokozi, Naomi L. Shitemi, and Saïda Yahya-Othman, eds., *Women Writing Africa: The Eastern Region* (Feminist Press at City University of New York, 2007), 140–143.

[2] Laura Fair, *Pastimes and Politics: Culture, Community, and Identity in Post-Abolition Urban Zanzibar, 1890–1945* (Ohio University Press, 2001), 48–51.

The war led to a decrease in the number of vessels available for shipping and thus to the closing of markets and an overall decline in exports such as coffee, cocoa, bananas, groundnuts (peanuts), sisal, tea, rubber, and other items. Just before the Second World War French West Africa exported 1.2 million tons of produce. Half of these exports came from Senegal's groundnut industry, which relied on the tedious, non-mechanized labor of migrant workers from Mali, eastern Senegal, Guinea, and Burkina Faso. In Senegal the production of peanuts plummeted from 70,000 tons in 1938 to 25,000 in 1941 and did not rebound to prewar levels until after the war ended.[11] On top of dealing with reduced income from exports, farmers had to pay a new tax in kind (crops) to help supply the Free French military and administration as part of the *effort de guerre* (war effort). Likewise, in British territories as well as southern Africa, exports had begun to recover from the global depression of the 1930s but declined drastically after 1939. In the late 1930s British Gold Coast (Ghana) and Nigeria, for example, exported half of the cocoa beans sold in global markets. Wartime interruptions led to overproduction, forcing Britain to purchase surpluses at very low prices. Unsurprisingly, Gold Coast cocoa producers protested this move. The British Colonial Office established the West African

[11] Frederick Cooper, *Decolonization and African Society: The Labor Question in French and British Africa* (Cambridge University Press, 1996), 165. On the longer history of labor practices in the Senegalese peanut industry, see Martin A. Klein, *Slavery and Colonial Rule in French West Africa* (Cambridge University Press, 1998).

Cocoa Control Board in 1940 to deal with the crisis. The board subsidized private companies to guarantee purchase of the crop and prevent bankruptcy among the producers. By 1942 the newly expanded West African Produce Control Board oversaw the production and sale of other West African crops as well, including palm oil, copra, and groundnuts.[12] In South Africa Britain agreed to purchase the bulk of excess wool produced, as it had done for Australia and New Zealand. While some products saw declining prices in their crops, other goods produced specifically for the "war effort" boomed. For instance, between 1937 and 1944, Nigeria's rubber trade nearly quadrupled and Mozambican cotton production increased almost sixfold.[13]

Decreased revenues devastated African economies and left many Africans struggling without a safety net. Without the cash value of exports, colonies were limited in their ability to import needed food crops. The combination of declining export income and limited local food production fueled inflation in African cities. By 1942 coastal towns in French West Africa saw a 50–75 percent increase in the cost of living. Officials attempted to limit the shock of inflation by instituting price controls on locally produced commodities, but, like the bulk purchasing of surplus goods, this adversely impacted African farmers and laborers.

During the war European imperial powers buckled down on the policy of self-sufficiency, what Bourdillon called the "fetish of the Balanced Budget." Investments in development had to come from either local revenues or nongovernmental sources. However, profit from colonial industries fluctuated greatly. Copper and gold mines were lucrative, but agricultural schemes were less reliable. Income from taxes on Africans posed another challenge. Herders had few possessions and most African farmers produced only enough to feed their families and engage in small-scale bartering. To make matters worse, European salaries bloated the overhead expenditures of colonial administrations, and development planning was costly and time-consuming. When crises emerged, as they did during the war, colonial administrations found it nearly impossible to put out the fires. As a result, the economic problems development was meant to solve grew exponentially. More often than not, the state identified the supply

---

[12]   David Fieldhouse, "War and the Origins of the Gold Coast Cocoa Marketing Board, 1939–40," in Michael Twaddle, ed., *Imperialism, the State and the Third World* (British Academic Press, 1992), 153–182.
[13]   Ashley Jackson, *The British Empire and the Second World War* (Hambledon Continuum, 2006), 221–223; Byfield, "Producing for the War," 35.

and quality of labor as the main obstacle to growth. Concerns about labor in Africa lay at the center of interwar and World War II development practices, but the problem of labor was much bigger and more involved than officials, economists, and entrepreneurs envisioned.

LABOR MOBILIZATION AND PROTEST

With declining revenues from exports and a food crisis on their hands, colonial states in Africa turned to conscripted labor during the war. Soldiers, nurses, cooks, and clerical staff worked for the French West African Tirailleurs Sénégalais, the British East African King's African Rifles, and other colonial militaries while civilians labored on government-owned farms or in private industries. In South Africa, Southern Rhodesia, and Kenya white farmers had the political clout to demand fixed minimum prices for their products and a guaranteed labor supply, a luxury out of reach for a majority of African producers. Massive wartime labor mobilization programs were also instituted in Swaziland, Sierra Leone, French Equatorial Africa, French West Africa, Nigeria, Morocco, Belgian Congo, and Tanganyika. The French imposed labor conscription quotas for each village, sometimes for each family. In Gabon Africans engaged in colonial industries like gold mining were recruited to build roads and collect rubber.[14] In Belgian Congo new demands for labor arose with the boom in the export of rubber and uranium, which the United States used to build the atomic bombs it deployed on Hiroshima and Nagasaki.[15] All able-bodied Africans in Belgian Congo and Ruanda-Urundi were required to work for the government for a minimum of 120 days annually. High labor demands and poor work conditions in wartime São Tomé and Príncipe echoed those of the islands' slave plantations in previous centuries. The demand for workers in both food and nonfood colonial industries during the war redirected labor that otherwise would have gone toward the cultivation of subsistence crops. These policies left many families vulnerable to starvation.

---

[14] Eric C. Jennings, "Extraction and Labor in Equatorial Africa and Cameroon under Free French Rule," in Byfield et al., eds., *Africa and World War II*, 200–219 at 204.
[15] Gabrielle Hecht, *Being Nuclear: Africans and the Global Uranium Trade* (MIT Press, 2012), 3–4.

Wartime labor demands and food crises had a devastating impact on Tanganyika (mainland Tanzania). The British colonial government forced 35,000 people, or about 11 percent of the workforce, to work for the "war effort" in 1944. Workers received minimum wages and had to work for nine months of the year. Most went to sisal farms, where unsanitary housing and miniscule food rations left many workers struggling to survive.[16] The removal of male labor, drought, and famine devastated the rural areas. Farmers sold off crops and herders unloaded cattle at below market prices to survive. These sacrifices, which the government considered the people's contributions to the war effort, made economic recovery after the war that much harder.

Africans grew tired of the "war effort" and particularly resented the forced labor programs. Inspired by earlier strikes in Africa and the Caribbean several protests erupted in colonial Africa, including the 1939 and 1940 Copperbelt Strikes in Northern Rhodesia (Zambia), the dockworkers' strike in Mombasa, and protests in Dar es Salaam in 1939. In Dakar a milder wave of dissent erupted in 1936 and 1937, but more serious strikes took hold of the city and spread throughout French West Africa after the war, culminating in the 1947–1948 railway strike that encompassed a large swath of French West Africa. Workers and soldiers demanded higher wages and better working conditions, rations, and housing. Workers on mines and in urban areas insisted on the right to bring their wives and children to the labor compounds and demanded a "family wage" to care for them. This launched debates about whether migrant workers were permanent residents in the cities and towns adjacent to colonial industries.

Protests and strikes arose out of frustration with forced conscription into armies and labor camps, disruption of families torn apart by migrant labor systems, a lack of social services like education and healthcare, and a decline in economic viability of African families everywhere. Men and women affected by these systems formed new social networks and relationships. New urban cultures led to the adoption of social values based as much on class and religion as on language or ethnicity.[17] Whether adopting the values of the civilizing mission or vying for rights as workers and soldiers, Africans began

---

[16]   Killingray, "Labour Mobilisation in British Colonial Africa," 85.
[17]   Michael O. West, *The Rise of an African Middle Class: Colonial Zimbabwe, 1898–1965* (Indiana University Press, 2002).

FIGURE 6.1 A troop of colonial soldiers consisting mainly of the Tirailleurs Sénégalais from West Africa marching on the Avenue des Champs-Élysées in Paris, July 14, 1939. Source: AFP via Getty Images

mobilizing politically by World War II. The political crisis around labor precipitated the overhaul of colonial development policies in the 1940s.

COLONIAL DEVELOPMENT AND WELFARE IN ANGLOPHONE AFRICA

The British Colonial Office, already dealing with protests in the Caribbean in the late 1930s, became concerned when labor strikes resurfaced in Africa. The Colonial Office was forced to see that social and political issues reflected problems with the system as a whole and were not simply a reflection of local circumstances. Lord Hailey's 1938 *African Survey*, sponsored by the American Carnegie Corporation, revealed trends in increasing poverty and declining health and economic status among Africans everywhere.[18] As the *African Survey* illustrated, the 1929 Colonial Development Act (CDA) repaired the British economy at the expense of the colonies. Furthermore, much of the money sent to African territories came in the form of loans with

[18] Lord Hailey, *An African Survey: A Study of Problems Arising in Africa South of the Sahara* (Oxford University Press, 1938).

high interest. In Nigeria, home to the "Lagos slums" Bourdillon mentioned, a third of the colony's revenue went toward repaying the capital and interest on development loans.[19] Given also the high cost of European officials' salaries and other overhead charges, colonial budgets had little left for social services and general welfare. After his visit to East Africa to investigate the question of education Parliamentary Under-Secretary of State for the Colonies Earl De La Warr stated that "the real development needed in Africa today is not the investment of large sums of capital, but the improvement of the human material."[20]

Britain's CDWA, passed in July 1940, superseded the 1929 CDA. The 1929 Act had funded British companies to carry out large infrastructural projects such as road and railway construction in the colonies in order to facilitate exports and to raise revenue for the British government and British private enterprise. The 1940 CDWA provided funding for both "development," meaning infrastructure necessary for the export economy, and "welfare," meaning better housing, education, and healthcare for colonial subjects. Though welfare was new to this empire-wide development program, it was not new to administrators in Africa; colonial officials in Africa had been arguing for at least a decade that investment in health, reproduction, child welfare, and other social projects produced a larger, more productive workforce and, therefore, greater economic profit.

Prior to 1940 monies spent on welfare in Africa came out of local revenues for each territory. During the early 1930s the Colonial Development Advisory Committee repeatedly stated that welfare schemes "fell outside the scope" of the 1929 CDA. By the end of the decade the committee began to pressure the Colonial Office to expand coverage of the legislation. Under the terms of the 1940 CDWA the Colonial Office provided £5 million annual funding for improvements in public health, education, agriculture, research, and other economic and social endeavors across all British colonies.

Staffing shortages caused by the war made it impossible to fully implement the 1940 CDWA. The funds the 1940 CDWA provided did not even amount to £5 million over the course of the next five years. Only about £835,000 per year was spent during the war, and

---

[19]   Hopkins, *An Economic History*, 190.
[20]   Earl De La Warr quoted in D. J. Morgan, *The Official History of Colonial Development*, Vol. 1 (Humanities Press, 1980), 59.

the West Indies received the bulk of this funding. Half of the money went toward agriculture, forestry, and veterinary services. The other half was split between social amenities like schools and hospitals, housing, public transportation, and communication services. The new secretary of state, Lord Lloyd, essentially put the legislation on hold in order to direct resources and energy toward the war effort.

The 1940 Act envisioned development funding as seed money to help colonies achieve economic self-sufficiency. Some Africans interpreted self-sufficiency as self-government, but even as the end of colonialism came into view, Colonial Office personnel framed self-sufficiency as a *prerequisite* for self-government. Colonies had to prove they could be financially independent for a sustained period of time, and Britain saw decolonization as a very gradual process. Britain passed a new CDWA just before the war ended in 1945 in order to make up for the lack of spending during the previous five years. The 1945 CDWA increased the amount of metropolitan funds available to £120 million over a ten-year period. The CDWA was intended to silence critics, like those Bourdillon referenced in 1941, who argued that imperial powers were not doing enough to take care of their colonial subjects.

During the war the British experimented with cost-saving development programs. In 1943, when it became clear that funds from the CDWA would not be readily available, the Colonial Office's Advisory Council for Education in the Colonies put forth a new policy for Africa called "mass education."[21] Mass education went far beyond schooling and literacy programs to include "soil conservation," "better sanitation," and "hygiene and infant and maternity welfare." Mass education trained Africans to carry out development work. By the early 1950s officials began using the term "community development" instead of "mass education" to disavow Africans of the notion that the government promised to provide universal schooling. While officials worried that expanded education would contribute to the rise of anticolonial movements, they hoped community development would buy the allegiance of African subjects.

[21]   Great Britain Colonial Office, *Mass Education in African Society* (London: His Majesty's Stationary Office, 1944).

6.2 Development and the rise of apartheid in South Africa after the Second World War

Though no longer a colony during the Second World War, the Union of South Africa received assistance from the Colonial Development and Welfare Fund as a member of the British Commonwealth. Despite inroads in education and welfare programs for indigenous Africans and the mobilization of labor unions, the 1940s brought drastic and unexpected changes to South African politics culminating in the establishment of apartheid ("separateness") in 1948.

The 1930s and 1940s was a time of rapid industrialization and economic growth in South Africa, especially in the gold mining regions. The income from gold was so extensive that it offset the country's wartime debts. For this reason, South Africa fared much better than other regions of the continent, and the boom brought new employment opportunities to Black South Africans. During World War II 150,000 whites, mostly Afrikaners (whites who spoke Dutch-based Afrikaans rather than English as their first language), joined the armed forces, vacating their positions in the mines and in other industries. A greater number of indigenous Africans migrated from the rural areas to cities like Johannesburg to occupy the semiskilled and skilled positions abandoned by white soldiers.

The Second World War was a time of optimism for Black South Africans when the radical African National Congress Youth League was founded, African labor unions successfully lobbied for better work contracts, and the CDWA allowed the state to expand its welfare programs for the urban poor. However, things shifted dramatically after the war. When white soldiers returned to South Africa, they found that African trade unions were demanding increased wages, better pensions, and other terms that would define Black workers as equal to white workers. Some responded by joining the Afrikaner-dominated National Party (NP) that advocated for increased racial segregation and whites' sustained control over the central government.

The rise to power of the NP and the apartheid state in South Africa's 1948 election was a backlash against the economic and political inroads Black South Africans made during the early and mid-1940s. By the end of the decade South Africa's ruling NP ushered in the policy of "separate development," which destroyed the state-based welfare system and intensified the impoverishment of nonwhites until apartheid ended in 1994. The legacies of this system are still widely apparent in the country's ongoing and widespread economic inequalities. South Africa may be an extreme example, but the apartheid policies of the late 1940s and 1950s mirrored the mindset of colonial officials and white minority governments elsewhere on the continent who feared Africans' greater political empowerment during the postwar era.

FIDES IN FRANCOPHONE AFRICA

The argument that postwar colonial development was a direct response to political upheaval was even more evident in francophone Africa than it was in the British colonies, though this political conflict centered on France itself. During the war France was fractured by German occupation and divided between the German-allied Vichy Regime and Free French Forces. Both sides used France's African colonies as pawns in their struggle to control Paris (see Figure 6.1). Charles de Gaulle, head of the Free French Forces, held a conference in Brazzaville, Congo in 1944 where he promised Africans citizenship as part of France *outre-mer* ("France overseas"). De Gaulle was seeking support among colonial subjects and anti-imperialist allies like the United States. These and other changes he proposed in 1944 did not go into full effect until the end of the war.

The establishment of FIDES on April 30, 1946, was the first major step toward realizing the ideals set forth at the Brazzaville Conference. The acronym FIDES also referred to the Latin word for "fidelity," which served as a useful rhetorical move to keep the colonies loyal to the metropole. The FIDES projects entailed funds dispersed from the metropole as well as contributions from the colonial accounts, funds collected from local taxes, and other sources of revenue. This funding structure set a precedent for France's policy of offering bilateral aid to its former colonies after independence. FIDES was a major shift from the prewar policies of *Pacte Colonial* (Colonial Pact), which, like British colonial development, insisted on economic self-sufficiency.

In October 1946 the creation of the Union Française (French Union) formally acknowledged French citizenship for Africans in France's colonies. The postwar era ushered in a gradual extension of the franchise among Africans and greater African political mobilization within French metropolitan politics. The French Union officially put an end to the *indigene* (indigenous) status of colonial subjects and gave Africans representation in the French Assembly. Also in 1946, the new government abolished the long-standing practice of *corvée* (forced labor). African representatives had limited power to shape French metropolitan politics, but they did wield considerable influence in Dakar. Alioune Diop, a prominent figure in the Négritude movement, was the *chef du cabinet* for the governor of Senegal. He and other African intellectuals and politicians checked the power of the French settler community in West Africa.

Like the British CDWA, FIDES was one of the first steps in declaring a new colonial policy designed to bind the colonies closer to the metropole and quash anticolonial sentiment. The French metropolitan government had provided direct loans to the colonies during the war, but FIDES offered large grants to the colonies for the first time. It had two divisions: the *section générale* (general section) and the *section d'outre-mer* (overseas section). The *section générale* included state grants for research as well as investment in public sector and public-private endeavors, whereas the *section d'outre-mer* earmarked funds for infrastructural development and the modernization of colonial economies. Development projects involved road and bridge construction, expansion of health and education services, town planning, the provision of clean water and electricity, and housing construction. Colonial officials used development funding to deal with some of the difficulties that arose from rapid urbanization and economic devastation of villages and towns before and during the war. These projects were by no means comprehensive. In large, predominantly rural territories public amenities such as paved roads, electricity, and access to sanitary water were limited to the urban centers.[22]

Between 1946 and 1956 nearly 65 percent of FIDES funding was spent on public works and other projects designed to build up the infrastructure of the colonies. The rest was divided between general social services and production of raw materials for export. In nearly all

---

[22] Martin Atangana, *French Investment in Colonial Cameroon: The FIDES Era (1946–1957)* (Peter Lang, 2009).

cases these funds had to be matched by money from local colonial revenues. When revenues through export income or local taxes did not produce the funds needed to match the FIDES aid, the colonies borrowed more money from the Caisse Centrale de la France d'Outre-Mer (Central Bank of France Overseas). FIDES partially contributed to colonies' indebtedness and perpetuated a relationship of dependency between the colonies and the metropole that became normalized by postcolonial loans from the World Bank and the IMF, a topic explored further in Chapter 7.

Neither the CDWA nor FIDES was successful in preparing colonies for economic self-sufficiency. Both policies pressured colonial governments to match metropolitan funding through local revenues or additional loans. Both Britain and France focused most of their energies on developing infrastructure to aid large-scale production and other export industries. During the 1950s many African families continued to face the same financial problems they encountered during the war. These experiences contradicted the notion that European imperial powers cared about the "improvement of human material" and the recognition of African citizenship. Furthermore, the lack of economic stability in the colonies became Europeans' primary justification for continued colonial rule with no end in sight.

6.3 The Dakar railway strike, 1947–1948

The Dakar railway strike of 1947–1948, which engaged 20,000 railway employees, their families, and their communities, is today remembered as a key moment marking the shift toward decolonization in French West Africa. The export of peanuts, timber, rubber, cotton, palm oil, cocoa, and other lucrative raw materials on the Dakar-Niger Railway nearly came to halt as the strikers disrupted traffic for more than five months. Building off earlier strikes at the ports and across Senegal in 1945 and 1946, the workers fought for higher pay, better housing, better leave terms, and accommodation for families. Most symbolically, the workers demanded that a *cadre unique* (a "single, nonracial job hierarchy") replace the colonial hierarchies, or *cadres*, that categorized laborers according to race and status.[1] The majority of African employees belonged to a rank that offered lower pay and fewer benefits than were available to workers of French descent.

As historian Frederick Cooper argues, they drew on the ideals of French assimilation more than on anticolonial sentiment to make their case for labor rights.[2]

The families of workers aided strikers by offering food, shelter, and the transfer of information. Ironically, the railway itself served as a conduit for the sharing of information and supplies among the protesters while its normal functions as the primary avenue for exports came to a stop. Writer and filmmaker Ousmane Sembène elegantly demonstrated this point in his novel *God's Bits of Wood* (1962), a dramatic take on the strike and its place as a centerpiece of Senegalese nationalist politics. Sembène also emphasized the central role of women in the strike, though he took some poetic license in manufacturing a women's march as a watershed event. Historians have taken issue with some of Sembène's interpretations of the strike, but they agree that the strike generated a sense of solidarity among the workers, their families, and the communities impacted by the railway.

The strike was somewhat disconnected from formal politics and some African politicians remained ambivalent during the event. Léopold Senghor, who had recently been appointed as a Senegalese representative to the National Assembly under the terms of the 1946 French Union, appeared to agree with the idea of a *cadre unique* in principle but never publicly endorsed the strike. The Senegalese strikers received political and financial support from railway workers across the region, including what is today Mali, Guinea, Ivory Coast, and Benin. The politicization of labor unions across French West Africa took a decidedly more class-centered rather than overtly anticolonial approach to politics. In the end, the railway companies, partly owned and controlled by the French West African government, offered concessions by raising the pay and status of certain categories of workers. The government did not eliminate the separate *cadres* until the passing of the Loi-Cadre of 1956, a broad set of reforms that set a clear path toward the decolonization of French African territories.

The Dakar railway strike of 1947–1948 highlighted the broken promises of wartime shifts in colonial development policies. European imperial powers declared their hopes for a new relationship with their African colonies wherein Africans would be treated more like citizens than subjects and development funding would be directed as much toward African welfare as it would toward projects guaranteed to generate profit. The railway strike was successful because it brought major concerns about colonialism to the surface of French West African politics even while the strikers focused on the gains particular to their cause. It is no wonder that it became celebrated by artists and historians as a turning point in Senegalese nationalist politics.[3]

[1] Cooper, *Decolonization*, 242.

[2] Frederick Cooper, "'Our Strike': Equality, Anticolonial Politics and the 1947–48 Railway Strike in French West Africa," *Journal of African History* 37:1 (1996) 81–118.

[3] See Cooper, "'Our Strike,'" and James Jones, *Industrial Labor in the Colonial World: Workers of the Chemin de Fer Dakar-Niger, 1881–1963* (Heinemann, 2002).

★★★

From the 1940s on colonial development had two fronts. The first angle of attack was through large infrastructural projects, many of which had been proposed in the 1920s and 1930s but had not yet materialized. The second approach aimed to develop human capital and the productivity of labor through the expansion of social welfare. These efforts were not to benefit Africa and Africans alone. As with the Great Depression, European countries destroyed by World War II looked to their colonies to revitalize metropolitan economies. Before the Second World War colonial administrations devoted minimal funds toward social welfare projects, and only those that were financially sound. While some people benefited from these efforts, they were designed to maintain a "balanced budget."

It was only when it became politically expedient to invest in the health and welfare of Africans that Britain and France adopted new approaches to development through the CDWA and FIDES, respectively. European officials hoped that the new development policies ushered in during and after World War II would help mitigate rising dissent among Africans. Labor unionization, strikes, and public protest forced imperial powers to recognize the need for economic relief, and perhaps a rethinking of colonial labor policies and practices. Workers demanded higher pay, better housing, support for their families, and recognition of their skills and status in companies. While many of these early wartime and postwar protests concentrated on terms of employment rather than the ideology of nationalism, they ignited a political fire that could not be extinguished.

African challenges to the development episteme during the Second World War forced European officials to reconsider colonial development policies. The principle of self-determination celebrated in the 1941 Atlantic Charter rang hollow among colonized Africans forced to fight and work for colonial oppressors. The contradiction between the anti-fascist rhetoric of the Allied forces and Africans' experience of colonialism during the war sparked new forms of dissent and planted the seed for nationalism. More and more, development had to simultaneously bolster colonial economies and address the day-to-day concerns of colonial subjects. As the next chapter demonstrates, postwar colonial development policies would offer only temporary relief for economic devastation and could not stop the rise of African nationalism.

Further Reading

To read more about food insecurity during the war see Lizzie Collingham, *The Taste of War: World War II and the Battle for Food* (Penguin, 2012); Bruce F. Johnston, *The Staple Food Economies of Western Tropical Africa* (Stanford University Press, 1958); and James Maddison Tinley, *South African Food and Agriculture in World War II* (Stanford University Press, 1954).

On labor mobilization and protest during and after the war see Judith A. Byfield, Carolyn A. Brown, Timothy Parsons, and Ahmad Alawad Sikainga, eds., *Africa and World War II* (Cambridge University Press, 2015); Frederick Cooper, *Decolonization and African Society: The Labor Question in French and British Africa* (Cambridge University Press, 1996); James Jones, *Industrial Labor in the Colonial World: Workers of the Chemin de Fer Dakar-Niger, 1881–1963* (Heinemann, 2002); and David Killingray and Richard Rathbone, eds., *Africa and the Second World War* (Palgrave Macmillan, 1986).

For more on shifting development policies and funding see Martin Atangana, *French Investment in Colonial Cameroon: The FIDES Era (1946–1957)* (Peter Lang, 2009); Anthony Hopkins, *An Economic History of West Africa* (Routledge, 2014 [orig. Addison Wesley Longman, 1973]); and D. J. Morgan, *The Official History of Colonial Development*, Volumes 1–5 (Humanities Press, 1980). See also the following British government reports: Great Britain Colonial Office, *Colonial Development Advisory Committee Reports, 1933–1940* (His Majesty's Stationary Office, 1934–1941); and Great Britain Colonial Office, *Colonial Development and Welfare Acts: Report on the Use of Funds Provided under the Colonial Development and Welfare Acts, and Outline of the Proposal for Exchequer Loans to the Colonial Territories* (Her Majesty's Stationary Office, 1959).

CHAPTER 7

From Modernization to Structural Adjustment

In an October 25, 1961 speech at Chatham House in London, Senegalese president Léopold Senghor stated, "We have chosen the African way to Socialism, which will be a synthesis of Negro-African cultural values, of western methodological and spiritual values, and Socialist technical and social values."[1] He argued for a balance between "*vertical solidarity* which binds us to Europe" and "*horizontal solidarity* with other African countries."[2] Senghor was a cultural nationalist who, nonetheless, embraced certain aspects of modernization, the economic argument that so-called traditional societies could "catch up" to "modern" ones by industrializing and integrating into the capitalist global economy. Senghor contended that modernizing Africa required Africanizing modernity, which entailed adapting the development episteme to African national contexts. Though framed in terms of greater social freedoms, protection of African cultures, and socialist ideals, Senghor's development policies celebrated the educated elite as the embodiment of knowledge and the harbingers of development.[3] Yoking modernization to educational expertise,

---

[1] The speech was published as Léopold Senghor, "Some Thoughts on Africa: A Continent in Development," *International Affairs* (*Royal Institute of International Affairs*) 38:2 (1962) 189–195 at 191.

[2] Ibid., 189–190.

[3] Mamadou Diouf, "Senegalese Development: From Mass Mobilization to Technocratic Elitism," transl. by Molly Roth and Frederick Cooper, in Frederick Cooper and Randall Packard, eds., *International Development and the Social Sciences: Essays on the History and Politics of Knowledge* (University of California Press, 1997), 291–319.

African nationalist leaders reinforced a key feature of the development episteme even as they insisted on the premier place of African cultures in national development.

Senghor and other African nationalist leaders of the 1950s and 1960s sought to (re)discover an African national identity and what it meant to be truly independent from European rule economically and politically. Many postcolonial leaders envisioned modernization as the solution to colonial and neocolonial economic dependence. However, modernization came at a price. Combined with nationalism, modernization in emerging African states called for big government and economic independence, yet modernization also required foreign development aid that had the power to bolster or undermine the authority of the new African leaders.

Historian Frederick Cooper has argued that, after the Second World War, "The development concept . . . allowed for an internationalization of colonialism."[4] As colonialism waned and African nation-states came into existence, international organizations and foreign governments replaced imperial powers as the primary investors in African development. The United Nations, the International Monetary Fund (IMF), and the World Bank were at the forefront of this movement. Swept up in the development episteme, African nationalists and the leaders of newly independent countries forged permanent ties to international development agencies, some staffed by former officials in the colonial development system. The development episteme also bound African countries to wealthy donor nations such as the United States and the Soviet Union, the post–World War II superpowers hoping to convince African rulers to support their side of the Cold War. The internationalization of African development expanded during the 1980s when the now widely criticized Structural Adjustment Programs (SAPs) of the IMF and the World Bank eroded both state power and state-sponsored social services in African countries. Rising political leaders who made big promises to their constituents in the era of independence during the 1960s found their hands tied by the internationalization of development and Cold War politics over the next two decades. Some, however, managed to play these politics to their advantage.

---

[4] Frederick Cooper, *Africa since 1940: The Past of the Present* (Cambridge University Press, 2002), 191.

MODERNIZATION THEORY IN POSTWAR PLANNING

After the Second World War western economists developed what holistically became known as "modernization theory," which provided a map for how a society could transform a "traditional" economy into a "modern" one. These economists reified Western Europe and the United States as the pinnacle of economic advancement and the epitome of modernity. Modernization theory was the capitalist version of 1950s-era futurism that envisioned all "modern" nations as industrialized. Industrialization had been part of the discourse on modernity since the Industrial Revolution of the eighteenth century. Western capitalist economists who employed the concept of modernization in the 1950s did so as a way to distinguish between a "modern" capitalist economy (a definitive feature of the west) and other economic modes, such as the bartering system, non-mechanized subsistence farming, and artisanal trades. Even though communists also touted state planning, industrialization, and modernization as central tenets of their societies, many western capitalists lumped communism in with "backward" economies during the era of the Cold War.

The defining feature of the modernist development discourse in the postwar era was the macroeconomic scheme. Paul Rosenstein-Rodan, who first outlined his big push theory in a 1943 article on Eastern Europe, was one of the first to promote this concept.[5] Rosenstein-Rodan argued that "backward" societies needed a "big push" to modernize their economies and catch up with western nations. From this perspective, small-scale welfare programs were inconsequential at best and wasteful of valuable resources at worst. In their place, he emphasized macroeconomic projects that promised high output and profits. Initially, the big push theory was designed to industrialize Eastern Europe after the Second World War, but Rosenstein-Rodan's ideas became central to African development projects during the independence era of the 1960s.

According to Rosenstein-Rodan, the "big push" took place over a series of steps. The first was industrialization, or the transformation

---

[5] Paul Rosenstein-Rodan, "Problems of Industrialisation of Eastern and South-Eastern Europe," *Economic Journal* 53:210/211 (1943) 202–211. See also Paul N. Rosenstein-Rodan, "The International Development of Economically Backward Areas," *International Affairs (Royal Institute of International Affairs)* 20:2 (1944) 157–165.

of a "feudal" society into a "capitalist" one. State-sponsored modernization of the agricultural sector would free up skilled labor for the newly established industrial sector. This differentiation of labor, combined with foreign investment and the growth of infrastructure, would launch the nation's economy into the global market. Increased production of exports and top-down economic planning would lay the foundation for domestic savings and investment in future growth. Small-scale industries, which were considered unproductive and unprofitable, would be phased out over time so that all labor could be redirected toward large, modern industrial pursuits.

By 1960 economist Walt Rostow expanded on Rosenstein-Rodan's big push theory. He proposed the following steps toward modernization in his *Stages of Economic Growth*:

1. Traditional society
2. Preconditions for take-off
3. Take-off
4. Drive to maturity
5. Age of high mass-consumption[6]

Economists like Rostow categorized African states as "traditional societies" with the exception of industrialized South Africa, and defined the continent by its lack of economic modernization. Rostow believed that nonindustrial societies (or "preindustrial," as he called them because all were destined for industrialization) existed in a status of equilibrium with a low cap on productivity and profit. Preindustrialized states could transform only when "modern" science and technology drove economic change. He estimated that a nation could "take off" in about twenty years and reach "maturity" after another four decades. He defined "maturity" as the stage at which the economy would be fully technology driven, diversified, and self-sustaining. The final stage of development was that of high mass consumption accompanied by population growth, two prominent characteristics of the American economy in the postwar era.

Rosenstein-Rodan's big push theory and Rostow's call for rapid technological advancement and mass consumption became models for the modernization of African nations after independence.

---

[6] Walt Rostow, *The Stages of Economic Growth: A Non-Communist Manifesto* (Cambridge University Press, 1960).

Modernization was more than industrialization; it was a comprehensive program meant to reshape the fundamental structures of African communities. However, modernization theory failed to recognize the ways in which African societies were already modern, even according to this definition. The notion that modernized societies were those that moved from a subsistence to a market economy presumed that they did not already have market economies. Instead of barter systems, "modernized" societies were those that used internationally recognized currencies, an ideal that failed to acknowledge the functional coexistence of barter and cash systems in Africa and many other places in the world.

The economic theory of modernization applied to political and social structures as well. Economists argued that political systems needed to develop democratic practices and cultures in order to bolster free trade, which boded well for Africans vying for independence from colonialism. In theory, a "modernized" society encouraged individual achievement and status criteria instead of ascriptive systems in which one's social status was defined at birth. Because of the focus on individual progress, however, extended families were meant to become less important to the overall economic system. Modernization of social groups implied reorganization into nuclear family units and a shift away from religion to secular political ideologies. Economic rationalists assumed that this process of modernization and industrialization would form organically out of societies in the same fashion as occurred in Western Europe and North America.

In this mid-twentieth-century debate, development amounted to a description of Western European historical change rearticulated as a model for the remainder of the world. It reiterated the fundamental theory behind the civilizing mission of the nineteenth century: all societies must be westernized in order to become modern. At the same time, because development and modernization were designed to create self-sustaining economies, these concepts became powerful political tools for African nationalists negotiating for independence from European colonial rule. Thus, development as modernization became a double-edged sword in the 1950s.

SUCCESSES AND FAILURES OF MODERNIZATION PROJECTS IN THE POSTWAR ERA

Postwar colonial development initiatives ushered in these new technologies and languages of improvement in African colonies. At the same time, colonial development brought a resurgence of the civilizing mission that reasserted Europe as both the model for progress and the source of the technology and funding deemed necessary for African progress. Colonial governments designed modernist economic and social programs to quell frustrations and stem the tide of nationalism, yet development also became the paradigm through which African nationalist leaders could claim self-reliance and demand self-rule.

Postwar colonial development concentrated on infrastructure and large-scale production. In British-controlled territories officials expanded social services for the attainment of "mass education" and improved transportation, electricity, water, and sanitation systems. Though social services became more pervasive in the late colonial era, the ultimate goal remained increasing profits from the export-driven colonial economy. Some large-scale initiatives, such as the Tanganyikan Groundnut Scheme, were notorious failures. Other projects that focused on infrastructural development, the expansion of educational and medical institutions and training programs, and investments in agriculture were more successful. In Nigeria and Ghana, for example, the introduction of centralized marketing boards for cash crops resulted in a substantial stabilization fund, which offered producers consistent prices for cash crops and avoided the erratic nature of global markets. African crops were still funneled through government-run railways and ports, and independent cooperatives were carefully regulated. Wages increased and social services expanded, but the expectations of the 1940 and 1945 Colonial Development and Welfare Acts (CDWA) far exceeded the outcomes in British colonial Africa.

7.1 The Tanganyikan groundnut scheme

Britain's infamous postwar Tanganyika Groundnut Scheme in present-day Tanzania was an ambitious five-year project that began with a plan to clear 60,000 hectares of tsetse-infested forest in the first year alone. The 1946 scheme also included construction of a deepwater port at Mtwara and the expansion of the railroad to facilitate the transport of nuts to the Indian Ocean and beyond. Unilever, a Dutch-British company that specialized in palm oil production in British West Africa, first proposed the idea, but the British government took on the task of implementing it. Officials hired 3,000 British employees and imported bulldozers to carry out the job as quickly as possible with minimal labor. The British government spent £35,870,000 on the project, an amount equal to the Tanganyikan colonial government's entire budget for those years.

The Groundnut Scheme faced three main obstacles resulting in its failure: a dearth of skilled laborers who could operate the machines, no maintenance plan for when the machines broke down, and ignorance of the environmental obstacles. The three main locations selected (Kongwa, Urambo, and Nachingwea) varied drastically in terms of annual rainfall and density of forest. Even the thinnest forest at Kongwa, where the project began, proved too much for the machines. The deep roots of the baobab trees, flooding, and an inexperienced workforce left abandoned bulldozers in the forest. By the end of 1947 only 3,000 of the first year's 60,000 hectares had been cleared. At the end of the following year only 20,000 hectares total had been cleared. A series of strikes involving dockworkers, railway workers, and groundnut workers demanding higher pay in late 1947 further challenged this and other development projects in the territory. A drought killed the plan for good in 1949, by which time the cost had far exceeded the initial budget.

News of the failed Tanganyikan Groundnut Scheme traveled far. A December 12, 1949, *LIFE* magazine article about this "scandal in peanuts" reported that the Overseas Food Corporation, the government entity overseeing the scheme, "issued a 156-page apologia for the failure of the peanut planning." The article included photos of bulldozers with twisted rakes and other machines trapped by trees with captions reading "useless road rollers." One photo featured women at work harvesting peanuts in order to show how "hired hands" had been employed in place of "inefficient machine harvesters."[1] A colossal and expensive failure, the Tanganyikan Groundnut Scheme demonstrated the need for greater understanding of local conditions and creating programs designed in collaboration with local communities.

[1] "Scandal in Peanuts: Britain Has Trouble Making a Nut Farm of Tanganyika," *LIFE*, No. 24, December 12, 1949, 46–48. See also John Iliffe, *A Modern History of Tanganyika* (Cambridge University Press, 1979), 440–442.

Development efforts in francophone Africa faced similar economic and political challenges to those in British territories in the postwar era. France's Fonds d'investissements pour le développement économique et social (FIDES) focused on infrastructure and the development of export commodities, and to a lesser extent, social services. FIDES, along with other postwar changes in colonial policy, was successful in reinforcing Africans' political and economic ties to France. The constitution of France's Fourth Republic (1946–1958) made concessions for African representation in the French Assembly and greater representation in the colonial administration, which opened new avenues for Africans to make political and economic demands. Frederick Cooper and others have argued that it was through the economic mobilization among labor unions and labor strikes that Africans articulated a "new vision of citizenship" based on political equality.[7] African workers demanded that France go beyond the abolition of the *indigénat* status and *corvée* (forced labor) to institute nonracial cadres and equal rights for African "citizens" of the newly created French Union. The promises of citizenship and incorporation into the French Union did not resolve the tensions of colonialism. The Algerian war for independence broke out in 1954 and blossomed into a crisis in 1958, by which time the call for independence had spread to other French territories on the continent. In response, Charles de Gaulle suspended the constitution and ordered the National Assembly to draw up a new one, leading to the establishment of the Fifth Republic in 1959. The African deputies and senators elected to the French Assembly between 1946 and 1960, including Léopold Senghor, helped to shape the discourse on modernization and development as African nationalists looked toward independence.

In many territories of francophone Africa FIDES-funded development projects created more problems than they solved. The postwar rhetoric on social and community development gradually gave way to schemes designed for maximum and immediate profit for private companies and external investors. For territories with extensive rural areas such as Chad, some funding went toward improvement of agriculture, forestry, and animal husbandry, but the majority of funds paid for the construction of roads, bridges, and airports in order to improve the transportation of exports into long-distance markets. Under the terms of FIDES, recipient territories had to match French development

---

[7] Frederick Cooper, *Citizenship between Empire and Nation: Remaking France and French Africa, 1945–1960* (Princeton University Press, 2014), 26.

funds from local revenue. Chad and other territories did so by borrow-ing heavily from the Caisse Centrale de la France d'Outre-Mer (CCOM), the French colonial bank, resulting in serious economic crises by the early 1950s. The French Treasury advanced large sums of capital to Cameroon including a deficit of more than 1 billion francs by the mid-1950s, which committed Cameroon to hefty annual repay-ments that ate away at the territory's resources. Tens of thousands of Cameroonians were laid off and Douala, the largest city, was devas-tated by unemployment and poverty. Meanwhile, the French brought in private companies to "develop" the exportation of coffee, ground-nuts, cotton, cocoa beans, and bananas. They returned to the kind of private development reminiscent of the charter and concessionary companies that established European colonies in Africa during the late nineteenth century. Resentment toward these interventions aided the rise of nationalism in the cocoa-producing regions of Cameroon.[8]

Some areas of francophone Africa saw a rise in profits after the war, but much of this can be attributed to community efforts and price controls rather than to FIDES directly. In stark contrast to the failure of the Tanganyikan Groundnut Scheme, expansion in the production of groundnuts in Senegal during the 1950s resulted primarily from the mobilization of the farmers and laborers by Murid religious leaders. Similarly, in what is now Ivory Coast, followers of Muslim leader Yacouba Sylla formulated their own vision of "Islamic development" during the late colonial era, which later informed President Félix Houphouët-Boigny's postcolonial modernization programs in the country.[9] FIDES tended to make the biggest impact through the expansion of transportation and communication structures that sup-ported local initiatives and existing industries.

It is important to follow the money trail in development projects in order to understand why some worked and others failed. Collaboration is another key factor. Many of the schemes that functioned well did so because of cooperation between officials and African community lead-ers or between government officials and scientists. The most successful case studies are those in which African leaders ensured that workers and their families would also benefit from the scheme.

---

[8] Martin Atangana, *French Investment in Colonial Cameroon: The FIDES Era (1946–1957)* (Peter Lang, 2009), 53–64.

[9] Sean Hanretta, *Islam and Social Change in French West Africa: History of an Emancipatory Community* (Cambridge University Press, 2009).

MODERNIZATION AND DECOLONIZATION

African nationalists of the 1950s and 1960s faced a conundrum. In order to claim the right to govern themselves, they first needed to convince colonial powers that they could be self-sufficient. They did so by embracing the development episteme, a theory that emulated the political, social, and economic structures found in western countries. In colonial Africa, where many economic resources were in the hands of European states, companies, and individuals, African negotiations for independence entailed assurances that their path toward development would not disrupt these economic relationships. Professing allegiance to modernization allowed nationalists to demonstrate their preparedness for independence and, at the same time, to promise their constituents and former colonizers a prosperous future. Despite political independence, African nations had to concede a degree of economic control to foreign investors if they wanted to succeed in the modern world. This compromise guaranteed the endurance of the development episteme in postcolonial Africa.

The history of landownership in Kenya's transition to independence demonstrates the continuation of colonial-era development policies into the postcolonial period. Land and cash crop agriculture were points of contention during the colonial era, as European settlers occupied the most fertile region of the territory and dominated the export industry beginning in the 1910s. During the anticolonial struggle of the 1950s, the British administration passed legislation that recognized individual landownership and Europeans' titles in legal battles over claims to land. When Kenya gained independence in 1963 under the leadership of Jomo Kenyatta, his administration sought to integrate Kenya into the world market. Kenyan landowners, previously confined to the production of subsistence crops for local consumption while European growers focused on cash crops, could finally break into the lucrative export markets by growing coffee and tea. Also, more Kenyans were able to purchase land. Kenyan historian William Ochieng' reported that by 1970 two-thirds of former settler farms had been transferred to African owners.[10] Yet many Kenyans were excluded from this deal. The percentage of people in the country living

[10]   William R. Ochieng', "The Kenyatta Era 1963–78: Structural & Political Change," in Bethwell Allan Ogot and William R. Ochieng', eds., *Decolonization & Independence in Kenya, 1940–93* (James Currey, 1995), 83–109 at 87–88.

below the poverty line rose steadily between 1964 (38 percent) and 1981 (48 percent).[11] Decolonization brought an end to white settler domination in the Kenyan highlands, but it did not terminate the inequalities produced by the colonial agricultural industry.

African nationalists embraced modernization and top-down development schemes, both of which required a unified, independent state with a powerful central government. Many nationalist leaders worked to embed their visions of modernization within African cultures and value systems. Some, like Léopold Senghor discussed at the beginning of this chapter, also engaged with socialist principles and relationships with socialist countries in order to counter the economic influence of former imperial powers. They pointed to the rapidly expanding economies of the USSR and China as evidence that socialism was not only compatible with modernization but constitutive of it.

Kwame Nkrumah, the first president of Ghana and a torchbearer for pan-Africanism, helped to popularize African socialism across the continent during the 1960s. Nkrumah's 1965 book, *Neo-colonialism: The Last Stage of Imperialism*, evoked Vladimir Lenin's anti-imperialist book, *Imperialism: The Highest Stage of Capitalism* (1917). Neocolonialism, he argued, was the continued economic exploitation of Africa by former imperial powers and other nations. Nkrumah also encouraged African leaders to adopt a policy of nonalignment during the Cold War. Though Nkrumah publicly criticized western capitalists, he welcomed the support of the IMF, the World Bank, and foreign companies for large state-centered modernization projects. His widely advertised Akosombo Dam project, the planning for which began under British colonial rule, promised to modernize Ghana's national economy. The primary purpose of the dam was to jump-start industrialization in Ghana through the vertical integration of bauxite mining to aluminum smelting. Vertical integration occurs when the same company that owns the supply chain controls the manufacture of the final product. The American company overseeing the Akosombo Dam project, Kaiser Aluminum, began constructing the dam in 1961. The scheme, which involved the forced and voluntary resettlement of 80,000 Ghanaians, became an economic and

---

[11] Francis M. Mwega and Njuguna S. Ndung'u, "Explaining African Economic Growth Performance: The Case of Kenya," in Benno J. Ndulu, O'Connell, Jean-Paul Azam, Robert H. Bates, Augustin K. Fosu, Jan Willem Gunning, and Dominique Njinkeu, eds., *The Political Economy of Economic Growth in Africa, 1960–2000: Vol. 2: Country Case Studies* (Cambridge University Press, 2008), 325–368 at 360.

political disaster for Ghana when Kaiser Aluminum refused to use Ghanaian bauxite while reaping much of the profit from the dam's cheap hydroelectric power.[12] Although Nkrumah espoused the rhetoric of African socialism and nonalignment, his willingness to embrace modernization and welcome foreign capital left Ghana vulnerable to neocolonial exploitation.

Julius Nyerere, the first president of Tanzania, ushered in a particular version of African socialism called *ujamaa* ("familyhood" in Swahili), which he outlined in the Arusha Declaration of 1967. As a nationalist politician in the late 1950s when Tanganyika was still a British Mandated Territory, Nyerere strategically adopted the term *maendeleo*, a Swahili word used widely to mean "development," in his plans for nationalist development and modernization. Its power came from the fact that colonial officials interpreted *maendeleo* as modernization and economic growth, but to the Swahili-speaking public it simply meant "progress" or "moving forward." In the context of *ujamaa*, the term *maendeleo* became shorthand for the economic and political progress of the independent nation.[13]

Nyerere's *ujamaa* program had mixed outcomes. It expanded and standardized Tanzania's education system and improved the health and standard of living of many Tanzanians. *Ujamaa* also promoted the philosophy of African socialism and community building that continues to hold sway in Tanzanian culture today. At the same time, it generated widespread frustration against the government for the hated Operation Vijiji (Operation Villages) program in which millions of Tanzanians (more than half the country's population) were forced to resettle into impoverished *ujamaa* village cooperatives. The 1973 oil crisis and the decline in value of key Tanzanian exports like coffee and cotton dealt a final blow to Tanzanian socialism. By the mid-1980s the country instituted neoliberal economic reforms.

In addition to the growing popularity of African socialism, modernization and decolonization unexpectedly contributed to a new wave of feminism in Africa, though after independence many African politicians turned their backs on the women who brought them to power. In

---

[12]   Stephan F. Miescher, "'No One Should Be Worse Off': The Akosombo Dam, Modernization, and the Experience of Resettlement in Ghana," in Peter J. Bloom, Stephan F. Miescher, and Takyiwaa Manuh, eds., *Modernization As Spectacle in Africa* (Indiana University Press, 2014), 184–204.

[13]   Priya Lal, *African Socialism in Postcolonial Tanzania: Between the Village and the World* (Cambridge University Press, 2015).

Kenya, Tanzania, Guinea, Algeria, Nigeria, Mali, Senegal, Zimbabwe, and elsewhere, women rallied political support for nationalist parties, joined in public efforts to "build the nation," and took up the nationalist cause on behalf of all mothers, wives, and working women. During the 1940s and 1950s women in Senegal and Kenya provided crucial supplies and information for anticolonial protesters and freedom fighters. In 1950s Guinea some female supporters of Ahmed Sékou Touré served as "shock troops" to suppress the opposition. In Tanganyika Muslim women like Bibi Titi Mohamed became central political organizers for the Tanganyika African National Union (TANU) before and after the country's independence in 1961. Women freedom fighters joined the front lines in the war against the Rhodesian Front in Zimbabwe during the 1960s and 1970s. Women who engaged in anticolonial movements perceived nationalism as the simultaneous liberation of the nation and of women. The promises of African feminism, however, suffered a debilitating blow with the arrival of independence. Very few women held elected positions in government, and national development came in the form of top-down, patriarchal modernization schemes spearheaded by "big men."[14]

Even while pressing for an African socialist approach to economic development, many leaders of new African nations accepted the basic principles of global capitalism. Decolonization promised freedom from colonial exploitation, but African leaders' allegiance to modernization theory created the perfect conditions for neocolonialism. Africa's postcolonial economic development entailed rapid industrialization and economic growth, which relied on investment from the global financial institutions (the IMF and the World Bank) as well as foreign nations, large banks, multinational corporations, and international development agencies.

THE INTERNATIONALIZATION OF DEVELOPMENT

Development became internationalized after World War II. International organizations argued that Africa's underdevelopment

---

[14] See, for example, Elizabeth Schmidt, *Mobilizing the Masses: Gender, Ethnicity, and Class in the Nationalist Movement in Guinea, 1939–1958* (Heinemann, 2005) and Tanya Lyons, *Guns and Guerilla Girls: Women in the Zimbabwean National Liberation Struggle* (Africa World Press, 2004).

was a global issue to be dealt with outside the framework of colonialism. This spurred tensions between the United Nations and imperialists, and it spawned new development organizations like the Commission de Coopération Technique en Afrique au Sud du Sahara (CCTA), established in 1954 to improve public health and medical care in francophone colonies.[15] In order to understand the framework for development for the second half of the twentieth century it is crucial to examine the international development specialists and the intellectual and scientific principles that informed their work. Professional training of development specialists occurred in tertiary education systems in Europe and, especially, the United States. The American GI Bill, also known as the Servicemen's Readjustment Act of 1944, helped to expand the US state university system, which subsequently trained numerous experts in the new development fields. Collectively, the United Nations, nongovernmental organizations (NGOs), universities, and other international organizations produced an international field of development science specialists. Some of these specialists had been trained for work in colonial technical services and joined the United Nations (UN) and its subsidiary organizations (such as the World Health Organization, the Food and Agriculture Organization, the International Labor Organization, UNESCO, and UNICEF) as "scientific consultants" after the collapse of imperialism in Africa. Whether trained under colonialism or not, these international specialists saw themselves as working toward the betterment of global society.

International macroeconomic development planning promoted a form of modernization that envisioned African nations as viable players on the world market and not merely the extensions of European capitalist centers. At the same time, international aid organizations framed their work within a set of intellectual narratives about Africa that were similar to the assumptions of former colonizers. Many believed that Africa must go through a process of rural and agrarian consolidation before reaching the higher stages of industrialization and capitalism, that Africans could not fully understand or adopt democracy until this process was complete, and that all development "problems" had technical solutions rather than political or social ones.

---

[15]   Daniel Vigier, "La Commission de coopération technique en Afrique au Sud du Sahara," *Politique étrangère* 19:3 (1954) 335–349.

Over time, internationalization transformed the bureaucratic, macroeconomic, government-centered model of development planning into one that reified the role of international specialists overseeing specific development projects. During the late colonial and early post-colonial periods governments oversaw long-term, regular improvements in the technical and social welfare sectors, but the foreign entities that took the reins on development projects during the late 1960s and 1970s tended to have short-term visions. This shift in approach continues to haunt African governments, which have little economic incentive to provide long-term support for programs with temporary funding from international sources.

The United States, in particular, became interested in African development as African nations gained independence. If Europeans "discovered" Africa in the nineteenth century, Americans "discovered" the continent in the 1960s. The United States looked to these new nations as a battleground for Cold War politics. Investment in African economies sought to ensure their future as American allies. The early 1960s was a time of hope in American visions of Africa. Africa became the newest addition to area studies in the academy with the establishment of the African Studies Association in 1957, the same year Ghana gained independence. John F. Kennedy inaugurated the Peace Corps in 1961 partly in order to bolster the image of Americans in Africa.[16] By this time the IMF and the World Bank had also switched their focus away from recovery of Europe in the immediate postwar era toward international development programs in the "Third World."

7.2 America's "discovery" of Africa in the 1960s

It is more accurate to say that the United States *rediscovered* Africa in the 1960s. Since the era of transatlantic trade, American missionaries, companies, humanitarian organizations, and politicians have had a long-standing fascination with the continent. The Anglo-American Corporation founded in 1917 invested heavily in South Africa. Liberia, a nation created by African American settlers and US politicians in the early nineteenth century, is still intimately linked to the United States, and the Firestone

---

[16] Larry Grubbs, *Secular Missionaries: Americans and African Development in the 1960s* (University of Massachusetts Press, 2009).

Corporation has maintained rubber plantations there since 1926. The United States also developed close ties to Ethiopia once it recovered from Italy's seven-year occupation between 1935 and 1942. In May 1953 the United States and Ethiopia signed a twenty-five-year treaty that allowed for American naval and air force bases and a communications center at the Kagnew Station in Asmara, now the capital of Eritrea. The United States provided aid to Ethiopia for the construction of schools, hospitals, infrastructure building, and agricultural development. Relations between the two countries remained strong until 1974 when Ethiopia became a socialist country and civil war erupted.

Decolonization in the 1960s offered American companies new business opportunities in Africa, which fit well with the development goals of both African and US political interests during the Cold War. Americans intervened in African politics extensively in order to stem the spread of communism and socialism. The Central Intelligence Agency (CIA) has been implicated in the death of Patrice Lumumba, the socialist-leaning popularly elected prime minister of Congo (now Democratic Republic of Congo, or DRC), in January 1961. During the 1960s, 1970s, and 1980s, the United States funded capitalist-leaning political parties and militias across the continent. Americans meddled in the civil wars of Angola and Mozambique by providing military aid for the National Union for the Total Independence of Angola (UNITA) as well as the Mozambican National Resistance (RENAMO), a group originally funded by the white-supremacist Rhodesian Central Intelligence Organization. While American involvement in political and military conflicts deflated public optimism about African development by the late 1960s, US businesses continued to profit by working with African political leaders.

African countries took advantage of the global power play during the Cold War era. For example, Kenya, Ethiopia, and Ghana actively sought aid from the United States while the socialist nations of Tanzania and Guinea looked to China and the USSR for assistance. The Tanzanian government sent young Tanzanians to the USSR for higher education and training in medicine, engineering, and other professions considered vital to national development. The Chinese government collaborated with Tanzania and Zambia to build the

FIGURE 7.1 Kenneth Kaunda, the prime minister of Zambia, and Julius Nyerere, the president of Tanzania, visiting a tunnel constructed by a Chinese engineering team in Uhuru, Tanzania, August 10, 1973. Source: AFP via Getty Images

TAZARA railway system with Chinese engineering expertise and the training of Africans (see Figure 7.1). Between 1973 and 1989 East Germany sent aid to Zimbabwe, Mozambique, São Tomé and Príncipe, Angola, Cape Verde, Guinea-Bissau, Guinea, Libya, Ethiopia, Zambia, Lesotho, and the Republic of Congo (today, People's Republic of the Congo), as well as communist-friendly political parties like the South West African Peoples' Organization (SWAPO) in Namibia and the African National Congress (ANC) in South Africa. In reality, most African nations played both sides of the Cold War, pledging sympathy for one in exchange for aid. Ghana was both a US ally and a proponent of socialism. Tanzania received funding from Canada as well as several European communist countries of the Eastern Bloc. The Cold War brought international attention and funding to Africa but did not necessarily result in sustainable economic development.[17]

---

[17] Elizabeth Schmidt, *Foreign Intervention in Africa: From the Cold War to the War on Terror* (Cambridge University Press, 2013).

THE IMF, THE WORLD BANK, AND STRUCTURAL ADJUSTMENT PROGRAMS (SAPS)

The IMF and the World Bank were born out of the Bretton Woods conference in 1944. These organizations facilitate international lending and aid, generally using funds collected from wealthier nations to invest in "least developed countries" (LDCs). Today the UN defines LDCs as "low-income countries confronting several structural impediments to sustainable development."[18] Both the IMF and the World Bank are owned and operated by member nations. Many African nations became members of the Bank within a decade of independence.[19] The membership of the two organizations is indistinguishable, but the functions of the IMF and the World Bank differ.

The World Bank (also known as the International Bank for Reconstruction and Development) was established to finance reconstruction of Western Europe after the Second World War. The purpose of the IMF was to ensure the economic stability of global markets amidst fluctuations in national currencies, imbalances in trade, and other issues influencing world markets. Essentially, the World Bank provides the funds and the IMF regulates the terms of those payments and the "code of conduct" for member nations.[20] The IMF also offers short-term emergency loans to its member countries, though this is not its primary function. The two organizations are interdependent, but most of the funding sent to Africa comes from the World Bank's International Development Association (IDA), established in 1960. The two decades after the inauguration of the IDA brought an eightfold increase in World Bank loans to Africa, mostly thanks to investment from members of the Organization of the Petroleum Exporting Countries (OPEC). Approximately one-third of these funds went toward agriculture, a quarter went toward transportation, and the remainder was split between education, water and sanitation, urban development, and general infrastructure.

---

[18]   United Nations Development Policy & Analysis Division, Least Developed Countries (LDCS), www.un.org/development/desa/dpad/least-developed-country-category.html, accessed January 3, 2020.

[19]   World Bank, Member Countries, www.worldbank.org/en/about/leadership/mem bers, accessed January 3, 2020.

[20]   David D. Driscoll, "The IMF and the World Bank: How Do They Differ?" International Monetary Fund website, www.imf.org/external/pubs/ft/exrp/differ/dif fer.htm, accessed January 3, 2020.

Despite their claims to political neutrality, the World Bank and the IMF served as tools for diplomacy in Cold War politics. For example, the World Bank and the IMF repeatedly aided the notoriously corrupt Mobutu Sese Seko during his thirty-two-year rule over Zaire (DRC) even after they discovered he embezzled funds and violently suppressed political enemies. Not until 1990, after the fall of the Berlin Wall and the fading of Soviet power, did these organizations discontinue payments to Mobutu.[21] As with direct American funding for political groups in Angola, Mozambique, and elsewhere, grants and loans provided by the World Bank and the IMF rewarded loyalty to the western cause. Corruption in African countries was the price paid for Cold War security.

The IMF and the World Bank became Africa's primary source of development funding by the 1980s. The IMF also regulates the terms for bilateral aid from richer countries to poorer countries. As such, these institutions have had and continue to have considerable control over African nations' economic and political positions vis-à-vis the global market. Independent African governments that embraced the top-down modernization agenda came under attack by international economists for their costly bureaucracy, subsidies to national industries, corruption, and other characteristics common to "developed" western nations but that were perceived as inefficiencies in Africa.[22] What African nations really needed, development economists argued, was to create an environment more attractive and open to foreign investment and trade. This was the logic behind the IMF and the World Bank's SAPs introduced in the 1980s.

The SAPs continued the macroeconomic trend of 1960s modernization but encouraged greater foreign control over African finances. Under the SAPs, African countries were expected to promote "free trade" in the form of relaxed tariffs and reduced regulations governing foreign companies operating in Africa. The international financial institutions required African nations to guarantee repayment of loans and returns on foreign investment before spending revenues on social services for their citizens. As occurred in colonial industries, foreign companies operating in postcolonial Africa were engaged in the extraction of raw materials and other exports for the global market. International development experts believed

---

[21]   Dambisa Moyo, *Dead Aid: Why Aid Is Not Working and How There Is a Better Way for Africa* (Farrar, Straus, and Giroux, 2009), 22–23.
[22]   See Kimberly Ann Elliott, ed., *Corruption and the Global Economy* (Institute for International Economics, 1997).

these changes would result in greater efficiency and rapid economic growth. During the debt crisis of the 1980s African nations desperate for external injections of money became especially vulnerable to the SAPs.

The SAPs failed to deliver on the promise of development. Though they resulted in meager increases in the gross domestic product (GDP) in select countries, these gains were overshadowed by a more significant increase in debt burdens due to the accumulation of interest on development loans. Meanwhile, African political leaders were stripped of their authority. The SAPs actually increased corruption because government officials had to contend with fewer and fewer resources.[23] The SAPs, which devoted very little attention and funding to poverty reduction, gender equity, and health services, adversely affected citizens in African countries. Since the early 2000s SAPs have required governments to earmark funding for poverty reduction and direct some resources toward reducing social inequalities. The long-term impact of these modifications is still unclear, but until recently SAPs have undermined African nations' ability to provide a safety net for their populations.

★★★

Attempting to modernize Africa into a mirror of western societies was a central tenet of the development episteme. The modernizing states of postcolonial Africa repeated some of the same mistakes as their colonial predecessors, and modernization opened the door to both nationalism and neocolonialism. Globalization of financial institutions and the creation of the IMF and the World Bank coincided with the decline of direct imperialism in Africa. The internationalization of development for Africa in the postcolonial era reinforced the notion that modernization centered on macroeconomic changes like industrialization. The United States and the USSR viewed newly independent African countries as pawns in the Cold War, yet throughout this period African regimes played their own game, vying for financial assistance and access to global markets. The citizens of African nations were the losers in the game of modernization as they suffered corrupt governments, declining social services, and ever-constricting resources.

Today African economies are still largely dependent on foreign investment, the export of raw materials, and the expansion of large-

---

[23]   Joseph Patrick Ganahl, *Corruption, Good Governance, and the African State: A Critical Analysis of the Political-Economic Foundations of Corruption in Sub-Saharan Africa* (Potsdam University Press, 2013), 33–35.

scale, export-oriented infrastructure projects. Serious concerns about social welfare faded into the background in the 1970s. The expansion of education and healthcare systems, the provision of clean water and electricity, and social services were common goals set out by leaders of newly independent nations, and some countries made limited progress in these areas. However, the primary concern for modernization theorists, nationalists, and international development experts who advocated structural adjustment was the individual countries' GDP and the rate of national economic growth over time. Lost in the "big push" of modernization was the plight of peasants, migrant laborers, traders, women, children, and others whose everyday labor fueled development. We see in the next chapter how international NGOs swooped in to fill this gap.

Further Reading

On African nationalism, decolonization, and socialism see Peter J. Bloom, Stephan F. Miescher, and Takyiwaa Manuh, eds., *Modernization As Spectacle in Africa* (Indiana University Press, 2014); Frederick Cooper, *Africa since 1940: The Past of the Present* (Cambridge University Press, 2002); William H. Friedland and Carl G. Rosberg Jr., eds., *African Socialism* (Stanford University Press, 1964); Priya Lal, *African Socialism in Postcolonial Tanzania: Between the Village and the World* (Cambridge University Press, 2015); Kwame Nkrumah, *Neo-colonialism: The Last Stage of Imperialism* (International Publishers, 1965); and Elizabeth Schmidt, *Mobilizing the Masses: Gender, Ethnicity, and Class in the Nationalist Movement in Guinea, 1939–1958* (Heinemann, 2005).

For discussions about modernization and development economics see Devesh Kapur, John P. Lewis, and Richard Webb, *The World Bank: Its First Half Century, Volumes 1: History and Volume 2: Perspectives* (Brookings Institution Press, 1997); Thandika Mkandawire and Charles C. Soludo, *Our Continent, Our Future: African Perspectives on Structural Adjustment* (CODESRA and Africa World Press, 1998); Walt W. Rostow, *The Stages of Economic Growth: A Non-Communist Manifesto* (Cambridge University Press, 1960); and Robert L. Tignor, *W. Arthur Lewis and the Birth of Development Economics* (Princeton University Press, 2006).

For more information about the internationalization of development in Africa see Larry Grubbs, *Secular Missionaries: Americans and African Development in the 1960s* (University of Massachusetts Press, 2009); Dambisa Moyo, *Dead Aid: Why Aid Is Not Working and How There Is a Better Way for Africa* (Farrar, Straus, and Giroux, 2009); and Peter J. Schraeder, *United States Foreign Policy toward Africa: Incrementalism, Crisis and Change* (Cambridge University Press, 1994).

CHAPTER 8

The New Missionaries

The rains failed to come again in 1983. It was the second year in a row that the Tigray and Eritrean regions of Ethiopia had this disaster visited upon them and the famine grew worse. The Derg, the military committee that ran Ethiopia after the 1974 coup, faced increasing armed resistance from opposition groups in these regions. The Derg found the famine a convenient weapon against the opposition and hoped to starve them into submission. Until 1984, many of the humanitarian groups working in Ethiopia collaborated with the Derg in an effort to reach some of the people who needed famine relief. In that year the government restricted humanitarian assistance to people who supported it in the conflict. At the same time, the US government refused to send relief aid as a pressure tactic against the Derg, who sat on the opposite side of the United States in the Cold War.[1] These political, environmental, and human conditions collectively transformed the famine into a crisis of epic proportions. The BBC filmed this crisis with excruciating detail in 1984. After watching the film, a spectacle of horrifying starvation, Irish singer Bob Geldof determined to help end the famine.

Geldof immediately gathered friends and recorded a song as a benefit for Band Aid, the nongovernmental organization (NGO) he had started. The single "Do they know it's Christmas" pathologized Africans, who would live in a place "where nothing ever grows, no rain or rivers flow." The lyrics called for Europeans to "say a prayer, to pray

[1]   Edmond J. Keller, "Drought, War, and the Politics of Famine in Ethiopia and Eritrea," *Journal of Modern African Studies* 30:4 (1992) 609–624.

for the other ones," and to "thank God it's them instead of you." Geldof's vision for development echoed that of missionaries like David Livingstone, who 120 years earlier gave public lectures in Europe urging that Christian salvation and western technological interventions would save Africans from poverty and the slave trade. "[R]ural poverty was spectacle," Maurice Amutabi explained. "NGOs ... presented similar historical similarities with European missionaries, with their production of the 'savage' needing to be 'saved' and 'civilized.'"[2] By replicating the relations of power embedded in the civilizing mission of earlier centuries, NGOs' emphasis on poverty and reliance on a discourse of saving seemed all too familiar to Africans. This chapter examines the shift in nongovernmental interventions in Africa's development from the civilizing mission of the late nineteenth century to the "NGOization" of African development in the twenty-first.

While the International Monetary Fund (IMF), the World Bank, and the United Nations (UN) have largely dictated African nations' development policies, NGOs have been the primary agents on the ground in Africa since the 1990s. Until recently, the vast majority of these NGOs have been international NGOs (INGOs) established, run, and funded by Europeans or North Americans. These were the new missionaries, the "secular missionaries."[3] Like their predecessors who came to end the slave trade and bring "civilization" to Africa a century earlier, NGOs function on a platform of humanitarianism, human rights, and development for the poor. Whether in the form of slave narratives collected by abolitionist missionaries or television commercials asking for donations to help feed starving African children, not-for-profit entities have thrived on the poverty of Africans and the industry of fundraising in order to "save" them. Both Christian missionaries and NGOs picked up the slack of government regimes by offering social services to people excluded from the wealth of the state. In this way, both missionaries and NGOs have acted as mediators between the people, on one side, and international funding agencies and governments, on the other.[4]

---

[2]   Maurice N. Amutabi, *The NGO Factor in Africa: The Case of Arrested Development in Kenya* (Routledge, 2006), 21.

[3]   Larry Grubbs uses the term "secular missionaries" to describe American development interventions in Africa since the 1960s. Grubbs, *Secular Missionaries: Americans and African Development in the 1960s* (University of Massachusetts Press, 2009).

[4]   Pádraig Carmody, *Neoliberalism, Civil Society and Security in Africa* (Palgrave Macmillan, 2007).

Beyond the religious aspect many differences have emerged between the European missionaries of earlier centuries and the NGOs working in Africa today. While missionaries and colonial offi-cials did not always see eye to eye, they generally found common ground. For example, European missionaries attending the 1910 World Missionary Conference in Edinburgh, Scotland agreed to instill respect for colonial authorities among their African congregations.[5] In contrast, NGOs often have few allegiances to African governments. They rely on African governments for access to their citizens or cooper-ation over development funding, but NGO employees and volunteers often view African bureaucracies as obstacles rather than facilitators.

While many NGOs have vastly different agendas for and approaches to development than missionaries, their relationship to civil society and their tendency to concentrate on issues like poverty and what we now call "human rights" replicates much of the work early missionary societies did leading up to and during the colonial era. As Walt Rostow, the author of *The Stages of Economic Growth* and a founding economist of modernization theory, reminisced, "most of us felt, I suspect, some kind of moral or religious impulse to help those striving to come forward through development. In that sense we were in the line that reached back a century and more to the missionaries from Western societies."[6] This desire to help and a belief that one could and should help develop African societies has driven humanitarian inter-ventions on the continent for the past 200 years.

POVERTY RELIEF IN PRECOLONIAL AFRICA

Many African societies had traditions of poverty alleviation and communal welfare systems long before the influx of European missionaries and colonial officials. African political leaders gained legitimacy by distributing largess to their constituents and allies. Africans were adept at protecting themselves and their families during times of crisis. Cattle, considered a valuable commodity, could act as a savings bank to be cashed in for food or other goods when necessary. Agricultural communities such as those of Great

---

[5] Brian Stanley, *The World Missionary Conference, Edinburgh 1910* (Eerdmans, 2009).
[6] Rostow quoted in Nils Gilman, *Mandarins of the Future: Modernization Theory in Cold War America* (Johns Hopkins University Press, 2003), 70.

Zimbabwe (ca. 1250–1450 CE) developed elaborate storage systems to ensure a steady supply of grain during the non-harvest seasons. If stored properly, grain could last months or even years. Farmers planted crops resistant to drought and a variety of crops with staggered harvests to protect against low yields or failures. Shared labor practices, customs governing land use and land-ownership, flexible terms regarding bridewealth payments, and adjustable bartering systems allowed flexibility for individuals and families to deal with fluctuations in crop outputs and food supplies.[7] Muslim brotherhoods (*tariqa*), mosques, and indigenous churches offered hospitality, health services, poverty relief, and other forms of charity. Ethiopian Christian organizations, for example, have a long tradition of catering to the destitute, elderly, and diseased.[8]

John Iliffe argues that before European colonialism most Africans faced primarily conjunctural poverty, temporary poverty resulting from a crisis such as warfare or famine. Structural poverty, or the "long-term poverty of individuals due to their personal or social circumstances," generally applied to slaves or those who were "incapacitated" and therefore incapable of performing labor.[9] The word used to describe a poor person in many African languages translated as someone without kin rather than someone without property or income. Iliffe explains that structural poverty was less common in many areas of the continent where land was abundant before the colonial era. Conjunctural poverty resulting from natural disasters, warfare, drought, or famine could lead to structural poverty, and some crises left permanent marks on African societies. When famine struck, some people went in search of fresh grazing and farming land. If this was not available, people resorted to more drastic measures such as warfare or pawning their children or themselves.[10] For instance, under Shona customary law in colonial Zimbabwe (Rhodesia) a man with no access to land or property could become an "adoptee" of a wealthy person

---

7   See, for example, Diana Wylie, *Starving on a Full Stomach: Hunger and the Triumph of Cultural Racism in Modern South Africa* (University Press of Virginia, 2001), 46.

8   John Iliffe, *The African Poor: A History* (Cambridge University Press, 2009 [orig. 1987]), 9–29.

9   Ibid.

10   Boubacar Barry, *Senegambia and the Atlantic Slave Trade* (Cambridge University Press, 1988), 108–109.

and was treated like a son.[11] He was bound to work for his "father" for the rest of his life. In exchange his adopted parent provided him housing, food, and sometimes even one of his daughters for marriage. To be sure, this was a relationship of servitude, but many preferred it to starving.

Temporary relationships of servitude were designed to help individuals or families deal with economic shocks. Parents temporarily pawned their children when they knew they could not feed them. They gave their children over to distant relatives with the resources to care for them, hoping their children could return in better times. Children could live and work with neighbors or kin to pay off debts their parents had incurred. Though during the height of the transatlantic slave trade these relationships more frequently led to permanent enslavement, the original intention of such institutions was temporary reprieve from a disaster and the prevention of permanent or structural poverty.

During the twentieth century, John Iliffe argues, structural poverty became more pervasive than conjunctural poverty and sometimes families became a liability rather than a resource. When European settlers and colonizers claimed land in Africa, they often introduced new practices of land tenure that emphasized individual ownership, which limited Africans' access to viable farmland. Migrant labor systems brought on new forms of structural poverty in which able-bodied young men and the families they left behind were regularly impoverished by unemployment and low wages.[12] The increase in monogamy among Christian Africans reduced the size of extended kin networks to call upon during times of crisis. Abolition of slavery also removed the possibility of pawning children and other forms of temporary servitude that helped families mitigate hardship. Some forms of poverty alleviation endured during the colonial era, such as charity and hospitality offered by Muslim brotherhoods or Christian churches. Overall, however, the social and economic changes that came with colonialism left more Africans facing structural, long-term poverty.

---

[11]   J. F. Holleman, *Shona Customary Law: With Reference to Kinship, Marriage, the Family and the Estate* (Manchester University Press, 1969 [orig. Institute for Social Research, University of Zambia, 1952]), 125.

[12]   Iliffe, *The African Poor*, 276.

8.1 Usufruct land tenure as a safety net

Usufruct land rights confer the rights to use land, usually on a temporary basis, to those who do not have ownership claims to the land. According to Ambe Njoh, land in the forest and coastal zones of West Africa "was always a collectively held usufruct" in the sense that individuals applied to chiefs or elders for permission to cultivate.[1] Though individual landownership was recognized in the Asante kingdom of Ghana during the nineteenth century, landless members of the kingdom were not left to starve. As historian Gareth Austin explains, "cultivation rights were virtually a free good. Land-owning stools offered the right to grow food, literally *didi asaseso*, 'to eat on the soil,' without charging anything that could be described as rent, to both subjects and non-subjects, providing that they performed the duties of subjects."[2] Similarly, a *mothami* (one with usufruct rights) in Kikuyuland, Kenya would be given access to land as long as he agreed to help with clearing, house building, and other communal tasks.[3] If he refused or caused disruptions in the community, his usufruct rights could be revoked. In colonial Zimbabwe the Shona community ward, or *dunhu*, conferred land use rights onto individuals.[4] Anyone recognized as a member of the *dunhu* had building and cultivation rights there. Community membership was based on residence rather than kinship, so as long as someone was accepted into the *dunhu* they could access these resources. These mechanisms for providing propertyless people access to land – whether temporary or permanent – helped alleviate hardship for many farmers and herders during the precolonial era. They offered individuals with no or few kin to support them a safety net and a way to build or rebuild their wealth and status.

While some of these practices continued during the twentieth century and in some cases still exist today, colonial policies of land tenure led to the alienation of land for many people. Jomo Kenyatta argued that European settlers who arrived in Kikuyuland in the early twentieth century exploited Kikuyu "generosity." Not only did they claim ownership over lands for which they had acquired only usufruct rights, but they did not fulfill their obligations to respect Kikuyu customs and ways of life. The British colonial administration upheld and in some cases conferred the settlers' right to landownership because they mistook communally held land as a resource up for grabs. The transition from kinship-based ownership and usufruct land rights to private, individual landownership, especially in agricultural societies, increased structural poverty. People without landed property became dependent on their labor, a less lucrative asset in the colonial economy, as their primary source of income. This is exactly the scenario that resulted in the impoverishment of "squatters" in Kikuyuland and ultimately sparked the Mau Mau anticolonial movement in 1950s Kenya.[5]

[1]   Ambe J. Njoh, *Tradition, Culture and Development in Africa: Historical Lessons for Modern Development Planning* (Ashgate, 2006), 73.
[2]   Gareth Austin, *Labour, Land, and Capital in Ghana: From Slavery to Free Labour in Asante, 1807–1956* (University of Rochester Press, 2005), 103.
[3]   Jomo Kenyatta, *Facing Mount Kenya: The Tribal Life of the Gikuyu* (Vintage Books, 1965 [1938]), 34–35.
[4]   Holleman, *Shona Customary Law*, 11–12.
[5]   Tabitha Kanogo, *Squatters and the Roots of Mau Mau, 1905–63* (James Currey, 1987).

MISSIONARIES AND COLONIAL DEVELOPMENT

Christian missionaries came to Africa equipped with the rhetoric of salvation and financial backing from Europe and North America. Their antislavery campaign offered a compelling justification for intervention. Western abolitionist discourses described African slavery as oppressive and unproductive, void of both humanity and economic development. Missionaries saw pawning and other forms of enslavement not as temporary means to deal with conjunctural poverty but rather as the fundamental impoverishment of African cultures. As Chapter 1 explains in greater detail, missionaries viewed Africa as a blank slate for spreading Christianity, "legitimate commerce," and "civilization." This religious movement for universal humanism launched the first foreign-led development initiative as well as what would become known as "human rights" in Africa.

The reality of mission work was quite different from the ideal. Missionaries did not anticipate that African leaders would perceive them as rival chiefs or that "legitimate" trade could perpetuate slavery rather than bring about emancipation. Many products Europeans encouraged, such as cloves from the Zanzibar Islands and rubber from the Belgian Congo, were produced, collected, or transported by enslaved or forced labor. By advocating for legitimate trade, missionaries (and, later, colonial officials) unwittingly supported industries that employed coercive labor tactics and reinforced or replicated master-slave relationships.[13] Furthermore, Africans who allied with missionaries often did so not for their message of salvation so much as their ability to access valuable foreign imports like guns, and for diplomatic reasons. Chief Moshoeshoe of the Sotho Kingdom in southern Africa invited the Paris Evangelical Missionary Society (PEMS) to his kingdom in 1832 to protect his people from invading rivals and raise his profile as a powerful and respected ruler. When the alliance became detrimental to his political authority, he distanced himself from the mission. Missionary interests conflicted with those of African leaders in the Buganda Kingdom as well. In 1888 a Muslim man named Kalema became the king of Buganda and drove out European missionaries and their Christians converts. British colonial forces came to the aid of the missionaries by ousting King Kalema and claiming a protectorate over Buganda in 1900.

The Buganda case reminds us that, whether intentional or not, missionaries paved the way for colonialism and colonial development programs. Missionaries relied on grants-in-aid from governments to run their churches and schools. In return, missionaries carried out much of the day-to-day work of colonial development and helped to forge the practical aspects of the development episteme. In Italian and Portuguese African colonies the Catholic Church and the state collaborated explicitly to "civilize" Africans, one parish at a time. Before the French West Africa administration imposed the separation of church and state in colonial affairs, religious leaders like Charles Lavigerie, founder of the White Fathers mission, held enormous sway in government affairs. British colonial welfare policies consistently relied on missionaries to carry out community development projects. Colonial welfare programs implemented across the continent in the 1920s, 1930s, and 1940s could not have existed without the volunteer efforts of private organizations. In emphasizing self-help, self-sufficiency, cooperatives, and neighborhood savings schemes, European officials looked to civil society to create its own safety net. When and where indigenous systems of support collapsed

---

[13] Frederick Cooper, *From Slaves to Squatters: Plantation Labor and Agriculture in Zanzibar and Coastal Kenya, 1890–1925* (Yale University Press, 1980).

under colonialism, Africans turned to missions for help. They sought out missions to educate their children, access medical care, find housing, and care for their families when food was scarce. Missionaries provided many of the social services that kin were unable and colonial governments were unwilling to offer, becoming the first line of defense against poverty.

Missionaries' role in the politics of colonial development became evident during the rise of nationalism in the 1950s. In Kenya, for example, missionaries joined the British government's effort to suppress the anticolonial movement, Mau Mau. The Christian Council of Kenya (CCK) directly intervened in the conflict by helping to "rehabilitate" suspected Mau Mau supporters among the Kikuyu. Missionaries made education, healthcare, and other social welfare benefits available to those who denounced Mau Mau. Many Kikuyu people obliged, though they had little choice in the matter. While clearly opposed to Mau Mau, the CCK did criticize the colonial administration for its violent and inhumane tactics against suspected rebels.[14]

By the 1950s and 1960s many missions that came to Africa in earlier decades had morphed into indigenous African churches with African leadership. From that point on the new foreign missionaries who arrived fell into the same category as any nonlocal, nongovernment development organization, what we now call INGOs (international nongovernmental organizations). Most Christian INGOs hired Africans to work for their organizations at the local level but kept westerners at the helm. The language of the missionary movement had shifted. As Firoze Manji and Carl O'Coill note, "It was no longer that Africans were 'uncivilized.' Instead, they were 'underdeveloped.' Either way, the 'civilized' or 'developed' European has a role to play in 'civilizing' or 'developing' Africa."[15] There are certainly ideological differences between the projects to free slaves, "civilize" and convert "heathens," and develop the poor. However, the pivotal role of contemporary INGOs in Africa's development work, their prevalence in African civil society, and their interventionist agendas expose their uncanny resemblance to colonial-era missionaries.

---

[14]   Caroline Elkins, *Imperial Reckoning: The Untold Story of Britain's Gulag in Kenya* (Henry Holt, 2005), 299–303.

[15]   Firoze Manji and Carl O'Coill, "The Missionary Position: NGOs and Development in Africa," *International Affairs* 78:3 (2002) 567–583 at 574.

8.2 Missionaries in the twenty-first century

Independence in Africa did not spell the end of Christian missionaries to the continent; quite the contrary, in fact. Between short mission trips, long-term missionaries, and gap-year mission trips for young people, more missionaries are going to Africa in the early twenty-first century than any time in the past. Some of the language of missionizing has changed; for instance, Methodists now send "mission cow-orkers" instead of "missionaries." Nevertheless, the goal of proselytization through development work remains remark-ably similar. Like missionaries of the nineteenth century, those of the twenty-first also build schools for Africans, in part so that converts can learn to read the Bible. The framing of missionizing has changed in the past fifty years from proselytism to humanitarian work, even though speak-ing about Christian doctrine is still a part of the process. Six of the seven most prominent international evangelical mis-sionary organizations concentrate their efforts on "relief and development."[1] The largest of these groups is World Vision with a budget of $2.6 billion and more than 40,000 employ-ees across the world. World Vision, which defines its employees as evangelical humanitarians, began in 1950 when American Bob Pierce sought to support the work of missionary organizations in Asia. He focused on orphanages and quickly pioneered child sponsorship programs, the leading method of fundraising for evangelical groups in the 1940s and 1950s. The fundraising combination of humani-tarian child sponsorship with Christianization still accounts for almost half of World Vision's annual budget. World Vision introduced programming in Africa once African countries gained independence in the 1960s and 1970s. Today religious groups constitute a significant minority of NGOs in Africa.

[1] David King, "The New Internationalists: World Vision and the Revival of American Evangelical Humanitarianism, 1950–2010," *Religions* 3:4 (2012) 922–949 at 924.

HUMANITARIANISM, HUMAN RIGHTS, AND THE NGO IN AFRICA

The idea of natural rights emerged from the Enlightenment and, more importantly, the Haitian, French, and American Revolutions, as well as the global antislavery movement. The discourse on human rights became more pervasive as humanitarian work became more secular during the twentieth century. The interwar period was a fertile time for discussions of human rights, humanity, and humanitarianism, but it was in the wake of World War II with the UN's Universal Declaration of Human Rights of 1948 and the rise of independence movements in Asia and Africa that the language of human rights became popular in Africa. No clear or single definition of "human rights" existed. Cultures, circumstances, and experiences produced widely disparate understandings of this concept.

The 1948 UN Universal Declaration of Human Rights listed thirty different articles defining universal human rights. Among others, the articles included freedom from discrimination due to "race, colour, sex, language, religion, political or other opinion, national or social origin, property, birth, or other status" (Article 2); freedom from slavery (Article 4); the "right to a nationality" (Article 15); the "right to freedom of opinion and expression" (Article 19); and the "right to take part in the government of his country, directly or through freely chosen representatives" (Article 21). Article 21 goes on to state that "the will of the people shall be the basis of the authority of the government" and that "universal and equal suffrage" shall be in place. The hypocrisy of imperial powers drafting this document in 1948 was not lost on Africans, most of whom remained under colonial rule until at least 1960.

Africans were likewise frustrated with the conception of human rights as enshrined in the UN's declaration because their position was proof that these rights were not "universal." Bonny Ibhawoh argues that African concepts of rights differed in three ways from those of the Enlightenment tradition in the west. First, rights are generally understood within the context of the family or community rather than the abstract individual. Second, African societies tended to link rights with duties, so that "[f]or every right to which a member of society was entitled, there was a corresponding communal duty."[16]

---

[16]   Bonny Ibhawoh, *Imperialism and Human Rights: Colonial Discourses of Rights and Liberties in African History* (State University of New York Press, 2007), 23.

Third, whereas Europeans and Americans defined and conferred rights through legal systems, Africans did so through negotiation, education, or other forms of socialization. Ibhawoh demonstrates that, in the case of Nigeria, many Africans adopted the western language of "human rights" after 1948 in order to argue for independence or, at the very least, greater representation in colonial administrations. In Africa the history of "human rights" as defined by the UN is therefore inextricably tied up with the history of anticolonial nationalism. African demands for human rights, now disconnected from a sense of duty, translated into all sorts of campaigns for equality: equal pay for equal work, men's and women's enfranchisement, the right to form labor unions and negotiate for better pay and benefits, and many other movements that fueled anticolonial sentiment in the 1950s and 1960s.

The growing importance of NGOs coincided with the standardization of human rights discourses and the secularization of humanitarian interventions in Africa and elsewhere. Usage of the term "NGO" or "nongovernmental organization" came out of the creation of the UN in 1945. The charter for the UN, which is an intergovernmental organization, gave non-state agencies observer status at UN meetings. This designation was initially used for international organizations not associated with any government or political party. Eventually, the term "NGO" gained greater usage, especially in the 1970s, and referred to any not-for-profit organization unaffiliated with a government. NGOs are no longer confined to international organizations and can be found at the local, regional, national, and international levels. Scholars have recently distinguished between internationally funded NGOs (INGOs) and local NGOs (LNGOs), a clarification that is key to understanding the history of development in Africa.

INGOs that arrived in African nations in the postcolonial era embraced the discourse on human rights, but they generally interpreted this to mean individualized rights, not collective ones. INGOs used the language of human rights to pressure development agencies and governments to fund the extension of education, healthcare, housing, and environmental resources. They framed these issues as African humanitarian problems that required a western development solution. Michael Barnett notes that "human rights activists argued in favor of a form of cultural relativism that accepted that Western peoples were indeed superior, but that also respected local cultures and envisioned that Africans would eventually attain the 'ability to run their own affairs.'"[17] This was a neocolonial version of the civilizing mission; Africans could eventually govern themselves, but not until they were enlightened through western intervention.

The discourse of human rights resurfaced in the 1990s and early 2000s when European politicians hypocritically condemned African leaders for not protecting their citizens' rights, the very rights European colonial powers denied Africans at the time of the UN's Universal Declaration of Human Rights. Western governments' push to identify human rights abuses in Africa allowed them to claim moral superiority without recognizing the legacies of colonialism. For example, when the World Bank withdrew Uganda's development funding in response to the country's anti-homosexuality law in 2014, it punished a postcolonial regime for doubling down on a law first implemented under British colonialism. It is important to disentangle the recent politics of human rights discourses, which largely characterize African leaders as despotic and inhumane, from the longer history of humanitarian intervention and the shifting meaning of "rights" in Africa.

THE NGOIZATION OF AFRICA

Anthropologist James Ferguson has stated that the IMF and World Bank's Structural Adjustment Programs (SAPs) were intended to counter state oppression by generating "a newly vital 'civil society'" and promoting "a new sort of 'governance' that would be both more democratic and more economically efficient." This is the essence of neoliberalism, or the revived call for economic liberalization (the "free market") and the notion that these economic policies foster a liberal social and political environment. Instead of democratic engagement between civil society and African governments, Ferguson argues, these changes brought on "swarms of new 'nongovernmental organizations' (NGOs)," drawn to Africa because of "the shift in donor policies that moved funding for projects away from mistrusted state bureaucrats and into what were understood as more 'direct' or 'grassroots' channels of implementation."[18]

---

[17] Michael Barnett, *Empire of Humanity: A History of Humanitarianism* (Cornell University Press, 2011), 74.
[18] James Ferguson, *Global Shadows: Africa in the Neoliberal World Order* (Duke University Press, 2006), 38.

The NGO has replaced the state as the primary entity directing development work in Africa. This process has been termed the "NGOization" of Africa. During the final decade of the twentieth century, the macroeconomic drive of nation-states gave way to NGOs, the non-state entities providing direct services and aid to local communities. In his study about the creation of "the Sahel" as a site for humanitarian intervention, Gregory Mann traces the origins of the NGOization of African societies back to the postwar period when emerging nationalists directed economic policies toward local communities and identified "social forces as the primary constraint on economic growth."[19] As newly minted nations embraced grand visions of modernization, development experts began to perceive rural and "traditional" social groups as obstacles. In the case of the West African Sahel, Mann argues, the NGO performed the work of management and intervention, or what is called "governmentality," that should have been done by the nation-state. This form of governmentality, which is actually "nongovernmentality," identifies local or regional communities ("the Sahel") – rather than the nation – as the target of specific development interventions. Such a focus on a particular region or group, especially one that did not exist within the boundaries of the nation, required an international approach by an INGO.

As Ferguson outlined it, NGOization has permeated African civil society. Many political scientists and sociologists agree that an active civil society is vital to a functional democracy, but the assumption in such a statement is that civil society consists primarily of citizens. However, by the end of the twentieth century, the majority of the organizations, institutions, and people that have comprised "civil society" in African countries originated in the west; they were not citizens of African countries. Even where citizens, locally owned business, and national or community-based religious organizations have actively participated in the public sphere and engaged in social and political movements, one often discovers the overwhelming influence of foreign financing and directives (see Figure 8.1).[20] This NGOization of African civil societies demonstrates the extent to which the development episteme and development funding has permeated everyday life in Africa.

[19] Gregory Mann, *From Empires to NGOS in the West African Sahel: The Road to Nongovernmentality* (Cambridge University Press, 2015), 8.
[20] Jane I. Guyer, "The Spatial Dimensions of Civil Society in Africa: An Anthropologist Looks at Nigeria," in John W. Harbeson, Donald Rothchild, and Naomi Chazan, eds., *Civil Society and the State in Africa* (Lynne Rienner, 1994).

FIGURE 8.1 NGO signs on the road leading into Balaka District in southern Malawi. Source: Photo taken by Donald J. Treiman. Printed with permission of photographer

AFRICAN WOMEN AND THE RISE OF THE LNGO

The NGOization of Africa has led to increased attention and funding for African women, but this is not the first time African women have entered the development spotlight. Nineteenth-century missionaries offered concubines refuge from the slave trade, humanitarian agencies such as St. Joan's Social and Political Alliance rallied against female circumcision and forced marriage of African girls in the 1920s and 1930s, and feminist-oriented NGOs of the twenty-first century continue to fight for the rights of African girls and women. The controversy over female circumcision (more recently called female genital cutting [FGC]), as discussed in Chapter 4, is one example, but other colonial campaigns were waged against forced marriage, child marriage, polygamy, bridewealth exchange, and Muslim practices of veiling or secluding women. Some African women embraced these efforts to change their lives, while others fought vehemently against what they considered "westernization." International feminist intervention into the lives of African women intensified in the postcolonial period and drew strength from African women's own political and social mobilization after the Second World War. Today much international and local funding has been earmarked for work specifically dealing with women and gender. African women and girls have become the key to unlocking valuable development dollars, but they have also taken advantage of this financial interest in their lives to build their own LNGOs.

The international campaign to save African women and girls took off during the 1930s and 1940s. European women's groups in Africa, such as the East African Women's League (EAWL) in Kenya and the Ligue pour la Protection de l'Enfance Noire in Belgian Congo, promoted work among African women to reduce infant mortality and improve child welfare. Some women's organizations in Africa were initially designed to aid white women living in the colonies and turned their attention toward African women after World War I. For example, until the mid-1920s the EAWL focused on white women's enfranchisement and fears about the sexual assault of European women by African men. Not until the 1930s did it advocate for African women's instruction in hygiene, nursing, sewing, and welfare.[21] Middle-class and elite African women in Nigeria, Mali, Congo, Gabon, Zanzibar, Zimbabwe, South Africa, Senegal, and elsewhere – those who viewed themselves as "modern" and respectable – launched their own campaigns to eradicate prostitution, child labor, crime, and diseases, and many fought to expand girls' education. These women launched some of the first LNGOs and helped to bolster an African civil society in the colonial and postcolonial era.

Women's issues became sidelined during the 1960s as national governments put their energies toward top-down modernization projects, but African women kept up the pressure. Activists such as Wangari Maathai, who established the Green Belt Movement in the late 1970s and fought hard for women's political and economic rights in Kenya in the 1980s and 1990s, helped to shift the focus of the development discourse back toward gender. Rather than emphasizing the impact of African culture on women, African women's rights activists have linked gender to development problems like political oppression and concerns about the environment. African women leaders continue to define development on their own terms and challenge the agendas of international development agents. The Maasai

---

[21] *East African Standard*, January 10, 1920, 12A, and June 19, 1920, 17; Kenya National Archives (KNA) AB/14/47, Report on the Education of Women and Girls in Kenya, 1944; KNA MSS/61/274, Circular from T. G. Benson, Principal of Jeanes School, Jeanes School Kenya, 1937.

Women's Development Organization (MWEDO) in Tanzania is a case in point. Dorothy Hodgson explains how this group of Maasai women created an LNGO to put their interests and needs ahead of those other women and development agents had identified for them. MWEDO not only decentered human rights in the development discourse, which others had defined as the need to eradicate FGM, but also challenged foreign and national stereotypes about Maasai communities.[22] By doing so MWEDO and other African women have challenged the push for individual versus collective rights.

Arturo Escobar contends that the increased "visibility" of women, peasants, and the environment in the development discourse does not necessarily represent their empowerment so much as it represents the power of this discourse to direct its gaze onto these objects of intervention.[23] The success of African women's LNGOs in their own countries and communities, however, indicates that African women have found ways to redirect this discourse and its gaze to their benefit. Community revitalization in Africa has depended on voluntary labor and women's grassroots organization. Despite the long history of international intervention in African development, especially where it concerns African women, LNGOs headed by African women have made a difference in development policies, and they have reshaped civil society to suit their needs and interests.

8.3 The Green Belt Movement

The late Wangari Maathai started the Green Belt Movement (GBM) in 1977 by organizing a group of women to plant trees and form a "green belt" in the city of Nairobi, Kenya. The Green Belt Movement is a "grassroots" NGO, which, according to Maathai, means that it works toward "community development" and insists that "the community must own the project."[1]

---

[22] Dorothy Hodgson, "'These Are Not Our Priorities': Maasai Women, Human Rights, and the Problem of Culture," in Dorothy Hodgson, ed., *Gender and Culture at the Limit of Rights* (University of Pennsylvania Press, 2011), 138–157.

[23] Arturo Escobar, *Encountering Development: The Making and Unmaking of the Third World* (Princeton University Press, 2012 [1995]), 155.

Maathai described how the movement spread in her 2006 memoir, *Unbowed*.

> By the mid-1980s, the Green Belt Movement had grown significantly and I had never been busier. I was working up to eighteen hours a day. By now, nearly two thousand women's groups were managing nurseries and planting and tending trees and more than a thousand green belts were being run by schools and students. Together, we had planted several million trees. Eventually, the Green Belt Movement would help establish more than six thousand nurseries, managed by six hundred community-based networks; involve several thousand women, and men, in its activities; and, by the early years of the twenty-first century, have planted more than thirty million trees in Kenya alone."[2]

Maathai's Green Belt Movement challenged the developmentalist agenda of the Kenyan state, which had pushed for infrastructural expansion and urbanization at the expense of the environment. The GBM was not only an environmental organization but also a women's community grassroots movement. Its success rested on the fact that women across Kenya and eventually in other areas of the continent worked tirelessly to organize their communities and restore the green spaces in their cities. The GBM became a model for what an LNGO should be: a community effort that challenged the state's destructive development schemes and fought for the rights of its citizens on their own terms.

[1] Wangari Maathai, *The Green Belt Movement: Sharing the Approach and the Experience* (Lantern Books, 2004), 86.
[2] Wangari Maathai, *Unbowed: A Memoir* (Anchor Books, 2006), 175.

★★★

Foreign humanitarianism has been a critical factor in Africa's welfare and development programs since the influx of European Christian missionaries during the nineteenth century. Like these missionaries the international nongovernmental organizations of the late twentieth and early twenty-first centuries view themselves as humanitarians, this time saving lives rather than souls. Both missionaries and INGOs used the rhetoric of western superiority, whether in terms of "civilization" or "development," to justify their intervention in Africa. Both also highlighted the issues of poverty and human rights, problems that became structural during the colonial era and intensified in the late twentieth century. Missionaries and NGOs have both set their sights on the local community (often an ethnic group), region, or continent rather than the colony or nation-state. This history recounting the rise of the NGO in Africa thus highlights the ways development has been broad in scope but narrow in practice and exposes the gaps in the macroeconomic policies of states and international development agencies. The ad hoc nature of development created a landscape of inequality, with differentiated experiences of education, health, and standards of living across Africa, a point we develop further in Part III of this book. This inequality, in turn, has perpetuated the demand for development interventions, and humanitarian nongovernmental organizations have responded in ways that hamstring postcolonial nations and attempt to remake African culture through human rights.

Africans have not been mere victims or recipients of development interventions. Many people have forged LNGOs that seek to revitalize African civil society and challenge the assumptions and tactics behind development policies of government authorities *and* INGOs. Some LNGOs have had to adopt western discourses of development in order to access funding that otherwise would go toward foreign development agents working in their communities. However, the work of LNGOs sheds light on the diverse interpretations of human rights and development that exist across the continent.

Further Reading

On poverty alleviation see John Iliffe, *The African Poor* (Cambridge University Press, 2009 [orig. 1987]); Nina Munk, *The Idealist: Jeffrey Sachs and the Quest to End Poverty* (Doubleday, 2013).

On the role of missionaries in development see Richard Elphick and Rodney Davenport, eds., *Christianity in South Africa: A Political, Social, and Cultural History* (University of California Press, 1997); Adrian Hastings, *The Church in Africa, 1450–1950* (Oxford University Press, 1994).

On humanitarianism and human rights see Bronwen Everill and Josiah Kaplan, eds., *The History and Practice of Humanitarian Intervention and Aid in Africa* (Palgrave Macmillan, 2013); Dorothy Hodgson, ed., *Gender and Culture at the Limit of Rights* (University of Pennsylvania Press, 2011); Bonny Ibhawoh, *Imperialism and Human Rights: Colonial Discourses of Rights and Liberties in African History* (State University of New York Press,

2007); Linda Mahood, *Feminism and Voluntary Action: Eglantyne Jebb and Save the Children, 1876–1928* (Palgrave Macmillan, 2009); Paul Tiyambe Zeleza and Philip J. McConnaughay, eds., *Human Rights, the Rule of Law, and Development in Africa* (University of Pennsylvania Press, 2011).

On development and NGOs see Gregory Mann, *From Empires to NGOS in the West African Sahel: The Road to Nongovernmentality* (Cambridge University Press, 2015); and Sarah Michael, *Undermining Development: The Absence of Power among Local NGOs in Africa* (James Currey, 2004).

On gender and development see Corrie Decker, *Mobilizing Zanzibari Women: The Struggle for Respectability and Self-Reliance in Colonial East Africa* (Palgrave Macmillan, 2014); Abosede A. George, *Making Modern Girls: A History of Girlhood, Labor, and Social Development in Colonial Lagos* (Ohio University Press, 2014); April Gordon, *Transforming Capitalism and Patriarchy: Gender and Development in Africa* (Lynne Rienner, 1996); and Michael Kevane, *Women and Development in Africa: How Gender Works* (Lynne Rienner, 2004).

Part III
"Problems" in the Development Episteme

CHAPTER 9

Reshaping Huts and Homes

The wife of a Portuguese official wrote the following description of domestic life in southern Africa's Delagoa Bay in 1891:

Lean dogs, cats, pigs, fowls, children (not lean), and sometimes goats, wander and play about the kraals, giving plenty of movement; and for scent! the odour of a long-worn, never-washed Kafir blanket, which is indescribably faint and nasty, and is often painfully apparent long before a kraal is entered. For sound there is the continual chattering or singing of the women, varied by a screaming child or the yelling of some wretched kicked and beaten dog.[1]

Nineteenth-century European travelers and settlers in Africa complained of the pungent assault from the cohabitation of animals and humans in African compounds. At the same time, many of these writers also remarked on the picturesque image of African settlements viewed from afar. European missionaries, explorers, and colonizers who began to travel more extensively in the interior of the continent in the nineteenth century recounted their initial impressions of African rural life as descriptions of huts and residential compounds. The development episteme homed in on domestic space as the first tangible development "problem" in Africa.

European proponents of the civilizing mission portrayed the hut as the quintessential icon of African rural domesticity and everything they thought was wrong with it: the use of semipermanent building materials; the isolation of communities; a lack of protection from slavers,

[1] Rose Monteiro, *Delagoa Bay: Its Natives and Natural History* (George Philip & Son, 1891), 139–140.

conquerors, and wildlife; inappropriate proximity of parents, children, and animals; "unhygienic" conditions for sleeping and eating; and a lack of order in community planning. Missionaries and colonial officials urged Africans to replace round huts with rectangular houses and reform the social, sexual, economic, and cultural characteristics of domestic life. To Europeans, huts represented Africans' inability to think long term or in a linear fashion. Clusters of African huts solidified the notion that African communities were acephalous (headless), without a central authority and that they were in need of strong (foreign) leadership. The fact that many Africans understood huts to represent both domestic and political authority evaded early European observers who believed wholeheartedly in the separation between a male public sphere and private female sphere. European interventionists sought to "civilize" Africans by reshaping huts into "modern" homes, reorganizing villages and towns into disciplined, ordered settlements, and "modernizing" African domestic units into nuclear families. From turning huts into homes in the nineteenth century to clearing "slums" in the twenty-first, campaigns to regulate residential spaces have been at the forefront of the development episteme in Africa.[2]

THE HUT IN AFRICA

European stereotypes about African huts obscured two facts: one, "that a variety of architectural styles, including rectangular, quadrangular, and octagonal, and a wide range of building materials, such as stone, wood, and clay, are of great antiquity throughout the continent," and two, that African forms of housing were rational responses to the environment and its available resources.[3] Homes across the continent came in the form of permanent, semipermanent, or temporary structures and were made of diverse materials, including mud, sticks, grass, leather, dung, and other resources from the local environment. African huts varied widely in size, shape, material, durability, and purpose. Africans were adept at protecting their homes from the

[2] Richard Hull, *African Cities and Towns before the European Conquest* (W. W. Norton, 1976).
[3] Ambe J. Njoh, *Tradition, Culture and Development in Africa: Historical Lessons for Modern Development Planning* (Ashgate, 2006), 177.

everyday dangers of weather, wild animals, and insects. Some African huts were made with dirt floors covered with mats, but more commonly, cow dung or ox fat was used to seal floors and walls. Cow dung was particularly effective at keeping dust down and sealing homes from moisture, vermin, and other nuisances. In southern Africa, many hut foundations were made of sand from ant heaps, which was sturdier and more resistant to moisture than other soils.[4] Thatched roofs made of wood and grass acted as weatherproofing. Some people, such as the Herero of present-day Namibia, spread ox hides over the top of huts to further insulate them. Rural communities along the Swahili Coast of East Africa and among the Ngoni of South Africa used mangrove poles from coastal forests as the main structures of support in mud and stone houses. Durable weatherproofing and constant upkeep made for more long-lasting structures. The fact that the huts of agriculturalists and mixed farmers took between a few weeks and several months to construct indicates that they were built to last years, sometimes decades, contrary to the European assumptions that these were temporary structures.

Pastoralist and other transhumant communities, such as the Fulbe or Fulani of West Africa, constructed less permanent abodes meant to last for a season or two, after which they would relocate in search of better grazing land for their livestock. Those who migrated every few weeks or months had little use for large, sturdy domestic structures. Given that less labor went into building pastoralist huts than those of more permanent settlement, they were more susceptible to rain and wind damage and required frequent repair. Materials used in hut construction were sometimes repurposed. For example, strips of leather affixed to the doorway in Maasai abodes of East Africa were transformed into a donkey saddle when the group moved to a new camp.[5]

Hut construction and the structure of compounds reflected local social and political relationships. Rarely in African societies did a nuclear family (a husband, wife, and their children) reside together

---

[4] Laurence P. Kirwan, "Recent Archaeology in British Africa," *Journal of the Royal African Society* 37:149 (1938) 496; Heinrich Vedder, Carl Hugo Linsingen Hahn, and Louis Fourie, *The Native Tribes of South West Africa* (Cape Times, 1928), 181; D. H. Reader, *The Zulu Tribe in Transition: The Makhanya of Southern Natal* (Manchester University Press, 1966), 43.

[5] Kaj Blegvad Andersen, *African Traditional Architecture: A Study of the Housing and Settlement Patterns of Rural Kenya* (Oxford University Press, 1977), 184.

in one hut. Often several people of different generations or ages resided in one house or compound. In many polygynous households separate huts existed for the husband and for each of his wives or concubines with their children. Households of Muslim Hausa communities in northern Nigeria included a central courtyard to ensure segregation of men and women, as well as a conical "entrance hut."[6] Once they reached a certain age (usually between eight and fifteen years old), boys in some African communities would leave their mother's homes to live with their fathers, stay on their own, or move in with other boys their age. Girls often stayed with their mothers until marriage. Sometimes pubescent unmarried girls lived together in their own huts, such as occurred among Luo communities of East Africa.[7] Whereas hut construction was often the responsibility of a young bachelor preparing for marriage, this was women's work in some Maasai communities and among the Elmolo of the Lake Turkana region.[8] In virilocal settlements women moved to their husbands' compounds. In some uxorilocal, matrilineal communities such as the Chewa of Malawi, a young man would go to his future wife's village and build a hut for himself and her there.

9.1 Architectural diversity in precolonial Africa

Many forms of residential and community settlements existed in precolonial Africa, including portable tents for long-distance traders in the West African Sahel, adobe brick houses in cities such as Gao and Timbuktu in Mali, square huts in the Asante Kingdom in Ghana, large coral and limestone houses in the Swahili cities of East Africa, and the stone structures of Great Zimbabwe (Zimbabwe) and of Engaruka in what is now Tanzania. Europeans admired these structures but often found other reasons to disparage them. For example, Europeans compared African homes to pigsties back home and assumed stone

---

[6] J. C. Moughtin, "The Traditional Settlements of the Hausa People," *Town Planning Review* 35:1 (1964) 21–34 at 26.

[7] Audrey Butt, *The Nilotes of the Anglo-Egyptian Sudan and Uganda* (International African Institute, 1952), 118.

[8] Bo Vagnby and Alan H. Jacobs, "Kenya: Traditional Housing of the Elmolo," *Ekistics* 38:227 (1974) 240–243 at 243.

structures were the work of visitors from other parts of the world.[1] In the 1920s British anthropologist P. Amaury Talbot noticed that the square homes he encountered in northern Nigeria were "well adapted to the climate." He explained, "they provide good protection from rain and storms and, though the rooms are small and close, yet those with thick clay walls are cool and the inmates are well guarded from the great variation in temperature."[2] Talbot even conceded that this square architecture may have been indigenous because of its suitability to the climate, but he went on to compare them to Greek, Roman, and Egyptian structures, implying that "foreign influences" must have led to this development in Nigeria. Despite this diversity in actual housing formations of precolonial Africa, the hut became the most salient symbol of African domesticity – and everything wrong with it – in the development episteme.

[1]   Klas Rönnbäck, *Labour and Living Standards in Pre-colonial West Africa: The Case of the Gold Coast* (Routledge, 2016), 141–142; R. N. Hall, "The Great Zimbabwe," *Journal of the Royal African Society* 4:15 (1905) 295–300.
[2]   P. Amaury Talbot, "Some Foreign Influences on Nigeria," *Journal of the Royal African Society* 24:95 (1925) 178–201 at 199.

African homes, often termed "wattle and daub" structures, epitomized the distinction between European and African civilizations for missionaries and colonial administrators, but not all Europeans found the African hut repulsive. Some seventeenth- and eighteenth-century European settlers and Trekboers in the Eastern Cape of South Africa adopted Khoikhoi methods of hut building along with other domestic practices like using animal skins for storing and processing food.[9] They found indigenous housing styles more effective at keeping out vermin and protecting the inhabitants from rain and wind. By the nineteenth century, however, Europeans perceived the African hut as the epitome of primitivism.

[9]   Richard Elphick and Robert Shell, "Intergroup Relations: Khoikhoi, Settlers, Slaves and Free Blacks, 1652–1795," in Richard Elphick and Hermann Buhr Giliomee, eds., *The Shaping of South African Societies, 1652–1840* (Wesleyan University Press, 1979), 184–239 at 228.

RESHAPING HUTS INTO HOMES

The first step in attempting to reshape African lifestyles was to reorganize compounds of round huts into parallel streets with rectangular homes. King Leopold II of Belgium instituted this policy of reform in the Congo Free State. In 1905, after some of Leopold's atrocities related to the rubber trade came to light, Mark Twain published the satirical *King Leopold's Soliloquy: A Defense of His Congo Rule*, in which he declared, among other things, that the Belgians burned the villages of the Congolese people. Two years later the Congo Free State administration issued *An Answer to Mark Twain*, which included more than thirty pages of photographs as evidence of the transformation of Congo from a country "steeped in the most abject barbary" to one "born to civilisation and progress." One set of photos showed the difference between villages of "the past," which were "untidy," and those of "the present," which were "kept according to Medical Officer's Instructions" (see Figures 9.1 and 9.2).[10]

The reshaping of round huts into square homes and compounds into neighborhoods with linear streets entailed simultaneous geometric restructuring of settled communities and reformulation of African minds and morals. Missionaries were the first to intervene on a grand scale because they had at their disposal a displaced community in freed slaves, whose need for homes made them the ideal targets of instruction. To missionaries freed slaves were blank slates, people in search of an identity and a community. They did not recognize the identities and cultures they brought with them to the mission stations. In addition to providing emancipated individuals with new clothing and new Christian names, missionaries had Africans build their own rectangular houses in order to reorient their "hearts and minds" toward the "civilizing" cause. In his history of Magomero, a nineteenth-century Christian Missionary Society settlement in Malawi, Landeg White explained,

Housing was an immediate necessity and so the Bishop with Scudamore ... began building, getting in the corner posts and frames of two houses within the week.

Corner posts! It was as deliberate a metaphor as Procter's "new ground." All the huts presented by Chigunda were round, with conical thatched roofs supported on posts which provided each hut with a circular shaded veranda. As at the Cape, where straight lines of rectangular houses with neat gardens

---

[10]   Anon., *An Answer to Mark Twain* (A. & G. Bulens Brothers, 1907), 6, 24–25.

were the sign of Christian dwellings, so at Magomero "civilisation" began by squaring the circle.[11]

Straight lines symbolized rationality, order, and discipline. These lines metaphorically delineated between the aspects of daily life: prayer, work, and leisure. They also signified new definitions of the "family" in terms of one man, one woman, and their children, now symbolically separated into different rooms for parents and offspring.

Africans learned how to reconstruct their homes by participating in missionary and colonial construction projects, often as voluntary or coerced unpaid labor. Freed slaves and converts living on mission stations built residential units, churches, schools, latrines, and even the missionaries' and officials' homes. During the colonial era students, soldiers, prisoners, villagers, and those who could not afford to pay taxes were compelled erect the infrastructure of the colonial state. Missionaries and colonial officials argued that participation in these construction projects manually trained Africans in modern building techniques *and* domestic roles, skills deemed necessary for their development.

These transformations were also intended to confine the domestic realm of daily life within the household. African compounds, villages, and states did not necessarily delineate so clearly between the domestic and the political, but colonial officials refused to recognize the importance of African women, marriage, and kinship to local lineages and political alliances. In French Guinea colonists literally and figuratively removed the household from the realm of politics.[12] Historian Emily Osborn argues that Baté state formation in Guinea must be told as a history of relationships between and among the men and women of the ruling Kaba household, symbolized by the fact that the royal residence served as the seat of governance. With the arrival of French colonialism in the early 1900s came an entirely new administrative center in which the courthouse, the train station, and government buildings were positioned at a distance from the homes of French administrators. Straight lines and rectangular buildings in French colonial architecture conveyed rationality and technology, while the distance between residential and administrative sectors of town symbolized the separation of the private from the public spheres and the personal from the political. Missionary and colonial transformations of

[11] Landeg White, *Magomero: Portrait of an African Village* (Cambridge University Press, 1987), 25.
[12] Emily Lynn Osborn, *Our New Husbands Are Here: Households, Gender, and Politics in a West African State from the Slave Trade to Colonial Rule* (Ohio University Press, 2011).

Untidy Villages

The past

FIGURES 9.1 AND 9.2 "Untidy Villages" of "The Past" vs. "Villages kept according to Medical Officer's Instructions" of "The Present" in the Congo Free State. Source: Anon., *An Answer to Mark Twain* (A. & G. Bulens Brothers, 1907), 24–25

Villages kept according to Medical Officer's Instructions

The present

FIGURES 9.1 AND 9.2 (cont.)

African homes reinforced and reinterpreted patriarchy in terms of the gendered division between a private, domestic, and female sphere and a public, political, and male sphere.

DOMESTICATING LABOR

As missionaries built new homes and stations from the ground up, European officials looked to huts as a source of revenue for the colony in the form of the hut tax. The hut became a tangible entity over which Europeans could assert their authority directly. The hut tax also provided the colonial administrations with crucial demographic information in the period before colonial censuses or social surveys. More importantly, the hut tax was intended to pressure Africans, especially young men, into the wage labor market for colonial industries. British businessman and parliamentarian Lord Hindlip (Charles Allsopp) wrote in 1905, "It seems that a tax on wives on the system in force in parts of South Africa would help to create a supply of labour. There can be no doubt that at some future period the hut tax will be superseded by a poll tax, which, though not applicable at present to outlying districts, would be beneficial in towns and near stations where loafers and general riff-raff not only abound but flourish amazingly."[13] French territories implemented a head tax rather than a hut tax from the start and eventually all colonial governments across the continent moved to the head tax as a tactic for labor recruitment. Even where the head or poll tax was in place, however, the tax collector often calculated the amount owed by counting the number of houses in a village and multiplying that by the estimated number of inhabitants per residence.

9.2 Fighting colonial hut taxes

Africans were no strangers to taxes. During the precolonial era, powerful chiefs and states asserted their dominance over neighboring communities by demanding tribute in exchange for protection. The difference under colonialism was the individual hut or human was now the unit by which this tax was calculated, and taxes became a much heavier financial burden on families. Regional chiefs

---

[13] Lord Hindlip, *British East Africa: Past, Present, and Future* (T. Fisher Unwin, 1905), 68.

responsible for paying tribute in the precolonial period were given monetary rewards and other incentives for collecting the fees from their constituents during the colonial era. Many Africans failed to see the logic in colonial tax policies. Why did they have to pay for homes they built, owned, and occupied? Why should they hand over tax on dependents for whom they maintained financial responsibility, especially when their dependents' labor was directed away from the lineage? Should not the colonial state compensate them for this loss of labor and encroachment on their land? Unsurprisingly, early attempts to impose hut and head taxes sparked widespread protest. Early tax rebellions arose in 1854 in southern Gold Coast, 1898 in Sierra Leone, 1905 in Kamerun (later split into the French-controlled Cameroon and British-controlled Cameroon), 1906 in South Africa, 1908–1909 in Nyasaland, 1913 in Togo, and 1929 in Nigeria. Resentment toward chiefs, soldiers, and other Africans who served as intermediaries counting huts and collecting colonial taxes grew to a crescendo in the 1920s and 1930s.[1]

---

[1] Michael Crowder (with LaRay Denzer), "Bai Bureh and the Sierra Leone Hut Tax War of 1898," in Michael Crowder, *Colonial West Africa: Collected Essays* (Routledge, 2012 [orig. 1978]), 61–103.

The amounts required under colonial tax laws varied widely, but were often quite burdensome. In nineteenth-century British territories one shilling (£0.05, equivalent to about $8 in 2019 US currency) per head was required in the Gold Coast whereas ten shillings (£.50, around $80 in 2019) per hut was the rate in Sierra Leone.[14] Other dues, such as the marriage registration fees and taxes on livestock, added to this burden. Across British Africa the goal was to set a tax at an amount equivalent to two months' wages, but tax rates varied in the different colonies and steadily increased during the twentieth century. Even where rates were relatively low, families with little access to the cash economy struggled to come up with the money for taxes.

Hut taxes in German territories varied. They were paid in marks or rupees and ranged from about $1.50 to $2.25 at the time (about $40 to $60 in 2019). When the hut tax was introduced in German East Africa in 1897 individuals who normally would have maintained separate huts

---

[14] All currency estimates are approximate calculations based on estimated inflation between the period 1900–1918 and 2018–2019 currency values and exchange rates.

resided together in one abode so as to reduce their tax payments. When German officials got wind of this strategy they replaced the hut tax with a head tax of two rupees (about $0.36 or $10 in 2019) per adult male.[15]

In French territories a head tax was imposed from the start and applied to all male Africans from the age of fourteen in French West Africa and eighteen in French Central Africa. Inconsistencies in calculating chronological ages meant that during the early colonial era some children many years younger than the stipulated ages were forced to pay or work for the state in lieu of payment, the more likely outcome. Rates varied and were generally low in the late nineteenth and early twentieth centuries, but after World War I tax amounts increased dramatically. The tax did not account for a significant portion of the revenue for the administrations, but it did exactly what it was intended to do: it directed many people into the state's forced labor system (*corvée*). Taxes were calculated in terms of labor time such that men between the ages of eighteen and fifty years were expected to provide up to ten days of work for the state per year as their "tax" contribution. In addition to the regular *corvée* labor/tax system, the lieutenant governors of French West African territories could at any time demand an additional labor tax called *prestation* specifically for public works projects.[16]

While hut and head taxes were imposed to coerce young men into the labor market, labor recruitment challenged colonial domesticity campaigns. Mine compounds, military barracks, and other large settlements for housing colonial laborers undermined missionary attempts to reorient Africans into nuclear families living in single-family homes. Several unrelated young men, often from different ethnolinguistic communities, would share rooms and live for months or years away from elders, wives, and children. By the 1940s and 1950s many laborers had successfully lobbied for married or family housing, an expense most colonial administrations and companies were loath to cover. Some missionaries and colonial officials supported workers' demands for a "family wage" and family housing because they echoed western patriarchal ideals around domesticity.

[15]   Arthur J. Knoll and Hermann J. Hiery, eds., *The German Colonial Experience: Select Documents on German Rule in Africa, China, and the Pacific 1884–1914* (University Press of America, 2010).
[16]   Babacar Fall, *Social History in French West Africa: Forced Labor, Labor Market, Women and Politics* (South-South Exchange Programme for Research on the History of Development [SEPHIS] and the Centre for Studies in Social Sciences, Calcutta [CSSC], 2002), 5–10.

9.3 Soldiers of the state

The colonial administration of German East Africa recruited African soldiers, called *askari*, who also served as the primary tax collectors. Many East Africans despised the *askari* for their violent methods of what appeared to some people as extortion. The government introduced the hut tax in 1897 as part of its campaign to quell the Hehe revolt. Tax collection and suppression of protest were equally important duties for the *askari*, particularly because the tax collector could take a cut of up to 10 percent. The lucrative job of the *askari* allowed him to establish himself as a patriarch, or "big man," on the military compound. The compound was called a *boma*, the term used in many local languages to mean everything from cattle enclosure to fortified village. Historian Michelle Moyd points out that the housing styles of the *askari* varied greatly depending on whether they were in an urban or rural district. Most compounds incorporated local architectural features or settlement patterns, such as a communal courtyard where meals were taken and a *baraza*, the seating area in front of the house where one visited with neighbors and friends. Moyd argues that the German colonial state tolerated a degree of autonomy in the *askari* settlements because it allowed the soldiers to amass dependents who provided free labor to their families and the state.[1] Unlike the large dormitories for miners in Belgian Congo, Northern Rhodesia, and South Africa – and certainly distinct from the slum-like African housing structures built on the outskirts of segregated cities such as Dakar, Bamako, Nairobi, and Johannesburg – *askari* compounds were symbols of the soldiers' elevated status and power in German East Africa.

[1] Michelle R. Moyd, *Violent Intermediaries: African Soldiers, Conquest, and Everyday Colonialism in German East Africa* (Ohio University Press, 2014), 148–181.

MAKING MODERN HOMES, CITIES, AND TOWNS

Whereas early twentieth-century colonial interventions were geared toward labor recruitment, by the interwar period (1920s and 1930s) officials concerned about the breakdown of African family structures and the poor health of laborers redirected the spotlight onto African domesticity. Two contradictory impulses influenced colonial policies and practices at this time: one that sought to preserve indigenous patriarchal structures keeping young people and women in check, and another that sought to modernize and "civilize" African homes and families. Whereas the former approach reified the authority of chiefs and male elders, the latter challenged African traditions like polygyny. Often colonial officials took the former approach and missionaries the latter, but in either case the physical transformation of the home – both external and internal – signified the degree to which the African family adopted "modern" domestic practices.

Even where officials aimed to preserve African social norms, they promoted "model villages" or "model huts" in an effort to educate the African public about domesticity. If Africans could not be convinced to give up the hut, then the hut had to adapt to "modern" conditions. Children were to sleep in spaces cordoned off from parents, and animals were to be kept outside. Cooking was to be done in a separate room from the center of the home or outside the hut where there would be better ventilation. French development schemes in Mali resettled families into ideal villages and homes with proper sanitation, irrigation, and transportation systems.[17] Colonial domesticity campaigns ignored the social logic of African families and indigenous practices of hygiene such as ablution rituals among Muslims or the use of cow dung to seal huts from weather and vermin. These reforms were intended to modernize African homes and, by extension, improve the health and productivity of African laborers. They also aided the capitalist marketing and distribution of European manufactured goods like soap, forks and knives, mirrors, shoes, blankets, radios, furniture, clocks, clothing, and other products moving through imperial trade networks.[18]

Though Europeans assumed Africans lived primarily in huts and villages, many Africans resided in urban centers before European settlement and colonization. The size and population of cities varied greatly, ranging anywhere from 5,000 to a few million

[17]   Monica M. van Beusekom, *Negotiating Development: African Farmers and Colonial Experts at the Office Du Niger, 1920–1960* (Heinemann, 2002), 33–56.
[18]   Timothy Burke, *Lifebuoy Men, Lux Women: Commodification, Consumption, and Cleanliness in Modern Zimbabwe* (Duke University Press, 1996).

people.[19] The cities across the continent had unique architectural traditions and spatial logics, from the narrow walkways in between the limestone houses of Swahili stone towns to the walled cities of Jenne, Great Zimbabwe, Notsé, Kano, and Katsina. Some cities were designed to facilitate long-distance trade and others were oriented toward the palaces of ruling families. For example, all major roads led to the Kabaka's palace in the center of the Buganda Empire located in what is now Uganda. People flocked to the central markets of Yoruba and Hausa cities in Nigeria to buy beautiful woven and dyed cloth, leather, and metal luxury items.[20] The Kongo Kingdom's capital at M'banza Kongo (contemporary Angola), located on a high plateau near the Luezi River, was both the center of the interior-coast slave trade route and the seat of power for the kingdom.

Urbanization expanded dramatically and rapidly during the colonial era. New cities like Nairobi sprang up alongside the railroad tracks and others like Johannesburg erupted into existence with the discovery of valuable minerals. In cities with a longer complicated colonial history like Dakar the layering of historical eras in architecture, town planning, and urban cultures makes it difficult to disentangle "precolonial" from "colonial" elements. Other cities that either came into existence or saw a large population increase during the colonial era did so from the influx of migrant laborers. The recruitment of rural young men for temporary or seasonal work in colonial cities posed a problem for city planners and urban residents. During the early 1900s colonial governments focused on town planning and public works projects to improve trade, transport, and communication avenues. These projects required large numbers of workers, but many colonial officials opposed the permanent settlement of African migrants in towns and cities. In Nairobi, Johannesburg, Lagos, Accra, Dakar, Brazzaville, Conakry, and elsewhere the question of who belonged permanently and where they would and could live dominated local politics and policies. One's gender, age, marital status, ethnicity, and racial identity influenced

---

[19] Dennis D. Cordell and Joel W. Gregory, eds., *African Population and Capitalism: Historical Perspectives* (University of Wisconsin Press, 1987).

[20] C. Magbaily Fyle, *Introduction to the History of African Civilizations: Volume I, Precolonial Africa* (University Press of America, 1999); Basil Davidson, *Lost Cities of Africa* (Back Bay Books, 1987); Graham Connah, *African Civilizations: An Archaeological Perspective*. Second edition (Cambridge University Press, 2001 [1987]).

one's ability to claim urban citizenship. Despite these restrictions, the population of cities ballooned and diversified after World War II. By the 1950s the need for permanent housing for urban laborers and their families became widely apparent, and more state planning and funding went toward the development of urban housing.[21]

Colonial-era urbanization increased demand for housing among laborers and others looking for new social and economic opportunities. Some government officials, African employees, and migrant laborers lived in European-style homes or tenement buildings. Most urbanites who did not live in labor compounds resided in temporary homes or rented rooms from wealthy landlords. Some Europeans pushed to destroy "native" style residences and replace them with European homes. Others sought to "improve" African homes by "modernizing" huts or refashioning African domestic space entirely by redefining the sleeping and social arrangements of family members.

Colonial and postcolonial campaigns for the rectangular home rested on a belief in the interdependency between "modern" home construction, higher standards of living, and increased productivity of labor. Interventions promoted distinct gender roles declaring women as caretakers of the home and family and adult men as the breadwinners and heads of households. The state imagined men as wage laborers and women as housewives whose domestic care optimized men's ability to perform their labor. These gender roles assumed that women oversaw the "private" space of the home and that men worked in the public sphere. In postwar southwestern Nigeria male railway workers embraced these principles as fundamental to their strikes in 1945 and 1946. Despite the fact that many Nigerian women brought significant income into the household through their trade activities, male laborers declared themselves the primary earners and heads of households based on their wage employment. As historian Lisa Lindsay explains, these men lobbied the colonial and postcolonial administrations for better wages and other benefits on the basis of their desire to build modern households with nuclear families.[22] The strikers reified the colonial concepts of masculinity and modern domesticity and evoked the colonial arguments about the connection between domesticity and

---

[21]   Richard Harris, "From Trusteeship to Development: How Class and Gender Complicated Kenya's Housing Policy, 1939–1963," *Journal of Historical Geography* 34:2 (2008) 311–337.

[22]   Lisa A. Lindsay, *Working with Gender: Wage Labor and Social Change in Southwestern Nigeria* (Heinemann, 2003).

labor productivity. In doing so, they convinced the state to provide better housing for themselves and their families.

Many people did not cooperate with the social engineering behind housing reforms. New domestic arrangements emerged in urban areas that challenged the colonial agenda, such as *métis* (racially mixed) families in Senegal, women-centered households in Nairobi, Black middle-class neighborhoods in Johannesburg, and short-term cohabitation in the mining compounds of Zambia. What and who defined the "modern" home in twentieth-century Africa was highly variable and contingent upon economic and social circumstances. For instance, when plastic became available in the mid-1960s it emerged as a staple material in "traditional" Hausa homes in Northern Nigeria.[23] This was not necessarily the innovation development experts envisioned. J. C. Moughtin, a scholar of urban design, wrote in 1964 that while he appreciated the "unique decorative character" of Hausa settlements and their relation to "social and religious customs," he maintained that these "must undoubtedly change to be replaced by a rectangular discipline based upon a regular blockwork construction."[24] Colonial interventions demonstrate that development efforts to reform African domestic architecture are rarely about design alone. Western planners insisted upon parallel lines and right angles in African homes in order to discipline the "African mindset" into accepting a "scientific" approach to residential planning. The assumption that western engineering is superior continued and continues to influence development housing reforms into the twenty-first century.

INFORMAL SETTLEMENTS IN THE MODERN CITY

As urbanization rapidly expanded during the colonial and postcolonial eras, cities struggled to deal with the eruption of informal settlements, commonly called "shantytowns" or "slums." For example, the city of Lagos in Nigeria went from an estimated population of 5,000 people in the late nineteenth century, to 325,000 by 1950, to a whopping 14.4 million people in 2020. With each successive wave of migration into cities during the twentieth and twenty-first centuries, the housing

[23] Moughtin, "The Traditional Settlements of the Hausa People."
[24] Ibid., 21, 33.

market has been unable to keep up. During the colonial period governments discouraged permanent relocation to cities by refusing to build viable housing infrastructure. Instead, many colonial governments turned a blind eye to the development of informal housing settlements on the edges of the urban centers. In many cases these "illegal settlers" squatted on land of questionable ownership, which later sparked conflict over land and housing rights. Colonial and postcolonial governments tacitly accepted the development of informal settlements because they provided a pool of cheap labor for businesses, elite households, and government modernization projects.

Informal settlements consist of temporary housing usually built of disposable materials, such as corrugated tin sheets, construction site debris, and other discarded items. As most informal settlements do not have access to electricity, running water, or sanitation, they have become symbolic and visible representations of Africa's obstacles to development. Given that African national governments have had limited ability to provide affordable housing in urban centers, informal settlements have expanded more rapidly across the continent since the 1960s. For example, whereas 16 percent of the global population live in informal settlements, this figure sits at 24 percent in South Africa. In some African cities, nearly 90 percent of the urban population live in informal settlements.[25]

Today the "shanty" has replaced the hut as a representation of Africans' inability to live a "civilized" and healthful life. African leaders of the early postcolonial era stressed the need to update African homes and communities with access to electricity, clean water, and sanitation. Massive resettlement projects such as those associated with the Akosombo hydroelectric dam scheme in 1960s Ghana and the villagization campaign of the *ujamaa* development program in 1960s and 1970s Tanzania uprooted rural people from their homes and villages in the name of modernization and development. In urban areas too the clearing of "slums," street children, and other "illegal" residents in the South African neighborhoods of Sophiatown and Alexandra during the 1950s and 1960s, in Harare, Zimbabwe as part of Mugabe's Operation Murambatsvina (Operation Drive Out Rubbish) in 2005, and more recently in

---

[25] For more information see the World Bank Blogs, Luis Triveno, "Eight Stubborn Facts about Housing Policies," July 5, 2016, https://blogs.worldbank.org/sustaina blecities/eight-stubborn-facts-about-housing-policies, accessed January 3, 2020.

Lagos, Luanda, and other African cities replicate colonial approaches to urban planning. Poor and working-class people's homes and neighborhoods in wealthy cities are discounted as illegal "slums" consisting of ill-equipped and unsanitary "shanties."

Informal settlements represent the "dark side" of development and modernization across the continent. Like the "slums" in cities of the global north, they serve as a stark reminder that the wealth gap is growing under late capitalism. African governments and the United Nations (UN) have sought to eliminate "slums" and "shantytowns" by providing modern housing for their citizens, yet these efforts take significant time to complete and they generate resistance from residents. Informal settlement dwellers face either relocation, often to outlying areas far away from their jobs and families, or significantly higher rents of new housing constructed in their neighborhoods. When informal settlement residents in Africa resist efforts to relocate them, the international development community reads this as evidence that Africans refuse to develop, a trope crystalized in the development episteme.

9.4 The KwaZulu-Natal Elimination and Prevention of Re-emergence of Slums Act, 2007

Upon his election as the president of South Africa in 1994, Nelson Mandela promised that the government would build more homes for people without them. The housing crisis in South Africa would not end overnight. A significant portion of urban dwellers in South Africa continues to live in large settlements consisting of thousands of informal shacks. The state considers them illegal because they are unregulated. Numerous governments and development organizations (including the UN) have set their sights on eliminating informal settlements globally. These "eyesores," as they are often called, are a constant reminder that "modernity" is the privilege of the few.

The UN's Millennium Development Goals (MDGs) of 2000 ranked reform of informal settlements the seventh most important goal on its list. Governments across Africa responded, not by attempting to improve access to quality housing but rather by eradicating informal settlements, often without alternative housing options for their inhabitants. While this was not the intention of the UN, it was one of the outcomes. In 2007 the regional government of KwaZulu-Natal, a province in South Africa, passed the Elimination and Prevention of Re-emergence of Slums Act, in line with the UN's MDGs. It gave the government the authority to destroy any informal settlements on public land and allowed owners of private land to evict shack dwellers.[1] All evicted residents were forced to live in temporary housing in transit camps indefinitely until the state could provide permanent housing for them. The transit camps were located outside of the cities, far from where most residents worked. This 2007 program was intended to act as a model for the rest of the country.

Former shack dwellers frustrated by the forced removals formed the Abahlali baseMjondolo (AbM) ("Residents of the Shacks"). The AbM protestors actively resisted the destruction of informal settlements sanctioned by the new "Slum Act" in Durban and took the KwaZulu-Natal government to court over the Act. Initially the government won in the regional court, though AbM appealed to the Constitutional Court of South Africa and prevailed in October 2009. The AbM successfully argued that the "Slum Act" contradicted the South African constitution and that the government and development organizations need to prioritize the social rather than the economic value of urban land.

While the UN's MDGs (recently renamed as Sustainable Development Goals) reifies older development assumptions about "modern" housing, the success of the AbM demonstrates that residents challenge this concept by demanding their right to determine where and how they live.

[1] Marie Huchzermeyer, *Cities with "Slums": From Informal Settlement Eradication to a Right to the City in Africa* (University of Cape Town Press, 2011).

★★★

Whether in the name of civilization, modernity, or modernization, interventions to transform the composite materials, structural designs, and locations of African homes represented the development agenda to reform and mobilize African domesticity and labor. Discourses on improvement masked the political and economic agendas at work and ignored the indigenous logic of African residential construction and organization in both rural and urban housing. The development episteme has demanded that Africans reform architectural and social domestic practices. The scientific work of early twentieth-century urban planners set the stage for what "modern" urban spaces would look like in African cities. Building square or rectangular houses meant embracing development.

Urbanization has far outpaced the ability of states and private enterprise to provide affordable, modern housing for citizens. Urban Africans have begun to fight back against the assumptions made about informal settlements by development specialists and city planners from the global north. These citizens, such as the members of the AbM in South Africa, are challenging their governments to see urban residential areas as social spaces that belong to all citizens, not just those wealthy enough to afford modern housing. In their challenge informal settlement dwellers are forcing the international development community to Africanize the development episteme.

Moreover, western scholars have begun to recognize the artistic and architectural value of African indigenous homes. The plethora of articles featuring African "traditional" architecture and house construction in the journal *African Arts*, established in 1967, demonstrates this renaissance in African residential construction.[26] Images of "shanty towns" have even become an artistic form of their own, for instance on pinterest.com and shutterstock.com, demonstrating the growing impact of African city dwellers' resistance to development stereotypes. The interplay between celebrating the vibrancy of African urban life and disparaging these urban settlements as unhealthy, unsafe, and illegal invokes colonial-era interventions into African housing that simultaneously admired African ingenuity and sought to reshape African domestic logic. Artistic and cultural forms cannot be separated from the economic and social realities that produce them. Perhaps efforts to develop African domestic spaces and families will soon take into consideration whether the new homes

---

[26] G. F. Rohrmann, "House Decoration in Southern Africa," *African Arts* 7:3 (1974) 18–21; Labelle Prussin, "Traditional Asante Architecture," *African Arts* 13:2 (1980) 57–87; Anitra C. E. Nettleton, "The Venda Model Hut," *African Arts* 18:3 (1985) 87–98; and Merrick Posnansky, "Dwellings of West Africa," *African Arts* 20:1 (1986) 82–83.

envisioned represent the economic, social, cultural, and political ideals of their inhabitants.

Further Reading

On housing practices related to the civilizing mission and early colonization see David Livingstone, *The Last Journals of David Livingstone, in Central Africa, from 1865 to His Death, 1866–1873 Continued by a Narrative of His Last Moments and Sufferings, Obtained from His Faithful Servants Chuma and Susi* (Library of Alexandria, 2012); Michelle R. Moyd, *Violent Intermediaries: African Soldiers, Conquest, and Everyday Colonialism in German East Africa* (Ohio University Press, 2014); and Landeg White, *Magomero: Portrait of an African Village* (Cambridge University Press, 1987).

On gender and domesticity see Lisa A. Lindsay, *Working with Gender: Wage Labor and Social Change in Southwestern Nigeria* (Heinemann, 2004); Emily Lynn Osborn, *Our New Husbands Are Here: Households, Gender, and Politics in a West African State from the Slave Trade to Colonial Rule* (Ohio University Press, 2011); and Luise White, *Comforts of Home: Prostitution in Colonial Nairobi* (University of Chicago Press, 1990).

On town planning and urban life see William Cunningham Bissell, *Urban Design, Chaos, and Colonial Power in Zanzibar* (Indiana University Press, 2011); Hilary Jones, *The Métis of Senegal: Urban Life and Politics in French West Africa* (Indiana University Press, 2013); Peter Marris, *Family and Social Change in an African City: A Study of Rehousing in Lagos* (Routledge, 1962); and Ambe J. Njoh, *Planning Power: Town Planning and Social Control in Colonial Africa* (Routledge, 2007).

CHAPTER 10

Lessons in Separate Development

A textbook used in French West African schools during the 1920s began one lesson with the following passage:

I live in Africa. I am an African. I have black skin. I belong to the black race. I am a black African. My teacher is French. He is a European. He has white skin. He belongs to the white race. He's a white man. The black has curly hair that he shaves completely. The white has straight hair blonde or black, which he combs with a brush with care. The black grows little beard. The white has a beard and a mustache which he can let grow or shave often. The black wears few clothes. He wears full and light cotton garments. The white is better dressed. He wears clothing made of woolen cloth.[1]

This textbook and others like it presented stereotypical images of Africans as villagers who lived in huts, worked on farms, and did simple crafts in contrast to "modern" Frenchmen who lived in "beautiful" towns with stone houses, hospitals, schools, telegraph stations, and administrative buildings. While colonial lessons distinguished between racially coded "African" and "French" worlds, education scholar Gail Kelly argues, students themselves created a new "separate world of educated Africans."[2] Colonial schools instilled in African students the notion that Europeans and Africans were on separate paths of development, but Africans did not accept these lessons passively. Kelly analyzes school essays in which African students wrote about their

[1] J. L. Monod, *Premier Livret de l'Ecolier Soudanais* (Delagrave, 1911), quoted in Gail P. Kelly, "Learning to Be Marginal: Schooling in Interwar French West Africa," *Journal of Asian and African Studies* 21:3–4 (1986) 171–184 at 173.
[2] Ibid., 172.

209

desire to work for the colonial government, live in European-style houses, and buy clothing from "French boutiques" for their wives.[3] At the same time, they celebrated African cultural aesthetics and dreamed of returning to their hometowns to help with farming. Students dismissed the dichotomies between African and French identities or "uncivilized" and "civilized" lifestyles. At the same time, the first generations of western-educated Africans believed they had attained a more advanced stage of development than their non-western-educated counterparts. To them, separate development was a class rather than racial distinction.

By the 1950s and 1960s African graduates of western schools across the continent viewed themselves as modern citizens who would guide their nations toward independence. Western education – introduced by missionaries, expanded by colonial administrations, and Africanized by nationalist leaders – was simultaneously a tool for indoctrinating Africans into colonial ideas about separate development and a weapon used by Africans to undermine the racist foundations of the development episteme.

Education comes in many forms and has many different purposes, such as socialization through art and literature, training in skilled labor, impartation of esoteric knowledge, and inculcation of national or societal values. African indigenous educational practices did all of these things before missionaries and colonial states introduced "formal" schooling. Colonial educators faced a conundrum; they sought to "civilize" Africans in western academic traditions and at the same time to reinforce ideologies of racial difference that undergirded colonialism and the development episteme. This conflict intensified as schools became a place for challenging these ideas and generating one's own ideas about development and nationalism. Some African nationalist movements and postcolonial reforms recentered African epistemologies in the schools. Today, institutions and scholars of the global north still claim to be the experts in technology, science, and medicine, the sciences necessary for solving development "problems," but many African institutions and scholars are at the forefront of development innovations designed for their own communities.

This chapter traces the transformation of the school from the site for instilling ideas about racial and class-based separate development during the colonial era into the key mechanism for ensuring African

---

[3] Ibid., 176–177.

political and economic development today. Modern schooling is here
to stay, but the role education plays in development is up for debate.

RELIGION, CIVILIZATION, AND THE DEVELOPMENT EPISTEME

The civilizing mission of the nineteenth century was not only a Christian
or colonial enterprise. Both Muslim reformers and Christian missionaries
launched campaigns to "civilize" Africans through religious education,
one of the foundations of the development episteme. Historically initiation practices, oral traditions, training and apprenticeships in arts and
crafts, and home-based instruction served as the primary forms of education in Africa. Sex-segregated initiation "schools" for boys and girls, such
as *chir* and *siwidhe* (Luo, Kenya), *jando* and *ukungwi* (Swahili, Tanzania),
bodika and *byale* (northern Sotho, South Africa), and *jow* (Bamana,
Mali), taught children about the history of their lineages and the proper
behaviors expected of men and women in their communities.[4] Rites of
passage often included songs, dances, and feats of strength or endurance
to test the initiates' preparedness for life's difficulties. Where Islam and
Christianity already existed, initiation practices and religious schooling
often coexisted and sometimes coincided. Some religious reformers of
the 1800s and 1900s criticized non-Muslim or non-Christian practices as
"uncivilized," but many Africans found ways to reconcile their cultures
with their religious beliefs.

Islamic education came to Africa with the spread of Islam during the
first millennium. Though elite centers of scholarship such as those at
Cairo and Timbuktu are nearly as old as Islam itself, "modern" Islamic
schools appeared in the nineteenth and twentieth centuries.[5] In

---

[4]   Bethwell A. Ogot, "The Construction of Luo Identity and History," in Luise White,
      Stephan F. Miescher, and David William Cohen, eds., *African Words, African Voices:
      Critical Practices in Oral History* (Indiana University Press, 2001), 31–52; Hans Cory,
      "Jando. Part I: The Construction and Organization of the Jando," *Journal of the Royal
      Anthropological Institute of Great Britain and Ireland* 77:2 (1947) 159–168; "Mishi wa
      Abdala," in Sarah Mirza and Margaret Strobel, eds. and transl., *Three Swahili
      Women: Life Histories from Mombasa, Kenya* (Indiana University Press, 1989),
      69–79; Eileen Jensen Krige, "The Place of North-Eastern Transvaal Sotho in the
      South Bantu Complex," *Africa: Journal of the International African Institute* 11:3 (1938)
      265–293.
[5]   Mansoor Moaddel, *Islamic Modernism, Nationalism, and Fundamentalism: Episode and
      Discourse* (University of Chicago Press, 2005).

Quranic schools Muslim boys and girls received instruction on the Quran, the holy book of Islam, and reading and pronunciation of Arabic. These lessons were intended to teach children to read, memorize, and recite the Quran, an important milestone for Muslim children. In most cases boys had more opportunities for advanced instruction than girls. Islamic modernist movements ushered in modern *madressas* (also spelled *madrasas* or *médersas*), schools that provided comprehensive instruction in Islamic studies as well as lessons in reading, writing, and mathematics. Many modernists also advocated for the education of girls and women.[6] Islamic education reforms arose in the context of European imperialist expansion, and some reformers sought to preempt or prevent westernization. For instance, Sultan Ali bin Hamud in the British Protectorate of the Zanzibar Islands recruited a teacher from Cairo's Al-Azhar University to ensure that Zanzibar's first modern boys' school opened in 1905 with a solid grounding in Islamic studies. The Muslim "civilizing mission" in Africa promoted both Islamic tradition and modern schooling.

Formal schooling was also essential to the modern Christian civilizing mission in Africa. Salvation required acculturation into European languages, values, and social practices, as well as biblical literacy. As discussed in Chapter 2, the civilizing mission dictated complete transformation of a student's daily routine, economic expectations and opportunities, and relationships with parents, elders, and chiefs. As the first Africans to speak, read, and write in European languages, mission school graduates became valuable aides for both colonial knowledge production and religious indoctrination.

The graduates of mission and colonial schools were eligible for the best government jobs open to Africans during the colonial era, but western education also generated new conflicts within communities. After Senegalese student Insa Bâ completed his training at the Lycee Imperiale in Algiers around 1901, French authorities appointed him as a chief, but his appointment did not last long. Historian Martin Klein points out that Insa Bâ's education became a wedge between him and his constituents, causing the French to replace him with his

---

[6] See, for example, Qasim Amin, *The Liberation of Women and The New Woman: Two Documents in the History of Egyptian Feminism*, transl. by Samiha Sidhom Peterson (American University in Cairo Press, 2000 [1992]).

brother.[7] Some Christian converts resented the racial exclusions they faced despite their achievements. One such individual was John Chilembwe, who established an independent African church and led the 1915 uprising in Nyasaland (Malawi). According to historian John McCracken, "Chilembwe threatened the prevailing belief in European hegemony."[8] In South Africa, where racist segregation policies restricted civil service jobs to whites, the products of mission schools such as Lovedale and Fort Hare established the South African Native National Congress, the precursor to the African National Congress (ANC), in 1912.

Muslim and Christian reformers preached against certain cultural practices they considered "backward" or "savage," but many Africans refused to recognize conflicts between culture and religion. The lessons in Muslim schools taught young people to abandon traditional healing practices and instructed girls to remain virgins until marriage.[9] Christian missionary schools also became sites of contention around customs like female circumcision, discussed in Chapter 4. Some European missionaries and African Christians compromised over custom. For example, in Malawi Presbyterian missionaries co-opted and adapted local initiation ceremonies into the church rituals.[10] Both the Christian and Muslim civilizing missions involved patriarchal efforts to undermine African men's and women's authority over the socialization of children. More often than not, they failed to destroy the African customs and beliefs they perceived as contrary to civilization and modernity. The civilizing missions that undergirded the development episteme drove educational reforms in nineteenth- and early twentieth-century Africa, but schooling also became a fruitful site for debating the meaning of development.

[7] Martin A. Klein, "Chiefship in Sine-Saloum (Senegal), 1887–1914," in Victor Turner, ed., *Colonialism in Africa, 1870–1960, Volume Three: Profiles of Change: African Society and Colonial Rule* (Cambridge University Press, 1971), 49–73 at 68–69.

[8] John McCracken, *A History of Malawi, 1859–1966* (James Currey, 2012), 133.

[9] See Adeline Masquelier, *Prayer Has Spoiled Everything: Possession, Power, and Identity in an Islamic Town of Niger* (Duke University Press, 2001), 95–96; and Laura Fair, "Identity, Difference, and Dance: Female Initiation in Zanzibar, 1890 to 1930," *Frontiers: A Journal of Women's Studies* 17:3 (1996) 146–172.

[10] Isabel Apawo Phiri, *Women, Presbyterianism and Patriarchy: Religious Experience of Chewa Women in Central Malawi* (Christian Literature Association in Malawi [Kachere Series, 2007 (orig. 1997)]), 32–36.

COLONIAL CURRICULUM AND SEPARATE DEVELOPMENT

Starting in the early 1900s European colonial administrations standardized education policies like the implementation of racial segregation in schools and institutionalized the notion that Africans were on a separate path of development from that of Europeans. Colonial schools trained Africans in agriculture, carpentry, tailoring, shoemaking, and other crafts to support the colonial economy. Meanwhile, African students and their parents viewed colonial schools as a gateway to lucrative government employment. Assimilationist schools promoted a curriculum similar to that of schools in Europe. Fourah Bay College in Freetown, Sierra Leone was known as the "Athens of West Africa" for its emphasis on western classics.[11] On the other hand, those in favor of "adapted" education for Africans, meaning a curriculum adapted to African social and cultural environments, advocated vocational training in agriculture and other local industries. Generally the French and, to a certain extent, German colonial powers took an assimilationist approach with an emphasis on learning European languages and cultures, whereas the British implemented an adapted education policy. Portuguese, Belgian, and Italian officials embraced the civilizing mission in theory but left schooling primarily in the hands of missionaries. Despite these pedagogical differences, all colonial schools sought to maintain racial difference as a fundamental characteristic of the colonial political economy and justification for separate development.

The French introduced a two-tiered schooling system with "European" schools for Europeans, *originaires* (original inhabitants of the French Four Communes), and *assimilés* or *évolués* ("civilized" Africans), leaving "African" schools to cater to the remainder of the population. In St. Louis (Senegal) the École d'Otages (literally, the "School for Hostages," renamed the School for the Sons of Chiefs and Interpreters in 1892) was opened in 1856 to train boys in clerical subjects like letter writing and bookkeeping to prepare them for work as colonial interpreters and clerks.[12] Other African students attended

---

[11] Daniel J. Paracka Jr., *The Athens of West Africa: A History of International Education at Fourah Bay College, Freetown, Sierra Leone* (Routledge, 2003).

[12] Hilary Jones, *The Métis of Senegal: Urban Life and Politics in French West Africa* (Indiana University Press, 2013), 223.

the two-year preparatory schools where they studied French language and culture. Each territory had an *École primaire supérieure* (higher primary or middle school) for boys from the regional schools who passed the competitive entrance exam. These schools provided four years of technical or administrative training free of charge and often led to government employment. More advanced students continued their schooling in the cities, where they took courses in history, geography, reading, writing, arithmetic, and hygiene. In 1934 on average 4.4 percent of school-aged children were enrolled in school in French West Africa, but educational development was uneven. For example, in Dakar, Senegal 18 percent of school-aged children were enrolled in government schools and nearly 30 percent in private schools, while in the predominantly rural region of Mauritania only 1.5 percent of school-aged children attended school.[13] The French also established Islamic-western hybrid schools and *madrassas* to teach French language and culture alongside religious instruction in regions with a significant Muslim population.

Increased funding of education by colonial powers during the interwar period resulted in more African teachers, agricultural experts, and medical and veterinary personnel available for development work. Professional training of teachers and clerical staff began in 1903 at the École normale William Ponty in Gorée, Dakar. In 1918 a medical school was added and in 1954 the William Ponty School became a university. The state established programs for training women for work as midwives, nurses, and pharmacists in the 1920s.[14] Whereas in the mid-1930s only about 5 percent of school-aged African children attended French colonial schools across West Africa, this number more than doubled in the decade after the establishment of the Fonds d'investissements pour le développement économique et social (the Investment Fund for Economic and Social Development) (FIDES) in 1946.

In contrast to the French, British colonial administrations financially supported and relied on missionaries and private organizations to educate Africans with an emphasis on vocational training. The

[13] W. Bryant Mumford, *Africans Learn to Be French: A Review of Educational Activities in the Seven Federated Colonies of French West Africa, Based upon a Tour of French West Africa and Algiers Undertaken in 1935* (Evans Brothers, 1939), 87, 158–171.
[14] Diane Barthel, "Women's Educational Experience under Colonialism: Toward a Diachronic Model," *Signs* 11:1 (1985) 137–154; Donna A. Patterson, *Pharmacy in Senegal: Gender, Healing, and Entrepreneurship* (Indiana University Press, 2015).

missionary-run Alliance High School, for example, was the only institution in Kenya at which students could take the Cambridge School Certificate examination, the highest-level examination for English-speaking secondary school graduates available to Africans during the colonial period. With the exception of a few missionary schools that covered instruction from the "infant" classes (preschool or kindergarten) up to Standard VI (sixth grade), most British colonial schools did not offer the full primary course. A typical "village" or "district" school instructed Africans in vocational skills like agriculture, carpentry, tailoring, and hygiene for two or three years. Only a few pupils would continue for another year or two of specialized training.

Some territories benefited more from education funding than others. In 1938 Southern Nigeria had thirty-three secondary schools while there was only one in the predominantly Muslim region of Northern Nigeria.[15] With the exception of a few missionary schools, British administrations in East Africa did not offer secondary education until the Second World War. The Colonial Office directed more funding and attention to education upon the advice of the American Phelps-Stokes Commission that toured Britain's African colonies in the mid-1920s.[16] Based on US experiences with African American education, the commissioners advocated the policy of "adapted education." Adapted education in Africa continued to offer a curriculum that emphasized agricultural training, training in small trades, and instruction in hygiene. Adapted education served as justification for racial segregation in the schools in both the United States and colonial Africa.

During and after World War II new funding from Britain's Colonial Development and Welfare Acts (CDWA) of 1940 and 1945 funneled significantly more money into education than the government spent previously. The postwar years witnessed the expansion of primary, secondary, and tertiary or college education across the continent. New colleges and universities offered professional programs in medicine, agriculture, education, and other arts and sciences.

In reality there was little difference between assimilationist and adapted colonial educational models; both sought to train a handful

[15]   Barbara Goff, *"Your Secret Language": Classics in the British Colonies of West Africa* (Bloomsbury, 2013), 15.
[16]   UKNA CO 323/1415/6 Advisory Council for Education in the Colonies, Memorandum on Community Education and Social and Economic Development Programmes in Rural Areas, 1937.

of skilled intermediaries to work for the state while providing basic instruction for the masses who would be expected to perform unskilled or semiskilled labor. In this way, colonial education policies reinforced separate development in racial and economic terms. The new class of African educated elites demanded access to more academic subjects, European language instruction, higher education, women's education, and professional programs. Many adhered to certain ideals of respectability as evidence of their elevated status. The respectability politics of the educated elite spoke to a different kind of separate development, one in which African elites claimed to deserve economic and social advantages over the "masses."

10.1 Respectability politics and the development episteme

The new colonized elites (the *évolué* in French and Belgian territories, the *assimilado* in Portuguese territories, and the "modern" or "civilized" in British territories) employed a politics of respectability to claim higher status under colonialism. In colonial Lagos the capital of the Protectorate of Southern Nigeria, Christians predominated among the political and economic elite though only about 25 percent of the city's population was Christian. According to historian Kristin Mann, by 1915 all of these elites had completed primary education, 80 percent had finished secondary school, and 30 percent went to a college in either Sierra Leone or Britain. Western-educated elites viewed themselves and their economic and social success as a model for other Africans to follow.[1]

Respectability politics rested on the adoption of new religious and moral codes, a new education system (and language), and new material cultures – the fundamental principles of the development episteme. Christian elites across Africa built square houses filled with the accoutrements of western life – tables, chairs, doors, books and bookcases, raised bed and blankets, and wardrobes full of western-style clothing. They adopted new rules around recreation as well. Africans reformed and redefined pastimes such as drinking and dancing as private, sex-segregated activities in order to bring them in line with Christian or western values.[2] "Respectable" elites also aided in European

colonial efforts to "develop" poor and rural African populations.
One example was the Lagos Women's League in Nigeria.
Historian Abosede George argues that the League led social
development campaigns to protect the virtue of Nigerian girls
and, symbolically, Lagos itself.[3] Educated elites urged young
men and women to conform to the gendered politics of respectability. New types of Islamic respectability also marked the rise of
a western-educated elite, many of whom were the products of
modernist schools with a grounding in Islamic studies.[4] The
respectability politics of African educated elites celebrated educational achievement, wealth and class status, and social causes
that reinforced the development episteme.

[1]   Kristin Mann, "Marriage Choices among the Educated African Elite in Lagos
      Colony, 1880–1915," *International Journal of African Historical Studies* 14:2
      (1981) 201–228.
[2]   Phyllis M. Martin, *Leisure and Society in Colonial Brazzaville* (Cambridge
      University Press, 1995).
[3]   Abosede George, *Making Modern Girls: A History of Girlhood, Labor, and
      Social Development in Colonial Lagos* (Ohio University Press, 2014).
[4]   Corrie Decker, *Mobilizing Zanzibari Women: The Struggle for Respectability and
      Self-Reliance in Colonial East Africa* (Palgrave Macmillan, 2014).

By the 1950s development programs began to envision universal
education as an attainable goal in the not-too-distant future.
According to a United Nations (UN) report, *Special Study on
Educational Conditions in Non-self-governing Territories*, primary school
enrollment in Africa increased noticeably between 1946 and 1951, the
years immediately following the passing of the CDWAs and the establishment of FIDES. The rates were wildly uneven. Only 2 percent of
school-aged children enrolled in schools in Burkina Faso and Chad. In
contrast, the Belgian Congo had an enrollment of 46.5 percent at the
elementary level. This relatively high rate of primary schooling is due in
part to the large number of missionaries there, which had increased
from 4,000 in the late 1930s to more than 7,000 by the late 1950s.
Table 10.1 shows percentages of school-aged children enrolled in
school in select territories. The biggest increase in enrollments during
the late 1940s occurred in British Somaliland, with a 317 percent
increase, and in French Equatorial Africa, which had a 173 percent
increase in enrollments. In both regions, though, the percentages in

Table 10.1 Percentage of school-aged children enrolled in select territories, 1950/1951

Percentage	Territories
0–10%	British Somaliland, French West Africa
11–20%	French Equatorial Africa, French Somaliland, Nigeria, Zanzibar
21–30%	Bechuanaland, South Africa
31–40%	Kenya, Swaziland, Uganda
41–50%	Basutoland, Belgian Congo, Gold Coast

Source: UN report, *Special Study on Educational Conditions in Non-self-governing Territories* (United Nations, 1954), 9

1946 were quite low (0.5 percent and 4 percent, respectively), and both remained woefully behind other regions even after the increases. Enrollment figures for indigenous populations in South Africa were comparable to those of colonial territories at around 30 percent. In general, increases in primary school enrollments in the late 1940s and 1950s coincided with new sources of funding through FIDES and CDWA.[17]

While nearly every territory increased school enrollment in the years following World War II, Bechuanaland (Botswana) was an exception. Its enrollments declined by 14.6 percent between 1946 (21,701 students) and 1951 (18,536 students) when a large number of boys and young men joined the migrant labor system to work in South Africa's booming mining industries. The gender breakdown of enrollments in 1950/1951 is also telling (see Table 10.2). Whereas many more boys than girls attended schools everywhere else in Africa, more girls than boys attended primary school in Basutoland (Lesotho), Bechuanaland (Botswana), and Swaziland (eSwatini), key regions of labor recruitment for South Africa. In the absence of older boys and men younger boys had to take on responsibilities like herding that kept them out of school.[18] The story of education in southern Africa reflects the enormous impact of South

[17] United Nations, *Special Study on Educational Conditions in Non-self-governing Territories* (United Nations, 1954), 14.
[18] John Charles Hatch, *Everyman's Africa* (Dobson, 1959), 228. This trend toward a greater percentage of girls in primary schools continued in Botswana, Lesotho, and Swaziland for decades after independence. See Fiona Leach, "Gender, Education and Training: An International Perspective," *Gender and Development* 6:2 (1998) 9–18 at 14.

Table 10.2 Percentage of female students in total enrollment in schools, 1950/1951

Territory	PS	SS
Basutoland	67.0%	34.4%
Bechuanaland	63.0	34.8
French Equatorial Africa	15.0	15.0
French West Africa	16.0	21.5
Gold Coast	25.0	11.6
Kenya	26.0	12.6
Nigeria	22.0	8.5
Swaziland	53.8	52.7
Uganda	24.0	13.5

Source: UN report, *Special Study on Educational Conditions in Non-self-governing Territories* (United Nations, 1954), 46. Some territories included in the estimates which appear in Table 10.1 were not included in this section of the report.

Africa's racialized separate development schemes during the apartheid era.

NATIONALISM, EDUCATION, AND DEVELOPMENT

Colonial education reinforced the notion of separate development, but it also offered a platform for social change, political mobilization, and – ultimately – national liberation. Nothing emphasizes this inherent contradiction more than the fact that the majority of African nationalist leaders were products of colonial schools. Missionary and colonial schools created opportunities for organizing beyond one's ethnic group or region. Western-educated elites bonded over their shared ability to speak European languages, participate in civil society, and claim elite respectability. A sense of solidarity united those who recognized that their academic achievements failed to result in equal treatment by missionaries or colonial officials. Eventually schools became the center of anticolonial and African nationalist movements.

Even before the spread of African nationalism of the 1950s and 1960s educated elites had been at the forefront of the anticolonial struggle. In the 1910s Louis Hunkanrin, an École William Ponty graduate, overtly criticized French policies in Dahomey (Benin). During the 1910s and 1920s educated elites in Malawi, Kenya, Ghana, and elsewhere became active critics of the colonial state and spokespeople for their communities. Protests among the educated elite generally centered around one of three issues: the lack of educational resources for Africans, the inequality of educated Africans in the social and political system, and the desire to protect African cultural identities from westernization.

Many leaders of new African nations, including Sylvanus Olympio (Togo), Kwame Nkrumah (Ghana), Jomo Kenyatta (Kenya), Léopold Senghor (Senegal), Nnamdi Azikiwe (Nigeria), Hastings Banda (Malawi), Philibert Tsiranana (Madagascar), and Julius Nyerere (Tanzania), attended universities abroad. These and other African elites were well positioned to negotiate with European colonial administrators and plan for a postcolonial future in part because colonial officials recognized highly educated Africans as their suitable successors. More importantly, these individuals were acutely aware of the contradictions built into the colonial philosophies of rule. Western education was their strongest weapon for overturning the system.

As colonialism came to a close African political leaders redeployed formal education toward nationalist movements. As discussed in Chapter 4, this sparked a body of literature that sought to undo the damage of colonial indoctrination. Novels such as Tayeb Salih's *Season of Migration to the North* (1966) and Ken Bugul's *The Abandoned Baobab* (1982) pointed to educated Africans' painful disillusionment at the racialization of western education even after the end of European colonial rule in Africa. Postcolonial literature became a tool for "decolonising the mind" and reclaiming African histories and identities.[19]

Since the 1970s efforts to provide universal primary education have been a cornerstone of many African nations' development policies. The World Bank and the International Monetary Fund's (IMF) Structural Adjustment Programs of the 1980s severely hampered these efforts by slashing the overhead expenditures of African nations. By the 1990s the push for universal primary education was taken up by nongovernmental and international organizations. It is Goal #2 of the UN Millennium Development Goals (MDGs). The MDG Monitor

---

[19] Ngũgĩ wa Thiong'o, *Decolonising the Mind: The Politics of Language in African Literature* (East African Educational Publishers, 1981).

claims to have made some progress toward this goal in sub-Saharan Africa, where the rate of enrollment in primary schools jumped from 52 percent in 1990 to 78 percent in 2012, with most of this growth occurring since 2000.[20] Providing universal primary education does not mean that school is free. For example, a for-profit company called Bridge International Academies (BIA) aims to work toward this goal by offering access to private primary education for a fee (see Box 10.2).

Since the early 2000s gender equity in schooling has also been a major development initiative for various African nations and the UN. Gender has become a major component of development projects and funding in general, and most people agree that gender equality begins with gender equity in primary, secondary, and tertiary schools. In 2015 the MDG Monitor cited Rwanda as the "leading" nation on gender equality, universal primary education, women's empowerment, child and maternal mortality, HIV prevention, and environmental sustainability.[21] At that time Rwanda was the only country in the world with a female majority among representatives in government. Rwanda has become the model for other African nations aiming for universal primary education and gender equality.

10.2 Development experiments in primary education

Shannon May and Jay Kimmelman, two social entrepreneurs, founded the for-profit company Bridge International Academies (BIA) in 2007 to help expand primary education worldwide. May and Kimmelman sought to build economies of scale into their education system in order to bring literacy and numeracy to millions of children. The BIA's focus on "leapfrogging" the global educational divide is reminiscent of Rosenstein-Rodan's "big push" theory of modernization, discussed in Chapter 7. The BIA encountered several challenges to primary education globally: teachers had limited training, many teachers did not show

---

[20]   MDG Monitor, MDG 2: Achieve Universal Primary Education, www .mdgmonitor.org/mdg-2-achieve-universal-primary-education/, accessed March 16, 2019.

[21]   MDG Monitor, Fact Sheet on Current MDG Progress of Rwanda (Africa), 2015, www.mdgmonitor.org/mdg-progress-rwanda-africa/, accessed March 16, 2019.

up to work or were not in their classrooms teaching, and school infrastructure was limited. In order to economize school costs and find enough suitable teachers, the BIA produces universal daily scripts designed for schools in each country and sends these plans to teachers via the Internet. Teachers then read the script, which is a complete lesson plan, from a tablet. The lesson plans tell teachers exactly what to say, what to ask of students, how many minutes they should focus on each topic, and so on. Teachers then submit a report on the educational outcomes, which is sent back to the international headquarters of the BIA in Cambridge, Massachusetts.[1]

The BIA's status as a for-profit company differs significantly from the usual development model. The BIA charges families $15–17 per month per student. While these numbers may seem low, the average Kenyan family with students in BIA schools earns $136 per month, meaning that 12.5 percent of the household income per child is paid to the school. The goal of the BIA is to educate 10 million students, but currently its enrollments hover around 100,000 students across Nigeria, Uganda, Kenya, India, and Liberia. This deficit of students means that the model has yet to become cost-effective. Thus far, BIA has made up the $12 million deficit through fundraising from major donors such as the Chan Zuckerberg Initiative and the International Finance Company, part of the World Bank. The BIA, a for profit company, is tapping the same institutions that fund nonprofit development organizations, which has created antagonism in the wider nongovernmental organization (NGO) community.

The BIA is the largest partner in Liberia's recent educational experiment, the Partnership Schools for Liberia (PSL). In 2016 Liberia contracted with six educational providers to take over half of its primary schools. The other half of the schools under the purview of the Liberian government act as a control group. The Liberian government gave each provider a budget of $50 per pupil, but the providers could put in more money if they wished. The BIA's schools cost an additional $613 per student. The initial report noted that the BIA schools had the biggest improvement in learning over the other partner schools, most of whom had a maximum of $100 per student in their budgets. However, the BIA schools refused to accept "underperforming" teachers and capped their classes at forty-five students, while the partner schools had around sixty-five students per class.[2] As the report noted, these distinctions likely affected the performance of the students.

May and Kimmelman's BIA project has faced significant criticism. In August 2017 174 NGOs made a public plea for funders to stop supporting the BIA.[3] They argued that for-profit schools exploited the global poor and left the poorest students without access to education, creating a bifurcated education system. Others have argued that students need to learn critical thinking skills, which does not happen in classrooms using the deeply scripted lessons found in BIA schools. Some critics also argue that the BIA's use of English in the classroom diminishes local cultures and languages. May and Kimmelman maintain that they are making significant improvement globally in access to literacy.

[1]   Jenny Anderson, "Bridging the Gap: The Controversial Silicon Valley-Funded Quest to Educate the World's Poorest Kids," *Quartz*, January 22, 2018, https://qz.com/1179738/bridge-school/, accessed January 4, 2020.
[2]   Mauricio Romero, Justin Sandefur, and Wayne Aaron Sandholtz, "Can Outsourcing Improve Liberia's Schools? Preliminary Results from Year One of a Three-Year Randomized Evaluation of Partnership Schools for Liberia," Center for Global Development, Working Paper 462, September 2017, www.cgdev.org/sites/default/files/partnership-schools-for-liberia.pdf, accessed January 4, 2020.
[3]   "Civil Society Call on Investors to Cease Support to Bridge International Academies," August 1, 2017, http://globalinitiative-escr.org/wp-content/upl oads/2017/07/Civil-society-call-on-investors-to-cease-support-to-Bridge-Int ernational-Academies.pdf, accessed January 4, 2020.

INTERNATIONALIZATION AND PRIVATIZATION OF UNIVERSITIES

While not one of the stated UN MDGs, expanding university education is a development priority for many African nations. Modern universities in Africa emerged out of African demands for higher education during the colonial era, but historically advanced educational institutions trained intellectuals, legal experts, and religious scholars. Long before Ethiopia opened its first official university in 1950, the Coptic Church introduced formal education and the training of priests as early as the sixth century when the region was known as the Kingdom of Axum.[22] Islamic universities like the University of al-Qarawiyyin in Morocco and Al-Azhar University in Egypt were established later in the first millennium. One of the oldest institutions in sub-Saharan Africa was the University of Timbuktu, a collection of scholarly centers in Mali that dates back to the beginning of the fifteenth century. In addition to literary and religious texts Timbuktu scholars wrote and preserved historical chronicles (*tarikhs*) in Songhay, Tamasheq, and Arabic dialects. Some manuscripts were destroyed during violent conflicts that broke out in Mali in 2012.[23]

Most modern universities in Africa began as missionary schools, secondary schools, or professional training centers. Cheikh Anta Diop University of Dakar in Senegal began as the École Africaine de Médecine de Dakar (the African Medical School of Dakar) in 1918. Makerere University in Kampala, Uganda opened first as a high school in 1922 and then expanded into a teacher training college in the mid-1920s and finally to a university in 1937. The University of Ghana (formerly the University College of the Gold Coast) in Accra grew out of the Achimota School founded in the 1920s. University education expanded rapidly across the continent in the postwar period. Nigeria's first university, the University of Ibadan, opened in 1948. The University of Kinshasa in the Democratic Republic of Congo (DRC, formerly Belgian Congo) began as the Catholic University of Lovanium, founded in 1954 out of a collection of Catholic schools in the colony. The present-day University of Nairobi in Kenya was also established in the mid-1950s. Many African universities were affiliated with institutions based in European imperial centers until African nations became independent in the early 1960s. At that time Makerere University, the University of Nairobi, and the University of Dar es Salaam, formerly attached to the University of London, collaborated to form the Federal University of East Africa, which lasted until 1970. Universities also provided new opportunities for women. In Sudan the Ahfad University for Women was established in 1966, though its origins go

[22] Tebeje Molla, *Higher Education in Ethiopia: Structural Inequalities and Policy Responses* (Springer, 2018), 15–18.
[23] Elias N. Saad, *Social History of Timbuktu: The Role of Muslim Scholars and Notables, 1400–1900* (Cambridge University Press, 1983).

back to the early 1900s when a local religious leader named Babicar Badri demanded a school for his daughters.[24]

Universities in Africa have been at the center of politics since the 1950s and 1960s, a trend that continues today. Education activists called for independence, decolonization of higher education, and Africanization of university staff and students. University students in Algeria, the Comoros Islands, Egypt, Ethiopia, Morocco, Mauritania, Senegal, South Africa, and Tanzania joined the global protests in 1968.[25] That year eminent Caribbean scholar Walter Rodney was in residence at Tanzania's University of Dar es Salaam, then a center for pan-Africanist scholarship and activism.[26] In South Africa and Zimbabwe the universities were key sites for Black nationalism and antiapartheid activism. In former Portuguese territories like Angola and Mozambique, where higher education had been controlled by the Catholic Church, independence led to the nationalization and secularization of universities. In Angola the Portuguese founded the University of Luanda (Universidade de Luanda, formerly Estudos Gerais Universitários de Angola) in the early 1960s. A few years after Angola gained independence in 1975 the institution became a nonracial public university. In 1985 it was renamed Universidade Agostinho Neto after Angola's first president who led the charge to decolonize higher education.[27]

Universities have also been important sites for preparing Africans for work in development. In the 1980s a decrease in funding to higher education and overall economic crises resulting from the World Bank and the IMF's Structural Adjustment Programs limited the universities' ability to produce graduates for this work.[28] A "brain drain" crisis ensued in the following decades as more Africans studied abroad in Europe and North America, many never to return. Given the mobility of labor, capital, and ideas in the digital age, some argue that

[24] Kathleen Sheldon, *Historical Dictionary of Women in Sub-Saharan Africa* (Scarecrow Press, Inc., 2005), 25–26.

[25] George Katsiaficas, *The Imagination of the New Left: A Global Analysis of 1968* (South End Press, 1987), 44.

[26] Andrew Ivaska, *Cultured States: Youth, Gender, and Modern Style in 1960s Dar es Salaam* (Duke University Press, 2011), 124–165.

[27] Adebayo O. Oyebade, *Culture and Customs of Angola* (Greenwood Press, 2007), 9. See also Y. G.-M. Lulat, *A History of African Higher Education from Antiquity to the Present: A Critical Synthesis* (Praeger, 2005).

[28] Horman Chitonge, *Economic Growth and Development in Africa: Understanding Trends and Prospects* (Routledge, 2015).

Africans who attend universities abroad now constitute a "brain-gain" rather than a "brain-drain."[29]

The 2000s ushered in a trend toward privatization of the university in Africa and across the globe. Today African universities partner with NGOs, humanitarians, and entrepreneurs in order to keep their doors open. One example is Stawa University in Kampala, Uganda. Stawa grew out of an NGO called Teach and Tour Sojourners (TATS), which hosts foreign scholars who give lectures and run workshops for Ugandan students. Stawa students get hands-on training in development by working in projects that in turn help to fund the university.[30] Internationalization and privatization of universities has led to a multiplication of universities. More than two dozen colleges and universities have been established in each of the countries of Algeria, Angola, Benin, Burundi, Ivory Coast, DRC, Egypt, Ethiopia, Ghana, Kenya, Libya, Malawi, Morocco, Mozambique, Nigeria, Rwanda, Somalia, South Africa, Sudan, Uganda, and Zambia. This trend mirrors the neoliberal push toward decentralization and privatization of development in general.

International development funding for university education in Africa has been insignificant compared to funding available for other types of education and training. This has contributed to the ongoing problem of the marginalization of Africans in the production of knowledge about Africa and Africans. The literature on development still largely ignores the work of African scholars. Some changes have emerged from partnerships between researchers and institutions of the global north with those on the continent, but much more work needs to be done to challenge the hegemony of the development episteme in creating knowledge about Africa and formulating educational policies in African nations.[31]

★★★

Formal schooling introduced during the colonial era contributed to racial and economic divisions by promoting the idea of separate

[29] Rubin Patterson, ed., *African Brain Circulation: Beyond the Drain-Gain Debate* (Koninklijke Brill NV, 2007).
[30] Interview with Corrie Decker, Laurence D. L. Maka, Vice Chancellor of Stawa University, August 1, 2019.
[31] Hanne Kirstine Adriansen, Lene Møller Madsen, and Stig Jensen, eds., *Higher Education and Capacity Building in Africa: The Geography and Power of Knowledge under Changing Conditions* (Routledge, 2016).

FIGURE 10.1 Students at the University of Cape Town, as part of the #RhodesMustFall movement, deface a statue of British colonial official and mining profiteer Cecil Rhodes as it is being taken down on April 9, 2015. Source: Rodger Bosch/AFP via Getty Images

development. Missionary and colonial education institutionalized the assumptions about racial difference embedded in the development episteme. Since the mid-twentieth century African and international development initiatives have sought to reverse these inequalities, but Africans still do not have much say in answering key questions such as: Who has the authority to set education policy? What/who are the sources of knowledge, the authors of textbooks, the teachers, and the models of educational development used in African schools? Should development funding go toward universal primary education, gender equity in schools, or expansion of universities? The marginalization of African epistemologies in formal education has contributed to the marginalization of African voices in the development discourse. The notion that education is necessary for African development is irrefutable, but innovations in development are needed in order to recenter African pedagogical practices in African schools.

Students in particular are an untapped resource. Students at the forefront of the "Arab Spring" in North Africa between 2010 and 2012, those leading the #RhodesMustFall and #FeesMustFall movements in South African universities in 2015, the central role of youth in Nigeria's 2019 election, and university students seeking peace amid ongoing violence in South Sudan all demonstrate the valuable role of students and young people in generating political change (see Figure 10.1). African students have also identified innovative energy sources, offered new ideas for environmental sustainability, and established businesses designed to keep profits in the hands of Africans. The conversation around education will have better results if it includes African educators, parents, and young people. International funders, NGOs, and African leaders who listen carefully to students and their parents may see their ideas pay off.

Further Reading

On the history of Islamic and Christian education in Africa see Roman Loimeier, *Between Social Skills and Marketable Skills: The Politics of Islamic Education in 20th Century Zanzibar* (Koninklijke Brill NV, 2009); Elias N. Saad, *Social History of Timbuktu: The Role of Muslim Scholars and Notables, 1400–1900* (Cambridge University Press, 1983). Rudolph T. Ware III, *The Walking Qur'an: Islamic Education, Embodied Knowledge, and History in West Africa* (University of North Carolina Press, 2014).

On colonial educational policies and practices see Kelly M. Duke Bryant, *Education As Politics: Colonial Schooling and Political Debate in Senegal, 1850s–1914* (University of Wisconsin Press, 2015); Meghan Healy-Clancy, *A World of Their Own: A History of South African Women's Education* (University of Virginia Press, 2014); Spencer D. Segalla, *The Moroccan Soul: French Education, Colonial Ethnology, and Muslim Resistance, 1912–1956* (University of Nebraska Press, 2009).

On education, nationalism, and postcolonial identity see Toyin Falola, *Nationalism and African Intellectuals* (University of Rochester Press, 2001); Kate Skinner, *The Fruits of Freedom in British Togoland: Literacy, Politics and Nationalism, 1914–2014* (Cambridge University Press, 2015).

On contemporary education, development, and universities in Africa see Catherine Griefenow-Mewis, ed., *On Results of the Reform in Ethiopia's Language and Education Policies* (Harrassowitz, 2009); Tim Livsey, *Nigeria's University Age: Reframing Decolonisation and Development* (Palgrave Macmillan, 2017); Edward Shizha and Michael T. Kariwo, *Education and Development in Zimbabwe: A Social, Political and Economic Analysis* (Sense, 2011).

CHAPTER 11

Capitalizing on Dis-ease

In the early 1830s Scottish explorer Macgregor Laird led an expedition up the Niger River. One of the officers who accompanied him, R. A. K. Oldfield, described Laird's condition upon reuniting with him after some time apart:

> I was shocked at the dreadful state in which I found Mr. Laird: pale and emaciated to the last degree, he appeared as if risen from the grave. He was suffering from a disease named by the natives "craw craw," – an inveterate form of scabies, which, I am informed, is epidemic. In the vessels almost every white man and officer, and all the Kroomen, had had it.[1]

By the time they returned home all but nine of the forty-eight Europeans in the expedition had perished. Laird and Oldfield survived to publish their accounts of the harrowing journey. Such stories of death and disease solidified the African continent as the "white man's grave" in the nineteenth-century European imagination.[2] The idea that "African" diseases are more dangerous than other diseases has not faded. The 2014–2015 Ebola outbreak in West Africa, for example, sparked global panic. Starting in October of 2014, people traveling to the United States from the African nations affected were carefully monitored for weeks after their arrival, and some members of Congress proposed a complete ban on travel from

---

[1] Macgregor Laird and R. A. K. Oldfield, *Narrative of an Expedition into the Interior of Africa, by the River Niger, in the Steam-Vessels* Quorra *and* Alburkah, *in 1832, 1833, and 1834 Vol. I* (Richard Bentley, 1837), 407–408.

[2] Pratik Chakrabarti, *Medicine and Empire: 1600–1960* (Palgrave Macmillan, 2014), 124–125.

the region.[3] The continent of Africa has been associated with disease in western discourses for at least 200 years.

This chapter investigates the history of medical research, the expansion of western medicine, and the emergence of public health programs in postcolonial Africa in order to highlight the two primary ways medicine and health became key "problems" in the development episteme. First, imperialist expansion necessitated efforts to make African territories more hospitable to European explorers, officials, and settlers. Second, colonial and national states invested in the health of their subjects and citizens because healthier, more productive laborers increased profits of local industries and presumably facilitated the growth of the state economies. Biomedical research and intervention has been essential to the development episteme since the Scramble for Africa in the late 1800s. European missionaries and explorers studied African healing methods and brought western medicines to ailing Africans. Even before 1800 western explorers and scientists were noting the medicinal properties of African plants and the therapeutic practices of African communities in order to adapt this knowledge for western medicinal knowledge.[4] Post–World War II colonial development funds, such as the British Colonial Development and Welfare Fund (CDWF) and the French Fonds d'investissements pour le développement économique et social (FIDES), solidified the link between development and public health by offering metropolitan development funding for medical research and public health projects. While Europeans portrayed Africa as the "white man's grave," many Africans viewed western medical interventions (and the diseases they were meant to cure) as symbolic of the dis-ease colonialism brought to their communities.[5]

The development episteme has perpetuated the idea that Africa is a place of disease and that Africans are resistant to treatments and cures. Colonial medical officials and practitioners looked to Africa as a "living laboratory" and viewed African bodies as "pathological

---

[3] Donald G. McNeil Jr. and Michael D. Shear, "U.S. Plans 21-Day Watch of Travelers from Ebola-Hit Nations, *New York Times*, October 22, 2014, www.nytimes.com/2014/10/23/health/us-to-monitor-travelers-from-ebola-hit-nations-for-21-days.html, accessed February 4, 2020.

[4] Londa Schiebinger, *Secret Cures of Slaves: People, Plans, and Medicine in the Eighteenth-Century Atlantic World* (Stanford University Press, 2017).

[5] Osaak A. Olumwullah, *Dis-ease in the Colonial State: Medicine, Society, and Social Change among the AbaNyole of Western Kenya* (Greenwood Press, 2002).

museums."[6] Africans continue to serve as inexpensive subjects available for medical research and experiments well into the twenty-first century.[7] Historian Melissa Graboyes argues that the history of medical research in Africa demonstrates "that problems are caused not by research per se, but by how it is done: the coercion, dishonesty, and misunderstanding that characterized so many encounters past and present."[8] Foreign healthcare workers and medical researchers frustrated with resistance or failures in Africa emphasize the misconceptions Africans have about western medicine, but Graboyes brings attention to the misconceptions foreign researchers have about Africans; some researchers portray Africans as "uneducated, unpredictable, and . . . yet to learn the benefits of biomedicine and scientific investigations."[9] Of course, many Africans have welcomed certain vaccinations, medicines, and other treatments, and some have integrated these with local healing technologies, but misinformed grumblings about African "superstitions" and mistrust or misuse of biomedicine persist.

This chapter traces the imperial history of racial and environmental medical research, the economic drivers behind public health initiatives, and the legacies of colonialism in medical research and public health interventions since the discovery of HIV/AIDS. Examining this history of African encounters with development interventions around health provides much-needed context for breaking down misconceptions about African resistance to or ignorance of western biomedical aid.

RACIAL SEGREGATION AND FEARS OF CONTAGION IN EARLY COLONIAL SETTLEMENT

The use of quinine as a malaria prophylaxis and other medical advancements facilitated widespread European exploration of the

[6] Helen Tilley, *Africa As a Living Laboratory: Empire, Development, and the Problem of Scientific Knowledge, 1870–1950* (University of Chicago Press, 2011); Melissa Graboyes, *The Experiment Must Continue: Medical Research and Ethics in East Africa, 1940–2014* (Ohio University Press, 2015), xii.
[7] P. Wenzel Geissler and Catherine Molyneux, eds., *Evidence, Ethos and Experiment: The Anthropology and History of Medical Research in Africa* (Berghahn Books, 2011).
[8] Graboyes, *The Experiment Must Continue*, 199.
[9] Ibid., xi.

continent after 1850, but it did not dispel the notion that Africa was a place of disease and death. Missionary/explorer Dr. David Livingstone embodied the overlap between exploration, medical intervention, and the civilizing mission. Livingstone and other scientists who traveled to Africa identified hundreds of new pathologies, viruses, bacteria, and other afflictions, and created what historian Osaak Olumwullah has called "a landscape of fear" in Africa.[10] As Africa became safer for European travel, it became more dangerous in the European imagination.

This discourse on diseased environments infected relationships between Europeans and Africans. From Senegal to South Africa imperialism frequently entailed European men's intimate connections with African women – both consensual and not, but theories of contagion mandated a different approach by the early twentieth century. During the 1910s, 1920s, and 1930s cross-racial relationships became less acceptable and racial segregation more commonplace, a shift some scholars have attributed to the arrival of European women.[11] European settlers established residential enclaves at high elevations, thought to be healthier and with a climate more suitable to whites than lowlands. "Native" spaces were portrayed as regions of extreme heat, a lack of sanitation, and illness. In European descriptions of the African environment dangerous tropical climes served as a metaphor for the lack of health and morality among African people.

11.1 Segregation in Algiers

The French colony of Algeria, established in 1830, was one of the earliest sites at which theories of racial contagion shaped colonial settlement policies. Land alienation in the rural areas began in the 1840s and 1850s, but the majority of the French settlers lived in the city of Algiers. The French administration established a "native quarter" (*village negre*) and a "Jewish quarter" to segregate local Muslims and Jews from European Christians. Urban

---

[10]   Olumwullah, *Dis-ease in the Colonial State*, 1.

[11]   Rachel Jean-Baptiste, *Conjugal Rights: Marriage, Sexuality, and Urban Life in Colonial Libreville, Gabon* (Ohio University Press, 2014), 194–216; and Carina E. Ray, *Crossing the Color Line: Race, Sex, and the Contested Politics of Colonialism in Ghana* (Ohio University Press, 2015).

segregation reinforced the ideology of biological difference between French people and Algerians and implied that cohabitation posed a significant threat to the white race. The "native quarter" in Algiers became known as a hovel "of breeding swarms, of foulness, of spawn, of gesticulations," and "a place of ill fame, peopled by men of evil repute."[1] The overcrowding of the "native quarter" and its limited access to the kind of public health resources available in the settlers' town ensured that its inhabitants were more susceptible to disease, which officials then used to justify continued racial segregation.[2]

[1] Frantz Fanon, *Wretched of the Earth* (Grove Press, 1966 [orig. 1963]), 42.
[2] Zeynep Çelik, *Urban Forms and Colonial Confrontation: Algiers under French Rule* (University of California Press, 1997).

Segregation policies reflecting European fears about racial contamination emerged in the cities of settler colonies in Algeria, South Africa, Kenya, Belgian Congo, and Southern Rhodesia. Kalina, the European district of Leopoldville (now Kinshasa) in the Belgian Congo, was separated from African settlements by a *cordon sanitaire*. Africans could cross this "sanitary barrier" into the European areas only for employment purposes between the hours of 9:00 AM and 6:00 PM. Similarly in Nairobi, River Road was thought to be a barrier to prevent the mixing of Indians, Africans, and Europeans. Racial segregation was an ongoing topic of debate in South Africa, where during the Segregation Era (1910 to 1948) administrators strictly limited the number of Africans who could enter the cities by creating "native townships" on the outskirts of towns. Arguments about the dangers African workers posed to the health of whites intensified during tuberculosis and syphilis outbreaks. Whether the urban townships were considered permanent settlements or temporary labor reserves, as the 1923 Urban Areas Act designated them, the notion that "white" industrial cities like Johannesburg and Kimberley should be protected from the influx of Black South Africans was entrenched several decades before the apartheid government came to power.[12] Theories of racial contagion were less pervasive in territories where interracial sex was a defining feature

[12] Saul Dubow, *Racial Segregation and the Origins of Apartheid in South Africa, 1919–36* (Palgrave Macmillan, 1989).

of conquest and colonial rule.[13] As ideas about racial difference shifted and pseudoscientific racism waned, interracial unions once again became more accepted, though the children of such unions often faced discrimination and social exclusion.[14]

MEDICINE, PUBLIC HEALTH, AND COLONIAL DIS-EASE

European encounters with so-called African diseases inspired new research in the medical sciences and new policies governing public health. Beginning with the London School of Tropical Medicine in 1899 academic institutions professionalized the study of diseases that Europeans "discovered" during their travels in Africa. In France the first forays into the field of tropical medicine occurred in the military where studies of diets, hygiene practices, and diseases compared the health of French people and Africans in racial terms.[15] On the continent missionary doctors and makeshift colonial health centers initiated biomedical examinations of Africans and created a trove of data about tropical diseases. Advances in microbiology and disease pathology helped colonial medical officers diagnose cases of sleeping sickness, cholera, malaria, tuberculosis, and other illnesses endemic to Africa.

Colonial officials tackled outbreaks of many diseases with both environmental and medical approaches. One of these diseases was trypanosomiasis ("sleeping sickness"), which first affected cattle and was spread via the tsetse fly in the forested regions of central and eastern Africa. David Livingstone drew on local knowledge about the tsetse fly in writing about its dangers in his travelogues. Severe outbreaks of sleeping sickness among humans occurred in the 1880s and 1890s in French Congo and Ubangi-Shari, 1901 and 1905 in Uganda, 1904 in German East Africa and in the Congo River basin, and 1908 in Northern Rhodesia and Nyasaland. Nearly 300,000 Ugandans died in the 1905 outbreak. Symptoms of trypanosomiasis included fever, headaches, joint pain, swelling of the lymph nodes, and, if left

---

[13] Hilary Jones, *The Métis of Senegal Urban Life and Politics in French West Africa* (Indiana University Press, 2013).
[14] Ray, *Crossing the Color Line.*
[15] Michael A. Osborne, *The Emergence of Tropical Medicine in France* (University of Chicago Press, 2014).

untreated, neurological symptoms, organ failure, and ultimately death.[16]

Colonial officials responded to the sleeping sickness outbreaks by relocating Africans away from areas inhabited by tsetse flies and mosquitoes and burning villages thought to be infested with these insects. These tactics destroyed indigenous communities and prevented Africans' access to their cattle, grazing land, and watering holes. Health officials extracted cerebrospinal fluid through a lumbar puncture in order to assess the stage of the disease in the patient, a practice that continues today (see Figure 11.1).[17] Colonizers in Africa employed

FIGURE 11.1 A European doctor and two African assistants giving an African boy a lumbar puncture near Yaoundé, French Cameroon, in order to determine the stage of sleeping sickness while French Governor Bonnecarrere and French MP Susset look on, March 1933. Source: AFP via Getty Images

[16] Maryinez Lyons, *The Colonial Disease: A Social History of Sleeping Sickness in Northern Zaire, 1900–1940* (Cambridge University Press, 1992), 42–45.
[17] Human African Trypanosomiasis, Symptoms, Diagnosis, and Treatment, The World Health Organization, www.who.int/trypanosomiasis_african/diagnosis/en/, accessed January 2, 2020.

systematized western biomedical practices to tackle sleeping sickness
and claim the power to control African populations and reform African
bodies. Unlike western biomedical discourses, African ideas about
health and healing did not necessary distinguish between physical,
social, and moral disturbances. The impact of sleeping sickness outbreaks on both cattle and humans around the turn of the twentieth
century was so sudden and pervasive that many people believed this
disease reflected the dis-ease brought on by European conquest and
settlement.[18]

Similar dynamics between colonial intervention and African mistrust
played out in Dakar, the capital of the French West Africa administration. In response to a 1914 bubonic plague epidemic, the French colonial government instituted a variety of mandatory sanitary interventions,
including the destruction of African homes, the cordoning off of the
"native quarter," and forced vaccinations of Africans. These measures
sparked a protest that closed down the central market for six days. Blaise
Diagne, the first African elected to the French Chamber of Deputies,
demanded that Governor William Merlaud-Ponty end the state's invasive tactics. Some of Diagne's supporters believed that the extreme
public health measures were carried out in retaliation for his election,
which occurred less than a month prior to the outbreak. Rumors spread
that French authorities planned to assassinate Diagne with poison dis-
guised as a vaccination dose. After a few weeks of protest, the government ended the state of emergency and removed the health regulations.
Efforts to impose harsh interventions like resettlement and racial segregation remained controversial in colonial Senegal. While French officials took a paternalistic approach, believing in the efficacy of western
biomedicine, many Senegalese viewed the outbreak as a sign that colonialism brought instability to the region.[19]

Rumors about the subversive dangers of western medicine were also
prevalent across eastern and central Africa, where some Africans spread
rumors that nurses and doctors were "vampires" who fed on the blood
and organs removed from ill (and ill-fated) victims.[20] During the
1904–1905 Maji Maji Rebellion in German East Africa local spiritual
healers sought to inoculate Africans from the infection of German

[18] Lyons, *The Colonial Disease*, 162–198.
[19] Myron Echenberg, *Black Death, White Medicine: Bubonic Plague and the Politics of
      Public Health in Colonial Senegal, 1914–1945* (Heinemann, 2002).
[20] Luise White, *Speaking with Vampires: Rumor and History in Colonial Africa*
      (University of California Press, 2000).

colonialism.[21] The *hongo* (spiritual expert) anointed warriors with a magical liquid (*maji*, or "water") that would make them disappear in battle and turn European bullets into water. Belief in the *maji* was a rejection of both European medicine and colonial conquest. The widespread distribution of the *maji* itself fueled the anticolonial uprising across much of southern Tanzania. Africans feared western health interventions, but Europeans also feared the political influence of African healers who led the charge against colonialism.

Experiments with state-run vaccination campaigns, such as those carried out after a smallpox epidemic in the Cape Colony of South Africa in the 1880s, blossomed into standardized public health regulations across colonial Africa in the 1910s and 1920s. Public health laws dictated and regulated medical examinations, vaccinations, and sanitary regimes. Christian missions used medical interventions and training to lure Africans to the mission stations. By World War I the colonial governments were building new hospitals, infirmaries, and dispensaries and took over training African medical assistants, nurses, dispensers, pharmacists, and eventually doctors. These developments facilitated medical research. Beginning in 1916 the Belgian Congo initiated an annual public health survey that catalogued cases of sleeping sickness, yaws, malaria, and measles. By the 1930s colonial institutions like prisons, schools, hospitals, and labor camps provided intimate access to African bodies for scientific study. Colonial officers could monitor Africans twenty-four hours a day and for months at a time. Day-to-day measurements of children's growth patterns, laborers' physical stamina, and prisoners' mental states provided fodder for eugenicist theories that race and culture were primary factors in mental and physical health. Colonial public health regulations transformed the western scientific doctrine of the development episteme into law and policy.

The first colonial health centers in Africa were located in cities near colonial schools, hospitals, and dispensaries. The interwar era brought new concerns about rural health to the fore, but services in rural areas remained patchy well after the end of colonialism. The introduction of western biomedicine did not replace indigenous health practices, but it did introduce new options. If medicinal herbs and rituals of local

---

[21] Jamie Monson, "War of Words: The Narrative Efficacy of Medicine in the Maji Maji War," in James Giblin and Jamie Monson, eds., *Maji Maji: Lifting the Fog of War* (Koninklijke Brill NV, 2010), 33–70.

healers did not work immediately, Africans could draw on the services of a missionary doctor or colonial dispensary, and vice versa. Some who benefited from and demanded access to western medicine viewed this as merely one option among a repertoire of possible solutions to health problems. Today it is difficult to distinguish between "western" and "African" healing practices because both have changed over time and health practitioners often rely on a combination of knowledge and approaches.

SEXUALITY, HEALTH, AND THE DEVELOPMENT OF LABOR

Sexually transmitted illnesses (STIs) were some of the first major health problems that colonial officials systematically catalogued. Sexually transmitted illnesses were common in Europe as well, a fact addressed by legislation passed in European countries between the late eighteenth and mid-nineteenth centuries.[22] Concerns about the impact of STIs on soldiers during World War I heightened awareness of the problem, and officials began linking STIs with the non-European destinations of European soldiers. In colonial Africa Europeans associated STIs with low birth rates, infant mortality, and declining population, issues that negatively impacted the labor pool. Europeans argued that African tendencies toward promiscuity accounted for the prevalence of diseases like syphilis. In Uganda and Malawi British doctors raised an alarm about the link between sexuality and syphilis outbreaks, though historian Megan Vaughan has pointed out that they often misdiagnosed cases of yaws, a non-venereal disease, as syphilis.[23] Despite western stereotypes about African sexuality and disease, many of the regions with the highest rates of STIs were those with a long history of contact with Europeans.

   In Africa as elsewhere women were identified as the vectors of STIs and were subject to forced medical examinations and deportation from cities. Typically, European and African men were treated while women were repatriated to their natal villages. The increase in STIs during the

[22] Philippa Levine, *Prostitution, Race, and Politics: Policing Venereal Disease in the British Empire* (Routledge, 2003).
[23] Megan Vaughan, *Curing Their Ills: Colonial Power and African Illness* (Stanford University Press, 1991), 137.

early twentieth century can be attributed in part to long-distance migrant labor schemes, rapid urbanization, and new forms of prostitution. Customary wife lending, concubinage, and slave marriages had long existed on the continent, but prostitution – the direct exchange of sex for cash – was generally a colonial invention. Luise White argues that sex work was tolerated and at times encouraged by the colonial administration in Kenya because it served to support the urban labor system by providing African men with access to the "comforts of home" necessary to regenerate their labor power.[24]

Concerns about venereal disease were simultaneously concerns about sexual morality and economics. European racial tropes perpetuating the myth of African promiscuity justified interventions into African sexual lives. Sexual immorality was connected to STIs, which many authorities considered the primary reason for high rates of infertility. Colonial states cared about infertility because it threatened the stability of the labor resources. Western attempts to control African sexuality and reproduction propagated both the economic goals of development and the racial ideologies of the development episteme.

11.2 The health of laborers

Despite the fact that they prioritized labor productivity, states did not always invest in the health of laborers. In South Africa, British East Africa (Kenya), French Equatorial Africa (Chad, Central African Republic, Cameroon, Republic of the Congo, and Gabon), the Gold Coast (Ghana), Northern Rhodesia (Zambia), Southern Rhodesia (Zimbabwe), and other colonies with large-scale colonial cash crop agriculture and resource extraction, state officials were preoccupied with the supply and condition of labor. South Africa's long-distance migrant labor system emerged in response to the late nineteenth-century Mineral Revolution with the discovery of gold and diamonds. In the early twentieth century mining officials became concerned about the severe and frequent outbreaks of tuberculosis (TB)

---

[24] Luise White, *Comforts of Home: Prostitution in Colonial Nairobi* (University of Chicago Press, 1990), 12.

among the miners. In the late 1920s more than 90% of Africans in the Transkei region of South Africa were infected with TB. Mining companies and state officials argued that Africans were responsible for the spread of the disease due to poor personal hygiene and sanitation practices. The collaborative organization established by the mining companies, the Witwatersrand Native Labour Association (WNLA), subjected workers to mandatory medical examinations, repatriated sick workers, and segregated the ill from the healthy in mining compounds. Meanwhile, officials, chiefs, and mining companies collaborated to ensure that healthy recruits were in constant supply. Historian Randall Packard argues that the poor living and work conditions on the mines facilitated the outbreaks. Inadequate medical care, limited food rations, unsanitary residential compounds, and grueling physical labor weakened miners' immune systems.[1]

South Africa was by no means unique. The primary concessionary company in the Belgian Congo, Union Minière de Haut-Katanga, performed regular medical exams on its laborers without acknowledging the impact of labor conditions on the workers' health. Recent studies place the origins of HIV/AIDS precisely in 1920s Kinshasa, where urbanization, migrant labor, and short-term relationships in mining compounds likely facilitated the spread of the disease.[2] Similarly, in Haut-Nyong, Cameroon, labor practices of the rubber industry and large-scale cocoa and coffee plantations contributed to a spike in sleeping sickness and syphilis and a rising rate of infant mortality by World War II.[3] Colonial economic development schemes, especially those dependent on migrant labor, exacerbated the very health problems many officials hoped to tackle.

[1] Randall M. Packard, *White Plague, Black Labor: Tuberculosis and the Political Economy of Health and Disease in South Africa* (University of California Press, 1989).

[2] Jacques Pepin, *The Origins of AIDS* (Cambridge University Press, 2011), 67–70.

[3] Guillaume Lachenal, "Experimental Hubris and Medical Powerlessness: Notes from a Colonial Utopia, Cameroon, 1939–1949," in Paul W. Geissler, Richard Rottenburg, and Julia Zenker, eds., *Rethinking Biomedicine and Governance in Africa: Contributions from Anthropology* (transcript Verlag, 2012), 119–140.

Colonial efforts to increase African exports for the global economy, commodify and regulate land and labor, and industrialize agricultural and mining brought on new health problems and new health interventions. Missionaries and officials introduced health education, midwifery training, and other medical training programs, and they provided treatment for syphilis, sleeping sickness, malaria, tuberculosis, and common ailments. Rather than promoting a healthy labor pool, colonial economic development was becoming detrimental to the health of African workers. Migrant labor systems in particular severely impacted the health and welfare of workers, as well as the women, children, and elders left behind in the villages. When they came home, migrant laborers infected their families with syphilis and tuberculosis. The removal of young men impoverished rural economies, resulting in widespread undernourishment and malnutrition. By the early 1940s some employers recognized the value of a permanent labor force and provided family housing for their workers.

The interwar period brought these issues into sharp focus, and officials implemented comprehensive health programs to treat and prevent the spread of deadly diseases and to increase the standard of living of Africans. Officials directed more funds toward improving the health of women and children and decreasing infant mortality. Women's health took center stage in the interwar period when more European women came to work in Africa. For instance the 1936 Annual Report for Nigeria listed school-based medical care for girls, medical and midwifery training for women, and child welfare and infant welfare centers among its recent innovations.[25] The ultimate goal remained the same as it did from the beginning of the twentieth century: to increase the population and improve the health of Africans in order to increase labor availability and productivity for the benefit of colonial economies. Colonial officials integrated a capitalist ethos with a modernizing impulse in devising African development policies.

NUTRITIONAL SCIENCE AS AFRICAN DEVELOPMENT

Malnutrition became a top health concern among western scientists and colonial officials during the interwar period. Prior to World War

---

[25] *Annual Report on the Social and Economic Progress of the People of Nigeria, 1936* (His Majesty's Stationary Office, 1938), 21–23.

I nutrition had been measured in terms of the "bread line," the daily minimum amount of food necessary for a person to be able to work, or the calories necessary for survival. The "bread line" determined workers' rations in colonial Africa. Breakthroughs in studies of the effects of vitamins and minerals in the late 1920s shifted the focus from undernourishment to malnutrition. Starvation among Europe's poor intensified during the Great Depression. Global concerns about hunger and malnutrition erupted in the 1930s.[26] In Africa social scientists studied malnutrition as a cultural problem rather than an economic one. John Boyd Orr and J. L. Gilks's 1926 nutritional study comparing the diet of the pastoralist Maasai with that of the agriculturalist Kikuyu suggested that the predominantly vegetarian culture of the Kikuyu made them less productive laborers.[27]

In 1938 the British Colonial Office sent a team to Nyasaland (Malawi) to compare the nutrition levels of three villages and one town. Anthropologist Audrey Richards, a medical doctor, an agricultural officer, a botanist, and a nutritionist were all hired to work under the leadership of Benjamin Platt. Platt hoped the project would set the standard for all succeeding nutrition surveys and development projects in British colonies. As historian Cynthia Brantley has argued, the scientists' misconceptions about the structure of African families made it difficult for them to recognize how much the migrant labor system impacted African diets. The scientists presumed that they would find micronutrient deficiencies. Instead, they discovered cases of seasonal hunger as communities ran out of food in the months before the harvest. Many households lacked enough labor to successfully feed themselves. Young men had been recruited into the migrant labor industries of southern and central Africa, and women were left to look after the farms. Women worked nine to ten hours a day in the best of circumstances – not counting the hours spent on childcare. There simply was not enough time for them to engage in agricultural work at a level that could sustain their families. Despite these findings, the researchers prescribed a development program focused on providing

[26] James Vernon, *Hunger: A Modern History* (Harvard University Press, 2007), 118–120.

[27] Cynthia Brantley, "Kikuyu-Maasai Nutrition and Colonial Science: The Orr and Gilks Study in Late 1920s Kenya Revisited," *International Journal of African Historical Studies* 30:1 (1997) 49–86; Michael Worboys, "The Discovery of Malnutrition between the Wars," in David Arnold, ed., *Imperial Medicine and Indigenous Societies* (Manchester University Press, 1988), 208–225.

supplements of vitamins and minerals, which directed attention away from the economic and political factors influencing African diets.[28]

In 1939, one year after the Nyasaland nutrition study, the British Colonial Office published a report on nutrition based on surveys conducted throughout the empire.[29] Officials in African territories attributed nutritional problems to local food cultures and African "ignorance" about nutrition, but the interviewees stated that poverty affected what they ate. Britain followed the report with "Health Propaganda Campaigns" to promote sanitation and nutrition in Africa, including instruction on how to prepare healthy meals. The state ignored evidence that economic hardship informed nutritional habits. In June 1940 the French administration in Senegal initiated its own policy for combating what it viewed as the interrelated problems of malnutrition and infant mortality.[30] Colonial researchers sought to trace the impact of nutrition on pregnant and nursing mothers and on children. Nutrition, fertility, maternity, and infant and child welfare were indicators of the overall health and viability of the population and, more specifically, the labor force.[31] Research on nutrition transformed African women and children into objects of scientific study and reified imperialist patriarchal claims to authority within the development episteme.

MEDICAL RESEARCH AND PUBLIC HEALTH IN THE AGE OF HIV/AIDS

Since the 1980s significant international funding and attention has been directed toward investigating and eradicating HIV/AIDS in Africa. The statistics are well known. In the hardest-hit regions of eastern and southern Africa, between 10 and 23 percent of the population were infected with HIV by the late 1990s. Around that time,

---

[28] Cynthia Brantley, *Feeding Families: African Realities and British Ideas of Nutrition and Development in Early Colonial Africa* (Heinemann, 2002).

[29] Great Britain, Economic Advisory Council, Committee on Nutrition in the Colonial Empire, *Nutrition in the Colonial Empire: First Report* (His Majesty's Stationary Office, 1939).

[30] Mor Ndao, "Colonisation et politique de santé maternelle et infantile au Sénégal (1905–1960)," *French Colonial History* 9 (2008) 191–211.

[31] Nancy Rose Hunt, "'Le Bebe en Brousse': European Women, African Birth Spacing and Colonial Intervention in Breast Feeding in the Belgian Congo," *International Journal of African Historical Studies* 21:3 (1988) 401–432.

American pharmaceutical companies developed effective antiretro-viral therapy (ART) for HIV/AIDS treatment, partly based on research conducted in African communities most impacted by the disease. The cost of these drugs was prohibitive and generic versions could not be produced until the patents expired. This sparked an intense debate over whether HIV/AIDS drugs should be provided at an affordable cost to those who need them in the global south. Pharmaceutical companies argued that they deserved a return on their investment in researching and developing the drugs, while others retorted that African volunteers who were subjected to invasive, sometimes harmful or deadly medical trials should be the first to receive the medications. The top pharmaceutical companies enjoyed an average profit margin of around 30 percent, and the rest around 18 percent. As one bioethi-cist for the National Institutes of Health explained, "It is not fair to place members of the population at risk without a reasonable expect-ation of a benefit to that population."[32] The question about the avail-ability and efficacy of ART prescription drugs was only one issue in debates about HIV/AIDS. Studies conducted in Africa reinforced colonial stereotypes about African "promiscuity" and "ignorance," and HIV/AIDS was labeled an "African" disease despite its global reach.[33] Anthropologist Johanna Crane argues that since drug therap-ies have become more available and affordable a new American "scramble" to conduct medical research on HIV in Africa has gener-ated new inequalities in treatment and overall medical care.[34]

Studies of HIV/AIDS have revealed the general inadequacies of healthcare services in African countries. The lack of attention and funding for cancer treatment is one example. The rates of cancers like Kaposi's sarcoma, related to HIV infection, have been on the rise, but the diagnosis rate of cancer is approximately half that of HIV infections. Furthermore, most people diagnosed with cancer are at a late stage with limited treatment options. Since public health initiatives during the past few decades have focused heavily on HIV/AIDS, malaria, and

[32] David B. Resnik, "Access to Affordable Medication in the Developing World: Social Responsibility vs. Profit," in Anton A. van Niekerk and Loretta M. Kopelman, eds., *Ethics & AIDS in Africa: The Challenge to Our Thinking* (David Philip, 2005), 111–126 at 115.

[33] Philip W. Setel, Milton Lewis, and Maryinez Lyons, eds., *Histories of Sexually Transmitted Diseases and HIV/AIDS in Sub-Saharan Africa* (Greenwood Press, 1999), 18.

[34] Johanna Tayloe Crane, *Scrambling for Africa: AIDS, Expertise, and the Rise of the American Global Health Science* (Cornell University Press, 2013).

other infectious diseases, diagnosis and treatment of cancer has remained a low priority. Now that ARTs are more widely available for HIV patients, some attention is being directed to other systemic health issues. The high cost and limited availability of treatments remains a major obstacle in cancer detection and treatment. Drug makers and nongovernmental organizations have formed partnerships to address the issue, but the vast majority of cancer patients receive only palliative care.[35]

Humanitarian and development healthcare projects in Africa today grapple with some of the same issues European colonial development experts faced during the early twentieth century. In addition to the misunderstandings between different cultures of healing, the World Health Organization (WHO) and other international funding agencies have to compromise between crisis response to outbreaks and long-term, comprehensive development of healthcare facilities and services. On the other end of the spectrum, individuals often make difficult choices, for example, between paying for expensive treatment and feeding their families. During the colonial era most people barely made enough cash to pay taxes, let alone cover routine or emergency medical care. While this is a conundrum for anyone living in a place with privatized healthcare, many Africans cannot access or afford the kind of health insurance common in places like the United States. Some international medical practitioners and researchers urge that healthcare is a human right, and they call on the leaders of African nations to build hospitals and dispensaries, to distribute prescription medications at low cost, and to train more Africans for biomedical work. The debate often glosses over some of the trickier questions about what healthcare means and how it should be provided. Will this involve coercive or invasive procedures? Will the resources be directed toward "African" disease like HIV/AIDS and malaria, or will people have access to more comprehensive health services? At what cost and to whom will these services be provided? Will Africa continue to be an inexpensive laboratory for western medical research? The answers to these questions lie in what Graboyes calls the "gray space of ethics, medicine, and the law," the very space where

---

[35] Donald G. McNeil Jr., "As Cancer Tears through Africa, Drug Makers Draw Up a Battle Plan," *New York Times*, October 7, 2017, www.nytimes.com/2017/10/07/health/africa-cancer-drugs.html?_r=0, accessed December 1, 2017. See also Julie Livingstone, *Improvising Medicine: An African Oncology Ward in an Emerging Cancer Epidemic* (Duke University Press, 2012).

misconceptions abound and neocolonial practices and perspectives resurface despite the good intentions of researchers.[36] Understanding the colonial capitalist impulse behind eradicating diseases and tackling nutrition problems in settler colonies and migrant labor populations helps to bring deep, long-standing issues into focus.

11.3 The 2014–2015 Ebola crisis in Liberia

The 2014–2015 Ebola crisis in West Africa, the largest outbreak of Ebola in recorded history, was both a medical and a public health crisis that spread fear and confusion across the globe. The country of Liberia, which had the most recorded deaths from the outbreak, became the center of debates over how the virus was spread and what could be done to stop it.[1] According to Garrett Ingoglia, then vice president of emergency response for Americares, the Ebola outbreak "highlighted inequalities in healthcare provision" in the countries affected.[2] Liberia had yet to fully recover from its civil wars of the 1990s and early 2000s. Healthcare facilities were woefully understaffed and under-resourced. Ingoglia estimated there were only about fifty Liberian doctors in the country at the time of the outbreak, and the international response came late. During the crisis, many healthcare facilities closed down because providers got sick or were afraid of contracting the disease. In their absence international aid organizations opened Ebola treatment centers. Doctors from all over the world came to Liberia to provide assistance. Given that international funding and expertise was focused primarily on Ebola, many people suffering from other ailments like malaria died because they had nowhere to go for treatment.

West Point, Monrovia, a densely populated peninsula of Liberia's capital city with about 70,000 residents, became the center of the outbreak. The settlement was already dealing with overcrowding and lack of water, sanitation, and hygiene (WASH) services. The early symptoms of Ebola are similar to those of malaria or the flu, which made the disease difficult to identify. Some people with these symptoms refused to go to the hospital for fear of contracting Ebola there, while others

---

[36] Graboyes, *The Experiment Must Continue*, 196.

questioned whether Ebola existed.[3] West Point residents resisted interventions by international aid workers partly because some residents believed aid workers were infecting people with Ebola. Researcher Leah Campbell explains, "The mood was a mixture of anger, suspicion and fear."[4] Government security forces instituted a mandatory quarantine around West Point, which sparked protest and violence between soldiers and residents. Eventually tensions eased once West Point community leaders stepped in to mediate the conflict and coordinate response efforts.[5]

It was not merely the government's extreme response to the Ebola outbreak that generated an environment of mistrust in West Point. Western medical intervention in Liberia has a deep and thorny history. The Republic of Liberia was established in 1847 by free Blacks from the United States as part of the "Back to Africa" movement. In 1926 the Liberian government offered Firestone Tire and Rubber Company a ninety-nine-year lease for up to a million acres of land in order to develop rubber plantations. That year, Firestone hired Harvard University scientists to conduct biological, ecological, and medical surveys in order to assess the region's potential for both rubber production and labor recruitment. Historian Gregg Mitman stated that this expedition "produced ways of seeing and knowing that both depended on and facilitated the development and industrialization of life in the tropics into new forms of biocapital."[6] Mitman's oral history interviews reveal that memories of this scientific colonization linger among the descendants of those displaced, and Firestone still dominates the Liberian economy today. In light of this history, the 2014–2015 Ebola crisis appeared as another chapter in a lengthy saga of Liberia's entanglement with American imperialism, extractive industrial capitalism, and western biomedical and biological science.

The failures and successes in tackling the recent Ebola outbreak in West Point offer some key points to consider. Not until West Point residents were involved in the negotiations with government did tensions cool. Policies regarding containment and treatment are more effective when members of the community are involved in their planning from the onset. Second, the rate of new infections began to slow once experts recognized Ebola was a global disease requiring a coordinated international response rather than merely an "African" disease in need of western scientific solutions. Third, health disasters can exacerbate economic and political inequalities as aid organizations tend to direct more funding toward crises than toward substantive, long-term changes. Ingoglia noted that, in this case, Americares' emergency response group was able to offer general training for West African health workers and help raise funding to expand the health system in Liberia.[7] Most importantly for the global community, the Ebola crisis in West Africa provided a rare opportunity for randomized controlled trials (RCTs) of an Ebola vaccine that showed success among people during the 2019 outbreak in the Democratic Republic of Congo.[8] Approaching an outbreak as a global issue erupting from longer histories of intervention and inequality – both local and global – results in more humane treatment of patients, better distribution of knowledge and resources, and more rapid and effective conclusions to crises.

[1]   Centers for Disease Control and Prevention, "2014 Ebola Outbreak in West Africa – Case Counts," www.cdc.gov/vhf/ebola/outbreaks/2014-west-africa/case-counts.html, accessed December 17, 2017.

[2]   Interview with Corrie Decker, Garrett Ingoglia, Vice President of Emergency Response for Americares, July 5, 2017.

[3]   Ingoglia, Interview.

[4]   L. Campbell, "Ebola Response in Cities: Learning for Future Public Health Crises," ALNAP Working Paper, 2017, ALNAP/ODI, available at www.urban-response.org/help-library/ebola-response-in-cities-learning-for-future-public-health-crises, accessed January 4, 2020, 18.

[5]   Adia Benton, "Whose Security? Militarization and Securitization during West Africa's Ebola Outbreak," in Michiel Hofman and Sokhieng Au, eds., *The Politics of Fear: Médecins Sans Frontières and the West African Ebola Epidemic* (Oxford University Press, 2017), 25–50.

[6]   Gregg Mitman, "Forgotten Paths of Empire: Ecology, Disease, and Commerce in Making of Liberia's Plantation Economy: President's Address," *Environmental History* 22:1 (2017) 1–22 at 8.

[7]   Ingoglia, Interview. See also Sharon Abramowitz, "What Happens When MSF Leaves? Humanitarian Departure and Medical Sovereignty in Postconflict Liberia," in Sharon Abramowitz and Catherine Panter-Brick, eds., *Medical Humanitarianism: Ethnographies of Practice* (University of Pennsylvania Press, 2015).

[8]   Shirin Ashraf and Arthur Wickenhagen, "Why Ebola Vaccine on Trial in the DRC Is Raising Hopes," *The Conversation*, February 10, 2019, https://theconversation.com/why-ebola-vaccine-on-trial-in-the-drc-is-raising-hopes-111126, accessed January 4, 2020.

★★★

African suspicion of western biomedical interventions has its roots in the imperial and colonial eras. Two primary motivations drove colonial policies around health and medicine in Africa: first, the protection of Europeans' health, and, second, the assurance of a constant supply of healthy African laborers. The nineteenth-century ad hoc campaigns to protect Europeans and segregate the sick from the healthy grew into state-sponsored public health programs during the interwar period. By World War II colonial development health discourses on Africa had shifted from the "white man's grave" to those addressing biopolitical concerns as states harnessed healthy bodies for productive purposes. Medical studies on declining populations, outbreaks of sleeping sickness or tuberculosis, STIs, and maternity and childcare sought healthcare solutions that would increase the productivity of labor. New hospitals, maternity centers, child welfare centers, and dispensaries brought some people relief and others terror. Whether dealing with a disease outbreak or researching endemic malnutrition, colonial officials relied on western biomedical solutions to these development problems. Scientists and officials used public health interventions and biomedical research to bolster the norms of the development episteme.

Given these legacies of colonial medicine, one might begin to under-stand why some people in Africa attribute a bout of malaria to witch-craft, believe HIV/AIDS was invented by western scientists to systematically infect Africans, or view colonialism and westernization as diseases in their own right.[37] Western medical interventions in Africa over the past two centuries instituted a culture of experimental research that still largely defines Africans' encounters with biomedicine today. Mutual misconceptions create conflict over the provision of services, such as occurred during the Ebola crisis in West Africa in 2014 and 2015. Some Liberians understandably mistrusted the intentions of govern-ment and foreign healthcare workers, and some international doctors and aid workers attributed this mistrust primarily to Liberians' ignor-ance about the disease and irrational fear of western medicine.[38] More

---

[37] Cindy Patton, *Inventing AIDS* (Routledge, 1990).
[38] The *New York Times* reported that "Health workers had been chased out of fearful neighborhoods." Kevin Sack, Sheri Fink, Pam Belluck, and Adam Nossiter, "How Ebola Roared Back," *New York Times*, December 29, 2014, www.nytimes.com/20 14/12/30/health/how-ebola-roared-back.html, accessed November 30, 2017. See also Adam Nossiter, "Fear of Ebola Breeds a Terror of Physicians," *New York*

nuanced analyses of this outbreak and other health crises in Africa require an acknowledgment not only of immediately relevant economic and political issues but also of a history of development. This history shows how health interventions have repeatedly pitted "ignorant" Africans against rational western scientists, all the while facilitating international capitalist interests on the continent. Africans working to redefine development within their own cultural and epistemological frameworks challenge state and local authorities to dissociate Africa and Africans from disease and death in the development episteme.

Further Reading

On health concerns linked to race, sexuality, and labor see Shane Doyle, *Before HIV: Sexuality, Fertility and Mortality in East Africa, 1900–1980* (Oxford University Press, 2013); Myron Echenberg, *Black Death, White Medicine: Bubonic Plague and the Politics of Public Health in Colonial Senegal, 1914–1945* (Heinemann, 2002); Lynette A. Jackson, *Surfacing Up: Psychiatry and Social Order in Colonial Zimbabwe, 1908–1968* (Cornell University Press, 2005); Randall M. Packard, *White Plague, Black Labor: Tuberculosis and the Political Economy of Health and Disease in South Africa* (University of California Press, 1989); Megan Vaughan, *Curing Their Ills: Colonial Power and African Illness* (Stanford University Press, 1991).

On medical knowledges and discourses see Steven Feierman and John M. Janzen, eds., *The Social Basis of Health and Healing in Africa* (University of California Press, 1992); Karen E. Flint, *Healing Traditions: African Medicine, Cultural Exchange, and Competition in South Africa, 1820–1948* (Ohio University Press, 2008); Melissa Graboyes, *The Experiment Must Continue: Medical Research and Ethics in East Africa, 1940–2014* (Ohio University Press, 2015); Nancy Rose Hunt, *A Colonial Lexicon of Birth Ritual, Medicalization, and Mobility in the Congo* (Duke University Press, 1999); Abena Dove Osseo-Asare, *Bitter Roots: The Search for Healing Plants in Africa* (University of Chicago Press, 2014); and Donna A. Patterson, *Pharmacy in Senegal: Gender, Healing, and Entrepreneurship* (Indiana University Press, 2015).

On colonial nutrition see Cynthia Brantley, *Feeding Families: African Realities and British Ideas of Nutrition and Development in Early Colonial Africa* (Heinemann, 2002); Jennifer Tappan, *The Riddle of Malnutrition: The Long Arc of Biomedical and Public Health Interventions in Uganda* (Ohio University Press, 2017); Diana Wylie, *Starving on a Full Stomach: Hunger and the Triumph of Cultural Racism in Modern South Africa* (University of Virginia Press, 2001).

Times, July 27, 2014, www.nytimes.com/2014/07/28/world/africa/ebola-epidemic-west-africa-guinea.html, accessed November 30, 2017.

CHAPTER 12

Manufacturing Modernization

In 2010 Irish musician Bono, a celebrity advocate for foreign aid in Africa, changed his tune about how to support African development. After long discussions with Ghanaian economist George Ayittey and Sudanese telecom billionaire Mo Ibrahim, among others, Bono urged that business partnerships are the solution to African underdevelopment.[1] He became convinced that neoliberal capitalism and the free market, what he calls "smart aid," would save Africa from poverty. This seemingly innovative direction in development thinking was actually not new. Since at least the 1860s when David Livingstone argued that "legitimate commerce" would end the slave trade, westerners have returned to the notion that global capitalism would "save Africa." Of course Africans and Europeans had been trading partners for centuries before colonization; what changed in the nineteenth century was the emergence of a moral imperative that commerce with the west would rescue Africans. The savior paradigm never portrays Africans as economic *equals*. Even Bono's concession for "partnerships" implies that the non-African "partner" will necessarily have enough economic influence to integrate the African partner into the global market.

Livingstone's campaign to bring European trade to the interior of the continent set the stage for international interventions to "modernize" African economies. Since the early twentieth century colonial economists pressed for modernization and industrialization in Africa,

---

[1] Bono, "Africa Reboots," *New York Times*, April 17, 2010, www.nytimes.com/2010/04/18/opinion/18bono.html?pag, accessed August 2, 2018.

but only to the extent that this aided the extraction of resources through the use of inexpensive labor. Modernization thus had its limits in Africa, and only very rarely emerged out of partnerships with Africans. Large-scale, colonial industrial projects supplied cheap raw materials and managerial jobs for Europeans. Governments and companies industrialized the mining sectors of segregated states in southern Africa in order to generate profit for themselves, not necessarily to aid the "modernization" of local economies. Even in postcolonial and postapartheid African states, industrialization has helped the few rather than the masses.

In light of this history and the current position of African economies in the global market, we must take Bono's well-meaning call for development partnerships with a grain of salt. Industrialization in Africa – and economic development more generally – may appear in very different forms than those development experts anticipate. Throughout the twentieth century Africans have established their own projects for developing agriculture, mining, and manufacturing in order to improve their societies. Murid peanut farming in Senegal, equal partnership in Botswana's diamond industry, and digital banking on mobile phones in Kenya (case studies discussed in this chapter) are just a few examples showcasing how Africans have taken the initiative to modernize their economies and form partnerships with governments and private funders on mutually beneficial terms. Despite the long history of western dominance over discourses on economic modernization, African industrialization and economic development does not always (and does not have to) look like western modernity.

COLONIZING AGRICULTURAL COMMODITIES

Agriculture has been central to trade in Africa for millennia, and the surplus farmers have produced has allowed for specialization of jobs, social stratification, and the rise of trading centers.[2] Both small-scale peasant and large-scale commercial agriculture were present in African societies before European colonialization. Some large empires, such as the Mali Empire, created plantations to feed their armies and produce

---

[2] Kevin Shillington, *History of Africa.* Third edition (Palgrave Macmillan, 2012), 22–41.

income for the state. African producers responded to the needs of the market and quickly adopted and adapted crops introduced from elsewhere. For example, cassava (known in the Americas as manioc) was brought to West Africa by Portuguese merchants in the sixteenth century. Africans began growing cassava in order to sell it to European merchants, especially slave traders, who needed to provide a large quantity of cheap food for the enslaved Africans being shipped across the Atlantic Ocean. Eventually cassava became a staple crop in many African diets, to the point that twelve of the top twenty cassava-producing countries today are in Africa.

European commercial desire for agricultural products brought foreign companies into the interior of Africa in the nineteenth century. Colonization of Africa began when European governments gave charters to these private companies and, along with them, exclusive rights to exploit the resources of designated regions in Africa. These charter or concessionary companies, as they were called, had administrative control over the colonies; initially private businesses rather than governments financed and oversaw colonial expansion. Charter companies then sold concessionary rights to others interested in conducting business in Africa. However, many of the early charter companies declared bankruptcy because of the high cost of building the burgeoning state's infrastructure as well as the "unexpected" expenditure of maintaining control over Africans fighting against colonization. When charter companies withdrew, European governments took direct control over African colonies. Colonial governments continued selling concessions in African territories to private corporations, but private entities no longer bore the cost of colonization. Concessionary companies were focused on short-term, profitable exploitation of African labor and resources. One of the worst excesses of this form of colonial commerce was seen in the Congo between 1885 and 1907, when private enterprises sought rubber to meet the high demands for the manufacturing industries in Europe and North America, but at a terrible human price.[3]

The early years of colonial agriculture introduced Africans to brutal forced labor regimes. Forced labor systems shifted African people's efforts away from subsistence farming toward commercial agricultural commodities. Some Africans actively resisted these regimes by fleeing

---

[3] Adam Hochschild, *King Leopold's Ghost: A Story of Greed, Terror, and Heroism in Colonial Africa* (Houghton Mifflin, 1998).

to other areas (such as occurred in the Belgian Congo and German Southwest Africa) or fighting wars against Europeans (like in French West Africa, Tanganyika, and South Africa). African resistance required European governments to maintain armies, which were costly and lowered the potential profits. Once European governments took over from private companies they modified coercive labor policies in order to lessen African resistance to colonialism. However, by requiring African peasant farmers to grow primarily commercial crops for export, colonization left many African communities on the edge of food insecurity and famine, as Chapter 6 details.

After World War I European powers designed colonial development schemes to furnish their own devastated economies back home with valuable raw materials. This also conveniently provided managerial employment opportunities for Europeans in the colonies. Most of these projects introduced western forms of technology and expansion of infrastructure to exploit peasant agricultural economies across the continent. In the process, Europeans brought several changes. First, they instituted taxes that had to be paid in cash rather than produce. The tax requirement incentivized Africans to seek out cash-paying jobs working for the colonial state or European settlers. Second, Africans in non-settler colonies were required to grow commodity cash crops such as cotton, sisal, tea, and coffee. This change created food insecurity, as many Africans no longer grew their own food but had to buy produce from other farmers. Third, European governments sponsored new "projects" and experimental farms that incorporated "scientific" methods to grow food and agricultural commodities. This research became one of the pillars of the development episteme. Colonial forms of agricultural commodity extraction required an industrialized approach.

COLONIAL INDUSTRIALIZATION

The rise of the Industrial Revolution in Europe heralded the links between economic industrialization, new technologies, and progressive ideas. From the western perspective, a "modern" society valued industrialized capitalism. Absent from this equation was the need for inexpensive raw materials and labor that could be readily exploited to produce the profits of industrialization at home and abroad. European businesses sought out new sources of cheap labor to produce exportable raw materials in late nineteenth-century Africa. During the twentieth century the colonial emphasis on the extraction of raw materials in Africa continued along with the push for industrialization and modernization.

Industrialization involves multiple stages of production of raw materials before they are turned into finished products. Around the end of World War I European exporters in eastern and western Africa began the first stage, which was to launch industrial processing in Africa. By moving production to Africa and using cheap African labor to do so European businesspeople improved their cost ratio on the finished products. These first-stage industries included extracting oil from groundnuts and palm kernels, ginning cottonseed, extracting and drying cocoa and coffee beans, tanning hides, and milling lumber. Most of this low-level production work was done onsite in rural regions before the items were moved to port cities for export.[4]

British and French colonial governments approached industrial policies differently. In some French colonies early efforts to industrialize went beyond first-stage production. For instance, in Ivory Coast the Établissements Robert-Gonfreville (ERG) built the first integrated textile factory in West Africa in 1921.[5] Eventually the factory included the spinning of thread, weaving of cloth, and production of finished garments. Historian Barbara Cooper has demonstrated that, before the establishment of the factory, Ivorian men and women worked together to produce cotton cloth, but the factory reshaped the gender dynamics of cloth production. Previously, because women produced the thread for cloth they had claims over some of the cloth their husbands wove. Regional factory production of spinning thread put women at an economic disadvantage.[6] By the 1950s Ivorian women began working as laborers in the factory, which restored their role in cloth production and gave them direct access to the cash economy.[7]

---

[4]   J. O. C. Onyemelukwe, *Industrialization in West Africa* (St. Martin's Press, 1984), 60.
[5]   Julien Clémençot, "Côte d'Ivoire: l'usine textile Gonfrevillegile un mauvais cotton," *Jeune Afrique*, September 22, 2015, www.jeuneafrique.com/mag/245660/economie/c ote-divoire-lusine-textile-gonfreville-file-un-mauvais-coton/, accessed February 4, 2020.
[6]   Barbara Cooper, "Cloth, Commodity Production, and Social Capital: Women in Maradi, Niger 1890–1989," *African Economic History* 21 (1993) 51–71 at 53.
[7]   Mona Etienne, "Women and Men, Cloth and Colonization: The Transformation of Production-Distribution Relations among the Baule (Ivory Coast)," *Cahiers d'Études Africaines* 17:65 (1977) 41–64 at 57.

Industrialization in British West African colonies differed from that in Ivory Coast. British officials allowed industrialization efforts that absorbed decommissioned soldiers, did not require imported machinery, and kept Africans outside of urban areas. British officials, who feared "detribalized" (and thus presumably uncontrollable) Africans living in cities, centered their industrial efforts on "village industrializing." Reminiscent of early European Industrial Revolution practices, the state provided villagers in the Gold Coast and Nigeria with spinning wheels to produce yarn.[8] When one company petitioned to set up a factory with mechanized spinners and looms that would employ 300 people in Nigeria, the Board of Trade in the United Kingdom refused to allow the export of the necessary machinery. The British, being far more protective of their home industries than the French, refused any industrialization efforts that would significantly challenge British businesses at home.

Colonial endeavors at industrialization outside of the mining regions in pre–World War II Africa were facilitated by either western business investments or officials working in the colonies. First-stage industrialization was more often under the control of the colonial state, wherein setting up of factories like those in Ivory Coast was done by private businesses. Early efforts at mechanizing focused on processing agricultural crops such as coconuts, cotton, coffee, and cocoa. In mineral-rich regions of the continent industrialization often developed on a much wider scale including vertical integration, where a company controls all of the different stages of production. First-tier production work often relied on coordination between colonial departments of agriculture, forestry, education, and health.

In the agricultural industry, officials connected industrial methods to education and better health for workers in order to instill in Africans western ideas of time management, efficient labor practices, how to save salaries, and other aspects of a "modern" capitalist workforce and society. Modernization slowly arrived with industrialization as Africans found ways to adapt industrialization to their needs in a colonial economy. This process of modernization, however, was not always welcomed by colonial officials, who worried about the effects of modernity on so-called primitive Africans.

---

[8] L. J. Butler, *Industrialisation and the British Colonial State: West Africa 1939–1951* (Frank Cass, 1997), 110–115.

MAKING AGRICULTURE MODERN

By 1910 colonial governments should have learned that mass coercion of people into commodity production sparks disruptive resistance from laborers. Nonetheless, they persisted in using coerced labor, though in some cases they limited the period of contracts from 10 to 100 days per year for infrastructural projects. Sometimes colonizers used economic incentives to recruit laborers to their farms and factories. After 1910 colonial governments established production around three areas: state-organized peasant production, settler plantations/farms, and mineral extraction. Non-settler colonies allowed African farmers the most independence in regard to production. However, colonial officials usually implemented quotas on the supply of particular cash crops. In most settler sites, colonial governments imposed head or hut taxes and forced African populations onto "reserves." On these small reserves it was virtually impossible for Africans to grow enough produce to pay their taxes and feed their families, forcing them to work on settlers' farms.[9] As opposed to the recruitment of single male laborers for mineral extraction, many settler farmers wanted African laborers to bring their whole families. This policy offered some stability to African families, but their landlessness forced them to work for European settlers in perpetuity. Male migrant labor systems in areas of mineral extraction separated families for long periods of time, and wives and extended kin often had to maintain family lands without the help of able-bodied men.

12.1 Pastoralism as a stage of development

Development theory in the mid-twentieth century argued that human societies went through "stages of development": from hunters and gatherers to pastoralists, then to agriculturalists, and finally to industrialists. The big push theory (discussed in Chapter 7) argued that industrial investment allowed less-developed societies to "jump stages." These theorists assumed that supposed holdovers from premodern stages, such as

---

[9] Blair Rutherford, "Another Side to Rural Zimbabwe: Social Constructs and the Administration of Farm Workers in Urungwe District, 1940s," *Journal of Southern African Studies* 23:1 (1997) 107–126.

pastoralists, would not want to maintain these livelihoods when faced with a "better" option. Pastoralism, or herding of livestock such as cattle and goats, is usually practiced in semiarid regions of Africa. Cattle are central to pastoralist cultures as they represent both individual and social wealth. A significant aspect of pastoralist culture is the nomadic movement for water sources during different times of the year. Governments and development specialists see nomadic communities as problematic because they ignore government policies regarding landownership, defy easy taxation, and at times come into conflict with settled agricultural communities. For these reasons, colonial and postcolonial governments sought to limit the movement of pastoralists.

By the 1970s development specialists argued that pastoralism was also aggravating environmental degradation.[1] Fears of environmental decline steered development officials to introduce irrigation projects in western and eastern Africa and to transform pastoralists into farmers. Many of these irrigation projects failed because they were not environmentally sound and they forced pastoralists into settled agriculture against their wishes.[2] As recently as 2011 the Ethiopian government announced a new large-scale irrigation scheme to expand agriculture. The president at the time, Meles Zenawi, stated that pastoralists "could even be involved in farming to improve their lives."[3] The idea that pastoralists should embrace farming presumes there is one form of modernity and that it does not include a nomadic lifestyle. However, many pastoralists embrace modernity in other ways. Today they use Afriscout, a mobile phone app, to find pasturage for their animals, set up breeding partners, and conduct other aspects of modern animal husbandry. Modern technologies can support different kinds of lifestyles outside the western paradigm of modernity.

[1] Report of the United Nations Conference on Desertification, held in Nairobi, Kenya August 29–September 9, 1977. The Action Plan is available online. www.ciesin.org/docs/002-478/002-478.html, accessed August 1, 2018.
[2] William M. Adams and David M. Anderson, "Irrigation before Development: Indigenous and Induced Change in Agricultural Water Management in East Africa," *African Affairs* 87:349 (1988) 519–535.
[3] Elliot Fratkin, "Ethiopia's Pastoralist Policies: Development, Displacement and Resettlement," *Nomadic Peoples* 18:1 (2014) 94–114.

The colonial governments tried to invest most of their energy and resources into organizing peasant agriculture for maximum efficiency. The question of irrigation was key. The Gezira irrigation scheme was one of the earliest and largest agricultural development projects undertaken by the British colonial government. Gezira is an area in the present-day Republic of Sudan between the Blue and White Nile Rivers. Farmers in Gezira had been using several different agricultural technologies to improve their yields for a millennium, including flood plain planting and *sagia* irrigation works, which used oxen-driven wheels to pump water. Despite the success of these earlier innovations, the British believed the introduction of western technology in Gezira would drastically improve agricultural output.

In 1900 Gezira was a high-producing region for sorghum, a grain widely consumed among East and North African populations but not Europeans. Europeans launched a massive irrigation scheme, which required building a dam on the Blue Nile at Sennar. This scheme would use mechanized pumping systems to control the flow of water, removing the need for oxen and the inconsistency of flood plain planting. When British officials realized the high cost of mechanization, they decided to replace sorghum with the more profitable cotton crop, a commodity highly valued in Britain.[10] However, the British governor-general of Sudan, Reginald Wingate, did not realize the extent of Gezira sorghum exports into communities around the Red Sea. His decision to promote cotton caused regional food shortages.

The scheme began in 1906 when an American industrialist created the Sudan Plantation Syndicate and, in cooperation with the British colonial government, moved farmers into an irrigated tenancy system. After developing several other schemes between 1908 and 1923, the government dammed the Nile River at Sennar in 1925. At that point the scale of the Gezira project had escalated to more than 247,000 acres. Suddenly, farmers in the area no longer had a choice about what they could grow, and they lost title to their lands. The 1921 Gezira Land Ordinance declared that Sudanese landowners were now land renters and required them to submit to the scheme rules in order to keep farming where they had farmed for generations. Some farmers refused and moved away, so the Syndicate brought in settlers from West Africa and Egypt. The scheme required 33 percent of all

<hr>

[10]   Arthur Gaitskell, *Gezira: A Story of Development in the Sudan* (Faber & Faber, 1959).

cultivated land to be under cotton production using particular inputs and fertilizers that had to be purchased from the Syndicate. This system created a type of serfdom for the laborers in Gezira. Scheme officials controlled all aspects of the planting schedule and evicted peasants deemed negligent in their duties. Gezira was initially run by a former military officer who lacked knowledge about agriculture, water, or the environment but who was keen to introduce Gezira workers to "discipline." This system reinforced western cultural views of time management and ownership of land in an effort to remake Africans into "modern" workers. Officials from the Colonial Office hoped to make the Gezira scheme a symbol of modernity for other parts of Africa to emulate.[11]

The British were not the only colonizers to put their hopes for agricultural development into irrigation schemes. The French colonial Office du Niger initiated an irrigation project in Mali to provide cotton for the French textile industry and rice for laborers in Senegal. In 1925 the government of French West Africa created the Service temporaire des irrigations du Niger (STIN) to begin small-scale work on developing dams on the Niger River. Originally, officials aspired to put more than 4.5 million acres of land under cultivation, but limited metropolitan funding slowed down the project.[12] By 1931 the Office du Niger scaled down its plans to cultivate only about half of that acreage. It completed the dams and canal work in stages throughout the 1930s and 1940s, and opened up four sections of the scheme to farmers between 1935 and 1952. Given the sparse population in this area of Mali, the administration relocated 25,000 farmers and their families into the region and forced them to build the dams and work on the farms. The French sought to "civilize" the settlers into monogamous, two-generation nuclear family units, which is not how most Malians lived. The plan backfired. The logistics of settling laborers was far more complicated than officials had expected. In the early years of the Office du Niger scheme settlers had to wait until their plots produced sufficient crops before they had access to proper housing, sanitation, and a regular source of food. Many settlers refused to work

[11]   Victoria Bernal, "Colonial Moral Economy and the Discipline of Development: The Gezira Scheme and 'Modern' Sudan," *Cultural Anthropology* 12:4 (1997) 447–479.
[12]   Monica M. van Beusekom, *Negotiating Development: African Farmers and Colonial Experts at the Office Du Niger, 1920–1960* (Heinemann, 2002).

toward French goals and disregarded French assimilationist efforts to remake their families.

By the end of World War II it was clear that mismanagement at the Office du Niger undermined the scheme. Officials assigned settlers to farmland without assessing its productive viability for the required crops. By the time of Mali's independence in 1960 the scheme had cultivated less than 3 percent of the originally planned 4.5 million acres. Moreover, as historian Monica van Beusekom explains, the French colonial government's attempts to "civilize" rural workers and "modernize" agricultural production utterly failed.[13]

Large-scale agricultural schemes were rife across Africa in both the colonial and postcolonial periods. The British attempted to replicate the successful groundnut production of Senegal's Muriddiya community (see Box 12.2) in northern Ghana and Tanzania, but they could not reproduce the unique conditions of groundnut production in French West Africa. As discussed in Chapter 6, British groundnut schemes in Tanzania (then Tanganyika) were colossal failures. Western efforts to industrialize agriculture in Africa suffered from miscalculation of African soils and environments and the insistence on large-scale, high-profile projects that ignored the realities of African lives. Attempts to remake African peasant farmers into western-style, modern, model citizens also seemed to fail, but these were secondary concerns. The fundamental purpose of colonial agricultural schemes was to produce raw materials as cheaply as possible for European industries, and most schemes fell far short of this objective.

12.2 Groundnut production by small farmers

The Muridiyya, a Senegalese Muslim Sufi sect begun by Amadou Bamba Mbacke in the late nineteenth century, came to dominate groundnut (peanut) agriculture in colonial Senegal. Amadou Bamba was initially exiled by the French colonial government from 1895 to 1912 because the French administration feared he would incite his followers to resist colonization. After 1900 the French slowly realized that Murid leaders (called marabouts) encouraged their followers

---

[13]   Ibid.

to grow food crops needed to feed the expanding urban centers. Eventually the French negotiated with Amadou Bamba and his marabouts to expand groundnut farming for export, which was greatly desired by French industry.[1] In exchange for Murid cooperation in groundnut production, the French stopped persecuting – although not surveilling – the Murids, kept western-style schools out of the Murid-dominated region of Senegal, and allowed them to build a large mosque in their holy city of Touba. The French government effectively created wide-scale groundnut production without having to invest any money or mechanize agriculture. They capitalized on the Murids' desire for religious freedom instead. In order to claim the Murid expansion of groundnut farming in Senegal as a success, however, the French had to abandon their modernizing goals of "civilizing" and westernizing African colonial subjects.[2]

[1] David Robinson, "The Murids: Surveillance and Collaboration," *Journal of African History* 40:2 (1999) 193–213.
[2] David Robinson, *Paths of Accommodation: Muslim Societies and French Colonial Authorities in Senegal and Mauritania, 1880–1920* (Ohio University Press, 2000).

MINING AND INDUSTRIALIZATION

Southern Africa, which Europeans began colonizing in 1652, became a regional center for industrialized mining in the late nineteenth century after the discovery of diamonds and gold. During this "mineral revolution" the government turned long-standing colonial racism into standardized policy. The segregationist policies of the late nineteenth and early twentieth centuries were solidified into the state-sanctioned system of apartheid ("separateness") in 1948. Apartheid denied Black South Africans citizenship in their own country, relegating them to "homelands" outside of urban centers. All movement of Black South Africans was controlled and only Blacks with work contracts could live in cities. These policies also artificially suppressed the wages of Black workers until the 1970s, which was a boon to manufacturing and mining businesses in the country. South Africa is often noted as the most industrialized nation in Africa, yet it was built on an economic foundation that benefited white settlers and deeply oppressed Black South Africans.[14]

The "mineral revolution" sparked a massive influx of Europeans, Americans, and Australians seeking to exploit the discovery of diamonds and gold in South Africa. In 1867 prospectors discovered diamonds in the area known as Kimberley, between the Vaal and Harts Rivers. The British, who already controlled the Cape Colony in South Africa, were at the forefront of this rush to stake claims over minerals, though other profit seekers from around the world laid claim to them as well. These mines brought tens of thousands of African migrant laborers to the region. Mining in South Africa expanded further in 1886 when gold was found in the Witwatersrand area. The city of Johannesburg quickly sprang up as 30,000 laborers flocked to the mines. As with the discoveries at Kimberley, whites gained control of the mining operations and relegated Black Africans to the lowest laboring positions.[15]

Mining brought rapid industrialization to South Africa and eventually to parts of present-day Zimbabwe, Zambia, Namibia, and the Democratic Republic of Congo (DRC). In most cases this industrialization did not bring the expected economic diversification to these countries because the wealth from mining remained in the hands of white settlers and multinational mining corporations. Segregation in settler-controlled states such as South Africa, Namibia, and Zimbabwe kept Black populations from enjoying the fruits of their labor. In Zambia and the DRC, while much of the wealth produced by the Copperbelt mines was extracted by Belgian, British, and South African firms, African populations had access to more possibilities for better housing, education, and healthcare. The distribution of benefits from industrial mining depended sharply on the politics of the state.[16]

In South Africa mine owners had to lure as many African laborers as possible to come and do the treacherous work because comparatively few Africans lived in the vicinity of the first mines. The living

[14] Hermanus S. Geyer, "Industrial Development Policy in South Africa: The Past, Present and Future," *World Development* 17:3 (1989) 379–396.
[15] John M. Smalberger, "The Role of the Diamond-Mining Industry in the Development of the Pass-Law System in South Africa," *International Journal of African Historical Studies* 9:3 (1976) 419–434.
[16] Hugh Macmillan, "Mining, Housing and Welfare in South Africa and Zambia: An Historical Perspective," *Journal of Contemporary African Studies* 30:4 (2012) 539–550.

conditions in the early mines were rough. There was limited housing, a dearth of affordable food, and a lack of sanitation, which made dysentery rife. Initially, the leaders of neighboring communities sent workers to the mines because the money they earned helped them buy the guns necessary to defend their land from marauding European settlers.[17] Once colonial governments realized some of the wages went toward purchasing firearms, they made it illegal to sell guns to Africans, and fewer local Africans came to work in the mines. With the consolidation of the mines into a few large corporations (such as Cecil Rhodes's DeBeers Company and Consolidated Gold Fields), mining employers built central compounds to house the workers and control their movements. Larger corporations with an ever-increasing need for labor established the Witwatersrand Native Labour Association (WNLA) to recruit workers throughout southern Africa, including contemporary South Africa, Mozambique, Angola, Malawi, Zimbabwe, Zambia, Namibia, Botswana, Swaziland, and Lesotho.

The migrant labor system brought workers on contracts ranging from four to twenty-four months, although most were for six to nine months.[18] In South Africa male workers (and they were all men) lived in single-sex compounds without access to their families (see Figure 12.1). This work was difficult and often unsafe. A late twentieth-century Sotho miner described his experience:

Working in the mines is an agonizing painful experience. . . . Your work is in an extremely dangerous place. Anything can happen to you at any place. Whenever you go down the shaft, you are not sure that you will come out alive. You don't want to think about it. But it keeps coming. Whenever an accident occurs and something is either killed or badly injured you think of yourself in the position, you think of your family and you become very unstable and lonely. You feel you want to see them for the last time, because the inevitable will come to you sometime. . . . Death is so real you keep on praying and thanking God each time you come out alive.[19]

For men on the mines in South Africa, the separation from their families was one of the most difficult aspects of their experience. Some South African mining companies began experimenting with

[17] Rob Turrell, "Diamonds and Migrant Labour in South Africa, 1869–1910," *History Today* 36:5 (1986) 45–50 at 46.
[18] T. Dunbar Moodie with Vivienne Ndatshe, *Going for Gold: Men, Mines, and Migration* (University of California Press, 1994), 19.
[19] Sotho miner quoted in ibid., 16–17.

FIGURE 12.1 Workers in a compound enclosed by wire netting, De Beer's diamond mines, Kimberley, about 1900. Source: Alamy, Image ID: J5P9MC

family housing in the 1970s when the price of gold was booming, but most migrant laborers continued to live in single-sex compounds.[20]

In other countries families of mine workers were welcomed and sometimes even expected to live in the vicinity of the mines.[21] While the mines of the Copperbelt in both the Belgian Congo (DRC) and Northern Rhodesia (Zambia) tried to create single-sex compounds, they quickly found that impractical. The sparsely populated region required the mine owners find ways to induce laborers to come work for them. Before World War II families who joined miners usually lived in the neighboring

---

[20] Wilmot James, "Capital, African Labour and Housing at South Africa's Gold Mines," *Labour, Capital and Society* 25:1 (1992) 72–86 at 75.
[21] Todd Cleveland, *Stones of Contention: A History of Africa's Diamonds* (Ohio University Press, 2014), 32.

towns. However, after the war the mines in Northern Rhodesia began building housing to accommodate families in the compounds.[22] For the mining corporations building family housing cost more but it stabilized the African labor force, and the overall costs were still substantially cheaper than recruiting white labor.

The wives and children migrant workers left behind experienced social and cultural change, sometimes for the better but often not.[23] Women were now responsible for producing food for the family *and* maintaining the homestead. They took on tasks like clearing land and harvesting that were formerly men's responsibilities. Moreover, family cohesion suffered as fathers spent less time with their children because of long periods away from home.[24] Before the 1970s migrant laborers working in South Africa generally intended to return to their homesteads. As the mining companies provided for their shelter and food, they could save the majority of their income to take home, to buy cattle, or to pay for improvements to their farms. However, many of these men ended up either staying permanently or remained in a constant cycle of returning to the mines. The farms in the rural areas gradually suffered from the effects of migration and environmental degradation. South African resettlement schemes in the 1960s overpopulated the "homelands" and further limited women's ability to eke out a living off agriculture. With the increase in wages in the mines in the 1970s, many African men gave up their hopes of a farming future and settled permanently in urban locations.[25]

In other regions of southern Africa the postcolonial era initially saw little change in the racial inequalities of the mining industry. The Congo was one exception in that Africans had more access to skilled labor jobs during the colonial era.[26] Racial wealth disparities remain because global financial institutions forced the governments of newly independent, Black majority-rule countries in the region, such as Zambia and the DRC, to recognize and honor the contracts between former colonial states and mining companies. This pressure came in numerous forms. When Congo became independent in 1960 the new prime minister, Patrice Lumumba,

---

[22] Miles Larmer, "Permanent Precarity: Capital and Labour in the Central African Copperbelt," *Labor History* 58:2 (2017) 170–184 at 176.

[23] Vusilizwe Thebe, "'Men on Transit' and the Rural 'Farmer Housewives': Women in Decision-Making Roles in Migrant-Labour Societies in North-Western Zimbabwe," *Journal of Asian and African Studies* 53:7 (2018) 1118–1133.

[24] Harriet Sibisi, "How African Women Cope with Migrant Labor in South Africa," *Signs* 3:1 (1977) 167–177.

[25] Moodie, *Going for Gold*, 32–33, 40–41.

[26] Larmer, "Permanent Precarity," 174.

hinted at the idea of nationalizing industries in the country. Within days of independence the mineral-rich province of Katanga had seceded under the ostensible leadership of Moise Tshombe. In contrast to Lumumba, who advocated for socialism, Tshombe was a willing figurehead for western mining interests in Katanga. By 1963 Patrice Lumumba had been assassinated and the United Nations brought the Katangan secession to an end. In 1965 Joseph Mobutu (later known as Mobutu Sese Seko) became president and would hold the office for more than three decades, in part due to support from the US government, which desired access to minerals and new alliances during the Cold War.[27] Other African nations took note of what happened in the Congo: flirting with nationalization of their industries, especially the mining sectors, would bring international interference and conflict to their nations. As a result, most African leaders, both well-meaning and venal, allowed mining operations to continue on similar terms to the colonial-era contracts that exploited African labor and resources.

Botswana offers an illuminating counterexample to the problems created in other mineral-rich countries. In 1966 when Botswana gained independence from Britain, it was a semiarid, landlocked country in southern Africa whose main export was cattle hides. One year after independence the South African DeBeers Corporation found diamonds in Botswana. The Botswana government, led by its elected president, Seretse Khama, negotiated with DeBeers to create a company called Debswana that shared profits equally with the Botswana government. The government of Botswana also received a 15 percent stake in the DeBeers Corporation. This income allowed the new government of Botswana to build schools, hospitals, and colleges.[28] The government worked to develop industry in the country, and as of 2015 Botswana had the fourth highest gross national income (GNI) in Africa and a literacy rate comparable to that of the United States. DeBeers was the same corporation that helped create the pass system and segregationist policies that disempowered so many South Africans.[29] The contrasting policies of

---

[27] Egged on by US business interests, Mobutu nationalized the Belgian mining interests in copper in 1967 but quickly backed down in the face of overwhelming international pressure. For more information see David Gibbs, "International Commercial Rivalries & the Zaïrian Copper Nationalisation of 1967," *Review of African Political Economy* 24: 72 (1997) 171–184.

[28] Thando D. Gwebu, "Botswana's Mining Path to Urbanization and Poverty Alleviation," *Journal of Contemporary African Studies* 30:4 (2012) 611–630.

[29] Smalberger, "The Role of the Diamond-Mining Industry."

DeBeers in Botswana and apartheid-era South Africa demonstrate that profit outweighs politics. These stories of mining in South Africa, the DRC, and Botswana recount the ongoing influence of global corporations in Africa and, in the case of Botswana, the positive impact that can result when African leaders negotiate relatively fair contracts for their countries.

12.3 The environmental costs of modernization

From the beginning of the nineteenth century the need to power steam engines on riverboats, railroads, and pumps used in mining – the engines of European exploration and exploitation – called for new sources of coal. Coal mining operations expanded across the continent from Nigeria to South Africa. Where coal was not available, local production of charcoal from felled trees increased, speeding up deforestation in some areas. Eventually colonial governments and foreign companies invested in the mining of other lucrative materials, like diamonds, gold, asbestos, uranium, coltan, and cobalt. In the postcolonial era the mining of "conflict diamonds" contributed to the civil wars in Sierra Leone and Angola, and "artisanal mining" of coltan and cobalt has perpetuated violence in the DRC.[1] Whether fueling colonial industries, modernizing the economy, or simply generating profit, the mining industry has generated conflict, disease, environmental devastation, and increased dependence on international corporations in Africa.[2]

In the mid-twentieth century development specialists called for large-scale hydroelectric plants to replace coal as the means to power future industrialization. Kariba Dam, opened in 1959 between the colonies of Northern and Southern Rhodesia (Zambia and Zimbabwe), was the first mega dam in sub-Saharan Africa. Dams in other countries appeared soon afterward, such as the Akosombo Dam opened in Ghana in 1965, the Aswan Dam opened in Egypt in 1970, and the Inga I dam opened in DRC in 1972. As with mining, multinational corporations benefit the most from hydroelectric power in Africa. Ghana had to guarantee that 80 percent of the power produced by the Akosombo Dam would be sold to the American-owned Volta Aluminum Company in order to secure the construction loan. Likewise, most of the power from the Kariba Dam is used by mining companies in Zambia and South Africa. Development specialists argue that African nations need to build hydroelectric power to create industry and diversify their economies, yet there is little to no measurable "trickle down" effect of these dams. The mega dams built in the 1950s and 1960s displaced hundreds of thousands of people from the reservoir areas behind the dams, reshaped downstream environments, and continue contributing to greenhouse gases from vegetation decaying in the reservoir lakes.[3] Despite these environmental costs, development experts continue to tout dam building as the solution to Africa's power needs, as seen with the ongoing plans for the Grand Inga Dam in the DRC and the Grand Ethiopian Renaissance Dam.

The development literature rarely addresses head-on the high human and environmental costs of modernization. These problems cannot be solved by development funders that encourage industrialization and trade in environmentally harmful commodities. Environmental concerns and development interests are often in direct competition, though more attention, research, and funding has been directed toward "sustainable development" in Africa since 2000.[4]

[1]   James H. Smith, "What's in Your Cell Phone?" in Dorothy L. Hodgson and Judith A. Byfield, eds., *Global Africa: Into the Twenty-First Century* (University of California Press, 2017), 289–297.
[2]   Lundy Braun, *Breathing Race into the Machine: The Surprising Career of the Spirometer from Plantation to Genetics* (University of Minnesota Press, 2014), 109–138; Gabrielle Hecht, "The Work of Invisibility: Radiation Hazards and Occupational Health in South African Uranium Production," *International Labor & Working-Class History* 81 (2012) 94–113; Jock McCulloch, *Asbestos Blues: Labour, Capital, Physicians and the State in South Africa* (James Currey, 2002); Michal Singer, "Towards 'A Different Kind of Beauty': Responses to Coal-Based Pollution in the Witbank Coalfield between 1903 and 1948," *Journal of Southern African Studies* 37:2 (2011) 281–296.
[3]   Allen F. Isaacman and Barbara S. Isaacman, *Dams, Displacement, and the Delusion of Development: Cahora Bassa and Its Legacies in Mozambique, 1965–2007* (Ohio University Press, 2013); Jacques Leslie, *Deep Water: The Epic Struggle over Dams, Displaced People, and the Environment* (Farrar, Straus and Giroux, 2005); Dzodzi Tsikata, *Living in the Shadow of the Large Dams: Long Term Responses of Downstream and Lakeside Communities of Ghana's Volta River Project* (Brill, 2006).
[4]   Moses K. Tesi, "Conceptualizing Africa's Environment: A Framework for Analysis," in Moses K. Tesi, ed., *The Environment and Development in Africa* (Lexington Books, 2000), 13; Bessie House-Soremekun and Toyin Falola, eds., *Globalization and Sustainable Development in Africa* (University of Rochester Press, 2011).

MODERNIZING MANUFACTURING

During the 1960s most of the political leaders of newly independent African states saw industrialization as the key to developing and modernizing their countries' economies. As seen with the efforts to implement major infrastructural projects, such as irrigation projects and mega dams, African leaders pursued industrial investment. The majority of western and eastern African states became independent during the height of the Cold War. Many African leaders sought to find a middle path in a binary world. Some participated in the Bandung Conference in Indonesia and joined the nonaligned movement claiming allegiance to neither western nor communist governments. In an effort to influence the interests of African governments, the US, USSR, Chinese, and European governments offered funding for infrastructural and industrial projects. Often donor governments built industrial projects and then handed them over to African governments.

Postcolonial African leaders encouraged manufacturing in order to expand employment rather than solely for profit. Profit-driven industrialization is focused on producing economic benefits for the owners, and in some cases shareholders in companies. Non-profit-driven industrialization, when factories are owned by the state, is often politically driven. The new political institutions in Africa at independence usually relied on fragile political leadership and national economies. At the same time the government-owned factories were often donated by non-African governments caught up in the politics of the Cold War. Thus, government-controlled industrialization, whether the government was colonial, democratic, or socialist/communist in structure, was deployed to hand out patronage and maintain the political alliances of national leaders. Even when NGOs introduced industrializing projects, they were less concerned with making profits than with offering employment. These businesses often ran with deficits that governments or donors made up because the main goal was political stability rather than profit. Given that there were few examples of profitable factories, international for-profit investors require higher interest rates and profit margins from their African investments.

The Urafiki textile factory in Tanzania is a classic example of postcolonial industrialization. During the 1960s the Chinese government built numerous factories designed to help African countries such as Guinea, Mali, Benin, Somalia, and Tanzania become more self-sufficient. The

Urafiki ("friendship" in Kiswahili) factory was a gift from the Chinese government to the Tanzanian government, and by 1969 it was wholly under Tanzanian management. Even though the sales of Urafiki cloth were strong, the factory had difficulty making a profit. The supply of electricity and water, crucial to the production process, fluctuated inconsistently. Political loyalty rather than productive value determined one's employment. By 1984 the cost of running the factory had become so prohibitive that the Tanzanian government asked the Chinese to resume control.[30] Eventually a private Chinese firm managed the factory, and as late as 2008 it was still running at a deficit now paid by the Chinese government. Cases like the Urafiki factory demonstrate the inefficiencies associated with politically motivated industrialization projects.

12.4 Technology and infrastructure

One of the most prohibitive aspects of industrialization has been the cost of building infrastructure to support industrial agriculture and manufacturing. Power grids are key to providing the electricity needed, but other forms of infrastructure are quickly being replaced through new technologies. In 2007 Safaricom launched M-Pesa in Kenya, a banking service that allows for the transfer of money between individuals and institutions via mobile phone networks. A Kenyan programmer developed the software for M-Pesa, which now has been adopted in other African, Asian, and European countries. In 2013 the Nigerian government began using this technology to transfer fertilizer subsidies to their farmers, approximately 90 percent of whom do not have access to bank accounts. In the past the government had to directly distribute fertilizer to improve agricultural outcomes, a costly process rife with corruption. Now the government is transferring the subsidies electronically to farmers, who can then purchase fertilizer from private sellers, expanding the economy through agricultural productivity and the development

---

[30]   Deborah Brautigam, *The Dragon's Gift: The Real Story of China in Africa* (Oxford University Press, 2009), 197–200.

of private fertilizer businesses. Within two years, 66 percent of farmers in Nigeria began using this technology, demonstrating the possibilities of African-driven technology for economic modernization.[1]

[1] https://ihub.co.ke/blogs/10800/how-nigeria-is-using-kenyan-technology, accessed August 4, 2018; www.cgap.org/blog/can-mobile-money-extend-financial-services-smallholder-farmers, accessed August 4, 2018.

***

Twentieth-century development theorists such as Walt Rostow argued that a modernized, developed, or progressive society must be based on western values of capitalistic industry. Development theorists have long held out industrialization as the means to a "better" life for Africans, often without defining what "better" means. Yet the reality in Africa over the past two centuries is that industrialization dominated by outsiders has rarely provided significant improvements in the lives of Africans. In efforts to bring industrial methods to agriculture, manufacturing, and mining on the continent, Africans have been treated like pawns in a game of profit that has left them with little material compensation. The recent movement of western and Asian agribusinesses into Africa has again illustrated that corporate efforts to make profits in Africa will benefit from the cheap labor of Africans without necessarily improving the lives of the workers themselves.

The rhetoric of "saving" Africans through industrialization is no longer a viable model. Most Africans are not looking to be "saved" but aspire to build partnerships that support their economic goals. Africans are building their future with the same technology one finds in the west but with distinctive approaches that fit their interests, needs, and goals. Only Africans can define the terms of these partnerships that will recognize culturally relevant ideas of what modernity and modernization should look like in Africa.

Further Reading

On the agricultural changes see Chima Korieh, *The Land Has Changed: History, Society and Gender in Colonial Eastern Nigeria* (University of Calgary Press, 2010); David Robinson, *Paths of Accommodation: Muslim Societies and French Colonial Authorities in Senegal and Mauritania, 1880–1920* (Ohio University Press, 2000).

On the development of irrigation agriculture in Africa see Monica van Beusekom, *Negotiating Development: African Farmers and Colonial Experts at the Office du Niger, 1920–60* (Heinemann, 2001); Victoria Bernal, "Colonial Moral Economy and the Discipline of Development: The Gezira Scheme and 'Modern' Sudan," *Cultural Anthropology* 12:4 (1997) 447–479.

On the building of dams and their effects on African communities see Heather Hoag, *Developing the Rivers of East and West Africa: An Environmental History* (Continuum, 2013); Allen Isaacman and Barbara Isaacman, *Dams, Displacement, and the Delusion of Development: Cahora Bassa and Its Legacies in Mozambique, 1965–2007* (Ohio University Press, 2013); Jacques Leslie, *Deep Water: The Epic Struggle over Dams, Displaced People, and the Environment* (Farrar, Straus and Giroux, 2005).

On the history of mining and migration in southern Africa see Todd Cleveland, *Stones of Contention: A History of Africa's Diamonds* (Ohio University Press, 2014); T. Dunbar Moodie with Vivienne Ndatshe, *Going for Gold: Men, Mines, and Migration* (University of California Press, 1994).

Epilogue
African Critiques of the Development Episteme

This book has demonstrated how development ideas and practices in Africa arose directly out of imperialism, colonialism, and neocolonialism. We have explored the gaps between development theory and practice, the successes and the failures of development projects, and the ways in which Africans have contended with colonial and postcolonial interventions. While the concept of progress that gave birth to the development episteme in Africa emerged from European post-Enlightenment traditions, it has been reshaped as much by the targets of development as by those who claimed expertise. Today the development discourse is a global debate in flux, and Africans have more influence than ever over reshaping the development episteme. This final chapter discusses recent debates about progress, modernity, and development in Africa and offers some closing thoughts on what development might mean for Africa's future.

FROM PROGRESS TO DEVELOPMENT

In his seminal work on African religions and philosophy John Mbiti wrote,

The linear concept of time in western thought, with an indefinite past, present and infinite future, is practically foreign to African thinking. The future is virtually absent because events which lie in it have not taken place, they have not been realized and cannot, therefore, constitute time. If, however, future events are certain to occur, or if they fall within the inevitable rhythm of nature, they at best constitute only *potential time*, not *actual time*. . . . *Actual time* is therefore what is present and what is past. It moves "backward" rather than "forward"; and people set their minds not on future things, but chiefly in what has taken place.[1]

Mbiti employs the Swahili words *sasa* and *zamani* to explain how people differentiate between a "Micro-Time" (*sasa*) with a "short future, dynamic present, and an experienced past" and "Big Time" (*zamani*), which "has its own 'past,' 'present' and 'future.'"[2] This concept of time, Mbiti argues, intertwines with African communities' economic livelihoods and rhythms of work. Mbiti notes that western observers who did not understand African concepts of time called Africans "lazy" when they refused to adhere to western work schedules and behaviors.[3] Mbiti's argument about these different concepts of time may offer some explanation for the conflicts between the western development episteme and African epistemologies, but there were and still are diverse ideas about historical and future change in African societies.

African ideas of progress long predate European colonialism. Ancient and medieval African texts such as the *Kebra Negast* (*The Glory of the Kings*) of Ethiopia, the *Kilwa Chronicle* from the Swahili Coast, and the *Ta'rīkh al-sūdān*, a history of the Songhay Empire written by a scholar based in Timbuktu, recount watershed events in local and regional histories.[4] All three accounts point to the arrival of monotheistic religion, whether Judeo-Christian beliefs in Ethiopia or Islam in Kilwa and Songhay, as the pivotal moment in history that broke from the past and established a progressive path toward "civilization." In *Ta'rīkh al-sūdān*, for example, author Al-Sa'idī wrote that before the arrival of Islam in the eleventh century the "pagans" were in "a dreadful state, hardly recognizable as human beings, blistered, dirty and naked, save for some tattered skins covering their bodies."[5] For

---

[1] John S. Mbiti, *African Religions & Philosophy*. Second revised and enlarged edition (Heinemann, 1999 [1969]), 16–17, emphasis in original text.

[2] Ibid., 22.

[3] Ibid., 19; Keletso E. Atkins, *The Moon Is Dead! Give Us Our Money! The Cultural Origins of an African Work Ethic, Natal, South Africa, 1843–1900* (Heinemann, 1993).

[4] Miguel F. Brooks, ed., *A Modern Translation of the Kebra Nagast (The Glory of Kings)* (Red Sea Press, 1995); Jack D. Rollins, *A History of Swahili Prose, Part One: From Earliest Times to the End of the Nineteenth Century* (E. J. Brill, 1983); John O. Hunwick, *Timbuktu and the Songhay Empire: Al-Sa'idī's Ta'rīkh al-sūdān down to 1613 and Other Contemporary Documents* (Koninklijke Brill NV, 2003).

[5] Al-Sa'idī quoted in Hunwick, *Timbuktu and the Songhay Empire*, 6.

him, the people's conversion to Islam was the most transformative occurrence in West African history.

Oral traditions offer similar explanations for dramatic, positive change over time. The well-known story of Sundiata, the founding king of the Mali Empire, is a good example. The Sundiata epic is a story about good conquering evil and the need to tell the great deeds of the past in order to inspire the leaders of the present to live up to this legacy in the future. Like *Ta'rīkh al-sūdān*, the epic of Sundiata identifies Islam as the dividing line between the barbaric past and the new age of the benevolent ruler. The "evil" King Soumaoro was defined by his use of charms, his brutality, and most of all, his lack of belief in Islam. The griot recounts, "At the time when Sundiata was preparing to assert his claim over the kingdom of his fathers, Soumaoro was the king of kings, the most powerful king in all the lands of the setting sun. The fortified town of Sosso was the bulwark of fetishism against the word of Allah."[6] Scholars have debated and speculated on whether Islam held such prominence during the thirteenth century when the Mali Empire was established, but this is something we cannot know for certain. What we do know is that these and other oral and written accounts about the history of Mali, similar to the *Ta'rīkh al-sūdān*, emphasize a turning point in history as evidence of progress. In these examples civilization is dependent on the adoption of religious truth, however defined, and all of the transformations that came with it.

Oral traditions from non-Islamic and non-Christian contexts also tell of watershed moments in history. They entail analyses of and commentaries on these events, usually organized in a way that legitimates either the ruler in power at the time of the recounting of the tradition or the lineage that maintains the tradition (and perhaps wishes to return to power). Jan Vansina, one of the first western academics to examine African oral traditions "as history," remarked that "the corpus of traditions in any given society provides an ideal model of how the society should function even though this never seems to have been the purpose for maintaining the traditions over time. Indeed, history in the telling like history in the writing often is the teacher of life (*magistra vitae*)."[7] Though the primary function of oral

---

[6] Dijbril Tamsir Niane, *Sundiata: An Epic of Old Mali* (Longman Group, 2006 [1965]), 41.

[7] Jan Vansina, *Oral Tradition As History* (University of Wisconsin Press, 1985), 106.

traditions was to legitimate existing dynasties, they also served as educational devices to teach young people about proper social behavior through cautionary tales and role models. Oral traditions, like West African writings about the arrival of Islam, simultaneously use the past as evidence of the greatness of the present and as a pedagogical tool to direct people toward a future that maintains or restores this greatness.

Starting in the late eighteenth century both Islamic and Christian religious movements in Africa embraced ideologies of progress and paved the way for the development episteme. It is no coincidence that Islamic revolutions of the eighteenth and nineteenth centuries in West Africa coincided with the Great Awakening, the abolitionist movement, and French and British colonial expansion there, or that the spike in Islamic conversion across the interior of East and West Africa checked the success of Christian missionaries during the nineteenth century.[8] These were parallel campaigns for spreading "civilization" across Africa, and both movements began with widespread religious conversion. These discourses entailed so much more than an abstract concept of progress. The populous Sufi movements of the nineteenth century emphasized social welfare and unity while the Christian civilizing mission relied on abolition of slavery and, as we know, set the stage for European colonialism. Both movements also promoted some version of modernity. They were battling for the authority to define not only the best path forward but also the most innovative and progressive – what was, in essence, the most modern approach to social change.

MODERNITY AS DEVELOPMENT

The term "modernity," which is a fundamental concept in the development episteme, has deeply ambiguous meanings. For example, in historical terms the "Modern Era" can refer to the period beginning between the sixteenth and eighteenth centuries, the post-Enlightenment period, or both in European history. In the United States the "Modern Era" generally signifies the period since the Second World War, with the rise of the United States as a global power. In courses on African history "Modern" often refers to the

---

[8] Gibril R. Cole, *The Krio of West Africa: Islam, Culture, Creolization, and Colonialism in the Nineteenth Century* (Ohio University Press, 2013); Felicitas Becker, *Becoming Muslim in Mainland Tanzania, 1890–2000* (Oxford University Press, 2008).

period since 1850 when colonialism began to take hold over the majority of the continent. Other references to "Modern Africa" situate this epoch squarely in the postcolonial period and sometimes go so far as to limit their scope to the twenty-first century. There is not one correct interpretation of what constitutes the "Modern Era" in Africa, and the concept of modernity itself has shifted over time.

As discussed in the early chapters of this book, nineteenth-century Europeans viewed Africa and Africans as holdovers from a distant past rather than their modern contemporaries. Describing the Victorian era of Britain (1837–1901), feminist scholar Anne McClintock wrote, "the agency of women, the colonized and the industrial working class [were] disavowed and projected onto anachronistic space: prehistoric, atavistic and irrational, inherently out of place in the historical time of modernity."[9] Nineteenth-century Europeans struggling to understand the differences between themselves and Africans described Africans as people who came from an ancient time and held onto ancient "traditions," thus making their existence in the presence appear "anachronistic." This contrast between modernity and tradition not only posed Africa as the "Other" to Europe but also excluded Africa and Africans from the present and the future of the "modern" world.

Some Africans embraced this dichotomy as a way to protect their identities and preserve their traditions in the face of colonial encroachment. Those whose legitimacy was based in their authority as "traditional" leaders (chiefs, spiritual healers, and leaders of cultural societies, for example) viewed colonial modernity as a threat. Many Africans viewed western modernity as a "contagion" during the 1930s because colonial urbanization, westernization, and racism threatened their livelihoods.[10]

To others, modernity offered opportunities to escape patriarchal authority or survive the economic pressures of colonialism. Young men and women who ventured into the towns in search of wage labor or other opportunities embraced "modern" lifestyles as a statement of their economic and social independence. They tested the limits of the civilizing mission by adopting European clothing, learning European languages, and demanding political or social

---

[9] Anne McClintock, *Imperial Leather: Race, Gender and Sexuality in the Colonial Context* (Routledge, 1995), 40.

[10] Jan-Georg Deutsch, Peter Probst, and Heike Schmidt, eds., *African Modernities* (Heinemann, 2002).

inclusion. Colonial officials concerned about these "detribalized" youth encouraged and sometimes forced them to return to their natal villages where they would be subject to the customary authority of elders and chiefs.

The categorization of Europe as "modern" and Africa as "traditional" was also at the heart of economic development policies of the late colonial and early postcolonial eras. Modernization theory was based on the notion that so-called traditional sectors of the economy had to "modernize" or catch up to the West by directly engaging with global capitalism and industrialization. The 1960s was a time of optimism in African development. African nationalist discourses offered different configurations for thinking about modernity and tradition. Though many bought into the idea that "modernity" came from Europe to Africa where it conflicted with "tradition," new African leaders attached different valences to these concepts. African nationalist discourses sought to reconcile the contradictions embedded in the ambiguity over colonial modernity. Is modernity good or bad for Africa? African politicians in newly independent states restated this question as: what can we take from modernity that will allow us to carve out a space in the global market without compromising our identity and sovereignty?

Léopold Senghor's vision for nationalist development in Senegal offered a potential answer. He challenged the notion that Africans lacked reason, technology, and other qualities associated with modernity. He embraced modernization primarily as an economic policy, urging that the development of African intellects and cultures continues on its own path. Senghor argued that Europeans and Africans employed different types of reasoning and logic. "However paradoxical it may seem, the vital force of the Negro African, his surrender to the object, is animated by reason. Let us understand each other clearly; it is not the *reasoning-eye* of Europe, it is the *reason of the touch*, better still, the *reasoning-embrace*, the sympathetic reason, more closely related to the Greek *logos* than to the Latin *ratio*."[11] Senghor clarified that this does not indicate that Africans are incapable of other types of reasoning.

[11]   Léopold Senghor, *On African Socialism* (Frederick A. Praeger, 1964), 73–75.

Does this mean, as certain young people would like to interpret my remarks, that the Negro African lacks discursive reason, that he has never used any? I have never said so. .... No civilization can be built without using discursive reason and without techniques. Negro-African civilization is no exception to this rule. Witness the astonishment of the earliest European navigators disembarking in Africa to discover well-organized states, with government, administration, justice, and army, with techniques (remarkable for that date) for working in wood, ivory, bronze, iron, basketry, weaving, and terra cotta, with medical and agricultural techniques worthy of Europe.[12]

Senghor challenged one of the basic principles of the civilizing mission, that Europe brought civilization to Africa. He argued that development must emerge from both African and European intellectual traditions and ideas of reason and disagreed that these were diametrically opposed. Though Senghor contended that "classical logic, Marxian dialectics, and that of the twentieth century" were necessary for the *"African road to socialism,"* he rejected many of the Eurocentric assumptions embedded in the modernity/tradition dichotomy.[13]

Senghor had been a founding member of the Négritude movement, which emerged in Africa during the 1930s just as Africans began to question the value of colonial modernity. At that time the broken promises of the civilizing mission and the disruptive effects of westernization and colonialism became the subject of the day. In the context of 1960s nationalism and modernization Léopold Senghor's words offered a balanced response that insisted upon recognition of Africa's contribution to modern human history at the same time that it called for European support in development. Scholars have since shown that Senegal's national development policies under Senghor reified western ideas of modernity and the "technocratic" state, but in the early 1960s Senghor's Afrocentric definition of development provided an important intellectual challenge to the development episteme.[14]

---

[12]   Ibid., 75.
[13]   Léopold Senghor, "Some Thoughts on Africa: A Continent in Development," *International Affairs (Royal Institute of International Affairs)* 38:2 (1962) 189–195.
[14]   See Mamadou Diouf, "Senegalese Development: From Mass Mobilization to Technocratic Elitism," transl. by Molly Roth and Frederick Cooper, in Frederick Cooper and Randall Packard, eds., *International Development and the Social Sciences: Essays on the History and Politics of Knowledge* (University of California Press, 1997), 291–319.

The modernity/tradition dichotomy did not disappear with African nationalism. In the 1980s and 1990s Africa continued to be placed in the "anachronistic space" of "tradition" in discourses on globalization. Whether referring to culture, economics, or transnational migration, globalization has often been described as the exposure of "traditional" communities to international influences, especially American culture. Well into the twentieth-first century we are still bombarded with media stories, images, and development projects that assume a conflict between "traditional" practices and beliefs and "modern" economic, social, cultural, or political forces.

DISILLUSIONMENT WITH MODERNITY AND DEVELOPMENT

The quest for modernity has been a driving force in development. The assumption that modernity originates in the West and has been brought to Africa through colonialism and development continues to shape the work of many people engaged in development projects in Africa today. While development professionals have become more attune to "the African perspective," African scholars and professionals have challenged their assumptions about modernity, development, and African cultures.

Philosopher Olúfẹ́mi Táíwò offers a biting critique of discourses on modernity in his book *How Colonialism Preempted Modernity in Africa*.[15] The title of his book invokes another well-known book on development, Walter Rodney's *How Europe Underdeveloped Africa*. Táíwò begins by pressing us to disentangle colonialism from modernity in our minds. Modernity in Africa did not originate with the West or with colonialism, he argues. Quite the contrary, colonialism sought in every way to prevent modern economic and political systems from emerging in Africa. Decoupling colonialism and modernity requires us first to recognize the ways in which Africans were modernizing prior to colonization and second to understand how colonialism sought to arrest the modernization of African societies. Colonial states checked the growth of capitalism and refused representative government, two pillars of "modern" development. Referring specifically to British indirect rule

[15]   Olúfẹ́mi Táíwò, *How Colonialism Preempted Modernity in Africa* (Indiana University Press, 2010).

policies, Táíwò states that colonial constructions of custom marked Africans as essentially and fundamentally "primitive" and therefore incapable of embracing modernity. Despite the fact that colonial ideology created and perpetuated the opposition between African tradition and western modernity, Africans contributed to and embraced modernity wherever possible. Táíwò's study highlights the power of representation in colonial development discourses. By labeling Africans as "traditional," colonial officials justified their exclusion of Africans from the political and economic rights "modern" Europeans had gained in the post-Enlightenment era.

Another scholar, historian E. S. Atieno Odhiambo, addressed the common trope in development discourse that African cultures and "traditions" constitute a "stumbling block" to development.[16] Despite more nuanced understandings of African cultures in academia by the early 2000s, development professionals continued to perceive African cultures as the reason for "Africa's failure at modernization and the mastery of modernity."[17] From this perspective, even where Africans became "modern" (for example, through the globalization of western culture), they failed to "develop" economically or politically. Odhiambo was not simply urging development experts to pay attention to African cultures, as this would only replicate a colonial anthropology in which "tradition" is captured, made static, and translated into a variable to plug into the development equation. He wrote, "So long as governments and the academy remain trapped in this prejudice against our cultures, and as long as we, the citizens of Africa, privilege them with the plentitude of power, there will be no meaningful development in Africa."[18] He warned developmentalists against proposing grand theories or large-scale models, even ones that claim to take local culture into account. If this continues to be the goal of development, Odhiambo advised, then "both the governments and the academy should leave the peasants alone."[19]

African scholars have also opened up the debate about the economic failures of development, especially in the wake of the International Monetary Fund (IMF) and the World Bank's Structural Adjustment Programs (SAPs) implemented during the

---

[16] E. S. Atieno Odhiambo, "The Cultural Dimensions of Development in Africa," *African Studies Review* 45:3 (2002) 1–16.

[17] Ibid., 2.

[18] Ibid., 11.

[19] Ibid., 12.

1980s and early 1990s.[20] Economist Dambisa Moyo's *Dead Aid* offers
a different approach to development, arguing that aid disables
African economies and makes them dependent on foreign
assistance.[21] The dependency theory is not new, of course. It emerged
in the 1970s with works such as Immanuel Wallerstein's *The Modern
World-System*. However, unlike the socialist-oriented world systems
theorists, Dambisa Moyo believes that neoliberal capitalism can offer
a solution to the problem. Her reputation as a leading world economist
lent credibility to her argument that capitalist trade and foreign investment will ween Africa off development aid and incorporate African
economies into the global market. The notion that aid is the culprit
also provides an out to nations and development organizations looking
for ways to pull back their financial commitments in Africa. Yet Moyo
did highlight one of the fundamental issues in the development episteme
and the discourse on modernity: that there is a one-way flow of ideas and
technology from the West (the haves) to Africa (the have-nots), and that
this dynamic has perpetuated a relationship of dependence. Was it the
transfer of development funding and knowledge or the *notion* that development funding and knowledge must be transferred from the West to
Africa that created this relationship of dependence? Moyo does not
resolve this issue, but her challenge to the idea of development aid is
one step away from the long-standing binary between the "developed"
West and the "undeveloped" or "least developed" African nations.

As Moyo's work indicates, development aid has emerged as an
industry in itself. A film released in 2014 entitled *Poverty, Inc.* brings
this point home. The film explains how the poverty industry creates
more opportunities for profit among international nongovernmental
organizations (INGOs), aid organizations, and for-profit corporations
than it does for poor people or developing nations. The film criticizes the
paternalism of development aid and the development discourse that
characterizes poor people as incapable of taking care of themselves.
This modern-day "white man's burden" sidesteps African-owned businesses, local NGOs, and indigenous innovations, perpetuates the
stereotype of Africans as helpless, and – even worse – undermines the
ability of Africans to participate directly in the local and global markets.

[20]   Thandika Mkandawire and Adebayo Olukoshi, eds., *Between Liberalisation and
       Oppression: The Politics of Structural Adjustment in Africa* (Codesria, 1993).
[21]   Dambisa Moyo, *Dead Aid: Why Aid Is Not Working and How There Is a Better Way for
       Africa* (Farrar, Straus, and Giroux, 2009).

Donated rice, t-shirts, mosquito nets, medicines, shoes, and other goods flood local markets with free goods and put African entrepreneurs out of business. The filmmaker asked Ghanaian software engineer Herman Chinery-Hesse about the notion that Africa is poor. Chinery-Hesse responded, "Africa has always been a reservoir for resources for the rest of the world. The countries they are calling poor are oil-rich, diamond-rich, timber-rich, land-rich, and gold-rich, and they are in good locations for tourism. The people here are not stupid. They are just disconnected from global trade, that's all."[22] African entrepreneurs have been excluded from the global market, and those who have managed to survive despite this disadvantage have been written out of the story of development.

This sense of frustration and disillusionment speaks to the challenges Africans face in attempting to decolonize development and reshape the development episteme. To be clear, disillusionment with neoliberal capitalism, or what has also been deemed "late capitalism," and its ideologies of progress is not limited to Africans. Many young people in the global north have expressed severe anxiety about their prospects for the future and do not believe they will be better off than their parents, one measure of capitalist growth and a marker of the "developed world." Development has not worked for everyone and in Africa it often has made life worse. Development has resulted in greater economic inequality, less local and national control over resources, and even a new "scramble for Africa" as investors from China and elsewhere buy up impoverished land in the name of development. It is not only that development projects have failed in Africa; the development episteme has failed to make sense to Africans. It is time to ask the question, is it Africans who most desperately need intervention or is it the development industry itself?

A WAY FORWARD

Europeans and Americans do not have a monopoly on discourses of progress, yet western perspectives still prevail in the development episteme. Because the majority of funding earmarked for African

---

[22] Michael Matheson Miller, James F. Fitzgerald Jr., Simon Scionka, and Robert A. Sirico, *Poverty, Inc.*, DVD video, directed by Michael Matheson Miller (Passion River Films, 2014).

development continues to originate outside the continent, this continues to be a problem. Those who make the decisions about funding have much control over how "development" in the formal sense is defined even if the recipients of this funding disagree. For many Africans development means a chance to "get ahead" by ensuring their survival and achieving some form of material success. This is the new modernity. After such a long history of ambiguous outcomes in development, modernity means recognizing the ways in which Africans envision themselves not as targets of foreign intervention but as agentive individuals who will draw on whatever resources they have to carve out a path for themselves and their communities.

Simultaneous with the rise of new nations in Africa, the artistic, cultural, literary, and philosophical movement that has come to be known as Afrofuturism has redefined the relationship between culture and modernity in the African Diaspora. The international popularity of the 2018 film *Black Panther* can be attributed partly to the global excitement around Afrofuturism (see Figure 13.1). The primary setting of the film was the imaginary Wakanda, a wealthy, technologically advanced African nation with a natural abundance of a powerful substance called vibranium. The film, which explored the cultural and political connections between Africa and the Diaspora, offered a completely different vision of Africa than that typically found in development studies. As Professor Abosede George of Barnard College explained, artistic representations in the film emerged from real-world historical and cultural experiences.[23] The intersection of imagined futures with African cultural ideals is a central characteristic of Afrofuturism. It is a reconceptualization of the future that centers African people and culture. In her 2017 TED Talk about science fiction in Africa writer Nnedi Okorafor recounted, "Growing up, I didn't read much science fiction. I couldn't relate to those stories preoccupied with xenophobia, colonization, and seeing aliens as others." Her "science fiction had different ancestors, African ones." Okorafor explained, "African science fiction's blood runs deep and it's old, and it's ready to come forth, and when it does, imagine the new technologies, ideas, and sociopolitical changes it'll inspire. For

---

[23] Abosede George on *Inside Edition*, "Is Wakanda Real? The Real-World Roots of 'Black Panther,'" www.insideedition.com/media/videos/wakanda-real-real-world-roots-black-panther-41131, accessed December 30, 2019.

FIGURE 13.1 Audiences watch *Black Panther* in 3D at the Movie Jabbers Black Panther Cosplay Screening in Nairobi, Kenya, on February 14, 2018. The film features Oscar-winning Mexico-born Kenyan actress Lupita Nyong'o. Source: YASUYOSHI CHIBA/AFP via Getty Images

Africans, homegrown science fiction can be a will to power."[24] Development has had complex and contradictory meanings. As the development episteme continues to place Africa and African cultures within the realm of the "traditional," the past, the out-moded, and the undeveloped, Africans are imagining alternative futures and visions of development that celebrate – rather than denigrate – African cultural ideals.

We argue that it is time to rethink development, to move past colonial-era paternalism and recognize the very different futures Africans see for themselves. Though we cannot claim to speak for Africans or truly represent African ambitions and plans for the future, we hope that this critical analysis of the idea of development in Africa contributes in some small way to the revolution already underway in Africa's place in global politics. The illusion of the omnipotence of the development episteme will be exposed only when we can see clearly the

[24] Nnedi Okorafor, "Sci-fi Stories That Imagine a Future Africa," TEDGlobal 2017, www.ted.com/talks/nnedi_okorafor_sci_fi_stories_that_imagine_a_future_africa/u p-next?language=en, accessed December 30, 2019.

crumbling stones out of which it was built. Development is not the powerful edifice it claims to be; it is a holdover of colonialism that is quickly losing relevance in our current world. Thus, we call for a decolonizing of the mind, not of Africans but of people living in the global north who see Africa as perpetually less than and of the self-professed development expert, whether African or foreign, in order to build on the efforts of Léopold Senghor, Olúfẹ́mi Táíwò, E. S. Atieno Odhiambo, Dambisa Moyo, Nnedi Okorafor, and others who have sought to reshape our world. If development scholars and professionals refuse to undergo such decolonization, then perhaps they should do what Odhiambo suggested and "leave the peasants alone."

Bibliography

PUBLISHED SCHOLARLY WORKS

Abi-Mershed, Osama. *Apostles of Modernity: Saint-Simonians and the Civilizing Mission in Algeria* (Stanford University Press, 2010).

Abramowitz, Sharon. "What Happens When MSF Leaves? Humanitarian Departure and Medical Sovereignty in Postconflict Liberia," in Sharon Abramowitz and Catherine Panter-Brick, eds., *Medical Humanitarianism: Ethnographies of Practice* (University of Pennsylvania Press, 2015), 137–154.

Abusharaf, Rogaia Mustafa. *Female Circumcision: Multicultural Perspectives* (University of Pennsylvania Press, 2006).

Achebe, Chinua. *The Education of a British-Protected Child: Essays* (Alfred A. Knopf, 2009).

Adams, William M. and David M. Anderson. "Irrigation before Development: Indigenous and Induced Change in Agricultural Water Management in East Africa," *African Affairs* 87:349 (1988) 519–535.

Adeleke, Tunde *UnAfrican Americans: Nineteenth-Century Black Nationalists and the Civilizing Mission* (University of Kentucky Press, 1998).

Adriansen, Hanne, Kirstine Lene, Møller Madsen, and Stig Jensen, eds., *Higher Education and Capacity Building in Africa: The Geography and Power of Knowledge under Changing Conditions* (Routledge, 2016).

Alavi, Hamza and Teodor Shanin, *Introduction to the Sociology of "Developing Societies"* (Palgrave, 1982).

Alexandre, Pierre. "Introduction," in Pierre Alexandre, ed., *French Perspectives in African Studies: A Collection of Translated Essays* (Oxford University Press for the International African Institute, 1973).

Allina, Eric. *Slavery by Any Other Name: African Life under Company Rule in Colonial Mozambique* (University of Virginia Press, 2012).

Allman, Jean. "Kwame Nkrumah, African Studies, and the Politics of Knowledge Production in the Black Star of Africa," *International Journal of African Historical Studies* 46:2 (2013) 181–203.

Amin, Qasim. *The Liberation of Women and the New Woman: Two Documents in the History of Egyptian Feminism*, transl. by Samiha Sidhom Peterson (American University in Cairo Press, 2000 [1992]).

Amutabi, Maurice N. *The NGO Factor in Africa: The Case of Arrested Development in Kenya* (Routledge, 2006).

Andersen, Kaj Blegvad. *African Traditional Architecture: A Study of the Housing and Settlement Patterns of Rural Kenya* (Oxford University Press, 1977).

Andersen, Margaret Cook. "Creating French Settlements Overseas: Pronatalism and Colonial Medicine in Madagascar," *French Historical Studies* 33:3 (2010) 417–444.

Asad, Talal, ed. *Anthropology and the Colonial Encounter* (Ithaca Press, 1973).

Atangana, Martin. *French Investment in Colonial Cameroon: The FIDES Era (1946–1957)* (Peter Lang, 2009).

Atkins, Keletso E. *The Moon Is Dead! Give Us Our Money! The Cultural Origins of an African Work Ethic, Natal, South Africa, 1843–1900* (Heinemann, 1993).

Austen, Ralph. *African Economic History: Internal Development and External Dependency* (James Currey, 1987).

Austin, Gareth. *Labour, Land, and Capital in Ghana: From Slavery to Free Labour in Asante, 1807–1956* (University of Rochester Press, 2005).

Bâ, Amadou Hampâté. *The Fortunes of Wangrin*, transl. by Aina Pavolini Taylor (Indiana University Press, 1987).

Bangham, Jenny. "What Is Race? UNESCO, Mass Communication and Human Genetics in the Early 1950s," *History of the Human Sciences* 28:5 (2015) 80–107.

Bank, Andrew. "Of 'Native Skulls' and 'Noble Caucasians': Phrenology in Colonial South Africa," *Journal of Southern African Studies* 22:3 (1996) 387–403.

Barnett, Michael. *Empire of Humanity: A History of Humanitarianism* (Cornell University Press, 2011).

Barry, Boubacar. *Senegambia and the Atlantic Slave Trade* (Cambridge University Press, 1988).

Barthel, Diane. "Women's Educational Experience under Colonialism: Toward a Diachronic Model," *Signs* 11:1 (1985) 137–154.

Bassett, Thomas J. and Philip W. Porter. "'From the Best Authorities': The Mountains of Kong in the Cartography of West Africa," *Journal of African History* 32:3 (1991) 367–413.

Beaudoin, Steven. *Poverty in World History* (Routledge, 2007).

Becker, Felicitas. *Becoming Muslim in Mainland Tanzania, 1890–2000* (Oxford University Press, 2008).

Becker, Felicitas. *The Politics of Poverty: Policy-Making and Development in Rural Tanzania* (Cambridge University Press, 2019).

Bennett, Brett M. and Joseph M. Hodge, eds. *Science and Empire: Knowledge and Networks of Science across the British Empire, 1800–1970* (Palgrave Macmillan, 2011).

Benton, Adia. "Whose Security? Militarization and Securitization during West Africa's Ebola Outbreak," in Michiel Hofman and Sokhieng Au, eds., *The Politics of Fear: Médecins sans Frontières and the West African Ebola Epidemic* (Oxford University Press, 2017), 25–62.

Berman, Edward H. *The Influence of Carnegie, Ford, and Rockefeller Foundations on American Foreign Policy: The Ideology of Philanthropy* (State University of New York Press, 1983).

Bernal, Victoria. "Colonial Moral Economy and the Discipline of Development: The Gezira Scheme and 'Modern' Sudan," *Cultural Anthropology* 12:4 (1997) 447–479.

Bigon, Liora. "Urban Planning, Colonial Doctrines and Street Naming in French Dakar and British Lagos, c. 1850–1930," *Urban History* 36:3 (2009) 426–448.

Bissell, William Cunningham. *Urban Design, Chaos, and Colonial Power in Zanzibar* (Indiana University Press, 2011).

Bloom, Peter J., Stephan F. Miescher, and Takyiwaa Manuh, eds. *Modernization As Spectacle in Africa* (Indiana University Press, 2014).

Bonner, Philip L., Amanda Esterhuysen, and Trefor Jenkins, eds. *A Search for Origins: Science, History and South Africa's "Cradle of Humankind"* (Wits University Press, 2007).

Bornstein, Erica. *The Spirit of Development: Protestant NGOs, Morality, and Economics in Zimbabwe* (Routledge, 2003).

Brantley, Cynthia. *Feeding Families: African Realities and British Ideas of Nutrition and Development in Early Colonial Africa* (Heinemann, 2002).

Brantley, Cynthia. "Kikuyu-Maasai Nutrition and Colonial Science: The Orr and Gilks Study in Late 1920s Kenya Revisited," *International Journal of African Historical Studies* 30:1 (1997) 49–86.

Brantlinger, Patrick. *Dark Vanishings: Discourse on the Extinction of Primitive Races, 1800–1930* (Cornell University Press, 2003).

Brantlinger, Patrick. *Rule of Darkness: British Literature and Imperialism, 1830–1914* (Cornell University Press, 1990).

Brantlinger, Patrick. "Victorians and Africans: Genealogy of the Myth of the Dark Continent," *Critical Inquiry* 12:1 (1985) 166–203.

Braun, Lundy. *Breathing Race into the Machine: The Surprising Career of the Spirometer from Plantation to Genetics* (University of Minnesota Press, 2014).

Brautigam, Deborah. *The Dragon's Gift: The Real Story of China in Africa* (Oxford University Press, 2009).

Brooks, George. *Eurafricans in Western Africa: Commerce, Social Status, Gender, and Religious Observance from the Sixteenth to the Eighteenth Century* (Ohio University Press, 2003).

Brooks, Miguel F., ed. *A Modern Translation of the Kebra Nagast (The Glory of Kings)* (Red Sea Press, 1995).

Bryant, Kelly M. Duke. *Education As Politics: Colonial Schooling and Political Debate in Senegal, 1850s–1914* (University of Wisconsin Press, 2015).

Burke, Timothy. *Lifebuoy Men, Lux Women: Commodification, Consumption, and Cleanliness in Modern Zimbabwe* (Duke University Press, 1996).

Butler, Lawrence J. *Industrialisation and the British Colonial State: West Africa 1939–1951* (Frank Cass, 1997).

Byfield, Judith A. "Producing for the War," in Judith A. Byfield, Carolyn A. Brown, Timothy Parsons, and Ahmad Alawad Sikainga, eds., *Africa and World War II* (Cambridge University Press, 2015), 24–42.

Byfield, Judith A., Carolyn A. Brown, Timothy Parsons, and Ahmad Alawad Sikainga, eds., *Africa and World War II* (Cambridge University Press, 2015).

Campbell, Chloe. *Race and Empire: Eugenics in Colonial Kenya* (Manchester University Press, 2007).

Carmody, Pádraig. *Neoliberalism, Civil Society and Security in Africa* (Palgrave Macmillan, 2007).

Çelik, Zeynep. *Urban Forms and Colonial Confrontation: Algiers under French Rule* (University of California Press, 1997).

Chakrabarti, Pratik. *Medicine and Empire: 1600–1960* (Palgrave Macmillan, 2014).

Chanock, Martin. *Law, Custom, and Social Order: The Colonial Experience in Malawi and Zambia* (Heinemann, 1998).

Chitonge, Horman. *Economic Growth and Development in Africa: Understanding Trends and Prospects* (Routledge, 2015).

Clark, Hannah-Louise. "Administering Vaccination in Interwar Algeria: Medical Auxiliaries, Smallpox, and the Colonial State in the Communes Mixtes," *French Politics, Culture & Society* 34:2 (2016) 32–56.

Cleveland, Todd. *Stones of Contention: A History of Africa's Diamonds* (Ohio University Press, 2014).

Cole, Gibril R. *The Krio of West Africa: Islam, Culture, Creolization, and Colonialism in the Nineteenth Century* (Ohio University Press, 2013).

Collingham, Lizzie. *The Taste of War: World War II and the Battle for Food* (Penguin, 2011).

Comaroff, Jean and John Comaroff. *Of Revelation and Revolution: Christianity, Colonialism, and Consciousness in South Africa* (University of Chicago Press, 1991).

Conklin, Alice L. "Colonialism and Human Rights, a Contradiction in Terms? The Case of France and West Africa, 1895–1914," *American Historical Review* 103:2 (1998) 419–442.

Conklin, Alice L. *A Mission to Civilize: The Republican Idea of Empire in France and West Africa, 1895–1930* (Stanford University Press, 1997).

Connah, Graham. *African Civilizations: An Archaeological Perspective*. Second edition (Cambridge University Press, 2001 [1987]).

Conte, Christopher A. *Highland Sanctuary: Environmental History in Tanzania's Usambara Mountains* (Ohio University Press, 2004).

Cooper, Barbara. "Cloth, Commodity Production, and Social Capital: Women in Maradi, Niger 1890–1989," *African Economic History* 21 (1993) 51–71.

Cooper, Frederick. *Africa since 1940: The Past of the Present* (Cambridge University Press, 2002).

Cooper, Frederick. *Citizenship between Empire and Nation: Remaking France and French Africa, 1945–1960* (Princeton University Press, 2014).

Cooper, Frederick. *Decolonization and African Society: The Labor Question in French and British Africa* (Cambridge University Press, 1996).

Cooper, Frederick. *From Slaves to Squatters: Plantation Labor and Agriculture in Zanzibar and Coastal Kenya, 1890–1925* (Yale University Press, 1980).

Cooper, Frederick. "'Our Strike': Equality, Anticolonial Politics and the 1947–48 Railway Strike in French West Africa," *Journal of African History* 37:1 (1996) 81–118.

Cordell, Dennis D. and Joel W. Gregory, eds. *African Population and Capitalism: Historical Perspectives* (University of Wisconsin Press, 1987).

Cosgrove, Denis and Stephen Daniels, eds. *The Iconography of Landscape: Essays on the Symbolic Representation, Design and Use of Past Environments* (Cambridge University Press, 1988).

Crane, Johanna Taylor. *Scrambling for Africa: AIDS, Expertise, and the Rise of the American Global Health Science* (Cornell University Press, 2013).

Crowder, Michael (with LaRay Denzer). "Bai Bureh and the Sierra Leone Hut Tax War of 1898," in Michael Crowder, *Colonial West Africa: Collected Essays* (Routledge, 2012 [orig. 1978]), 61–103.

Curtin, Philip D. *The Image of Africa: British Ideas and Action, 1780–1850* (University of Wisconsin Press, 1964).

Davidson, Basil. *Lost Cities of Africa* (Back Bay Books, 1987).

Davie, Grace. *Poverty Knowledge in South Africa: A Social History of Human Science, 1855–2005* (Cambridge University Press, 2014).

Decker, Corrie. *Mobilizing Zanzibari Women: The Struggle for Respectability and Self-Reliance in Colonial East Africa* (Palgrave Macmillan, 2014).

Desai, Gaurav. *Subject to Colonialism: African Self-Fashioning and the Colonial Library* (Duke University Press, 2001).

Deutsch, Jan-Georg, Peter Probst, and Heike Schmidt, eds. *African Modernities* (Heinemann, 2002).

Diouf, Jean Léopold. *Dictionnaire wolof-français et français-wolof* (Karthala, 2003).

Diouf, Mamadou. "Senegalese Development: From Mass Mobilization to Technocratic Elitism," transl. by Molly Roth and Frederick Cooper, in Frederick Cooper and Randall Packard, eds., *International Development and the Social Sciences: Essays on the History and Politics of Knowledge* (University of California Press, 1997), 291–319.

Doyle, Shane. *Before HIV: Sexuality, Fertility and Mortality in East Africa, 1900–1980* (Oxford University Press, 2013).

Dubow, Saul. *Racial Segregation and the Origins of Apartheid in South Africa, 1919–36* (Palgrave Macmillan, 1989).

Dubow, Saul. *Scientific Racism in Modern South Africa* (Cambridge University Press, 1995).

Dubow, Saul, ed. *Science and Society in Southern Africa* (Manchester University Press, 2000).

Echenberg, Myron. *Black Death, White Medicine: Bubonic Plague and the Politics of Public Health in Colonial Senegal, 1914–1945* (Heinemann, 2002).

El Shakry, Omnia. *The Great Social Laboratory: Subjects of Knowledge in Colonial and Postcolonial Egypt* (Stanford University Press, 2007).

Elkins, Caroline. *Imperial Reckoning: The Untold Story of Britain's Gulag in Kenya* (Henry Holt, 2005).

Elliott, Kimberly Ann, ed. *Corruption and the Global Economy* (Institute for International Economics, 1997).

Elphick, Richard and Robert Shell. "Intergroup Relations: Khoikhoi, Settlers, Slaves and Free Blacks, 1652–1795," in Richard Elphick and Hermann Buhr Giliomee, eds., *The Shaping of South African Societies, 1652–1840* (Wesleyan University Press, 1979), 184–242.

Elphick, Richard and Rodney Davenport, eds. *Christianity in South Africa: A Political, Social, and Cultural History* (University of California Press, 1997).

Escobar, Arturo. *Encountering Development: The Making and Unmaking of the Third World* (Princeton University Press, 2012 [1995]).

Estrada-Villalta, Sara and Glenn Adams. "Decolonizing Development: A Decolonial Approach to the Psychology of Economic Inequality," *Translational Issues in Psychological Science* 4:2 (2018) 198–209.

Etherington, Norman. "A False Emptiness: How Historians May Have Been Misled by Early Nineteenth Century Maps of South-Eastern Africa," *Imago Mundi* 56:1 (2004) 67–86.

Etienne, Mona. "Women and Men, Cloth and Colonization: The Transformation of Production-Distribution Relations among the Baule (Ivory Coast)," *Cahiers d'Études Africaines* 17:65 (1977) 41–64.

Everatt, David. "The Undeserving Poor: Poverty and the Politics of Service Delivery in the Poorest Nodes of South Africa," *Politikon* 35:3 (2008) 293–319.

Everill, Bronwen. *Abolition and Empire in Sierra Leone and Liberia* (Palgrave Macmillan, 2013).

Everill, Bronwen and Josiah Kaplan, eds. *The History and Practice of Humanitarian Intervention and Aid in Africa* (Palgrave Macmillan, 2013).

Eze, Michael Onyebuchi. *Intellectual History in Contemporary South Africa* (Palgrave Macmillan, 2010).

Ezra, Elizabeth. *The Colonial Unconscious: Race and Culture in Interwar France* (Cornell University Press, 2000).

Fabian, Johannes. *Out of Our Minds: Reason and Madness in the Exploration of Central Africa* (University of California Press, 2000).

Fair, Laura. "Identity, Difference, and Dance: Female Initiation in Zanzibar, 1890 to 1930," *Frontiers: A Journal of Women's Studies* 17:3 (1996) 146–172.

Fair, Laura. *Pastimes and Politics: Culture, Community, and Identity in Post-Abolition Urban Zanzibar, 1890–1945* (Ohio University Press, 2001).

Fall, Babacar. *Social History in French West Africa: Forced Labor, Labor Market, Women and Politics* (South-South Exchange Programme for Research on the History of Development [SEPHIS] and the Centre for Studies in Social Sciences, Calcutta [CSSC], 2002).

Falola, Toyin. *Nationalism and African Intellectuals* (University of Rochester Press, 2001).

Falola, Toyin and Emily Brownell, eds. *Landscape, Environment and Technology in Colonial and Postcolonial Africa* (Routledge, 2012).

Fanon, Frantz. *Black Skin, White Masks* (Grove Press, 1967).

Fanon, Frantz. *Wretched of the Earth* (Grove Press, 1966 [orig. 1963]).

Feierman, Steven and John M. Janzen, eds. *The Social Basis of Health and Healing in Africa* (University of California Press, 1992).

Ferguson, James. "Anthropology and Its Evil Twin: 'Development' in the Constitution of a Discipline," in Frederick Cooper and Randall Packard, eds., *International Development and the Social Sciences* (University of California Press, 1997), 150–175.

Ferguson, James. *Global Shadows: Africa in the Neoliberal World Order* (Duke University Press, 2006).

Fieldhouse, David. "War and the Origins of the Gold Coast Cocoa Marketing Board, 1939–40," in Michael Twaddle, ed., *Imperialism, the State and the Third World* (British Academic Press, 1992), 153–182.

Flint, Karen. *Healing Traditions: African Medicine, Cultural Exchange, and Competition in South Africa, 1820–1948* (Ohio University Press, 2008).

Fratkin, Elliot. "Ethiopia's Pastoralist Policies: Development, Displacement and Resettlement," *Nomadic Peoples* 18:1 (2014) 94–114.

Freire, Paulo. *Pedagogy of the Oppressed* (Bloomsbury, 2014 [1970]).

Friedland, William H. and Carl G. Rosberg Jr., eds. *African Socialism* (Stanford University Press, 1964).

Fyle, C. Magbaily. *Introduction to the History of African Civilizations: Volume I, Precolonial Africa* (University Press of America, 1999).

Ganahl, Joseph Patrick. *Corruption, Good Governance, and the African State: A Critical Analysis of the Political-Economic Foundations of Corruption in Sub-Saharan Africa* (Potsdam University Press, 2013).

Geissler, P. Wenzel and Catherine Molyneux, eds. *Evidence, Ethos and Experiment: The Anthropology and History of Medical Research in Africa* (Berghahn Books, 2011).

George, Abosede A. *Making Modern Girls: A History of Girlhood, Labor, and Social Development in Colonial Lagos* (Ohio University Press, 2014).

Geyer, Hermanus S. "Industrial Development Policy in South Africa: The Past, Present and Future," *World Development* 17:3 (1989) 379–396.

Gibbs, David. "International Commercial Rivalries & the Zaïrian Copper Nationalisation of 1967," *Review of African Political Economy* 24:72 (1997) 171–184.

Gil-Riaño, Sebastián. "Relocating Anti-Racist Science: The 1950 UNESCO Statement on Race and Economic Development in the Global South," *British Journal for the History of Science* 51:2 (2018) 281–303.

Gilman, Nils. *Mandarins of the Future: Modernization Theory in Cold War America* (Johns Hopkins University Press, 2003).

Ginio, Ruth. "Negotiating Legal Authority in French West Africa: The Colonial Administration and African Assessors, 1903–1918," in Benjamin N. Lawrance, Emily Lynn Osborn, and Richard Roberts, eds., *Intermediaries, Interpreters, and Clerks: African Employees in the Making of Colonial Africa* (University of Wisconsin Press, 2006), 115–138.

Glick, Thomas. "The Anthropology of Race Across the Darwinian Revolution," in Henrika Kuklick, ed., *A New History of Anthropology* (Blackwell, 2008), 225–241.

Goff, Barbara. *"Your Secret Language": Classics in the British Colonies of West Africa* (Bloomsbury, 2013).

Gordon, April. *Transforming Capitalism and Patriarchy: Gender and Development in Africa* (Lynne Rienner, 1996).

Gould, Stephen Jay. "The Hottentot Venus," *Natural History* 91:10 (1982) 20–27.

Gould, Stephen Jay. *The Mismeasure of Man* (Norton, 1981).

Graboyes, Melissa. *The Experiment Must Continue: Medical Research and Ethics in East Africa, 1940–2014* (Ohio University Press, 2015).

Griefenow-Mewis, Catherine, ed. *On Results of the Reform in Ethiopia's Language and Education Policies* (Harrassowitz, 2009).

Grubbs, Larry. *Secular Missionaries: Americans and African Development in the 1960s* (University of Massachusetts Press, 2009).

Gulde, Anne-Marie and Charalambos Tsangarides, eds. *The CFA Franc Zone: Common Currency, Uncommon Challenges* (International Monetary Fund, 2008).

Guyer, Jane I. "The Spatial Dimensions of Civil Society in Africa: An Anthropologist Looks at Nigeria," in John W. Harbeson, Donald Rothchild, and Naomi Chazan, eds., *Civil Society and the State in Africa* (Lynne Rienner, 1994), 215–230.

Gwebu, Thando D. "Botswana's Mining Path to Urbanization and Poverty Alleviation," *Journal of Contemporary African Studies* 30:4 (2012) 611–630.

Hale, Dana S. *Races on Display: French Representations of Colonized Peoples, 1886–1940* (Indiana University Press, 2008).

Hanretta, Sean. *Islam and Social Change in French West Africa: History of an Emancipatory Community* (Cambridge University Press, 2009).

Harlow, Barbara and Mia Carter, ed. *Archives of Empire*, Vol. 2 (Duke University Press, 2003).

Harris, Richard. "From Trusteeship to Development: How Class and Gender Complicated Kenya's Housing Policy, 1939–1963," *Journal of Historical Geography* 34:2 (2008) 311–337.

Hastings, Adrian. *The Church in Africa, 1450–1950* (Oxford University Press, 1994).

Healy-Clancy, Meghan. *A World of Their Own: A History of South African Women's Education* (University of Virginia Press, 2014).

Hecht, Gabrielle. *Being Nuclear: Africans and the Global Uranium Trade* (MIT Press, 2012).

Hecht, Gabrielle. "The Work of Invisibility: Radiation Hazards and Occupational Health in South African Uranium Production," *International Labor & Working-Class History* 81 (2012) 94–113.

Herbert, Sandra. *Charles Darwin and the Question of Evolution: A Brief History with Documents* (Bedford St. Martins, 2011).

Hoag, Heather. *Developing the Rivers of East and West Africa: An Environmental History* (Continuum, 2013).

Hochschild, Adam. *King Leopold's Ghost: A Story of Greed, Terror, and Heroism in Colonial Africa* (Houghton Mifflin, 1998).

Hodge, Joseph Morgan. *Triumph of the Expert: Agrarian Doctrines of Development and the Legacies of British Colonialism* (Ohio University Press, 2007).

Hodge, Joseph M., Gerald Hödl, and Martina Kopf, eds. *Developing Africa: Concepts and Practices in Twentieth-Century Colonialism* (Manchester University Press, 2014).

Hodgson, Dorothy. *Once Intrepid Warriors: Gender, Ethnicity, and the Cultural Politics of Maasai Development* (Indiana University Press, 2001).

Hodgson, Dorothy. "'These Are Not Our Priorities': Maasai Women, Human Rights, and the Problem of Culture," in Dorothy Hodgson, ed., *Gender and Culture at the Limit of Rights* (University of Pennsylvania Press, 2011), 138–157.

Holmes, Rachel. *African Queen: The Real Life of the Hottentot Venus* (Random House, 2007).

Hopkins, Anthony. *An Economic History of West Africa* (Routledge, 2014 [orig. Addison Wesley Longman, 1973]).

House-Soremekun, Bessie and Toyin Falola, eds. *Globalization and Sustainable Development in Africa* (University of Rochester Press, 2011).

Huchzermeyer, Marie. *Cities with "Slums": From Informal Settlement Eradication to a Right to the City in Africa* (University of Cape Town Press, 2011).

Hull, Richard. *African Cities and Towns before the European Conquest* (W. W. Norton, 1976).

Hunt, Nancy Rose. "'Le Bebe en Brousse': European Women, African Birth Spacing and Colonial Intervention in Breast Feeding in the Belgian Congo," *International Journal of African Historical Studies* 21:3 (1988) 401–432.

Hunt, Nancy Rose. *A Colonial Lexicon of Birth Ritual, Medicalization, and Mobility in the Congo* (Duke University Press, 1999).

Ibhawoh, Bonny. *Imperialism and Human Rights: Colonial Discourses of Rights and Liberties in African History* (State University of New York Press, 2007).

Iliffe, John. *The African Poor: A History* (Cambridge University Press, 2009 [orig. 1987]).

Iliffe, John. *A Modern History of Tanganyika* (Cambridge University Press, 1979).

Ireton, Barrie. *Britain's International Development Policies: A History of DFID and Overseas Aid* (Palgrave Macmillan, 2013).

Isaacman, Allen F. and Barbara S. Isaacman. *Dams, Displacement, and the Delusion of Development: Cahora Bassa and Its Legacies in Mozambique, 1965–2007* (Ohio University Press, 2013).

Ivaska, Andrew. *Cultured States: Youth, Gender, and Modern Style in 1960s Dar es Salaam* (Duke University Press, 2011).

Jackson, Ashley. *The British Empire and the Second World War* (Hambledon Continuum, 2006).

Jackson, John P. Jr. *Science for Segregation: Race, Law, and the Case against Brown v. Board of Education* (New York University Press, 2005).

Jackson, Lynette A. *Surfacing Up: Psychiatry and Social Order in Colonial Zimbabwe, 1908–1968* (Cornell University Press, 2005).

James, Wilmot, "Capital, African Labour and Housing at South Africa's Gold Mines," *Labour, Capital and Society* 25:1 (1992) 72–86.

Jean-Baptiste, Rachel. *Conjugal Rights: Marriage, Sexuality, and Urban Life in Colonial Libreville, Gabon* (Ohio University Press, 2014).

Jennings, Eric C. "Extraction and Labor in Equatorial Africa and Cameroon under Free French Rule," in Judith A. Byfield, Carolyn A. Brown,

Timothy Parsons, and Ahmad Alawad Sikainga, eds., *Africa and World War II* (Cambridge University Press, 2015), 200–219.

Jezequel, Jean-Hervé. "Voices of Their Own? African Participation in the Production of Colonial Knowledge in French West Africa, 1910–1950," in Helen Tilley, ed., with Robert J. Gordon, *Ordering Africa: Anthropology, European Imperialism, and the Politics of Knowledge* (Manchester University Press, 2007), 145–172.

Johnston, Bruce F. *The Staple Food Economies of Western Tropical Africa* (Stanford University Press, 1958).

Jones, Gareth Stedman. *An End to Poverty: A Historical Debate* (Columbia University Press, 2005).

Jones, Hilary. *The Métis of Senegal: Urban Life and Politics in French West Africa* (Indiana University Press, 2013).

Jones, James. *Industrial Labor in the Colonial World: Workers of the Chemin de Fer Dakar-Niger, 1881–1963* (Heinemann, 2002).

Kanogo, Tabitha. *Squatters and the Roots of Mau Mau, 1905–63* (James Currey, 1987).

Kapur, Devesh, John P. Lewis, and Richard Webb. *The World Bank: Its First Half Century, Volumes 1: History* and *Volume 2: Perspectives* (Brookings Institution Press, 1997).

Katsiaficas, George. *The Imagination of the New Left: A Global Analysis of 1968* (South End Press, 1987).

Katz, Michael B. "The Urban 'Underclass' As a Metaphor of Social Transformation," in Michael B. Katz, ed., *The "Underclass" Debate: Views from History* (Princeton University Press, 1993).

Keim, Curtis. *Mistaking Africa: Curiosities and Inventions of the American Mind.* Third edition (Westview Press, 2013).

Keller, Edmond J. "Drought, War, and the Politics of Famine in Ethiopia and Eritrea," *Journal of Modern African Studies* 30:4 (1992) 609–624.

Kelly, Gail P. "Learning to Be Marginal: Schooling in Interwar French West Africa," *Journal of Asian and African Studies* 21:3–4 (1986) 171–184.

Kevane, Michael. *Women and Development in Africa: How Gender Works* (Lynne Rienner, 2004).

Killingray, David. "Labour Mobilisation in British Colonial Africa for the War Effort, 1939–46," in David Killingray and Richard Rathbone, eds., *Africa and the Second World War* (Macmillan, 1986), 68–96.

King, David. "The New Internationalists: World Vision and the Revival of American Evangelical Humanitarianism, 1950–2010," *Religions* 3:4 (2012) 922–949.

Klausen, Susanne. *Race, Maternity, and the Politics of Birth Control in South Africa, 1910–39* (Palgrave Macmillan, 2004).

Klein, Martin A. "Chiefship in Sine-Saloum (Senegal), 1887–1914," in Victor Turner, ed., *Colonialism in Africa, 1870–1960, Volume Three: Profiles of Change: African Society and Colonial Rule* (Cambridge University Press, 1971).

Klein, Martin A. *Slavery and Colonial Rule in French West Africa* (Cambridge University Press, 1998).

Knoll, Arthur J. and Hermann J. Hiery, eds. *The German Colonial Experience: Select Documents on German Rule in Africa, China, and the Pacific 1884–1914* (University Press of America, 2010).

Korieh, Chima. *The Land Has Changed: History, Society and Gender in Colonial Eastern Nigeria* (University of Calgary Press, 2010).

Kuklick, Henrika. "The British Tradition," in Henrika Kuklick, ed., *A New History of Anthropology* (Blackwell, 2008), 52–78.

Lachenal, Guillaume. "Experimental Hubris and Medical Powerlessness: Notes from a Colonial Utopia, Cameroon, 1939–1949," in Paul W. Geissler, Richard Rottenburg, and Julia Zenker, eds., *Rethinking Biomedicine and Governance in Africa: Contributions from Anthropology* (transcript Verlag, 2012), 119–140.

Lal, Priya. *African Socialism in Postcolonial Tanzania: Between the Village and the World* (Cambridge University Press, 2015).

Larmer, Miles. "Permanent Precarity: Capital and Labour in the Central African Copperbelt," *Labor History* 58:2 (2017) 170–184.

Law, Robin, Suzanne Schwarz, and Silke Strickrodt. "Introduction," *Commercial Agriculture, the Slave Trade and Slavery in Atlantic Africa* (James Currey, 2013), 1–27.

Lawrance, Benjamin N., Emily Lynn Osborn, and Richard L. Roberts, eds., *Intermediaries, Interpreters, and Clerks: African Employees in the Making of Colonial Africa* (University of Wisconsin Press, 2006).

Leach, Fiona. "Gender, Education and Training: An International Perspective," *Gender and Development* 6:2 (1998) 9–18.

Leslie, Jacques. *Deep Water: The Epic Struggle over Dams, Displaced People, and the Environment* (Farrar, Straus and Giroux, 2005).

Levine, Philippa. *Prostitution, Race, and Politics: Policing Venereal Disease in the British Empire* (Routledge, 2003).

Lewis, Martin W. and Kären E. Wigen. *The Myth of Continents* (University of California Press, 1997).

Lindsay, Lisa A. *Working with Gender: Wage Labor and Social Change in Southwestern Nigeria* (Heinemann, 2003).

Livingstone, Julie. *Improvising Medicine: An African Oncology Ward in an Emerging Cancer Epidemic* (Duke University Press, 2012).

Livsey, Tim. *Nigeria's University Age: Reframing Decolonisation and Development* (Palgrave Macmillan, 2017).

Loimeier, Roman. *Between Social Skills and Marketable Skills: The Politics of Islamic Education in 20th Century Zanzibar* (Koninklijke Brill NV, 2009).

Lulat, Y. G.-M. *A History of African Higher Education from Antiquity to the Present: A Critical Synthesis* (Praeger, 2005).

Lumumba-Kasongo, Tukumbi. "Rethinking Educational Paradigms in Africa: Imperatives for Social Progress in the New Millennium," in Philip Higgs, Ntombizolile Vakalisa, Thobeka Mda, and N'Dri Thérèse Assié-Lumumba, eds., *African Voices in Education* (Juta, 2000), 139–157.

Lyons, Maryinez. *The Colonial Disease: A Social History of Sleeping Sickness in Northern Zaire, 1900–1940* (Cambridge University Press, 1992).

Lyons, Tanya. *Guns and Guerilla Girls: Women in the Zimbabwean National Liberation Struggle* (Africa World Press, 2004).

Macmillan, Hugh. "Mining, Housing and Welfare in South Africa and Zambia: An Historical Perspective," *Journal of Contemporary African Studies* 30:4 (2012) 539–550.

Macqueen, Norrie. "A Community of Illusions? Portugal, the CPLP and Peacemaking in Guiné-Bissau," *International Peacekeeping* 10:2 (2003) 2–26.

Mahood, Linda. *Feminism and Voluntary Action: Eglantyne Jebb and Save the Children, 1876–1928* (Palgrave Macmillan, 2009).

Manji, Firoze and Carl O'Coill. "The Missionary Position: NGOs and Development in Africa," *International Affairs* 78:3 (2002) 567–583.

Mann, Gregory. *From Empires to NGOs in the West African Sahel: The Road to Nongovernmentality* (Cambridge University Press, 2015).

Mann, Kristin. "Marriage Choices among the Educated African Elite in Lagos Colony, 1880–1915," *International Journal of African Historical Studies* 14:2 (1981) 201–228.

Mann, Kristin and Richard L. Roberts, eds., *Law in Colonial Africa* (Heinemann, 1991).

Manning, Patrick. *Francophone Sub-Saharan Africa 1880–1995* (Cambridge University Press, 1988).

Marris, Peter. *Family and Social Change in an African City: A Study of Rehousing in Lagos* (Routledge, 1962).

Marsters, Kate Ferguson. "Introduction to Mungo Park," in *Travels in the Interior Districts of Africa* (Duke University Press, 2000).

Martin, Phyllis M. *Leisure and Society in Colonial Brazzaville* (Cambridge University Press, 1995).

Masquelier, Adeline. *Prayer Has Spoiled Everything: Possession, Power, and Identity in an Islamic Town of Niger* (Duke University Press, 2001).

Mathers, Kathryn. *Travel, Humanitarianism, and Becoming American in Africa* (Palgrave MacMillan, 2010).

Maul, Daniel Roger. "The International Labour Organization and the Struggle against Forced Labour from 1919 to the Present," *Labor History* 48:4 (2007) 477–500.

Mbiti, John S. *African Religions & Philosophy*. Second revised and enlarged edition (Heinemann, 1999 [1969]).

McClintock, Anne. *Imperial Leather: Race, Gender and Sexuality in the Colonial Context* (Routledge, 1995).

McCracken, John. *A History of Malawi, 1859–1966* (James Currey, 2012).

McCulloch, Jock. *Asbestos Blues: Labour, Capital, Physicians and the State in South Africa* (James Currey, 2002).

McGregor, JoAnn. "The Victoria Falls 1900–1940: Landscape, Tourism and the Geographical Imagination," *Journal of Southern African Studies* 29:3 (2003) 717–737.

McLaughlin, Fiona. "Can a Language Endanger Itself? Reshaping Repertoires in Urban Senegal," in James Essegbey, Brent Henderson, and Fiona McLaughlin, eds., *Language Documentation and Endangerment in Africa* (John Benjamins, 2015), 131–152.

McMahon, Elisabeth. "Becoming Pemba: Identity, Social Welfare and Community during the Protectorate Period" (PhD diss., Indiana University, 2005).

McMahon, Elisabeth. "Developing Workers: Coerced and 'Voluntary' Labor in Zanzibar, 1909–1970," *International Labor and Working-Class History* 92 (2017) 114–133.

Memmi, Albert. *The Colonizer and the Colonized* (Orion Press, 1965).

Merchant, Emily Klancher. "A Digital History of Anglophone Demography and Global Population Control," *Population and Development Review* 43:1 (2017) 83–117.

Michael, Sarah. *Undermining Development: The Absence of Power among Local NGOs in Africa* (James Currey, 2004).

Miescher, Stephan F. "'No One Should Be Worse Off': The Akosombo Dam, Modernization, and the Experience of Resettlement in Ghana," in Peter J. Bloom, Stephan F. Miescher, and Takyiwaa Manuh, eds., *Modernization As Spectacle in Africa* (Indiana University Press, 2014), 184–204.

Mitchell, Michele. "'The Black Man's Burden': African Americans, Imperialism, and Notions of Racial Manhood 1890–1910," *International Review of Social History* 44:7 (1999) 77–100.

Mitman, Gregg. "Forgotten Paths of Empire: Ecology, Disease, and Commerce in Making of Liberia's Plantation Economy: President's Address," *Environmental History* 22:1 (2017) 1–22.

Mkandawire, Thandika and Adebayo Olukoshi, eds. *Between Liberalisation and Oppression: The Politics of Structural Adjustment in Africa* (Codesria, 1993).

Mkandawire, Thandika and Charles C. Soludo. *Our Continent, Our Future: African Perspectives on Structural Adjustment* (CODESRIA and Africa World Press, 1998).

Moaddel, Mansoor. *Islamic Modernism, Nationalism, and Fundamentalism: Episode and Discourse* (University of Chicago Press, 2005).

Molla, Tebeje. *Higher Education in Ethiopia: Structural Inequalities and Policy Responses* (Springer, 2018).

Monson, Jamie. "War of Words: The Narrative Efficacy of Medicine in the Maji Maji War," in James Giblin and Jamie Monson, eds., *Maji Maji: Lifting the Fog of War* (Koninklijke Brill NV, 2010), 33–70.

Moodie, T. Dunbar with Vivienne Ndatshe. *Going for Gold: Men, Mines, and Migration* (University of California Press, 1994).

Morgan, D. J. *The Official History of Colonial Development*, Vol. 1 (Humanities Press, 1980).

Moyd, Michelle R. *Violent Intermediaries: African Soldiers, Conquest, and Everyday Colonialism in German East Africa* (Ohio University Press, 2014).

Moyo, Dambisa. *Dead Aid: Why Aid Is Not Working and How There Is a Better Way for Africa* (Farrar, Straus and Giroux, 2009).

Mudimbe, V. Y. *The Idea of Africa* (Indiana University Press, 1994).

Mudimbe, V. Y. *The Invention of Africa: Gnosis, Philosophy, and the Order of Knowledge* (Indiana University Press, 1988).

Muh'd, Zeyana Ali. "Wartime in Zanzibar," in Amandina Lihamba, Fulata L. Moyo, M. M. Mulokozi, Naomi L. Shitemi, and Saïda Yahya-Othman, eds., *Women Writing Africa: The Eastern Region* (Feminist Press at City University of New York, 2007), 140–143.

Mukhopadhyay, Carol "Getting Rid of the Word 'Caucasian,'" in Mica Pollock, ed., *Everyday Anti-Racism: Getting Real about Race in School* (New Press, 2008).

Munk, Nina. *The Idealist: Jeffrey Sachs and the Quest to End Poverty* (Doubleday, 2013).

Mwega, Francis M. and Njuguna S. Ndung'u. "Explaining African Economic Growth Performance: The Case of Kenya," in Benno J. Ndulu, Stephen A. O'Connell, Jean-Paul Azam, Robert H. Bates, Augustin K. Fosu, Jan Willem Gunning, and Dominique Njinkeu, eds., *The Political Economy of Economic Growth in Africa, 1960–2000: Vol. 2: Country Case Studies* (Cambridge University Press, 2008), 325–368.

Nandy, Ashis. *The Intimate Enemy: Loss and Recovery of Self under Colonialism* (Oxford University Press, 1983).

Ndao, Mor. "Colonisation et politique de santé maternelle et infantile au Sénégal (1905–1960)," *French Colonial History* 9 (2008) 191–211.

Nettleton, Anitra C. E. "The Venda Model Hut," *African Arts* 18:3 (1985) 87–98.

Newbury, Catharine and David Newbury. "A Catholic Mass in Kigali: Contested Views of the Genocide and Ethnicity in Rwanda," *Canadian Journal of African Studies* 33:2/3 (1999) 292–328.

Nisbet, Robert. *History of the Idea of Progress*. Fourth edition (Routledge, 2017 [orig. 1980]).

Njoh, Ambe J. "The Experience and Legacy of French Colonial Urban Planning in Sub-Saharan Africa," *Planning Perspectives* 19 (2004) 435–454.

Njoh, Ambe J. *Planning Power: Town Planning and Social Control in Colonial Africa* (Routledge, 2007).

Njoh, Ambe J. *Tradition, Culture and Development in Africa: Historical Lessons for Modern Development Planning* (Ashgate, 2006).

Nyambariza, Daniel. "Les Efforts de Guerre et la Famine de 1943–1944 au Burundi, d'Après les Archives Territoriales," *Cahiers CRA Histoire* 4 (1984) 1–18.

Ochieng', William R. "The Kenyatta Era 1963–78: Structural & Political Change," in Bethwell Allan Ogot and William R. Ochieng', eds., *Decolonization & Independence in Kenya, 1940–93* (James Currey, 1995), 83–109.

Ocobock, Paul. *An Uncertain Age: The Politics of Manhood in Kenya* (Ohio University Press, 2017).

Odhiambo, E. S. Atieno. "The Cultural Dimensions of Development in Africa," *African Studies Review* 45:3 (2002) 1–16.

Ogot, Bethwell A. "The Construction of Luo Identity and History," in Luise White, Stephan F. Miescher, and David William Cohen, eds., *African Words, African Voices: Critical Practices in Oral History* (Indiana University Press, 2001), 31–52.

Olejniczak, William. "Royal Paternalism with a Repressive Face: The Ideology of Poverty in Late Eighteenth-Century France," *Journal of Policy History* 2:2 (1990) 157–185.

Olumwullah, Osaak A. *Dis-ease in the Colonial State: Medicine, Society, and Social Change among the AbaNyole of Western Kenya* (Greenwood Press, 2002).

Onyemelukwe, J. O. C. *Industrialization in West Africa* (St. Martin's Press, 1984).

Osborn, Emily Lynn. *Our New Husbands Are Here: Households, Gender, and Politics in a West African State from the Slave Trade to Colonial Rule* (Ohio University Press, 2011).

Osborne, Michael A. *The Emergence of Tropical Medicine in France* (University of Chicago Press, 2014).

Ospovat, Dov. *The Development of Darwin's Theory: Natural History, Natural Theology, and Natural Selection, 1838–1859* (Cambridge University Press, 1981).

Osseo-Asare, Abena Dove. *Bitter Roots: The Search for Healing Plants in Africa* (University of Chicago Press, 2014).

Ovadia, Jesse Salah. *The Petro-Developmental State in Africa: Making Oil Work in Angola, Nigeria and the Gulf of Guinea* (Hurst, 2016).

Oyebade, Adebayo O. *Culture and Customs of Angola* (Greenwood Press, 2007).

Packard, Randall M. *White Plague, Black Labor: Tuberculosis and the Political Economy of Health and Disease in South Africa* (University of California Press, 1989).

Paracka, Daniel J. Jr., *The Athens of West Africa: A History of International Education at Fourah Bay College, Freetown, Sierra Leone* (Routledge, 2003).

Patterson, Donna A. *Pharmacy in Senegal: Gender, Healing, and Entrepreneurship* (Indiana University Press, 2015).

Patterson, Rubin, ed. *African Brain Circulation: Beyond the Drain-Gain Debate* (Koninklijke Brill NV, 2007).

Patton, Cindy. *Inventing AIDS* (Routledge, 1990).

Pepin, Jacques. *The Origins of AIDS* (Cambridge University Press, 2011).

Phiri, Isabel Apawo. *Women, Presbyterianism and Patriarchy: Religious Experience of Chewa Women in Central Malawi* (Christian Literature Association in Malawi [Kachere Series, 2007 (orig. 1997)]).

Plaatjie, Sebeka Richard. "Beyond Western-Centric and Eurocentric Development: A Case for Decolonizing Development," *Africanus* 43:2 (2013) 118–130.

Poovey, Mary. *Making a Social Body: British Cultural Formation, 1830–1864* (University of Chicago Press, 1995).

Posnansky, Merrick. "Dwellings of West Africa," *African Arts* 20:1 (1986) 82–83.

Pratt, Mary Louise. *Imperial Eyes: Travel Writing and Transculturation* (Routledge, 1992).

Prussin, Labelle. "Traditional Asante Architecture," *African Arts* 13:2 (1980) 57–87.

Pybus, Cassandra. "'A Less Favourable Specimen': The Abolitionist Response to Self-Emancipated Slaves in Sierra Leone, 1793–1808," *Parliamentary History* 26:4 (2007) 97–112.

Ray, Carina E. *Crossing the Color Line: Race, Sex, and the Contested Politics of Colonialism in Ghana* (Ohio University Press, 2015).

Reid, Richard J. *A History of Modern Africa: 1800 to the Present* (Wiley-Blackwell, 2009).

Resnik, David B. "Access to Affordable Medication in the Developing World: Social Responsibility vs. Profit," in Anton A. van Niekerk and Loretta M. Kopelman, eds., *Ethics & AIDS in Africa: The Challenge to Our Thinking* (David Philip, 2005), 111–126.

Robinson, David. "The Murids: Surveillance and Collaboration," *Journal of African History* 40:2 (1999) 193–213.

Robinson, David. *Paths of Accommodation: Muslim Societies and French Colonial Authorities in Senegal and Mauritania, 1880–1920* (Ohio University Press, 2000).

Rodney, Walter. *How Europe Underdeveloped Africa* (Howard University Press, Revised ed. 1982 [orig. Bogle-L'Ouverture Publications, 1972]).

Roediger, David. *The Wages of Whiteness: Race and the Making of the American Working Class* (Verso, 1991).

Rohrmann, G. F. "House Decoration in Southern Africa," *African Arts* 7:3 (1974) 18–21.

Rollins, Jack D. *A History of Swahili Prose, Part One: From Earliest Times to the End of the Nineteenth Century* (E. J. Brill, 1983).

Rönnbäck, Klas. *Labour and Living Standards in Pre-Colonial West Africa: The Case of the Gold Coast* (Routledge, 2016).

Rutherford, Blair. "Another Side to Rural Zimbabwe: Social Constructs and the Administration of Farm Workers in Urungwe District, 1940s," *Journal of Southern African Studies* 23:1 (1997) 107–126.

Saad, Elias N. *Social History of Timbuktu: The Role of Muslim Scholars and Notables, 1400–1900* (Cambridge University Press, 1983).

Said, Edward. *Orientalism* (Pantheon Books, 1978).

Schiebinger, Londa. *Secret Cures of Slaves: People, Plans, and Medicine in the Eighteenth-Century Atlantic World* (Stanford University Press, 2017).

Schmidt, Elizabeth. *Foreign Intervention in Africa: From the Cold War to the War on Terror* (Cambridge University Press, 2013).

Schmidt, Elizabeth. *Mobilizing the Masses: Gender, Ethnicity, and Class in the Nationalist Movement in Guinea, 1939–1958* (Heinemann, 2005).

Schneider, William. "The Long History of Smallpox Eradication: Lessons for Global Health in Africa," in Tamara Giles-Vernick and James L. A. Webb Jr., eds., *Global Health in Africa: Historical Perspectives on Disease Control* (Ohio University Press, 2013), 25–41.

Schneider, William. "Toward the Improvement of the Human Race: The History of Eugenics in France," *Journal of Modern History* 54:2 (1982) 268–291.

Schraeder, Peter J. *United States Foreign Policy toward Africa: Incrementalism, Crisis and Change* (Cambridge University Press, 1994).

Schumaker, Lyn. *Africanizing Anthropology: Fieldwork, Networks, and the Making of Cultural Knowledge in Central Africa* (Duke University Press, 2001).

Segalla, Spencer D. *The Moroccan Soul: French Education, Colonial Ethnology, and Muslim Resistance, 1912–1956* (University of Nebraska Press, 2009).

Setel, Philip W., Milton Lewis, and Maryinez Lyons, eds. *Histories of Sexually Transmitted Diseases and HIV/AIDS in Sub-Saharan Africa* (Greenwood Press, 1999).

Sheldon, Kathleen. *Historical Dictionary of Women in Sub-Saharan Africa* (Scarecrow Press, 2005).

Shillington, Kevin. *History of Africa*. Third edition (Palgrave Macmillan, 2012).

Shillington, Kevin. *History of Southern Africa* (Macmillan, 1987).

Shizha, Edward and Michael T. Kariwo. *Education and Development in Zimbabwe: A Social, Political and Economic Analysis* (Sense, 2011).

Showers, Kate B. "Prehistory of Southern African Forestry: From Vegetable Garden to Tree Plantation," *Environment and History* 16:3 (2010) 295–322.

Sibeud, Emmanuelle. "The Elusive Bureau of Colonial Ethnography in France, 1907–1925," in Helen Tilley, ed., with Robert J. Gordon, *Ordering Africa: Anthropology, European Imperialism, and the Politics of Knowledge* (Manchester University Press, 2007), 49–66.

Sibisi, Harriet. "How African Women Cope with Migrant Labor in South Africa," *Signs* 3:1 (1977) 167–177.

Silva, Tiloka de and Silvana Tenreyro. "Population Control Policies and Fertility Convergence," *Journal of Economic Perspectives* 31:4 (2017) 205–228.

Singer, Michal. "Towards 'A Different Kind of Beauty': Responses to Coal-Based Pollution in the Witbank Coalfield between 1903 and 1948," *Journal of Southern African Studies* 37:2 (2011) 281–296.

Skinner, Kate. *The Fruits of Freedom in British Togoland: Literacy, Politics and Nationalism, 1914–2014* (Cambridge University Press, 2015).

Sklair, Leslie. *The Sociology of Progress* (Routledge & Kegan Paul, 1970).

Smalberger, John M. "The Role of the Diamond-Mining Industry in the Development of the Pass-Law System in South Africa," *International Journal of African Historical Studies* 9:3 (1976) 419–434.

Smith, James H. *Bewitching Development: Witchcraft and the Reinvention of Development in Neoliberal Kenya* (University of Chicago Press, 2008).

Smith, James H. "What's in Your Cell Phone?" in Dorothy L. Hodgson and Judith A. Byfield, eds., *Global Africa: Into the Twenty-First Century* (University of California Press, 2017), 289–297.

Spear, Thomas and Richard Waller, eds. *Being Maasai: Ethnicity and Identity in East Africa* (Ohio University Press, 1993).

Stanley, Brian. *The World Missionary Conference, Edinburgh 1910* (Eerdmans, 2009).

Steinmetz, George. *The Devil's Handwriting: Precoloniality and the German Colonial State in Qingdao, Samoa, and Southwest Africa* (University of Chicago Press, 2007).

Surun, Isabelle, "French Military Officers and the Mapping of West Africa: The Case of Captain Brosselard-Faidherbe," *Journal of Historical Geography* 37 (2011) 167–177.

Symonds, James. "The Poverty Trap: Or, Why Poverty Is Not about the Individual," *International Journal of Historical Archaeology* 15 (2011) 563–571.

Táíwò, Olúfẹ́mi. *How Colonialism Preempted Modernity in Africa* (Indiana University Press, 2010).

Tallis, Vicci. *Feminisms, HIV and AIDS: Subverting Power, Reducing Vulnerability* (Palgrave Macmillan, 2012).

Tappan, Jennifer. *The Riddle of Malnutrition: The Long Arc of Biomedical and Public Health Interventions in Uganda* (Ohio University Press, 2017).

Tesi, Moses K. "Conceptualizing Africa's Environment: A Framework for Analysis," in Moses K. Tesi, ed., *The Environment and Development in Africa* (Lexington Books, 2000), 13–38.

Thebe, Vusilizwe. "'Men on Transit' and the Rural 'Farmer Housewives': Women in Decision-Making Roles in Migrant-Labour Societies in North-Western Zimbabwe," *Journal of Asian and African Studies* 53:7 (2018) 1118–1133.

Thiong'o, Ngũgĩ wa. *Decolonising the Mind: The Politics of Language in African Literature* (East African Educational Publishers, 1981).

Thiong'o, Ngũgĩ wa. *Moving the Centre: The Struggle for Cultural Freedoms* (James Currey, 1993).

Thomas, Lynn M. *Politics of the Womb: Women, Reproduction, and the State in Kenya* (University of California Press, 2003).

Tignor, Robert L. *W. Arthur Lewis and the Birth of Development Economics* (Princeton University Press, 2006).

Tilley, Helen. *Africa As a Living Laboratory: Empire, Development, and the Problem of Scientific Knowledge, 1870–1950* (University of Chicago Press, 2011).

Tilley, Helen, ed., with Robert J. Gordon. *Ordering Africa: Anthropology, European Imperialism, and the Politics of Knowledge* (Manchester University Press, 2010).

Tinley, James Maddison. *South African Food and Agriculture in World War II* (Stanford University Press, 1954).

Tsikata, Dzodzi. *Living in the Shadow of the Large Dams: Long Term Responses of Downstream and Lakeside Communities of Ghana's Volta River Project* (Brill, 2006).

Turrell, Rob. "Diamonds and Migrant Labour in South Africa, 1869–1910," *History Today* 36:5 (1986) 45–50.

Ukadike, N. Frank. "Western Film Images of Africa: Genealogy of an Ideological Formulation," *Black Scholar* 21:2 (1990) 30–48.

Unger, Corinna. *International Development: A Postwar History* (Bloomsbury Academic Press, 2018).

Vagnby, Bo and Alan H. Jacobs. "Kenya: Traditional Housing of the Elmolo," *Ekisties* 38:227 (1974) 240–243.

Vail, Leroy, ed. *The Creation of Tribalism in Southern Africa* (James Currey, 1989).

Van Beusekom, Monica M. *Negotiating Development: African Farmers and Colonial Experts at the Office Du Niger, 1920–1960* (Heinemann, 2002).

Vansina, Jan. *Oral Tradition As History* (University of Wisconsin Press, 1985).

Vaughan, Megan. *Curing Their Ills: Colonial Power and African Illness* (Stanford University Press, 1991).

Vernon, James. *Hunger: A Modern History* (Harvard University Press, 2007).

Wallerstein, Immanuel. "After Development and Globalization, What?" *Social Forces* 83:3 (2005) 1263–1278.

Wallerstein, Immanuel. *World-Systems Analysis: An Introduction* (Duke University Press, 2004).

Ware III, Rudolph T. *The Walking Qur'an: Islamic Education, Embodied Knowledge, and History in West Africa* (University of North Carolina Press, 2014).

Wariboko, Waibinte E. *Race and the Civilizing Mission: Their Implications for the Framing of Blackness and African Personhood* (Africa World Press, 2010).

Weindling, Paul. "Julian Huxley and the Continuity of Eugenics in Twentieth-Century Britain," *Journal of Modern European History* 10:4 (2012) 480–499.

West, Michael O. *The Rise of an African Middle Class: Colonial Zimbabwe, 1898–1965* (Indiana University Press, 2002).

Westcott, Nicholas. "The Impact of the Second World War on Tanganyika, 1939–49," in David Killingray and Richard Rathbone, eds., *Africa and the Second World War* (Palgrave Macmillan, 1986), 143–159.

White, Landeg. *Magomero: Portrait of an African Village* (Cambridge University Press, 1987).

White, Luise. *Comforts of Home: Prostitution in Colonial Nairobi* (University of Chicago Press, 1990).

White, Luise. *Speaking with Vampires: Rumor and History in Colonial Africa* (University of California Press, 2000).

Woloch, Isser and Gregory S. Brown, *Eighteenth Century Europe: Tradition and Progress, 1715–1789*. Second edition (W. W. Norton, 2012).

Worboys, Michael. "The Discovery of Malnutrition Between the Wars," in David Arnold, ed., *Imperial Medicine and Indigenous Societies* (Manchester University Press, 1988), 208–225.

Wylie, Diana. *Starving on a Full Stomach: Hunger and the Triumph of Cultural Racism in Modern South Africa* (University Press of Virginia, 2001).

Young, Crawford. *The African Colonial State in Comparative Perspective* (Yale University Press, 1994).

Zeleza, Paul Tiyambe and Philip J. McConnaughay, eds. *Human Rights, the Rule of Law, and Development in Africa* (University of Pennsylvania Press, 2011).

Ziai, Aram. *Development Discourse and Global History: From Colonialism to Sustainable Development Goals* (Routledge, 2016).

Zimmerman, Andrew. "'What Do You Really Want in German East Africa, Herr Professor?' Counterinsurgency and the Science Effect in Colonial Tanzania," *Comparative Studies in Society and History* 48:2 (2006) 419–461.

PUBLISHED PRIMARY SOURCES

African Development Bank. *African Economic Outlook, 2017: Entrepreneurship and Industrialisation* (African Development Bank, Organisation for

Economic Co-Operation and Development, United Nations Development Programme, 2017).

Annual Report on the Social and Economic Progress of the People of Nigeria, 1936 (His Majesty's Stationary Office, 1938).

Anon. *An Answer to Mark Twain* (A. & G. Bulens Brothers, 1907).

Biko, Steven. *I Write What I Like* (Harper & Row, 1979).

Burton, Richard F. *First Footsteps in East Africa, or, An Exploration of Hārar* (Longman, Brown, Green, and Longmans, 1856).

Burton, Richard F. *The Lake Regions of Central Africa: A Picture of Exploration* (Longman, Green, Longman and Roberts, 1860).

Burton, Richard F. *Wanderings in West Africa from Liverpool to Fernando Po* (Tinsley Brothers, 1863).

Burton, Richard F. *Zanzibar: City, Island, and Coast* (Tinsley Brothers, 1872).

Butt, Audrey. *The Nilotes of the Anglo-Egyptian Sudan and Uganda* (International African Institute, 1952).

Buxton, Thomas Fowell. *The African Slave Trade and Its Remedy* (John Murray, 1840).

Christie, James. *Cholera Epidemics in East Africa* (Macmillan, 1876).

Cory, Hans. "Jando. Part I: The Construction and Organization of the Jando," *Journal of the Royal Anthropological Institute of Great Britain and Ireland* 77:2 (1947) 159–168.

Curtin, Philip D. *African Remembered: Narratives by West Africans from the Era of the Slave Trade* (Waveland Press, 1967).

Darwin, Charles. *Descent of Man, and Selection in Relation to Sex*, Vol. 1 (John Murray, 1871).

Darwin, Charles. *Descent of Man, and Selection in Relation to Sex*. Second edition revised and augmented (John Murray, 1874).

Dundas, Charles. *Kilimanjaro and Its People: A History of the Wachagga, Their Laws, Customs and Legends, Together with Some Account of the Highest Mountain in Africa* (H. F. & G. Witherby, 1924).

Ehrlich, Paul R. *The Population Bomb* (A Sierra Club Ballantine Book, 1968).

French-Sheldon, Mary. *Sultan to Sultan: Adventures among the Masai and Other Tribes of East Africa* (Arena Publishing Company, 1892).

Gaitskell, Arthur. *Gezira: A Story of Development in the Sudan* (Faber & Faber, 1959).

Great Britain Colonial Office. *Colonial Development Advisory Committee Reports, 1933–1940* (His Majesty's Stationary Office, 1934–1941).

Great Britain Colonial Office. *Colonial Development and Welfare Acts: Report on the Use of Funds Provided under the Colonial Development and Welfare Acts, and Outline of the Proposal for Exchequer Loans to the Colonial Territories* (Her Majesty's Stationary Office, 1959).

Great Britain Colonial Office. *First Interim Report of the Colonial Development Advisory Committee Covering the Period 1st August 1929–28th February 1930* (His Majesty's Stationary Office, 1930).

Great Britain Colonial Office. *Mass Education in African Society* (His Majesty's Stationary Office, 1944).

Great Britain, Economic Advisory Council, Committee on Nutrition in the Colonial Empire. *Nutrition in the Colonial Empire: First Report* (His Majesty's Stationary Office, 1939).

Hailey, Lord. *An African Survey: A Study of Problems Arising in Africa South of the Sahara* (Oxford University Press, 1938).

Hall, R. N. "The Great Zimbabwe," *Journal of the Royal African Society* 4:15 (1905) 295–300.

Hatch, John Charles. *Everyman's Africa* (Dobson, 1959).

Hindlip, Lord. *British East Africa: Past, Present, and Future* (T. Fisher Unwin, 1905).

Hofmann, Corinne. *The White Masai* (Bliss, 2005).

Holleman, J. F. *Shona Customary Law: With Reference to Kinship, Marriage, the Family and the Estate* (Manchester University Press, 1969 [orig. Institute for Social Research, University of Zambia, 1952]).

Hunwick, John O. *Timbuktu and the Songhay Empire: Al-Saʿidī's Taʾrīkh al-sūdān down to 1613 and Other Contemporary Documents* (Koninklijke Brill NV, 2003).

Isaacs, Nathaniel. *Travels and Adventures in Eastern Africa, Descriptive of the Zoolus, Their Manners, Customs, Etc. Etc. with a Sketch of Natal* (Bradbury & Evans Printers, 1836).

Johnson, H. T. "The Black Man's Burden," *Voice of Missions* 7 (Atlanta: April 1899), Reprinted in Willard B. Gatewood Jr., *Black Americans and the White Man's Burden, 1898–1903* (University of Illinois Press, 1975), 183–184.

Johnston, Harry H. "Sir Harry Johnston's Address on Retirement from the Presidency," *Journal of the Royal African Society* 20:78 (1921) 83–88.

Kant, Immanuel. "An Answer to the Question: What Is Enlightenment?" in Allen W. Wood, ed., *Basic Writings of Kant* (Modern Library, 2001).

Kenyatta, Jomo. *Facing Mount Kenya: The Tribal Life of the Gikuyu* (Vintage Books, 1965 [1938]).

Kingsley, Mary H. *The Story of West Africa* (H. Marshall & Son, 1899).

Kingsley, Mary H. *Travels in West Africa: Congo Francais, Corisco and Cameroons* (Macmillan, 1897).

Kipling, Rudyard. "The White Man's Burden," *New York Sun*, February 10, 1899.

Kirwan, Laurence P. "Recent Archaeology in British Africa," *Journal of the Royal African Society* 37:149 (1938) 494–501.

Krige, Eileen Jensen. "The Place of North-Eastern Transvaal Sotho in the South Bantu Complex," *Africa: Journal of the International African Institute* 11:3 (1938) 265–293.

Laird, Macgregor and R. A. K. Oldfield. *Narrative of an Expedition into the Interior of Africa, by the River Niger, in the Steam-Vessels* Quorra *and* Alburkah, *in 1832, 1833, and 1834*, Vol. I (Richard Bentley, 1837).

Livingstone, David. *The Last Journals of David Livingstone, in Central Africa, from 1865 to His Death, 1866–1873 Continued by a Narrative of His Last Moments and Sufferings, Obtained from His Faithful Servants Chuma and Susi* (Library of Alexandria, 2012).

Livingstone, David. *Missionary Travels and Researches in South Africa, Including a Sketch of Sixteen Years' Residence in the Interior of Africa, and a Journey from the Cape of Good Hope to Loanda on the West Coast; Thence across the Continent, Down the River Zambesi, to the Eastern Ocean* (John Murray, 1857).

Lugard, Frederick D. *The Dual Mandate in Tropical British Africa* (Frank Cass, 1922).

Lugard, Frederick D. "The International Institute of African Languages and Cultures," *Africa: Journal of the International African Institute* 1:1 (1928).

Maathai, Wangari. *The Green Belt Movement: Sharing the Approach and the Experience* (Lantern Books, 2004).

Maathai, Wangari. *Unbowed: A Memoir* (Anchor Books, 2006).

"Mishi wa Abdala," in Sarah Mirza and Margaret Strobel, eds. and transl., *Three Swahili Women: Life Histories from Mombasa, Kenya* (Indiana University Press, 1989), 69–79.

Monod, J. L. *Premier Livret de l'Ecolier Soudanais* (Delagrave, 1911).

Monteiro, Rose. *Delagoa Bay: Its Natives and Natural History* (George Philip & Son, 1891).

Moughtin, J. C. "The Traditional Settlements of the Hausa People," *Town Planning Review* 35:1 (1964) 21–34.

Mumford, W. Bryant. *Africans Learn to Be French: A Review of Educational Activities in the Seven Federated Colonies of French West Africa, Based upon a Tour of French West Africa and Algiers Undertaken in 1935* (Evans Brothers, 1939).

Niane, Dijbril Tamsir. *Sundiata: An Epic of Old Mali* (Longman Group, 2006 [1965]).

Nkrumah, Kwame. *Neo-colonialism: The Last Stage of Imperialism* (Thomas Nelson, 1965).

Reader, D. H. *The Zulu Tribe in Transition: The Makhanya of Southern Natal* (Manchester University Press, 1966).

Rollins, Jack D. *A History of Swahili Prose, Part One: From Earliest Times to the End of the Nineteenth Century* (E. J. Brill, 1983).

Rosenstein-Rodan, Paul. "Problems of Industrialisation of Eastern and South-Eastern Europe," *Economic Journal* 53:210/211 (1943) 202–211.

Rosenstein-Rodan, Paul N. "The International Development of Economically Backward Areas," *International Affairs (Royal Institute of International Affairs)* 20:2 (1944) 157–165.

Rostow, Walt. *The Stages of Economic Growth: A Non-Communist Manifesto* (Cambridge University Press, 1960).

Saitoti, Tepilit Ole. *The Worlds of a Maasai Warrior: An Autobiography* (University of California Press, 1986).

Senghor, Léopold. *On African Socialism* (Frederick A. Praeger, 1964).

Senghor, Léopold. "Some Thoughts on Africa: A Continent in Development," *International Affairs (Royal Institute of International Affairs)* 38:2 (1962) 189–195.

Speke, John Hanning. *Journal of the Discovery of the Source of the Nile* (Harper, 1864).

Spencer, Herbert. *Essays: Scientific, Political, and Speculative, Volume I* (D. Appleton, 1910).

Stanley, Henry Morton. *The Congo and the Founding of Its Free State: A Story of Work and Exploration* (Harper, 1885).

Talbot, P. Amaury. "Some Foreign Influences on Nigeria," *Journal of the Royal African Society* 24:95 (1925) 178–201.

Vedder, Heinrich, Carl Hugo Linsingen Hahn, and Louis Fourie. *The Native Tribes of South West Africa* (Cape Times, 1928).

Vigier, Daniel. "La Commission de coopération technique en Afrique au Sud du Sahara," *Politique étrangère* 19:3 (1954) 335–349.

United Nations. *Special Study on Educational Conditions in Non-self-governing Territories* (United Nations, 1954).

United Nations. United Nations Educational, Scientific and Cultural Organization, "The Race Question," 1950, https://unesdoc.unesco.org/ark:/48223/pf0000128291, accessed February 5, 2020.

United Nations. United Nations Educational, Scientific and Cultural Organization, "Statement on the Nature of Race and Race Differences," Paris, June 1951, https://unesdoc.unesco.org/ark:/48223/pf0000122962, accessed February 5, 2020.

White, Arthur Silva. *The Development of Africa* (George Philip & Son, 1890).

Wilson, Godfrey. "147. Anthropology in Northern Rhodesia," *Man* 38 (1938).

Wilson, Godfrey. *An Essay on the Economics of Detribalization in Northern Rhodesia*, Rhodes-Livingstone Papers No. 5–6 (Rhodes-Livingstone Institute, 1941–1942).

ONLINE REPORTS AND WEBSITES

"About NEPAD," http://nepad.org/content/about-nepad, accessed June 12, 2019.

African Development Bank. *Board Documents*, "Statement of Voting Powers As at 28 February 2019," www.afdb.org/en/documents/document/afdb-statement -of-voting-powers-as-at-28-february-2019–108964, accessed February 4, 2020.

Campbell, L. "Ebola Response in Cities: Learning for Future Public Health Crises," ALNAP Working Paper, 2017, ALNAP/ODI, available at www.ur ban-response.org/help-library/ebola-response-in-cities-learning-for-future-public-health-crises, accessed January 4, 2020, 18.

Centers for Disease Control and Prevention. "2014 Ebola Outbreak in West Africa: Case Counts," www.cdc.gov/vhf/ebola/outbreaks/2014-west-africa/ case-counts.html, accessed December 17, 2017.

"Civil Society Call on Investors to Cease Support to Bridge International Academies," August 1, 2017, http://globalinitiative-escr.org/wp-content/up loads/2017/07/Civil-society-call-on-investors-to-cease-support-to-Bridge-I nternational-Academies.pdf, accessed January 4, 2020.

Driscoll, David D. "The IMF and the World Bank: How Do They Differ?" International Monetary Fund website, www.imf.org/external/pubs/ft/exrp/ differ/differ.htm, accessed January 3, 2020.

"Human African Trypanosomiasis, Symptoms, Diagnosis, and Treatment," World Health Organization, www.who.int/trypanosomiasis_african/diagno sis/en/, accessed January 2, 2020.

"Life of a Maasai Warrior," www.bush-adventures.com/maasai-warriors/, accessed December 26, 2017.

Millennium Development Goals (MDG) Monitor, Fact Sheet on Current MDG Progress of Rwanda (Africa), 2015, www.mdgmonitor.org/mdg-progress-rwanda-africa/, accessed March 16, 2019.

Millennium Development Goals (MDG) Monitor, MDG 2: Achieve Universal Primary Education, www.mdgmonitor.org/mdg-2-achieve-universal-primary-education/, accessed March 16, 2019.

Report of the United Nations Conference on Desertification, held in Nairobi, Kenya August 29–September 9, 1977. The Action Plan is available online. www.ciesin.org/docs/002–478/002–478.html, accessed August 1, 2018.

Romero, Mauricio, Justin Sandefur, and Wayne Aaron Sandholtz. "Can Outsourcing Improve Liberia's Schools? Preliminary Results from Year One of a Three-Year Randomized Evaluation of Partnership Schools for Liberia," Center for Global Development, Working Paper 462, September 2017, www.cgdev.org/sites/default/files/partnership-schools-for-liberia.pdf, accessed January 4, 2020.

The Rusty Radiator, http://radiaid.com/, accessed June 12, 2019.

"The Samaritans," www.aidforaid.org/, accessed June 12, 2019.

"Spot the Africa," www.youtube.com/watch?v=AHO1a1kvZG0, accessed June 12, 2019.

United Nations Development Policy & Analysis Division, Least Developed Countries (LDCS), www.un.org/development/desa/dpad/least-developed-country-category.html, accessed January 3, 2020.

United Nations Development Programme (UNDP) Sustainable Development Goals, www.undp.org/content/undp/en/home/sustainable-development-goals.html, accessed June 12, 2019.

Williams, Kirsten C. "INGOS Relocating to the Global South," *K4D Helpdesk Report*. UK Department for International Development, September 10, 2018, https://assets.publishing.service.gov.uk/media/5bb226d9e5274a3e10 bd9394/438_INGOs_relocating_to_the_South.pdf, accessed February 4, 2020.

World Bank, Member Countries, www.worldbank.org/en/about/leadership/members, accessed January 3, 2020.

World Bank Blogs, Luis Triveno, "Eight Stubborn Facts about Housing Policies," July 5, 2016, https://blogs.worldbank.org/sustainablecities/eight-stubborn-facts-about-housing-policies, accessed January 3, 2020.

The World Bank in Africa, www.worldbank.org/en/region/afr, accessed June 12, 2019.

NEWSPAPER ARTICLES AND OTHER MEDIA SOURCES

"Africa Rising: The Hopeful Continent." *The Economist*, December 3, 2011, www.economist.com/leaders/2011/12/03/africa-rising, accessed February 4, 2020.

Anderson, Jenny. "Bridging the Gap: The Controversial Silicon Valley-Funded Quest to Educate the World's Poorest Kids." *Quartz*, January 22, 2018, https://qz.com/1179738/bridge-school/, accessed January 4, 2020.

Ashraf, Shirin and Arthur Wickenhagen. "Why Ebola Vaccine on Trial in the DRC Is Raising Hopes." *The Conversation*, February 10, 2019, http://thecon versation.com/why-ebola-vaccine-on-trial-in-the-drc-is-raising-hopes-1111 26, accessed February 4, 2020.

Bono. "Africa Reboots." *New York Times*, April 17, 2010, www.nytimes.com /2014/07/28/world/africa/ebola-epidemic-west-africa-guinea.html, accessed February 4, 2020.

Clémençot, Julien. "Côte d'Ivoire: l'usine textile Gonfrevillegile un mauvais cotton." *Jeune Afrique*, September 22, 2015, www.jeuneafrique.com/mag/2 45660/economie/cote-divoire-lusine-textile-gonfreville-file-un-mauvais-cot on/, accessed February 4, 2020.

Cole, Teju. "The White-Savior Industrial Complex." *The Atlantic Monthly*, March 21, 2012, www.theatlantic.com/international/archive/2012/03/the-white-savior-industrial-complex/254843/, accessed February 4, 2020.

George, Abosede. *Inside Edition*. "Is Wakanda Real? The Real-World Roots of 'Black Panther,'" www.insideedition.com/media/videos/wakanda-real-real-world-roots-black-panther-41131, accessed December 30, 2019.

Jasanoff, Maya. "With Conrad on the Congo River." *New York Times*, August 18, 2017, www.nytimes.com/2017/08/18/opinion/joseph-conrad-congo-river.html, accessed February 4, 2020.

McNeil, Donald G. Jr., "As Cancer Tears through Africa, Drug Makers Draw Up a Battle Plan." *New York Times*, October 7, 2017, www.nytimes.com/2017/10/07/health/africa-cancer-drugs.html, accessed February 4, 2020.

McNeil, Donald G. Jr., and Michael D. Shear. "U.S. Plans 21-Day Watch of Travelers from Ebola-Hit Nations." *New York Times*, October 22, 2014, www.nytimes.com/2014/10/23/health/us-to-monitor-travelers-from-ebola-hit-nations-for-21-days.html, accessed February 4, 2020.

Miller, Michael Matheson, James F. Fitzgerald, Jr., Simon Scionka, and Robert A. Sirico. *Poverty, Inc.*, DVD video, directed by Michael Matheson Miller (Passion River Films, 2014).

Nossiter, Adam. "Fear of Ebola Breeds a Terror of Physicians." *New York Times*, July 27, 2014, www.nytimes.com/2014/07/28/world/africa/ebola-epidemic-west-africa-guinea.html, accessed February 4, 2020.

Okorafor, Nnedi. "Sci-fi Stories That Imagine a Future Africa." TEDGlobal 2017, www.ted.com/talks/nnedi_okorafor_sci_fi_stories_that_imagine_a_future_africa/up-next?language=en, accessed December 30, 2019.

Sack, Kevin, Sheri Fink, Pam Belluck, and Adam Nossiter. "How Ebola Roared Back." *New York Times*, December 29, 2014, www.nytimes.com/2014/12/30/health/how-ebola-roared-back.html, accessed February 4, 2020.

"Scandal in Peanuts: Britain Has Trouble Making a Nut Farm of Tanganyika." *LIFE*, No. 24, December 12, 1949, 46–48.

"Uganda Fury at David Cameron Aid Threat over Gay Rights." BBC News, October 31, 2011, www.bbc.com/news/world-africa-15524013, accessed January 12, 2018.

Yasukawa, Olivia and Thomas Page. "Lion-Killer Maasai Turn Wildlife Warriors to Save Old Enemy." CNN World, February 8, 2017, www.cnn.com/2017/02/07/africa/maasai-tanzania-wildlife-warriors/index.html, accessed February 4, 2020.

INTERVIEWS

Interview with Corrie Decker, Garrett Ingoglia, Vice President of Emergency Response for Americares, July 5, 2017.

Interview with Corrie Decker, Laurence D. L. Maka, Vice Chancellor of Stawa University, August 1, 2019.

ARCHIVES

Kenya National Archives

AB/14/47, Report on the Education of Women and Girls in Kenya, 1944.

MSS/61/274, Circular from T. G. Benson, Principal of Jeanes School, Jeanes School Kenya, 1937.

United Kingdom National Archives

CO 323/1415/6 Advisory Council for Education in the Colonies, Memorandum on Community Education and Social and Economic Development Programmes in Rural Areas, 1937.

CO 533/384 Confidential Report on Johnstone Kenyatta.

CO 533/601, East Africa, Reestablishment of the Amani Institute, May 1926.

CO 859/81/15, B. H. Bourdillon to Lord Moyne, October 24, 1941, Correspondence Marked "Secret and Personal."

CO 879/121/4, Memorandum Prepared by Professor Julian Huxley and Dr. W. K. Spencer for Advisory Committee on Education in Tropical Africa, 1928.

CO 879/123/11, Professor Julian Huxley, MA, "Biology and the Biological Approach to Native Education in East Africa" (Printed for the Colonial Office, April 1930).

FO 881/2572, Report by Frederic Holmwood on East Africa, 1874.

British Library, United Kingdom

East African Standard, British Library Newspaper Collections.

Index

Made in the USA
Las Vegas, NV
24 December 2020